iment · Lost in █████████████ s ·
he Grey Seas Unc██████████er-
eople · Ordeal by Ice · Owls
oil · The Black Joke · Never
ncient Norse in Greenland and
f the Viking Grave · Canada
e Quest for the North Pole ·
Ieritage Lost · The Boat Who
ale for the Killing · Tundra:
nts of Arctic Land Voyages ·
Snow Walker · Canada North
l No Birds Sang · The World
er · My Discovery of America
n Fossey · The New Founde
nversations with the Green
Iemories of War and Peace ·
vels in a Post-War World ·
Reader · Walking on the Land

FARLEY

Also available from Steerforth Press

The Farfarers

High Latitudes

Walking on the Land

FARLEY

THE LIFE OF FARLEY MOWAT

JAMES KING

STEERFORTH PRESS
SOUTH ROYALTON, VERMONT

First published in Canada by Harper*Flamingo*Canada, Toronto, 2002

For information about permission to reproduce
selections from this book, write to:
Steerforth Press L.C., P.O. Box 70,
South Royalton, Vermont 05068

Library of Congress Cataloging-in-Publication Data

King, James, 1942–
    Farley : the life of Farley Mowat / James King. — 1st Steerforth ed.
        p. cm.
    ISBN 1-58642-055-0
    1. Mowat, Farley. 2. Authors, Canadian — 20th century — Biography.
I. Title.
PR9199.3.M68 Z75 2003
808'.0092—dc21

2002151149

FIRST STEERFORTH EDITION

For my grandson,
PATRICK

Contents

Photographs

EXCEPT where noted, all photographs are courtesy of Farley and Claire Mowat.

Acknowledgements

I COULD not have written this book without the cooperation, encouragement, assistance and warm hospitality of Farley and Claire Mowat. My greatest obligation is to them. I learned a great deal from speaking with the late Frances Mowat, and I have also benefited enormously from time spent with John Mowat, Rosemary Mowat and Sandy Mowat.

In interviews the following have provided me with much needed and appreciated information: Pierre Berton, Anita and David Blackwood, Janice Boddy, Silver Don Cameron, Elizabeth Campbell Cox, Peter Davison, Dorothy and John de Visser, Mary Elliott, Beryl Gaspardy, Ole Gjerstad, Jack Granatstein, Harold Horwood, Marie Heydon Johnston, Jack McClelland, Lily Miller, Wade Rowland, Ed and Lily Schreyer, Andy Thomson, Ervin and Janice Touesnard, Vi Warren, Catherine Wilson and Ron Wright. For help in uncovering vital details, I wish to thank Stephen Cummings, Janet Friskney, Muriel Maxwell, Lorrie Minshall, Suzanne Mullett, Robin Russell, Sheila Turcon and Shirley Turner. Stephen Harding served briefly as my research assistant, and I am deeply grateful to him for sorting through the Angus Mowat papers at the University of Western Ontario.

John Orange, author of *Farley Mowat: Writing the Squib*, has been generous with assistance and encouragement. John Lutman at the University of Western Ontario Library and Apollonia Steele at the

Research Collections at the University of Calgary Library have given me much needed assistance. As is their custom, Carl Spadoni and Charlotte Stewart at the Research Collections at the McMaster University Library have done all in their power to aid me. Anne McDermid has been unflagging in providing assistance and comfort.

I am deeply grateful to Stephanie Fysh for copyediting this book with great thoroughness and sensitivity. Proofreader Vivien Leong, as well as Nicole Langlois and Roy Nicol at HarperCollins, made many useful suggestions. From the outset, Phyllis Bruce has been a strong booster of this project. I have benefited enormously from her enthusiasm, acumen and kindness.

Preface

ON January 6, 1999, a reader wrote to the *Globe and Mail*, "When will you finally move Farley Mowat and [his 1997 non-fiction book] *The Farfarers* into the fiction column of the National Bestsellers List? After all, everyone in Canada knows that Farley Mowat is, himself, a purely fictional character." Years after the fact, Farley is convinced that his adoption of a public persona—the outspoken and more than a trifle exhibitionistic young man—was really the brainchild of his publisher and close friend, Jack McClelland: "I think we were having one of our liquid lunches, and as we reeled back toward the office, Jack said, 'You have to present an image.' So I listened and I worked out my image: a kilt-wearing, swaggering, mooning, drinking Farley Mowat. It was always a cardboard cutout, and it was very useful. I could carry it in front of me, and be my own self behind it. I don't need it any more."

The cutout may be cardboard, but Farley still wears it when it suits him—and when he needs it. "I like a good fight if there's a good reason for doing it," he admits, and adds: "I'll break my ass to save whales or to do something for people in distress." When the writer and broadcaster Peter Gzowski interviewed him at the Harbourfront International Festival of Authors in 1999 and debated with him about the number of facts a non-fiction writer owed his readers, Farley bellowed, "Fuck the facts!"

But behind this facade is a private person hidden from the public, a man quite unlike the public Farley Mowat. A non-fiction writer with superb narrative instincts, he remains a tireless advocate of the Inuit, wolves, whales and a host of other endangered peoples and species. Whatever the subject, he writes with finesse, allowing his stories the breathing room they need to hit their mark.

He is perhaps the best-known Canadian writer of all time, but what is his place in Canadian literature? Perhaps the most apt comparison is with the American transcendentalist writer and prophet Henry David Thoreau, who withdrew to Walden Pond in 1845, observed everything about him and then drew comparisons between the integrity of the natural world and the vainglory of the human. Like Thoreau, Farley had the instinct to become a hermit; like Thoreau, Farley resisted that impulse and wrote of humanity's struggle to become a compassionate overseer of planet Earth.

In this biography, I have attempted to portray the "real" Farley Mowat by bringing the public and private together and, in the process, to provide a multi-layered biography of a man who, it turns out, is more fascinating than the legend he has crafted.

My interest in Farley was piqued when I began writing my biography of Jack McClelland. From the outset, Farley was strongly supportive of that project, feeling that McClelland's immense contribution to the cultural history of Canada was on the verge of being forgotten. At our first meeting in 1997, at Farley's summer home in Nova Scotia, the conversation centred on McClelland, but there were many interesting asides that day, enough to make me realize that a life of Farley Mowat would be an even more intriguing activity than I had previously imagined.

Only when I had completed my life of McClelland did I broach the question to Farley of writing his biography. That was a matter, he promptly told me, to which he would have to give a lot of thought. Later he informed me that he might be willing to cooperate with such a venture but that he might wish to attach "conditions." He left the matter that way for several weeks and then phoned me to announce that he would like to cooperate with me and that he would impose absolutely no conditions on the resulting book and would make all his embargoed papers available to me.

Although biographers are finicky creatures who do not like to be instructed how to write their books, they should pay keen attention to any clues, subtle or not, placed in their way by helpful biographees. As Farley and I talked about his father, Angus, I began to become aware of just how delicate and precarious the relationship between the two men had been. I was astounded, however, when I began exploring the huge Angus Mowat archive at the University of Western Ontario, an assortment of papers never seen by Farley. In those documents, detailed evidence of the intricacies of the complicated struggle and deep bonding between father and son emerged. Since the two men wrote to each other regularly and often intimately, the exchanges of letters are very revealing. In fact, the Angus Mowat papers provided many leads on all aspects of the life of his famous son.

This book contains new, sometimes startling information about every aspect of Farley Mowat's existence, but at its centre it is very much a father-and-son story about a relationship which was, for both men, touching, maddening, angering, destructive, rehabilitating and, in the final analysis, transformative.

The biographer, in dealing with a living subject, is part journalist, part antagonist, part friend, part father confessor. Although the biographer must extract as much information as possible, there is a corresponding obligation to understand, empathize and then explain. From the beginning, I was convinced that the best biography of Farley Mowat would be one in which I could show the reader both how Farley Mowat saw the world and how Farley Mowat saw himself in the world. In other words, who is Farley Mowat and why did he become the person he is?

As I worked on this book—interviewing Farley, Claire, their friends and their enemies, following in his footsteps and, in the process, piecing together the various strands that constitute my subject—I uncovered the frequently fragile, often tentative, mostly hidden and sometimes darker sides of his character. In the process, I discovered a new Farley Mowat, a robust figure of remarkable proportions and depth, and it is to this larger-than-life character that I have devoted this book.

This "real" Farley Mowat has been my subject. Yet no one should expect someone as varied and as contradictory as Farley Mowat to be pinned down in a single phrase. The various epithets given to the chapters of this book—Bunje, Plausible Ike, Billy, Squib II, Raging Boy, Saga-Man, Nomad, Happy Adventurer, Keeper of the Whale, Wayfarer, His Father's Son, Prophet of Doom, Keeper of the Faith—provide some idea of the remarkable diversity of this man—exuberant, mercurial, kindly, tormented, melancholic, gregarious and generous.

PART ONE

A Dutiful Son

I

Bunje

1921–1928

ACCORDING to his father, Angus, himself a teller of fantastical autobiographical adventures, Farley Mowat was begotten either under the grandstand at the Canadian National Exhibition in Toronto or in a green canoe in the Bay of Quinte. "That's quite an amazing feat . . . in any colour canoe," one person to whom Angus confided the second legend rejoined. Although a canoe afloat on water would be a challenging place to conceive a child, such a daring deed might explain Farley's subsequent interest in water and the creatures that dwell there. However, on another occasion, Angus just as improbably claimed that it was *he* who had been conceived in a green canoe. There is a third scenario provided by Angus: "Farley was not, as has been asserted, conceived at the Canadian National Exhibition. It was at night, after returning from the Exhibition, when his mother was too tired to say 'No.' "[1]

Even before Farley's birth in Belleville, Ontario, on May 12, 1921, to Helen and Angus Mowat, he was a bit of a scapegrace. As his father

3

recalled, Farley from "his earliest years had some disregard for the conventional. In the first instance he tried to get out when his mother was in a taxi cab on the way to the hospital. He nearly did, too. Then in the hospital, he'd be damned if he'd wait for the doctor, who was something of a slow-poke, so out he popped all over everything. The nurse said the first thing she knew there he was. She said he rolled over, propped himself up on one elbow and gave her a kind of drunken leer."[2]

From the outset, Farley was also a bit of a conundrum, as his father comically lamented: "I much wanted a son who would become a salt-water sailor, perhaps a deep-sea captain. Well Neptune puts his mark on those fated to go down to the sea in ships. They are born with a caul over their heads. This is Neptune's guarantee that they will never drown or, if they do, they will become Mermen and enjoy a rollicking hereafter among the Mermaids." Always the rebel, Farley was born without the least hint of a caul.

He was in every way an exceptional child, even as a three-year-old, as can be seen in this recollection: "I see, in my mind's eye, a large and strikingly marked honey bee standing on an anthill near where I sit. This bee is resolutely and briskly directing traffic away from me." This is Farley's earliest memory. Like many incidents in his subsequent life, it has been subjected to rigorous questioning. "Bees do not act like that," he has been assured many times. His response: "Nonsense. I *know* I was taken under the protection of the bees, and the proof is that I have never been stung by one. . . . I believe I was adopted into their tribe, and ever since I have been as kindly disposed to them as they to me."

There may be more than a small dose of sprightly myth-making in both the retelling of the memory and its recipient's assurance that it is accurate. What cannot be denied is the young child's sense of fusion with nature, his feeling that he could from the very start of his existence find common ground with—and sympathy and understanding for—the non-human creatures of the planet.

*   *   *

Helen Mowat, circa 1920

Born in the town of Ridgeway, Ontario, in 1896, Farley's vivacious mother, Anne Helen Lillian—always called Helen—was the eldest daughter of Henry (Hal) Thomson, a bank manager with Molson's Bank. The Thomson family—a Scots family who had first arrived in Canada in 1795—had its notables, including Helen's grandfather, Rev. C.E. Thomson, rector of Toronto's St. Mark's Church, and her great-grandfather, Alexander Grant, administrator (equivalent to lieu-tenant-governor) of Upper Canada. Helen grew up in Trenton, where Hal had been transferred, and when she was a young adult, Hal, after making some injudicious loans, was banished hundreds of miles away, to Port Arthur (now Thunder Bay) on Lake Superior in north-ern Ontario. Hal's professional ineptness made him reclusive. His wife, Georgina—rangy, long-nosed and skittish—took charge of him and her four sons and two daughters and their rambling old house.

Angus was born on the edge of Prince Edward County, a tiny corner of southeastern Ontario populated by United Empire Loyal-ists, pro-British refugees who had left the United States in the 1780s

Angus Mowat, circa 1939

and 1790s to settle in Upper Canada. The area's largest settlement, Belleville, on Lake Ontario, was named after Arabella, the wife of Francis Gore, administrator of Upper Canada. The town became an important sawmilling centre, a divisional point of the Grand Trunk Railway and the centre of a thriving cheesemaking industry. Sir John A. Macdonald practised law at the courthouse in nearby Picton before he became Canada's first prime minister. So prosperous did the town grow that its citizens petitioned Queen Victoria to make their community the capital of Canada.

Then as now, the coast of the county had unspoiled white sandy beaches, and the picturesque towns and villages contained splendid examples of Georgian architecture. To escape the heat, the wealthy Belleville families summered in places such as Wellington, where they built "cottages" on the lakeshore. The Mowat and Thomson families were members of the upper middle class: well educated and well placed. But they were also slightly déclassé. Neither Hal Thomson nor Robert McGill Mowat, Angus's father, had retained much of the family status, a fact which weighed heavily upon them. Angus was soon to join their ranks.

Before the onset of the Great War, Angus had been one among many determined suitors for Helen's hand. Her parents did not approve of him, and Helen considered him merely a pushy little fellow—she preferred a young artillery lieutenant. But when the lieutenant died during the great influenza epidemic of 1918, Angus renewed his claim to Helen's hand, and she finally accepted. Even after her marriage, Helen attracted a long line of would-be lovers. Her son is certain she never gave in to temptation, but she could be coquettish: "This did not bother my father; in fact, he may have felt it gave him licence."

Handsome, mustachioed Angus was a man who took considerable liberties with life. A great admirer of the silver-screen exploits of the swashbuckling Douglas Fairbanks and the debonair John Barrymore, he took every opportunity to play a number of roles with élan. His

Robert McGill and Mary Ann Mowat

imagination and his energy knew no boundaries. Fire ranger, soldier, sailor, librarian and writer, he did many things well.

While Angus's sense of himself could be all-encompassing, it could also be a bit evasive. He once told Farley, "I was granted, had, fell into, an almost perfect childhood. . . . I have long been convinced that nothing could have been improved on my behalf."[3] Yet the real circumstances of Angus's birth on November 19, 1892, and of his early life in Trenton do not support this assertion. For one thing, Angus's mother, Mary Ann Jones, the daughter of a Brockville furniture manufacturer, was a dour, uncompromising person who constantly reminded her husband, Robert McGill Mowat, a hardware merchant, that he had never lived up to the high standards of her family—or his own.

The Mowat family was distinguished. John Mowat, who immigrated to Canada from Caithness, Scotland, to fight in the War of 1812, took a land grant in 1814, settled in Kingston in 1819 and married Helen Levack. The eldest of their five children was Oliver, later Sir Oliver Mowat and premier of Ontario. John Bower, the third son, who became a Presbyterian minister, was one of the first three students to be admitted to Queen's University in Kingston, Ontario; he accepted the ministry at St. Andrew's, Niagara-on-the-Lake, and was later appointed to the Chair of Theology and Hebrew at Queen's University, a position he held for forty-three years. With his first wife, Janet McGill, whose father was also a Presbyterian divine, John had one child, Robert McGill (Gill) Mowat, Angus's father.

Gill was expected to go far either in the Church or at the bar, but he was lackadaisical and not suited for either profession. He was seconded to the Jones family business but proved so ineffectual, he was banished to sleepy little Trenton, a few miles from Belleville, to run his own hardware store. He was such a daydreamer that he once filled an order for a dozen candles with an equal number of sticks of dynamite. After he went bankrupt for the third time, he became a full-time remittance man, living off his wife's inheritance.

Attempting to improve upon the reality of his father's depressed existence, Angus wrote: "Robert McGill was a romantic man, a dreamer, a writer of terrible poetry; and he tried to be a man of business. . . . but when the business failed for the third time the family refused to rally round again. So he retired—and sailed a small sloop named *Nancy Lee* and wrote more poetry till he died. He drank a little." The great accomplishment of Robert's life was—according to his son—to "beget" him. Overlooked was Jean, Angus's older sister.

As a child, Angus was sickly. Lydia LaBelle, the Mowats' French-speaking servant, often wept over him: "Oh, Madame Mowat, you'll never raise *lui*." At school he was nicknamed "Puke," but Angus was certain that he acquired the sobriquet because he had at the age of five stolen a cigar from his father, smoked it in front of his peers and then vomited. He was proficient at lacrosse until he received a serious wound. From boyhood, he was an excellent sailor, noted for the twin traits of pluck and perseverance. On a number of occasions, the youngster managed to drink a great deal of whiskey intended for an elderly uncle, who lived with the family, by substituting his mother's homemade cherry brandy for his uncle's "Blended Pap."

In 1912, at the age of nineteen, Angus enrolled at Queen's University, where he was a particularly good student in European history. In the summer of 1914, he worked as a fire ranger in the Temagami region in northern Ontario, living in idyllic circumstances in a remote cabin and making patrols by canoe. That July he penned the sentimental "A Wanderer's Dream of the Bay," which reads in part: "The distant loon laughs loudly, the marsh-bird croons her love, / And our Bay of wondrous beauty gently dreams." In September, filled with a desire to serve his country in battle, he joined the Queen's University Officer Training Corps and was commissioned as a lieutenant on September 14, soon after the Great War began. He trained with the Canadian Engineers and departed for war.

Angus left on the troopship *Northland*, which departed Halifax on April 9, 1915. As he crossed the North Atlantic, he wrote to his parents, telling them of a dream in which he was in a movie theatre but did not know if he was a member of the audience or a character in the film.

His actual experience of war a year later—Angus had transferred to the 4th Battalion (Infantry) of the Canadian Expeditionary Force—

was short and fierce. Like the other young Canadians dispatched to France, he was thrown into some of the worst—and most suicidal—situations a soldier can experience. As a member of the Canadian Corps, he fought in the battle of the Somme in 1916 and then in the battle of Vimy Ridge in 1917; on April 10, 1917, he was severely wounded at Vimy and evacuated. While recuperating at the Queen Alexandra Hospital in London, he wrote to his father about the severity of the damage to his right arm: "The old wing, you will be sorry to hear, has been objecting again. It has been sore for several days, and this morning a piece of bone as large as a small bean came out. It feels much better already and the discharge stopped at once."[4] After he was wounded, all he "had to cling to was [his] love for Helen."[5] Although Angus was "struck off the strength" on July 22, 1918, he retained his commission in the militia, with the Hastings and Prince Edward Regiment (HPER, the "Hasty Pees"), an infantry unit composed of countrymen and townsmen from the two counties in southeastern Ontario.

The wound marked Angus for life, leaving him with a stiff arm that looked like a ragged claw. Some men might have been self-conscious about a crippling wound; for Angus, it was a badge of honour—although he carefully avoided allowing his disability to be captured by photographers. Despite the wound and his relatively short height (5'6"), it was a dashing Angus Mowat attired in army uniform who once again presented himself to Helen Thomson, now living in Port Arthur. She quickly informed him that she still did not love him and would not marry him. At that time Angus's arm was still in a cast, "hurting like hell," and the pain spurred him on. His persistence finally won Helen's hand.

Angus returned to a Canada that wanted to forget the war, to get on with the business of making its way in the twentieth century. Like many First World War veterans, Angus was emotionally rudderless, seeing little purpose to or sense in life after having witnessed the carnage unleashed by "the war to end all wars." In the face of the meaninglessness of much of life, he discovered only one solution:

escape—which, he observed, a man must take as he takes a mistress. Even before the war, he had been restless. He summarized his early life as an attempt to exchange his family home for the "pillars—[which] turned out to be plaster ones—of a college cloister." That was a failure, so "seizing upon a romantic opportunity, I flung my gown aside and, wearing very shiny buttons and uttering loud cries of daring-do, I plunged into the glory of a great war! Alas! The buttons soon turned green and glory faded like a cloud; and I just barely managed by the skin of my teeth to escape out of that escape and into a hospital cot."[6] In addition to assuaging his own sense of purposelessness, Angus had the additional burden of worrying about Gill, who in his son's absence had managed to get everything at home into yet another hopeless financial mess.

The restlessness continued. After Angus and Helen married on May 28, 1919, they spent the summer fire-ranging at Orient Bay, Lake Nipigon. Before that, Angus had worked at the Port Arthur shipyards and at a stave mill in Trenton making barrels; during the winter of 1920–21, the couple lived briefly in Toronto, where Angus worked in the grocery business and in a sash factory. In the spring of 1921, just before Farley was born, they returned to Trenton and moved into a house—called "Bingen on the Rhine"—overlooking the Bay of Quinte. The owners of Bingen, the eccentric Posts, were beekeepers. The house's huge drawing room was used by the Posts every autumn and winter as a repository of over a hundred hives. For a while, Angus himself kept bees, thinking to establish himself as a professional apiarist.

Angus Mowat and Helen Thomson,
March 1918

Angus was a rebel against the class into which he had been born. Dispirited by the war, he was not inclined to pursue any of the traditional paths of success: the ministry, business or the law. Helen, raised as a lady, was living (not from choice) what can only be called—by the standards of her family—a lower-culture existence. From infancy, Farley's inclination to be an outsider was fostered by his parents' behaviour.

Angus loved names. At Queen's, he had reinvented himself as "Squib," a small but strong charge used to detonate major explosions. Farley was named after Helen's younger brother, who had been killed in a fall from a cliff, but before the baby was three months old, Angus decided his name should be "Bunje," after a character in an H.G. Wells novel. When Helen protested, Angus replied that "Bunje" was a "working title" to be used until their son made up his own mind as to what he wanted to be called. Angus may have been implying that Farley was somehow "on approval" and would have to earn his own—or better—name according to his future conduct.

Bingen—so-called because a previous tenant had seen some resemblance between this rat-infested Gothic ruin and the ancient fortress on the Rhine sometimes called Mouse Tower because the vermin there destroyed their evil owner—was given the simpler name of "The Fortress" by Angus. Yet the truth was that by any name the Mowat home was unsavoury. It was dirty, draughty and, of course, filled with rodents. The couple had so little money that their diet consisted mainly of porridge, soda biscuits, oatmeal and honey.

Porridge was not one of Farley's favourite foods. At the age of three, the toddler refused to touch a large bowl of it given to him by Helen. He was deaf to her pleas to eat. As his father recalled, he waited her out, "looking pleasant, until he thought the time ripe; then he slowly lifted up the bowl . . . and crowned himself with it."[7] The young child seemed invulnerable: "At the age of two all the ceiling plaster in his room fell down and ought to have snuffed him out; but I found him sitting up in his crib chortling."[8]

During the summer of 1923, a pestilence called "foul brood" wiped out the bees. Angus then briefly tried his hand at selling insurance, but he disliked it so much that he would cross to the other side of the street if he saw a prospect heading his way. Things got even worse when the chimney in Bingen's enormous kitchen caught fire and collapsed. The family of three took shelter in the nearby decrepit "Swamp House," which stunk of rotten wood. Then the Mowats' fortunes swung upwards when the despotic spinster who ran the Trenton Public Library threatened to resign if she did not get her own way. The chairman of the board accepted her offer with alacrity and offered the job to Angus at the salary of five hundred dollars a year.

The move back to Trenton had been done on Angus's initiative, as his son recalled: "This was a decision in which Helen had no part. In truth she seldom had any significant say in major family decisions then or later. She was generally phlegmatic about this, although she once ruefully told me that being married to a man who always knew precisely what was best for all of us could be trying."[9] Whether he was certain or uncertain that he was the master of his own destiny, Angus always acted as if he were infallible.

Later, Angus summarized the stages of his escapism: "into fire-ranging—which I gave up when the government changed—into bolting in a shipyard—which I liked because it provided time for meditation; and into librarianship. In the shipyard I contemplated rather too long in one place on a winter's day, and froze a foot and got fired. But I liked it. Librarianship, on the other hand, was a disappointment. . . . It was with deep chagrin and a sense of having been cheated, that I discovered the sad truth about librarians, namely, that they do their reading after midnight and all the rest of the time they work."[10] For Angus—who had an intuitive understanding of what libraries should do for their patrons and an extraordinary grasp of how to operate them—his chosen profession was very much a second-best choice. Like his father before him, he was—and remained—a disappointed man, one whose calling did not really reflect his aspirations.

The impoverished family now took two rooms in the autumn of 1923 at the home of Mrs. White, a railway worker's widow. But the

Mowats moved quickly from there after an inebriated Angus came home from hunting without his key late one night, removed the storm window from his and Helen's upstairs bedroom, fell to the ground and awakened the entire household. Their next home was a two-bedroom apartment above a clothing store on Front, the main street of Trenton.

Angus chose that residence because it was near the harbour at Trenton and allowed quick access to the Bay of Quinte. Soon after taking up his new post, Angus bought—using up one-fourth of his annual salary—*Little Brown Jug*, a seventeen-foot Akroyd sailing dinghy. Unfortunately, the summer of 1924 was cold and blustery, and *LBJ*, as the boat was nicknamed, was built solely as a racing machine. It had no cabin and its occupants were at the mercy of unkind elements. This led to a protracted battle of wills between Angus and Helen: "Helen resolutely refused to go cruising again unless in a much larger boat, one with a comfortable and waterproof cabin." Naturally worried about her son's survival, she put her foot down and was a deemed "balky as a bloody mule" by her spouse.

Angus held out for an entire year before selling *LBJ* and purchasing *Stout Fella*, an old twenty-six-foot Lake Ontario fishing boat propelled by a ten-horsepower, single-cylinder gasoline engine. Since the boat did not even have a sail, Angus felt he had really come down in the world. He was certainly completely undermined on the day the boat got stuck in the middle of the area occupied by the open central span between the causeway and the swinging bridge that connected Prince Edward County to the town of Belleville. Farmers bound for the Belleville market were irate; "Why didn't you just pull the plug and let that bathtub sink?" one of them yelled. Helen burst into tears. Demonstrating remarkable grace under pressure, Angus calmly worked the vessel free, leapt ashore and then smiled cheekily at his tormentors. "All right, Bunje-boy," he exclaimed. "You can tell your mother it's safe to come on deck again." The only time Helen ever swore was another time Angus grounded their boat. He offered a feeble excuse, to which she replied, "Balls!"[11]

Despite all the drawbacks, Farley's memories of life aboard ship are ecstatic, filled with the comradery he shared with Angus and Helen.

(both photos) Stout Fella, *September 1927*

At sea, there were fish aplenty for the taking; farmers often insisted on giving them vegetables, milk, cream, butter and eggs; farm wives would press fresh bread and pies, jars of preserves and pickles, bottles of maple syrup, and chicken and ham on Helen.

Farley's job was to row ashore each morning to collect milk from a nearby farm. He made friends with the children, who were allowed on board for hours at a time. There were other ways to pass the time too. For instance, there was the companionship of the local drunks and hobos who assembled outside the abandoned cold storage plant, the windowless limestone walls of which towered like those of a medieval fortress. These men drank a solidified kind of alcohol called "Canned Heat." "We children were allowed to consort with these ragamuffins," he recalls, "and I especially remember a lanky redhead called Bunny-Boy who had once worked in a circus and could juggle half a dozen cans of 'Canned Heat' at a time." Four-year-old Farley proved such an apt sailor that Angus told him he was grown up enough to have either sugar or rum on his porridge; Farley chose rum.

Farley loved to visit Charlie Haultain's fox ranch—a half acre of wasteland on the edge of a swamp. In the corner of the enclosure devoted to the pens, he could climb a rickety ladder to a tower of peeled poles about thirty feet high that supported a tiny cabin. There he had a window onto the secret lives of the animals. The little boy's imagination transformed the ranch into a fur trader's post. In Farley's eyes, Charlie was a truly romantic figure: "He was swarthy, swift of movement. . . . He would have been perfectly at ease clothed in buckskin with feathers on his head. In fact, he was generally clothed in the powerful aroma of dog-fox, which is similar to skunk. It permeated his cabin, and his garments, which he did not often change."[12] Charlie once declared he would make a proper woodsman of Farley, but then the older man lost interest in the foxes and went off to northwest Ontario to prospect for gold.

Then there was a brief friendship with the "Marsh Boy," the son of a poacher. The two played on and under decaying old steamer docks and in the hulks of abandoned barges. His new friend led Farley into the world of animals—muskrat houses, snapping turtle nests, the domain of the huge, thick, black water snakes—until Farley desperately wanted to become the Marsh Boy, to be an inhabitant of the murky landscape, half land, half water, of his new friend.

The wild child visited the Mowats' home only once. From under his ragged tangle of black hair, he stared suspiciously at them. Not impressed by the meal of macaroni and cheese offered him, he pulled a knotted handkerchief from his pocket, untied it and spread some hard-boiled eggs on the kitchen floor. These were not ordinary eggs: one was from a heron, two from a helldiver, and one from a gull. While the astonished Mowats looked on, he cracked each egg against his forehead, peeled off the shell and gulped down the contents. He departed immediately after finishing his meal and refused to visit his hosts' civilized habitation again.

From the beginning, Farley's adventures were a real worry to Helen. When her son was about four years old, the family of three were staying with some friends who had a cottage on the south shore of the Bay of Quinte not far from the mouth of Murray Canal. There were a bunch of derelict shacks and cabins nearby, including an old ice house, where tons of blocks were stored between layers of sawdust. One day, Farley and a group of three or four other children congregated there. As on many other days, they imagined the place to be an igloo or a polar bear's den. Then someone slammed the door shut and the children were locked in. They yelled and screamed, but no one could hear them because of the building's thick insulation. One of the little girls buried her face in Farley's neck. For the first time in his life, he felt terror. Fortunately, one of the inhabitants of a nearby cottage came to get ice and released the children. For weeks afterwards, the small boy had nightmares about this incident. He cried so despairingly that he woke up with his face drenched in tears.

By the age of five, Farley, who had become a skilled rower, went the half-mile offshore to a nearby island while a desperate Helen wrung her hands and a proud Angus cheered his son. At that time, Farley weighed only thirty pounds. Worried that her son might have some sort of wasting disease, Helen pestered the local doctor for tonics and potions. These did no good and so Helen took her son by train to Toronto to see Dr. Alan Brown, Canada's foremost pediatrician. After a brief examination, the physician brought Farley back to

Farley, April 1927

the waiting room. "Who's Mrs. Mowat?" he asked. Helen identified herself, whereupon the doctor thundered, "Well, Madam, what do you mean wasting my time? This boy is as healthy as an ox. As for his size—if you'd wanted a prize fighter for a son, you should have married one. Good day to you!"[13]

In photographs of young Farley with his parents, Helen looks at the camera with genuine pleasure. Angus, almost always wearing his tam-o'-shanter, strikes a pose. They are a handsome couple, obviously bursting with pride in their offspring.

Angus and Helen were well aware of their young son's precociousness. One night at Bingen, Farley awoke to find an enormous bear in his room. The intruder, standing upright by the window, wore a checked tweed cap with a matching visor. He was a friendly creature, but Farley tensed up and called for his parents, who arrived within seconds. They assured the boy it had all been a dream, but for him the animal had been all too real. Later Farley hoped it would return: "But he never came back, and I think I know why. My parents were partially correct. It was a dream all right, but *it was the bear's dream*. And I think we scared the bejesus out of *him*."[14]

Farley's parents, not surprisingly, differed in their attitudes towards parenting. Helen was a very traditional mother, although one perfectly capable of dealing with a deeply imaginative child. She wanted to bring her son up well. For her, an Anglican who had completed her education at a Roman Catholic convent school, that meant instilling in him a respect for the conventions of polite society and organized religion. Helen, though, lacked the glamour or seductiveness of Angus. At first glance, he seemed every boy's ideal father: he was a war hero, an excellent sailor, a man who encouraged his son's early fascination with nature. A skeptic as far as religion was concerned, he often defied the conventional or held it in contempt—a lesson he taught his son well.

And yet, although he amply demonstrated his love for Farley, Angus—perhaps because his own father was a failure and he feared the same fate for himself—made it clear from the outset that he had high expectations of his son. And he wanted those expectations to be met. Expecting Farley to be exact, precise and unfaltering in posture and conversation, Angus was rigid, militaristic and judgemental in dealing with him. Angus was charming to the world, but with Farley, he always held back—more than he did with any other person. And lurking behind that reticence is a question: Was Farley cherished as a child by Angus? Or was the son a bit of a disappointment? Then and later, if Farley did what his father wanted, Angus was supportive. If Farley failed to do what was expected of him, Angus withheld his approval.

In Farley's lyrical and moving account of his early years, *Born Naked*, one crucial anecdote is missing. At the age of four or five, he had asked for an electrical train set for Christmas; he had made it clear to his parents that he was desperate to have such a choice gift. When he woke up on Christmas morning, the little boy found instead a small wooden toy train by his bed. Distraught, he tried to hide his anguish by running to the bathroom, where he burst into tears. Only then was he led to the electrical train set, which had been set up in another room. Angus was testing Farley's stoicism and self-control—Helen would have never initiated such a scheme. The boy failed the examination.

Towards the end of his life, Angus tried to analyze his relationship with Farley, wondering if intimacy had been impossible with him because earlier his own father had been distant from him:

Angus, Farley and Gill aboard Stout Fella, *September 1927*

Having time on my hands [recently] I have been thinking about [Gill] for days—and of course knew I would have to confront not just his incompetence in business only but domestically and in his relations with others—pleasantly polite but miles distant. And that was pretty much as he was with me too. He never gave me any of his confidence and he, very kindly mind you, refused mine. Now this may have been my fault too. I don't know. He was quietly affectionate with me when I was little, much more than mother ever was. But I think now that he drew back as I grew up. I wonder why. And I wonder if somehow I could not have prevented it. Actually I gave up trying.

Having come to this painful conclusion, Angus wrote to his son: "Do you suppose I am a little like that too?"[15]

Plausible Ike

1928–1932

HAVING dedicated himself to becoming a librarian, Angus threw himself wholeheartedly into that profession. He was an excellent organizer, and he devoted himself to making books attractive to the reading public; in the process, he became a leader in encouraging the greatest possible use of public libraries. Throughout his career, he was especially concerned that marginalized individuals (particularly indigenous peoples and the working class) be made aware of the opportunities libraries offered for self-directed learning.

Within seemingly narrow confines, Angus could be a maverick: "How are we the librarians to face the responsibility of leading the public toward the Mecca of all library ideals—the reading of the best books in the language?" The misplacement of books was the perfect solution: "I choose from among my non-fiction books, certain works which I know, or believe, to have a more or less strong popular appeal. These I place on the fiction shelves, arranged alphabetically, according to author, just as though they were fiction. The aims in doing this are twofold: the perfectly obvious one of bringing better books before the patron's eye, being assured that he will borrow at least some of them, and hoping that having borrowed, he will read; and, secondly, the more important, which naturally follows, that having read, his interest will be sufficiently aroused to lead him to ask for something further of the same nature."[1]

In the summer of 1926, when Farley was five, both Angus and Helen attended the Ontario Library School in Toronto. Two years later, at the age of thirty-six, Angus was offered the librarianship of the Corby Public Library in Belleville, the county seat, a much larger and more prosperous place than Trenton. In his new job, Angus even had a part-time assistant. More importantly, his salary tripled.

The new Mowat residence was somewhat of an improvement, a high-ceilinged, wide-windowed apartment occupying the second floor of the library building, an austere three-storey limestone structure poised on the terraced slope of a hill overlooking the Moira River. The family's hand-me-down furniture did not sit well within the grandeur of their new home, which now looked as if squatters had taken up residence in a castle.

The move to a larger town also meant that Farley had even more opportunity to get into mischief. Directly across the street from the library stood the ornate brick mansion of Dr. Sobie and his family. There were two children: Jean, a year or two older than Farley, and Geordie, who was Farley's age. Quite soon after they met, Geordie and Farley made the garage behind the Sobie house into their own private bat- and swallow-infested hideaway. Of particular fascination to the lads were the leftovers from Dr. Sobie's office that were stored in the loft, scores of brown, green and red glass jugs containing medicinal syrups, some of which were laced with codeine and other narcotics. Two or three times, the boys liberally sampled these potions, fell soundly asleep and were late for dinner.

The two boys prowled the shores of the Moira River. Rather than attempting to explore its beauties, the two scamps gathered where the huge sewage pipes poured forth waste. Thousands of suckers assembled there to gorge themselves, and the boys would fish for them, catching only a few suckers but snaring a lot of condoms. One day, they filled these balloons with water and dropped them on passersby walking in front of the library.

Farley—who had at an early age developed a penchant for appearing in the nude—was embarrassed one summer day while playing Ping-Pong with Jean and some of her friends. All of a sudden, the girls began to twitter uncontrollably and crowed, "We can see your dinkie!" This time Farley had been caught unawares: his penis had wiggled out from under his shorts. He had forgotten to put on his underwear that morning. Nonetheless, Farley was quite happy to play the patient for the five girls who lived next door. Years later one of these ladies told him, "You were a big help to us in Belleville. We had most of Dad's old medical books to study but pictures aren't enough. We learned a lot from checking you over. You were sort of our own little male cadaver, if you know what I mean."[2]

Left by himself in the apartment one rainy Saturday afternoon, Farley used his mother's perfume bottles to weigh down pellets of cotton wool, which he shot through a tin peashooter. When his parents returned home and smelled the thick scent of Attar of Roses, Farley vehemently denied having tinkered with his mother's toiletry. Helen burst into tears, and Angus gave his son seven whacks on each hand with a razor strap. Afterwards, Angus shook hands with Farley and informed him he had been punished for lying, not for stealing the perfume.

Farley now took to thieving on a small-time basis. He would pocket the odd penny his father left on top of his bureau. When he had five cents, he would buy a chocolate bar. He felt so guilty about this infraction that he never ate the candy, although he turned the cardboard wrappers—designed for the purpose—into gliders. One time, coming upon his father's .45 Colt service revolver under a pile of underwear, he showed it to Geordie. Although he was afraid to touch the sinister-looking thing, he did steal a bullet; he gained a great deal of prestige among his peers until an older boy took it from him.

There was a Horatio Alger as well as a Tom Sawyer side to Farley. He and a friend, Alan Evans, decided to manufacture raspberry cordial. They made gallons of the stuff but drank more than they sold. Then they decided to trap mice, skin them and make their fortune selling mouse fur. "The idea," Farley recalls, "originated from my having read about moleskin smoking jackets. If moles—why not mice?" The next scheme was a rabbit ranch. This venture went askew when their pregnant doe, Buffy, was eaten by a cat. Then Alan suggested the former gatehouse where he lived be turned into a hotel offering accommodation for two cents a head, with raspberry cordial thrown in. The only takers were two teenage couples from the wrong side of town. "They were interested in the beds in the upstairs rooms, raddled with mildew and mouse nests as these were. Alan and I were turfed out of our own hostelry with the emphatic adjuration not to return or tell anyone what was going on or 'you'll get your little asses kicked up to your ears.' "

In the autumn of 1927, when Farley began attending Grade 1 at Lord Dufferin School, a fellow classmate, the Marsh Boy, gave him a painted turtle the size of a small dinner plate. Hercules was allowed to range around the apartment at will. One day, he gave out a cry and laid an egg, which never hatched. The following spring, she was given her liberty in the swamps of her birth.

Shortly thereafter, the young boy experienced what might best be called an epiphany:

> I was daydreaming in a swing sofa when a sudden movement caught my eye. I looked up to see a huge spider in the centre of its web battling an equally enormous hornet. The duel was taking place only a hand's breadth away, and I felt myself being drawn directly into the world of the combatants and, in some inexplicable way, associated with them. I watched in wonder- ment as the velvet-clad black spider feinted warily, avoiding the dagger thrusts of the golden hornet's sting. Suddenly the spider drove its curved jaws—in the tips of which tiny jewels of liquid poison gleamed—into the back of the hornet's neck. At the same instant, the hornet curved its abdomen and buried its dagger in the spider's belly. The web, which had been shaking wildly, grew still as death overwhelmed the duellists. And I slowly emerged from something akin to a trance having, for the

first time in my life, consciously entered into the world of the Others—that world which is so infinitely greater than the circumscribed world of Man.

In one of the finest passages in his writings, Farley vividly describes the balances and checks Nature provides to the Others. This is a world of instinct rather than intellect, a place where survival is based on strength, need and dominance. In this sequence, both participants fail, but they die living according to their essential selves. The human world is severely hampered because humankind, which is busy destroying the Others, has lost touch with its essential self.

Earlier, Farley had made his way through the anthropomorphic confections of Beatrix Potter, Mother Goose, Aesop's Fables, A.A. Milne's Christopher Robin books and *The Wind in the Willows*. In fact, Farley gained early notoriety in March 1929 when Toronto's *Mail and Empire* carried the story of the letter he sent to Christopher Robin:

> I like your father's books very much. I like Pooh better than all my books. I have read it five times. Daddy is getting me the new one. I wish you would come and visit me at Belleville. We have a sailboat and we will go crooging [cruising] on the lake.
> Yours truly,
> Bunje Mowat

The reply delighted Farley: "Dear Bunje, Thank you for your letter. I love the snapshots [of Farley aboard a tugboat named *M. Sicken*]. I wish I had a boat of my own. I like rowing. Pooh sends his love. With love from Christopher Robin."

After making contact with the Others, Farley turned briefly to the Dr. Doolittle books and then became fascinated with Kipling's *Just So Stories*, predictably identifying with Mowgli. Next he turned to the more naturalistic depictions of the animal world in the writings of Ernest Thompson Seton and Charles G.D. Roberts. Nothing in his father and mother's library was forbidden to him. The representations of farting and pissing in an illustrated edition of Rabelais' *Gargantua and Pantagruel* thrilled him, as did the privately printed erotic novels given to Angus by book salesmen.

Helen was pregnant when the Mowats moved to Belleville, and in the spring of 1929—just before Farley turned eight—she went into hospital for the delivery, which proved difficult and protracted. The baby girl died. "One day," Farley recalls, "I visited my mother [in hospital] bringing a bouquet of lilacs I had picked myself. To my perplexity and distress, that caused her to burst into tears. Only later did I learn that the lilacs had been in full and early bloom the week that I was born, and she had believed them to be a token of good luck." After two further miscarriages, Helen gave up the attempt to have another child.

Not only did Helen have to endure the loss of the baby girl and the subsequent miscarriages, but she also soon discovered that Angus was being unfaithful. Either he became careless in covering his tracks or he told outrageous stories to explain his absences because Helen (who thought Farley was out when he was reading in his room) confronted Angus about them in about 1929. Hearing loud voices coming from the direction of the kitchen, and curious as he had never heard such sounds before, Farley padded into the hall, where he saw his father squatting in front of the icebox. Helen was standing right behind him, waving both her fists in the air. She hit Angus and followed with a kick in the rump that sent him tumbling into the icebox, hitting his head with enough force to make it bleed. Overcome by her own violence, she fell to the floor in a faint.

Farley the boy—according to Farley the man—was not traumatized by the event. In fact, a "delightful shiver," a combination of fear and excitement, ran down his spine: "Had I been older I might have been tempted to applaud." Knowing that it would be a serious mistake to reveal his eavesdropping, he crept silently back to his room while his parents patched up their quarrel.

In describing this time in *Born Naked*, Farley maintains a genial tone perfectly in accord with recounting what he feels may have been the happiest and most trouble-free years of his life. He does not connect the death of his sister with his father's adulteries, but there is a link. The deaths of her daughter and the other babies wounded Helen deeply, and she turned increasingly to the comforts of religion. She was no longer a willing sexual partner, and Angus's propensity to roam accelerated at an ever more rapid rate. At some level, Helen remained perfectly aware of her husband's peccadillos, although she turned a blind eye to them. Divorce was not much of an option in those days, and in any event, Helen probably thought her wandering husband would return to her. Nonetheless, while he does not admit to it in his autobiography, the domestic landscape of Farley's childhood darkened in 1929, when he was eight years old.

Some of the tensions in the Mowat household were lightened by the distraction of relocating in 1930 to Windsor, where Angus was appointed librarian, with a staff of six. Despite his earlier rebellion against settling into a profession, Angus had chosen one with considerable mobility, especially in the midst of the Great Depression.

For Farley, the move to the Border City was daunting: "Just across the river lay the vast, smoky sprawl of Detroit, Michigan, the Motor City, where nearly half the automobiles that were already dominating the lives of North Americans had been or were being built." Since many men from Canada worked in the auto plants in the nearby United States, Windsor and Detroit were sometimes referred to as the Twin Cities. For the three Mowats, however, Detroit was alien ground and its inhabitants were foreigners. Farley dated his fierce anti-Americanism from those days: "Living on the borders of a foreign nation which so obviously believed in its Manifest Destiny as the eventual master of the continent helped instil in me the fervent nationalism I still proudly maintain."

The new Mowat home was a ground-floor apartment in a brick fourplex on Victoria Avenue, a mile from downtown and the public library. Victoria School was three times the size of the one Farley had attended in Belleville. New in school, the little mite of a boy was teased mercilessly by the others, who called him "squirt." They also pronounced his name "Fart-ley," and briefly he changed his name to

"Farleigh," as if this would make any difference. Farley's small size—and his disinclination to play sports—distanced him from many of his peers. He made a few good friends, but he was also a reflective child who enjoyed his own company. For him, solitariness was a virtue, not something to be shunned. Finding solace in this way allowed the child to enter freely into the natural world.

With one new friend, Hughie Cowan, Farley explored the riverbank, the factory dumps and the big patches of wasteland surrounding the city. Rabbits, foxes and raccoons there were aplenty, but this landscape was also populated by the destitute, in hobo jungles where the boys were offered spoonfuls of beans and mouthfuls of tea. In his encounters with these men, Farley learned what he considered to be an early but salutary lesson in the way capitalist economies function.

Farley's reading now turned to James Fenimore Cooper's *The Last of the Mohicans* and other narratives dealing with the indigenous peoples. Like many boys of his generation, he was absorbed by Indian lore, but it was not until he fell under the spell of Ernest Thompson Seton's *Two Little Savages* that he decided to become an Indian himself.

Farley and Hughie formed a tribe of two. In the late spring of 1931, the Mowats—accompanied by Hughie—discovered the many pleasures of Point Pelee, the most southerly point in Canada and a short drive from Windsor. Within the forest and on the sandy beaches, dunes and marshes that border this part of Lake Erie, the boys were allowed to camp out and construct their own wigwam. Unfortunately, the hunt for moose went unrewarded since none live in that area of Ontario, but they did come across some Americans, whose covered wagon was a big Buick. When these invaders were within range, the boys let fly two blunt-headed arrows at their enormous tent. Hearing an almighty bellow, the would-be Indians quickly retreated. That evening, a pair of policemen arrived at the Mowat tent inquiring about local archers: one of the arrows, after penetrating the tent, had struck one of the palefaces in the ribs. After the departure of the police, Farley fessed up to what he had done, emphasizing that his prey were Americans. This particular detail was enough in Angus's eyes to save their hides.

The entrepreneurial streak in Farley was rekindled when he and Hughie attempted to sell the seeds that fell from the great sycamores that shaded the library. Farley even wrote a letter to the *Border City Star* extolling these as "the rarest and beautifulest trees I have ever seen in my life and should be spread." The publication of the letter did not help the non-existent sales. Indeed, Farley was not deeply sympathetic to other salespeople. When a woman peddling magazines door to door called on the Mowats, Farley, alone at home, regaled her with a description, in gruesome detail, of the practical difficulties porcupines experienced in their sex lives.

He wrote a long narrative poem about an obnoxious schoolmate. As he later recollected, this piece of juvenilia set the scene for much of what was to follow in his later career. Unfettered by facts—he suggested his schoolmate was the unfortunate result of a mating between a pig and a porcupine—he gained acclaim from his schoolmates.

Hughie and Farley also organized a circus in the Mowat backyard. When Hughie tried to do a handstand on top of the back fence, he crashed to the ground with such violence that several little girls screamed. Then, playing a ghost, Farley almost became a real one: blinded by his own disguise, he ran full tilt into a concrete pillar and knocked himself out, leaving a permanent depression in his left temple. The circus finally closed after a distraught mother discovered that Farley had persuaded her eight-year-old daughter to display her talents as a dancer in the nude.

A succession of animals graced the Windsor home of the Mowats. First there was Miss Carter, a stray kitten named after their landlady, who lived a few doors down the street. Since Angus did not like the woman, this gave him the opportunity to insult her: every night he stood on the front steps calling the cat by name, adding, "Come home, you little tramp!" Then there was Limpopo, a Florida alligator that was a starving, six-inch weakling when he first arrived as the gift of a fiendish relative. Eventually—when he had grown to two feet long—Limpopo was released on the banks of the St. Clair River. Years later, Farley was delighted when he read about the discovery of a six-foot alligator in the Detroit sewer system.

Jitters, a black squirrel, imprinted himself on Farley. The squirrel's one bad habit was to torment the feline Miss Carter. The squirrel, who was allowed the freedom of the house, entertained visitors "by racing around the edges of the living-room floor until he had gained maximum velocity whereupon, like a circus motorcyclist, he would begin spinning around the walls, spiralling higher and higher until he reached the picture rail up under the ceiling." This party trick proved Jitters's nemesis when he raced around the outside walls of the apartment building, lost his grip, shot off the corner of one of the eaves and then thudded down to the pavement. He died a few minutes later in Farley's arms.

Farley could be a predator. Curious about butterflies and moths—perhaps a throwback to his earliest memory of the honeybee—he acquired a butterfly net and a killing bottle. "The cyanide fumes would almost instantly kill any insect placed in the bottle and, I now realize, could have killed me had I taken a few deep breaths of the fumes myself." The boy's real fascination was with moths, and he spent countless summer evenings patrolling beneath the street lights on Victoria Avenue to see and snare them. "I can still smell the fragrance of those summer nights and feel the wild exhilaration of capturing a rare specimen." Although he would no longer commit such atrocities, "I cannot," he admits, "honestly censure the boy-who-was for what he did then."

In December 1931, Farley acquired his first dog. He and his parents had paid a weekend visit to one of Helen's Trenton friends, who had moved to Cleveland, Ohio. Her purebred Boston terrier had been courted by a travelling male—from the look of the litter, he may have been a dachshund—and had given birth to a litter six weeks earlier. Farley pleaded for one of the pups. Angus replied that there were restrictions about importing dogs into Canada, whereupon Helen volunteered to smuggle the puppy across the border in the folds of her coat. Billy, as the puppy was named, was so badly mauled by an Alsatian in the spring of 1932 that he had to be destroyed. Then Miss Carter disappeared. Farley suspected the Alsatian was guilty of her murder, and he penned his first poem about this incident, one couplet of which runs, "I'd like to choke him full of mud, / And drown him in his own foul blood."

*   *   *

Angus's love of the water was renewed in Windsor on yachting cruises with the wealthy bourgeoisie of Windsor. Although he had once complained loudly about the powered vessels of such people as "stink pots," he now took considerable enjoyment in such trips. Dressed in white flannels and a blue blazer with gold buttons, Angus, who was a bit of a Sunday socialist, could easily have been mistaken for one of the stars of the silver screen. Helen, as she wryly informed Farley, did not share her husband's pleasure in associating with the rich: "He would buy the fanciest yachting togs for himself but there never seemed to be money for me to dress so I could feel at ease amongst all those swells. Quite often I stayed home with you which, I am sure, didn't cramp your father's style at all."

There were unexpected excursions away from Windsor. Farley spent the Christmas holiday of 1930 with Helen's parents in Belleville. He was told this was because his parents had both come down with influenza, but as an adult, he suspected it was because there had been a major rupture in their marriage, perhaps due to another in Angus's long string of infidelities. Farley did not particularly enjoy visiting his paternal grandparents at "Greenhedges," the house in Oakville to which they had moved from Trenton. Angus's sister, Jean Cond, and her son Larry, who was a few years older than Farley, also lived in the house. One day Farley found three catfish in a pond and took them home as pets. Having no proper receptacle for them, he placed them in the toilet. Late that night, when she needed to use that facility, Grandmother Mowat was startled out of her wits. Upon seeing the fish, Larry flushed the toilet. That cousin also teased Farley relentlessly, for instance by giving him salt instead of sugar.

In the summer of 1932, Helen and Farley visited her parents at their cottage at Kazabazua on Danford Lake in the Gatineau Hills northeast of Ottawa. Farley loved this primitive white-pine structure pungent with the scent of turpentine. There was no running water and no electricity. The light of the Aladdin lamps made the planks of the cabin glow golden at night. There were no other children nearby, but the boy found ample companionship with the deer, beaver, squirrels, skunks and otters he found in the woods.

One day he came upon a young black bear, and they stared at each other for what seemed like ages. "I was thinking about my dream bear at Bingen and I wondered how this one would look in a checked cap. The idea set me giggling. The bear cocked his head quizzically for a moment then lumbered off into the woods as if, perhaps, doubting my sanity."

There were pike and bass to be caught, berries to be picked, and little red-bellied snakes and wood frogs to be snared and secreted in tins and jars under his bed. That month in the cottage was "no mere interlude" in Farley's life—it was a revelation: "Thereafter the desire to become one with wilderness and its native inhabitants would grow even stronger within me."

During the years in Belleville and Windsor, Angus gave Farley a new nickname to replace "Bunje": "Plausible Ike." To Angus, "plausible" meant a person who was uncertain and deferential in his opinions rather than firm and steadfast. Angus found mere plausibility beneath contempt; he respected only unwavering, strong sentiments. "Plausible Ike" carried a message for the youngster, who Angus felt was much too indefinite about things: if Farley wanted to become a man like his father, he had a long way to go. Although nicknames sometimes have a comic ring to them—this one certainly does—they can be bestowed as a way of controlling the recipient. In the case of "Plausible Ike," the tone of failed expectations lingers.

In part to win his father's approval, Farley was enthusiastic when Angus was offered in January 1933 the job of chief librarian in Saskatoon, Saskatchewan. "Surely you wouldn't do such a thing?" Helen asked her husband. "It would be like taking us to Siberia." Western Canada was suffering particularly hard from the Great Depression. But Angus was determined to make the move, and Farley backed him: "We were men, and Adventure was calling." The twelve-year-old's fertile imagination "assured [him] that the world of the Wild West was still alive."

3

Billy

1933–1939

WITH the benefit of hindsight, Farley Mowat reflected in later years that he had always felt both restless and rootless—a real outsider; he wondered if the constant moves to which he was subjected as a child (four towns before the age of eleven) took a toll on him. As a youngster, he thrived on change, but he was never really able to settle into any of those places. Though the shifts provided exciting opportunities for new and fun-filled exploits, they also produced a man prone to wanderlust.

From the outset, Angus, in charge as always, determined that the trip west would be neither modern nor sensible. "Now," his son recalled, "we would become as one with the early pioneers and head out in a covered wagon." Angus called it a gypsy caravan although what he actually had in mind was a prairie schooner, which he would design, build and pilot himself. The trip would, as much as possible, be done in nautical fashion. He spent six months building a ship's cabin eight feet wide and fifteen feet long mounted on the four-wheel frame of a Model T Ford truck. An outer skin of marine canvas was stretched over a frame made of steamed white oak ribs sheathed in tongue-and-groove cedar planking. The resulting structure was christened *Rolling Home*, but some wags called it "Angus's Ark." The schooner was to be pulled by *Eardlie*, the family's pea-green Model A Ford roadster.

The maiden voyage on August 5, 1933—two days from Windsor to Oakville for a two-week visit with Angus's parents—did not start propitiously. The unwieldy vehicle escaped her captain's control and ricocheted off a curb, knocking several wooden spokes out of a front wheel. While Angus drove *Eardlie* back to search for a new wheel, a passerby counselled Helen, "Nope. You'd best haul her onto the nearest bit of ground, Missis, and plant some flowers out in front, and settle right down here." Helen wished she were able to take advantage of such sensible advice. In Oakville, the senior Mowats were depressed by the family's departure. Gill took comfort in a bottle of whiskey, Angus's parting gift; Mary Ann withdrew to her bedroom, labelling this venture "more foolish nonsense of the sort that has distinguished the Mowat men for generations."

Farley, squeezed in between Helen and Angus on *Eardlie's* narrow front seat (the rumble seat was full of luggage), grew restive after the resumption of the long journey. Finally, Angus asked if he would like to ride inside the Ark. "What a question!" Farley later recalled. "Would I have liked to skipper the *Queen Mary*? Would I have liked to pilot the *Graf Zeppelin*?" In his new home, Farley gave his imagination free rein; one of the roles he assigned to himself was that of a First World War ace piloting a Vimy bomber.

Eardlie and *Rolling Home* attracted a great deal of derogatory attention from those unlucky enough to get caught behind them on the highway. "Angus," his son recalled, "would bare his teeth at such displays of incivility and fling pungent epithets back while Helen, who hated displays of raw emotion, cringed in the seat beside him." Since no road yet spanned the land north of Lake Superior, the Mowats crossed into Michigan, headed towards Wisconsin, and re-entered Canada at Portal, North Dakota. Most of the roads they travelled on, with brief exceptions in the United States, were unpaved.

During their stops along the way, the family witnessed more clearly the effects of the Great Depression. One day they came across a motley assortment: an old skeleton of a man, dirty and stockingless, accompanied by three lads from ten to fourteen years of age clad in tattered overalls, along with two girls and a very young baby. This group was from Texas, had been on the road for six months and were heading north to hoe potatoes. Angus thought them deprived but shiftless. Although Helen was frightened of them, she offered them a plateful of cookies. Farley thought them greedy because of the locust-like haste in which they devoured them: "Much later, while reading Steinbeck's *Grapes of Wrath*, I would remember the cookie incident with a pang of shame, but at the time I had no comprehension of the miseries and degradation to which that family and several millions like them were being subjected."

The Mowats' first stop in Saskatchewan was near Estevan, where drought-like conditions had made the farmers' lives a misery. Still, they found people like the Gents, immigrants from England, cheerful and optimistic. In fact, Mrs. Gent secretly pressed a fifty-cent piece— probably the only cash she possessed—into Farley's hand when the Mowats were taking their leave after camping for a night as guests on the Gents' land.

For Farley, the trip west was a study in contrasts. He beheld lonely, treeless, dust-filled landscapes and unpainted houses from which ragged children poured out to gape at *Eardlie* and *Rolling Home*; yet the land was rich with cattle, gophers, rattlesnakes, hawks, ducks in the thousands, partridges, prairie chickens, and red-winged and yellow-headed blackbirds. The landscape of Saskatchewan was more fecund than its American counterpart. There were saffron-coloured wheat fields still yielding harvests, fewer abandoned farms, and large sloughs filled with water.

After almost four weeks on the road, the Mowats finally reached their destination. Founded three decades earlier as a Methodist temperance colony, Saskatoon was beginning to outgrow its roots— the town was now a place where Galicians, Mennonites, Ukrainians and British converged. Farley was delighted when the family stayed at the municipal tourist park attached to the city zoo while Angus searched for a house to rent; briefly, two camels, a bison and a pair of elk were their next-door neighbours.

Helen, having grown up surrounded by the Victorian architecture of Ontario, hated Saskatoon. Dust storms, even in daylight, overshadowed the city oppressively. And Helen recalled: "The place all looked so *new* and, well, *temporary*. . . . All those boxy little bungalows covered with grey stucco and those great, wide streets with numbers instead of names, and the wind whistling down from the North Pole in winter and up from the desert in the summer." The Mowats' new home was one of those "grungy little boxes."

Afraid of being scapegoated again because of his name, Farley registered at Victoria School as "Billy." The change did him little good because he shared none of the interests of the other boys, who were addicted to hockey: "I was not prepared either to learn to skate or swing a stick, since I knew I would certainly make a fool of myself if I tried." The one friendship Farley made was short-lived:

> One Saturday afternoon down in [the Mowat] cellar, he introduced me to bestiality, onanism and homosexuality all in one fell swoop by first masturbating his dog, then himself, and finally me. He was successful with himself and the dog but gave up on me and then delivered the shattering opinion that my dick wouldn't work because it was too small. The truth was that I was terrified of discovery, for my mother was in the kitchen overhead and might have descended the cellar stairs at any moment in order to attend to our fractious furnace.

Helen, who suffered from chronic neuralgia, found the extreme cold of a western winter almost unbearable. Farley and Angus, on the other hand, developed a love affair with arctic winter conditions; the high point of that winter for them was the day the thermometer fell to 52°F below zero.

The advent of spring replaced the snow and ice with thick, non-porous muck called "gumbo." That April Farley was made aware for the first time of the importance of conserving the environment. Emerging from a bluff, he confronted a tall, unshaven, hawk-faced butterfly-catcher by the name of Alistair McPherson, who promptly told the child to call him Tom. "Tell me now, what rare creatures have ye spied today?" Tom's father had been a ghillie, an attendant to a Highland chief, but the son, who did not take to the gentry, immigrated to Canada, where he worked as a baker. Although he collected butterflies and birds' eggs, he told the young boy, "Ye may take one of each kind, mark ye laddie, and nae mair!"

Farley thrived. He was especially pleased when a neighbour gave him a pair of white rats, which quickly multiplied to ten. The young naturalist, outraged when some neighbours threatened to report the animals to the Public Health, penned his first defence of animal rights in his school's newspaper:

> This small animal has helped mankind more than we can guess. When Pasteur was attempting to find a cure for rabies the rat played perhaps the most important role of all. It was this little creature that took the deadly injections of dried rabbit brains by which Pasteur was able to determine whether his cure was effective. Most hospitals now have a room set aside for breeding White Rats for medicine. They give their lives that ours might be saved. . . . Not only are they useful but they are very amazing as pets. They are exceedingly loving towards each other and when a male and female are separated for a few days they show every possible affection when re-united.

Unfortunately, the affection became so great that the Mowat basement smelled like a barn, and the rats were soon exiled to the biology building of the university.

Farley's closest friend was the dog Mutt, originally given the improbable and cumbersome name of Diggory Venn by Angus. Mutt, who had been acquired just before Farley's thirteenth birthday, became

Mutt, 1936

the subject of one of Farley's most celebrated books: *The Dog Who Wouldn't Be*, which tells in an exaggerated fashion the real-life exploits of this extraordinary canine.

Mutt's appearance was perfectly timed as far as Helen was concerned. For a long time, her husband had been speaking of acquiring a proper hunting dog against her expressed wish. When a little boy holding a wicker basket in front of him called at the Mowat household and asked Helen if she wanted to buy a duck for a dime, she espied a bedraggled pup among the starving ducklings. She engaged the boy in conversation and learned of the sad plight of his farming family. Not interested in the fowl, she asked about the pup, which was offered to her for a nickel. She hesitated and then involuntarily allowed her hand to touch the basket. When the pup leapt at her, the astute salesman seized his advantage: "He likes you, lady, see? He's yours for just *four* cents!"

That is how the arrival of Mutt is presented in *The Dog Who Wouldn't Be*, but he was actually given to the Mowats by a man named Fuesdale, who had bought him from a small child selling puppies door to door. The real and the fictional Mutt—part black-and-white setter and part everything else—shared one trait, an indomitable knowledge that he was neither canine nor human:

> At some early moment in his existence Mutt concluded there
> was no future in being a dog. And so, with the tenacity which

38

marked his every act, he set himself to become something else. Subconsciously he no longer believed that he was a dog at all, yet he did not feel, as so many foolish canines appear to do, that he was human. He was tolerant of both species, but he claimed kin to neither.

Mutt's uniqueness was the character trait that made him so appealing. Unwilling to be the retriever desired by Angus, he nevertheless became, on his own terms, a hunting dog par excellence of comic proportions. Mutt was also heroic in his refusal to allow any obstacle to get in his way: "My family and I were electrified one morning to discover Mutt halfway up a tree in our back yard. He was climbing awkwardly but determinedly, and he got fifteen feet above the ground before a dead branch gave beneath his weight and he came bouncing down again. He was slightly bruised, and the wind was knocked out of him; but he had proved that climbing was not impossible for a dog, and from that moment he never looked down."

The trip from Ontario to Saskatoon whetted Angus's appetite to explore farther west. So a trip to the Pacific Ocean in the summer of 1934 was their new adventure. *Rolling Home* was to be used again, but a concerned friend, a Scotsman, warned Angus, "if ye did manage to drag it awa' up into they mountains ye'd likely end up, the lot of ye, tipped into the bottom of aye canyon." The advice was heeded, and a tent substituted for the caravan. Angus, Helen, Farley and Mutt set out, all four wearing motorcyclists' goggles. From the start, Mutt had decided opinions—as Angus recalled—on how to conduct himself: "He sat proudly upon the highest peak of the deck load and snarled at roadside curs to the accompaniment of ribald wit from numerous small boys. We tried to ignore his bad manners, nonchalantly, as though he were not our dog, or, if he were, we had not heard the rumpus."[1]

At first the trip was a misery. The sloughs they travelled past were bone dry, and water for bathing was rarely available at the various campsites where they spent the night. The mosquitoes were numerous and hungry, so that the tent had to be buttoned up during the hot, muggy nights. As they approached the Rockies, the landscape became more lush. In the mountains, there were countless hairpin turns and missing guardrails. The travellers were on edge, expecting the worst.

Not long after they had begun their descent of the Selkirk Range, a big touring car with its top down overtook them too closely, the young carefree passengers waving bottles at the Mowats. Angus cursed them and braked to a halt. There was a blur of movement as the big car suddenly vanished from sight. Farley and Mutt, running to the point where the car had disappeared, looked over the edge. The car had landed upside down on a ledge of rock, all its occupants apparently killed. The little boy was sick to his stomach.

Angus's memory of this incident was quite different. On the way to Lake Louise on the return portion of the trip, Angus became aware in his rear-view mirror of an "old fashioned, high backed touring car of the open air type with a ballooning, wind filled hood, swaying after us at a reckless forty. In her eagerness she was literally rolling down the trail and we hastily pulled into the cliff to let her pass. She thundered by like an angry bull elephant, roared into a straight-away bit of road that lay ahead and, to our amazed consternation, leapt suddenly, straight into the air, dived into the bush on the off side, turned over twice, swiftly, writhingly, with the spasmodic movement of a shot rabbit, and settled to rest in a cloud of dust." Farley "became very white of face" and stopped himself from becoming sick. When the Mowats reached the scene of the accident, they discovered that the driver had been thrown clear and had broken some ribs; the Mowats then helped the three passengers free of the wreckage. One of these—a pretty girl—burst into tears and complained to the driver, "You bust up your own car last night and now see what you've done to Mr. Walker's!"[2]

In *Born Naked*, Farley reworks the car crash into a coming-of-age story in which he confronts a grim reality: excessive, carefree displays of emotion can lead to violence and even death. If the passengers did not die in his memoir, the story would be far less poignant. Although the details of the story are heightened in the retelling, and in the process embellished, its essence remains intact. As a writer, Farley—an exceptionally close observer of detail and nuance—often bypasses the "truth" of a situation in order to grasp what might be called its "essential truth." He follows this procedure to make his writing more dramatic, but he also does it to recapture the feelings that animated the original situation, emotions that might be lost if he stuck to the "real" facts. In other words, he does what all writers of fiction or non-fiction should do: he takes liberties.

The Okanagan Valley was a relief to Farley after days of brooding mountain peaks. Mutt soon became addicted to cherries: "He was certainly a vision as he sat in the rumble seat, goggles pushed high up on his forehead, eating cherries out of a six-quart basket. After each cherry he would raise his muzzle, point it overside, and nonchalantly spit the pit" out through his front teeth. Often, Mutt had to give pride of place in his owner's attention to various Others: elk, mountain goats, wolves, black bears—once to a mother grizzly with its cub.

At Rathtrevor Beach near Nanaimo on Vancouver Island, Farley discovered the world of the ocean. So immersed did he become in that world that, as he recalls, "it is a wonder I did not begin to grow gills." At low tide, he burrowed in the sand and mud flats. "At high tide I was a beachcomber pausing to stare seaward through my field glasses at the flashing fins of what were probably killer whales, and at the bewhiskered faces of seals, who stared right back." Angus and Helen had to drag Farley away, although they allowed him to take with him a huge number of crabs and other sea creatures, which promptly decomposed in the heat of the return journey to the Prairies.

Soon after their arrival back in Saskatoon, the Mowats moved into a substantial house (owned by a professor on sabbatical) on Saskatchewan Crescent, a ritzy street high above the broad river valley. Thirteen-year-old Farley, although he did not much care for the comforts of his new home, was grateful for its proximity to natural parkland inhabited by foxes and coyotes.

Since their large new home required a lot of care, the Mowats hired Rachel, nineteen years old, as a maid. "I immediately fell in love with her," Farley recalled, "not in any overt sexual way but as with the sister I had never had. And I think Helen came to feel Rachel was the daughter she did not have." At times, Helen, now bedridden with neuralgia, allowed Rachel to run the household. And Rachel, who came from a poor farming family and had recently married a logger working in a bush camp in The Pas, was glad to find work with a family who appreciated her. An outsider to city life, she saw teenaged Farley as someone who had trouble adjusting to a new environment. Years later she told him, "Your dog was your best friend. Saturday mornings you and Mutt would disappear down the riverbank into the bush, or out on the prairie. Sometimes you'd come back with your pockets full of owl pellets, balls of bone and feathers." She also noticed that the boys from the Catholic school would chase him home: "You always played innocent but I used to wonder what you did to get them so mad that a half-a-dozen of them on their bikes would come flying after you right into our front yard." Rachel did Farley's math homework for him, and in exchange, he taught her about the world of the Others.

In many ways, Farley the teenager had become something of a Marsh Boy, someone who found kinships with those who were segregated from others. Fred was one of these new acquaintances, someone who was not a "reassuring sight. He was clad in tattered bib overalls, had tangled hair hanging to his shoulders, and a truly fearsome face which, I later learned, had been disfigured from birth." In exchange for lessons about the natural world, Fred taught his new friend how to open locks and gave him a set of picklocks. Through Fred, Farley met Whitey and became acquainted with some new facts of life. For a nickel she would allow a boy to accompany her to the riverbank, where she would show him her "private parts"; for a chocolate bar—a Sweet Marie—she would allow some sort of coitus, standing up. She did have her standards: she considered it "dirty" to do anything in a horizontal position.

Aware of the distance between Farley and his peers, Helen wanted her son to make friends with ordinary children. First he was forced to attend Sunday school at the Anglican church on the other side of the river. When Farley found all kinds of excuses to absent himself,

Angus gave him a modified nickname: "Alibi Ike," a name bestowed "with some admiration, for he was secretly on my side, never having been able to abide Sunday School himself."

Then Farley was forced into the Cubs. He escaped this indignity by casually remarking at dinner that his scout master was "really chummy. I guess he thinks a lot of me because he keeps patting me on the behind." Next, Farley was volunteered for Saskatoon's Little Theatre Group in a pantomime based on *Alice in Wonderland*, in which he played the Dodo. One evening, he inadvertently bumped into the Mad Hatter. After that performance, Helen apologized to the cast: "He can't really help himself. He gets it from his father. He has to be the centre of attention, no matter what." Helen's final endeavour to socialize her wayward son was to enroll him in the Children's Choir. At the fourth rehearsal, he fainted in the middle of the "Ave Maria" and emptied his bladder. He also taught himself to make strategically placed, high-pitched farts that embarrassed his mother.

In his own attempt to establish normal peer relations, Farley started the Beaver Club of Amateur Naturalists, which consisted of four boys and three girls. The founder was a strict taskmaster: each would-be member had to list from memory one hundred birds, twenty-five mammals, and fifty fish, reptiles or insects; to take at least one ten-mile nature walk a month; to write a four-page essay once a month; and to make a donation to the Saskatchewan National Animal Museum, begun by Farley a few months earlier.

The large wood-panelled room in the Mowat basement was lined with glass-fronted bookshelves. One Saturday afternoon, when Angus and Helen were away, the group pulled the absent professor's hundreds of tomes off the shelves and hauled them into the garage. In their place were substituted the contents of the museum: buffalo bones, the joined skulls of a two-headed calf, an umbrella stand made from the lower leg and foot of an elephant, a grossly discoloured human kidney in a jar of alcohol, a stuffed black bear cub and mounted tropical birds. The latter were, in turn, home to legions of moths and to little beetles called dermestids. The grand opening of the museum was abruptly cancelled when the moths and beetles invaded the closet where Helen kept her raccoon coat. This discovery precipitated an investigation by Angus and the rapid dispersal of the contents of the museum. Undaunted, Farley began a magazine: *Nature Lore—The Official Organ of the Beaver Club of Amateur Naturalists*.

A bit later, Farley convinced the editor of the Saskatoon *Star Phoenix* to publish a weekly column about bird life in its Saturday children's supplement, "Prairie Pals." Farley was paid five dollars a week for his weekly column, "Birds of the Season," which ran from March 14 to May 9, 1936. His career ended abruptly when he penned a piece describing, in graphic detail, the underwater mating habits of the ruddy duck. Farley was fired because the lazy editor, who never bothered to read submissions before publication, was inundated by complaints.

At the same time as Farley was becoming more and more involved with the world of the Others, he became aware of the plight of the human misery unleashed by the Depression. Helen unpacked and distributed bales of clothing sent from Ontario; she also worked as a nursing assistant tending children in the Municipal Hospital. Disgusted by the government's paltry attempts to help the destitute, she and Angus became members of the socialist Co-operative Commonwealth Federation (CCF), the forerunner of the New Democratic Party (NDP).

Farley's encounter with a Polish-born couple and their two children provided him with a vivid glimpse into the world of the poor and unemployed. Rachel took him to visit these people, who had lost their farm to foreclosure and been forced to take refuge in the city. They existed "in a gaunt shell of a frame house beyond the end of a streetcar line. . . . I can vividly remember the repulsive smell of the one occupied room, all the space the family could hope to heat with the green poplar which was what they had to burn."

At thirteen, Farley was still capable of being extremely mischievous. Unable to obtain information on the manufacture of explosives from his chemistry set, he spent some hours in the reference section of his father's library and learned about the manufacture of high explosives.

Most of the ingredients—ammonium nitrate, potassium nitrate, powdered charcoal, sulphur, nitric acid, mercury—were readily available from farm supply stores and drug stores. On the evening Farley decided to mix the ingredients together, a farewell party was in full swing for Helen, who was escaping to Ontario for a visit. Suddenly there was a bang, which blew out the cellar windows and filled the house with thick smoke. "It sounded," Angus later recalled, "as if somebody had dropped a trench mortar shell down the chimney." Although her nerves were shattered, Helen made her departure on time. Her final words of parting, conveyed to Angus, were priceless: "Tell the sweet little lamb he musn't play about with matches."

Farley and Mutt sometimes conspired together to annoy Angus, who was writing his first novel, *Then I'll Look Up*, on the dining-room table. Boy and dog once became so vociferous that he threw four volumes of the *Encyclopaedia Britannica* at them.

That spring, interest in the Beaver Club waned. The boys wanted to play baseball, and the girls wanted to play with the boys. Farley's attention became focused on Muriel Pinder, who was regarded as "hot stuff" by most of the young men. He wrote and mailed her a poem:

No bird that flies in summer skies,
No mouse that lurks in sacred church,
No fish that swims in river dim,
No snake that crawls on sunny walls
Can stir my heart the way you do
With raven hair and eyes so blue.

She returned the poem immediately with a single word—"Ugh!"—emblazoned on it. As Farley later remarked, she "may not have had a taste for me but her literary taste was impeccable."

In a bid to make his sex life more interesting than wet dreams, Farley forged an alliance with Munro Murray. Although only a year older than Farley, Munro looked nineteen, had peach fuzz on his upper lip and was regarded as a "whiz" with girls. Not only did he go to parties with them, he parked with them afterwards along the river bend. Farley was certain he had gone "all the way." In order to find his own "way to paradise," Farley hung around Munro as much as possible. The problem was that Farley still looked young for his years, like everyone's idea of a kid brother. Munro did his best. He arranged a blind date for Farley: "The plan was for us to take the girls to a movie, buy them a soda, then drive to a secluded spot near the ski jump where we would neck and—maybe—do it." Munro borrowed his mother's make-up kit and tried to make Farley look older, in the process making him look like Dracula. Unfortunately, while Munro and his date steamed up the front of the car, Farley got nowhere with Violet, who finally exclaimed, "Doesn't this here kid ever shut up?" Devastated, Farley got out of the car and walked home. The next day, the much more experienced Munro advised Farley to use his hands more and his mouth less. He also offered to recruit his own girlfriend's twelve-year-old sister. Farley decided to remain celibate.

Farley never forgot the humiliating time when Angus insisted not only that he perform the role of maid at a cocktail party but also that he pass himself off as a woman: "The thought of dressing up like a girl was enough to chill the blood of any boy of my age." On the other hand, Christmas was approaching and he desperately wanted a good camera for photographing birds. Taking this crucial circumstance into consideration, Farley decided to go along with his parents' suggestion that the imposture would be a good practical joke. In turn, he turned the enterprise against his parents by serving excessively strong drinks which inebriated the whole group, who managed to do serious damage to the rented house. Even more chaos ensued when Angus proceeded to demonstrate his new double-barrelled twelve-gauge shotgun on the front lawn. The targets were plates, which were sent spinning into the air over the riverbank; the police arrived shortly thereafter. Since Angus had spent so much money—a month's salary—on the new shotgun, Farley did not get his camera.

Farley's obsession with birds was so overwhelming that he obtained an official bird-bander's permit (No. 1545), becoming the youngest person to hold one in Canada. He no longer counted himself a mere "amateur naturalist. I had officially entered into the Realm of Ornithology wherein I expected to spend the rest of my mortal days." He found two baby owls in the woods—Wol and Weeps—and made pets of them. They later became characters in *The Dog Who Wouldn't Be* and the protagonists of their own children's book, *Owls in the Family*.

Quite soon, Farley's would-be career as a naturalist was in open conflict with his pursuit of hunting. From youth, Angus had shot duck for fun and food; later he became a sport hunter. Years later, he explained it this way: "It was the *hunt*, you understand. Getting up shivering in the dark for bacon and eggs and a mug of tea, and then the sounds and smells of an autumn dawn. Sheer ecstasy!" The son had a different memory, emphasizing the camaraderie this activity can generate:

> Not only did he become an avid sport killer in Saskatoon,
> Angus made it his business to turn me into one too. This wasn't
> too difficult. Nothing could have been more attractive than the
> opportunity to be buddy-buddy with my father in a shared
> enterprise. Besides which, Angus was right: the desire to hunt,
> if not to kill, comes naturally to most young males.

Although it took him some time, Angus became an excellent sport hunter. Farley was a lukewarm participant in all their outings. He wanted to be like his father, but he could not put his heart into it. He accompanied his father, but he wanted to look at the birds, not destroy them.

One day, Angus and Farley were in pursuit of Canada geese, snow geese and wavies. In the early morning light, father and son could see almost nothing, but then suddenly they heard the sound of wings:

> My father saw them first. He nudged me sharply and I half-
> turned my head to behold a spectacle of incomparable grandeur.
> Out of the storm scud, like ghostly ships, a hundred whistling
> swans bore down upon us on stately wings. They passed directly
> overhead not half a gunshot from us. I was transported beyond
> time and space by this vision of unparalleled majesty and mystery.
> For one fleeting instant I felt that somehow they and I were one.

(top) *Farley with a hawk, circa 1939*
(above) *Farley with Fang, his pet coyote, 1939*

Despite his feelings of oneness, Farley took aim a few minutes later when a flock of Canada geese flew overhead; this was "more a conditioned reflex than a conscious act." Although father and son had not really aimed at a specific bird, one fell, "appearing gigantic in the tenuous light as it spiralled sharply downward. It struck the water a hundred feet from shore and I saw with sick dismay that it had been winged. It swam off . . . its neck outstretched, calling . . . calling . . . calling after the vanished flock."

The adolescent felt he had broken his compact with nature. His sense of loss was so great that he never went sport hunting again. There was, Farley fondly recalled, a much less traumatic excursion, "a singularly memorable excursion one Christmas when the family, at Angus's instigation, went north to Prince Albert in the private car of a local railroad mogul, then by open lumber truck, horse-drawn sleigh and finally by dog-team to spend the festive season with a trapper in the forests."

Years later, reflecting on how warmly Farley had rendered his early years in Saskatchewan in *The Dog Who Wouldn't Be*, Angus made a paradoxical observation:

> I guess that Farley was at the moment which comes, not to all men, but to men who are meditative when he was still close to his past youth and he felt the urge to catch at it—not to try, foolishly, to hold it—but just to touch it before it all went back into memories. And I surmise that Farley had a particularly happy childhood and youth; and I surmise that, in his wrong-headed way, he somehow blamed me; and I surmise that the only way he could say so was in jest—in apparent jest.[3]

Though Farley saw the happiness he experienced as a child as attributable in large part to his father, a man he desperately wanted to emulate, their relationship was so complicated that something good was perceived as a fault. The love of father and son was real, but it was seldom expressed directly.

★   ★   ★

Angus naturally took an active interest in his son's sexual development. Farley's testicles did not fully descend until he reached adolescence. One day, the boy overheard Angus saying to a friend, "I think the little bugger's balls are finally coming down." The father was also quite liberal on the subject of masturbation. At breakfast one morning, when the two were alone together, he looked his son in the face and said, "In the army, we used to call it pulling the pud. Everybody did it. Nothing wrong with it either. Nothing wrong with *you* playing with *yourself*, Bunje, so long as you don't get caught by a minister, or any of the other old women whose idea of pleasure is attending a good hanging. So carry on until you can try something better." At such moments, Angus relinquished the role of father in favour of that of older brother or best friend.

To assist Farley in getting "something better," Angus announced at dinner—in the face of yet another of Helen's long visits back east—that he had hired a maid, Louise. "To this day I don't know whether Angus hired Louise because he thought I was in need, or because he was in need, or genuinely as someone to clean the house and wash and cook. Maybe all three." In any event, Louise was a nineteen-year-old knockout with a husky voice, gleaming black hair and eyes and a curvaceous figure. She was totally incompetent in housekeeping except for making and consuming huge quantities of chocolate fudge. Within one week of Helen's return home, Louise was dismissed. Helen's comment to her son is quietly revealing: "It wasn't so much what Louise *couldn't* do. It was what she could."

Farley idolized his great-uncle Frank Farley, a distinguished ornithologist who had homesteaded in Camrose, Alberta. The two had exchanged letters but had never met before the summer of 1936, when the lean, over six-foot-tall man in knee-length, lace-up boots presented himself at the Mowat home. Farley was ecstatic. "His head, under a soft felt hat, was a mountain crag dominated by the famous (in the family) Farley nose. He had the washed-out stare of a turkey vulture." Frank was so powerful that Farley felt like squealing when the older man gripped his shoulder. Frank and another ornithologist,

Albert Wilks, had come to take Farley to Churchill on the west coast of Hudson Bay to study arctic birds and collect their eggs.

The trio left Saskatoon in the first week of June and travelled for three days and nights in the caboose of a train up through The Pas. Then they and their fellow passengers, including two Catholic missionaries, some trappers and several Cree, continued by train all the way up to Churchill. At Mile 400, Farley saw the boreal forest give way to the dwarf trees of the Barrens. At Mile 410, he saw an amazing sight: "A flowing, brown river was surging out of the shrunken forest to the eastward, plunging through the drifts to pour across the track ahead of us. But this was no river of water—it was a river of life." This was *la foule* ("the throng"), the mass migration of the caribou.

For six weeks, Farley explored the tundra, finding nests and collecting eggs, but he became more and more agitated by the wanton killing of birds at the peak of their nesting season. Frank Farley was blunt with him: "Don't be soft. There's millions more out there. We're doing this for science. I measure every specimen. I shoot and note the condition of its plumage. Science needs to know these things." At that time the boy assented, but later he would come to the realization that "collecting expeditions such as ours were little more than high-grade plundering operations conducted in the hallowed name of Science."

Farley had one close call. He and Wilks were collecting hawks' eggs. The two had delivered the contents of two nests to Frank when a group of outraged parents, "like a squadron of attacking fighter aircraft swooped on [Farley], talons outstretched and beaks gaping wide. The first one missed by no more than a foot and made me cower against the cliff wall. The second struck home. My head was buffeted hard against the rock by fiercely beating wings. I raised an arm to protect myself and it was raked from wrist to elbow by sharp talons. For a horrible instant I thought I was going to fall; then Frank's shotgun bellowed and my attacker spun away." Frank was stern with Farley: "You must have done something to upset them."

That summer Farley encountered the Dene Indians (then called Chipewyan) from the interior of northern Manitoba, the most primitive people he had ever glimpsed: "Small, dark, solemn (in our presence), they spoke a peculiar language of rustling sibilants. They were partly dressed in caribou-skin clothing which was shedding and looked singularly ratty. About twenty of them were living in squat little tepees of soot-blackened canvas full of rips and patches."

At Churchill, Farley was awed by the sight of several hundred belugas, the small, friendly white whales that sport there. That serene encounter was blasted by the noise of two motorboats that appeared suddenly, their crews blazing away at the animals with heavy-calibre rifles. Soon the surface of the water was filled with splashes of crimson as the belugas tried to escape the onslaught.

Back in Saskatoon, Angus did not allow a lack of proper sailing water to deter him from purchasing a sixteen-foot sailing canoe, which he restored, remodelled and christened *Concepcion*. Attempts to sail it on the Saskatchewan River, however, were unsuccessful. Undeterred, he and another landlocked romantic determined to build a boat and sail from Saskatoon to Halifax. They did not get very far: the boat sank twelve times in the first six miles. Born and bred in the Bay of Quinte, Angus soon began to tire of the Prairies. Within four years of arriving in Saskatoon, he decided to seek a post back in Ontario. Helen was delighted her husband had at last come to his senses.

The trouble was that Farley had fallen in love with the West. Between September 22, 1935, and March 22, 1936, his notebooks record thirty-four bird hikes covering more than three hundred miles. He had made good friends with Murray Robb, one of the members of the now disbanded Beaver Club. At Nutana Collegiate, his first high school, Farley had at long last found congenial teachers. Gnarled-faced Frank (Monkey) Wilson was an excellent instructor in biology; the math specialist, "Jelly Belly," was fascinated by Indian lore; and the English teacher, Mrs. Edwards, allowed her charges to write on topics of their own choosing.

The announcement early in 1937 that Angus had been appointed Inspector of Public Libraries for the Province of Ontario completely devastated his son: "I was going to be deported from the one place I had ever really felt at home. I became depressed and, in classic teenage style, grew sullen and uncommunicative." Helen noted in her diary, "This has changed poor Bunje into a perfectly horrid boy." Nevertheless, she was sympathetic. Angus was not. He informed his son, "It'll be the best thing that ever happened to you. Going back to where you came from will do you the world of good. Chin up and take it like a soldier and a man!" But Farley was neither. In the privacy of his third-floor room, he made plans to run off and become a cave-dwelling hermit.

In the spring of 1937, the Mowats returned east, again by caravan. Farley spent the summer at Kazabazua in the Gatineau Hills and "suffered" his first love affair. His beloved was Mary, a Mennonite who had become the Mowats' new maid in April and whom Farley seduced the following month; in retrospect, he said, she was "the first to make a man of me—sort of."[4] In the Gatineau Hills, Mary met and eventually married a young Québécois, an event that inspired Farley, the abandoned lover, to write a melancholic sliver of verse, which ends with this serio-comic putdown of himself and his longings:

> Still his unseeing, dull and lidless stare
> Earnestly scans the long blue air;
> A corpse's gaze—save where a clinging fly
> Scuffs busily across the sunken eye.

During that summer, Farley discovered that with the advent of adolescence and all its attendant pangs, his early attachment to his grandparents' cottage had almost vanished. That autumn, his past disappeared even more when the Mowats moved into a house at 90 Lonsdale Road in Toronto and Farley attended North Toronto Collegiate. Still very much a solitary, he often wandered into cemeteries in order to find some room in the big city. One Toronto adventure involved a surreptitious attempt to use a quarter-plate Graflex—about as big as a shoe box and almost as noisy to operate as a farm tractor—to photograph a striptease artist named Fanny la Fanny at the Casino burlesque on Queen Street, which resulted in his being ejected by three burly bouncers.

Hove To, Richmond Hill

Farley took almost no part in school activities: all his spare time was spent in the company of ornithologists. In visits back east from Saskatchewan, he had passed many happy hours at the Royal Ontario Museum (ROM) in Toronto; he continued this habit upon his return. One other activity—very much a sideline—was the writing of what he later called "dark, obscure, and frightfully bad verse."[5]

In the summer of 1938, accompanied by his closest friend, Andrew Lawrie, a fellow student at North Toronto Collegiate, he hitchhiked back to Kazabazua on a scientific field trip. The friends spent a month in the region shooting small birds and trapping small mammals, which they converted into museum specimens. The two lads also learned further "rudiments of human biology from the daughters of some cottagers in the vicinity."[6] When he had been in the Barrenlands with his great-uncle two years earlier, Farley had wanted to be simply a "naturalist observer"; this summer he became, very much in the manner of Frank Farley, a collector.

In the autumn, the Mowats, who had soon sickened of Toronto, rented a house in the country at Elgin Mills, some thirty miles north of the city. A year later, in 1939, they bought a house—their first—in nearby Richmond Hill, then a village of four hundred people. The new home, in Angus style, had to have a name; Angus christened the clapboard house on Elizabeth Street "Hove To," a nautical expression for a temporary resting place. By this time, the family had lived in nine houses.

Farley's next romance was with Marie Heydon, a fellow student at Richmond Hill High School. She remembers herself and Farley as only children, who were, as a result, exceptionally close to their parents. She had trouble persuading Farley to go to dances—he disliked all such public events. Farley could be easygoing, but sometimes she could see a real glint of determination and stubbornness in his eyes. He could also be deceptively quiet for a long time before offering an observation. Once they went to a concert in Toronto; not until after it was over did Farley, with great disgust, inform her that her hat had blocked the view of other members of the audience.

As before, Farley's lack of interest in sports kept him a loner among the other boys. Another early friend, Bette Campbell, remembers him as a funny-looking little guy with a Scotch tam and a lot of swagger. She also fondly remembers his special trick of playing "Bolero" on the piano with one finger.

Farley made a new friend in Harris Hord, then working as a bank teller in Richmond Hill. Out of the blue, Farley approached the shy young man and asked him to go sailing. Later that day, Farley introduced Hord to the local speakeasy, a place he evidently knew very well. The young man from Saskatoon told his new friend that he was entering Queen's University in Kingston in the autumn and was determined to become an ornithologist.

In the summer of 1939, together with Hord and Frank Banfield—who owned their means of transport, a 1937 Dodge—Farley made a two-month field trip to Saskatchewan to begin an ornithological survey of that province. As a way of subsidizing this venture, Banfield and Mowat had convinced the ROM to purchase any specimens they caught. Banfield's interest was in small mammals, while Farley and Hord wanted to collect birds. The three, outfitted as for an African safari and with enough arms and ammunition to start their own war, drove to Saskatoon, where they picked up Murray Robb and then went north to Emma Lake. After ten days there, they headed south to Fort Carleton for a week, then to Dundurn and the Cypress Hills. At one point they were seized by a posse of Mounties who mistook them for bank robbers. They went home, with crates of birds and animal skins and one live coyote, to Ontario by way of

Idaho, Wyoming and Montana so they could visit Yellowstone National Park, the home of Old Faithful, the geyser that erupts at frequent intervals.

A serious ornithologist Farley may have been, but he did have time for more age-typical pursuits. This is his description of one evening's adventure out drinking: "Things got wild and wicked. Finally a cute little blonde called Tiny, as high as I was (in the two ways) came over and greeted me. . . . In a couple of minutes we were highland flinging to the amusement of sundry sober people. Tiny's boyfriend kept following me around insisting I should have her phone number. Finally, he wrote it on my shirt and went away hiccupping happily."[7]

As he approached his twentieth year, Farley knew himself to be a person whose opinions and beliefs set him apart from most of his contemporaries. He cultivated a decidedly eccentric veneer and interests that were outside the mainstream. A prairie boy who had been, against his will, transported back to his point of origin, he found it increasingly difficult to know what he wanted to do with his life.

Farley's dilemma became compounded by the increasingly ominous events in Europe, which led to the outbreak of the Second

Andrew Lawrie and Mutt, summer 1938

World War in the summer of 1939 just as he and the two other young Canadians were leaving Yellowstone. The young men found that their Canadian money was now considered valueless in the United States, and, for almost a week, they subsisted on a diet consisting mainly of oatmeal, something Farley had much experience with; their limited American funds had to be spent on gas to get them back to the border.

Like many young men of his generation, Farley realized that his immediate future lay in the battlefields of Europe; like his peers, he knew many of their lives would be lost in that conflict. He decided, therefore, not to go to university: Canada's predestined role would be to assist England and the Allies in the fight against Nazism, and he knew Angus would expect him to enlist.

But even as late as early 1940, war for Farley still remained a grim fantasy. A more immediate tragedy was the death of his beloved Mutt near Elgin Mills in April 1940, killed by a speeding truck driver. "The pact of timelessness between the two of us was ended, and I went from him into the darkening tunnel of the years."

4

Squib II

1939–1946

ON September 2, 1939, Angus, his face flushed with excitement, pulled into the driveway at Hove To: "Farley, my lad, there's bloody big news! *The war is on!* Nothing official yet, but the Regiment's been ordered to mobilize, and I'm to go back in with the rank of major, bum arm and all. There'll be a place for you too. You'll have to sweat a bit for it, of course, but if you keep your nose clean and work like hell there'll be the King's Commission" in the Hasty Pees.

Farley shared his father's conviction that the Munich Pact, which surrendered the Sudetenland to Germany, had been a sellout and that the Nazi threat to world order had to be eradicated. But he did not wish to join the infantry. Instead, he dreamed of soaring in the stratosphere as a member of the Royal Canadian Air Force. That dream fell to earth when the recruiting sergeant in Toronto told him he was not interested in "peach-faced kids." Undaunted, Farley, who was both short (5'7") and slight and accustomed to being called "shrimp" or "baby face," pulled out his birth certificate. The sergeant was distinctly unimpressed: "Eighteen, eh? You still can't go for air crew. Too young, and anyway we got a waiting list ten miles long. You might come back in six months." On May 13, 1940, the day after his nineteenth birthday, Farley returned to the recruiting station and was allowed to take a physical. Although he was in perfect health, he weighed 4 pounds less than the official minimum of 120. Once again, he was dismissed.

"What do they need pilots built like King Kong for?" a humiliated Farley asked Angus. Soothed by his father's assurance that the Air Force was both elitist and pretentious and then cunningly reminded by him that there were still openings in the 2nd (Reserve) Battalion of the Hasty Pees (the 1st had been on active service in England since Christmas 1939), Farley was persuaded to take the Army medical. The examining doctor, a good friend of Angus's, advised Farley to drink as much water as possible. So ballasted, he passed this medical with flying colours and was duly enlisted as a private soldier, serving at Picton as a batman (officer's servant) to the newly appointed lieutenants his own age.

These ploys were arranged by Angus, who firmly believed that any officer who had not served in the ranks would be useless as a leader of fighting men. "And," as Farley recalled, "he was determined that this is what I was going to become." At an unconscious level, Farley resented his father for having pushed him into the Hasty Pees. A few years later, while fighting in Europe, he had a magnificent dream of "being a fighter pilot, wheeling high and free in the cool mercy of some northern sky." Then the dream became a nightmare when "a sudden flaming rage against my father for having inveigled me into the clutches of the Infantry" arose—apparently from nowhere. This eruption of anger against his father both amazed and frightened him, for he had not known he carried within himself such hostility.

Any dreams of glory in battle were held firmly in abeyance for a long time. Through the summer of 1940 and into early autumn, Farley served as a batman and, briefly, as an officers' mess corporal at Picton and then at Trenton. That winter, he served as an acting second lieutenant in the 2nd Battalion HPER at Trenton, where he pioneered

Angus, Helen and Farley, summer 1938

ski-training techniques. Since Trenton was where young pilots trained, Farley's resentment would have been reinforced by the condescension the dashing airmen regularly bestowed on members of the infantry. Farley's spare time was spent sailing aboard Angus's new ketch, *Scotch Bonnet*. He had a few, mainly abortive, affairs. And he increased his knowledge of birds.

At Trenton, he faced another major obstacle. Years later Angus recalled, "Some ass posted Farley to my Company and we both had a bad time of it since I was a good disciplinarian and worshipped the Regiment and, well, you can't show favours to your own son, can you? I daresay I must have been pretty bad but I didn't know how bad till one day [when I was at] Camp Borden the three other sub-alterns of my Company asked if I would grant them an interview. They had something on their minds. I forget the words, but the gist of it was, 'For Christ's sake, Sir, we can see you hate your son, but do you have to break his back on that account? And him the best officer in the Company?' "[1]

Ignoring this advice, Angus called Farley aside: "You may be my son, in fact I'm fairly confident you are, but in this regiment you're just another snotty-nosed little subaltern who has to be taught to change his diapers and respect his betters." However much Angus made certain he was far tougher on Farley than on the others in his command, another side—that of proud parent—was moved by the transformation he beheld: "I watched you breaking out of the happy dream of birds and facing up to the hard realities, and overcoming the natural misgivings at what then lay ahead."

Towards the end of 1941, Angus was posted to District Military Headquarters in Kingston, where Helen and their dog Elmer joined him in a rented cottage, also called Hove To. Two years later, he was transferred to National Defence Headquarters in Ottawa, where he established a book distribution scheme for troops in Ottawa.

Meanwhile, in February 1941, Farley was taken on strength at Fort Frontenac, Kingston, as a second lieutenant. For four months he faced dreary, routine army work and boarded at the home of the Noonans, where he fell in love with the daughter of the house, Molly. In the next few months, he took an officer training course at Brockville to qualify as a full lieutenant and was then posted to the A10 Infantry Training Centre at Camp Borden, near Barrie, Ontario.

The long wait to see action awakened his mischievous side. Farley and a chum, disillusioned by the lack of proper training facilities, disguised themselves as privates and ran off to Toronto for a good time. When the two were apprehended, the entire incident was treated as a joke by their superiors. That November, Farley's rebelliousness came to the fore when he tried without success to organize a Young Officers' Revolt to challenge the King government. The young men—volunteers all—were furious at Mackenzie King's weak stand on conscription, which was based on the prime minister's fear of insurrection in the province of Quebec, where the war was viewed as a European problem.

There was also the sheer boredom of waiting for the experience of war to begin, as Farley confided to his mother: "Borden is the nuts. . . . What about my status? Can you find out where we stand and what chances we have of seeing a fighting country before Xmas? If

I'm stuck here for a winter it ought to about decide me to join the blinking dodos." The men would still have to wait in England because the stock of fighting men at the front had not been exhausted, but action of any kind seemed preferable to boredom.

Finally, in July 1942, Farley was posted overseas to Whitley, on the edge of the Salisbury Plain, as a reinforcement officer, remaining there as a training officer until October. At Whitley, Major Stan Ketcheson, an old friend of Angus's, gave Farley the nickname "Squib," which rightly belonged to Angus. Reluctant to accept the designation, Farley nevertheless began to sign some letters home "Squibb," the extra "b" marking him as Squib the Second. Angus began to write letters to "Squib [Mark II]." In her letters, Helen continued to address Farley as Bunje.

Farley still looked terribly young, much too boyish to be a leader of men in battle. In photographs from the time, he looks barely sixteen. He tried to change his image by growing a moustache, but the sparse-growing thatch above his lips only brought scorn from his superiors.

When he took a battle-drill course, he wound up spending four weeks in hospital in Maidenhead with damaged knees. In October 1942 he was posted to Waldron, near Horam in Sussex, where, as acting battalion intelligence officer, he spent most of his time experimenting with high explosives:

> Fooling with bombs and other bangers became something of an addiction with me that winter. After four months with my Regiment, I was uncomfortably aware that I was still regarded in some quarters more as a mascot than a fighting soldier. Some of my superiors tended to be a shade too kindly, my peers a whit too condescending. I needed to excel at something martial and reasonably risky and it seemed to me that a flirtation with things that go bang in the night might earn me soldierly merit and the respect of my fellows.

This lack of respect must have been devastating as he was painfully aware that Angus expected great things of him.

Battalion Headquarters, which was set up in the vicarage at

Waldron, allowed Farley the opportunity in his off hours to explore the countryside and its bird life. Later he accompanied his regiment on manoeuvres to Loch Fyne near Inveraray, Scotland, where, briefly, he was exposed to battle-like conditions; he then returned to Surrey and Sussex for the balance of the winter. In the spring of 1943, he was assigned to act as air liaison officer in mock battles, which meant he had to call in air strikes for both sides. He remained on this assignment until June, when he was recalled to the Regiment, which was soon to go into action. He was given command of Five Platoon of Able Company, and the Regiment proceeded north to Darvel, Scotland, to practise procedures for assault landings. The soldiers knew something big was coming; many were certain they were to be part of the European invasion. The wait was frustrating, but during it Farley made friends with Al Park, a fellow platoon commander. Earlier, in September 1942, he had acquired the services of a batman, gnarled, squeaky-voiced but experienced "Doc" Macdonald.

When he could snatch some free time, Farley began to put together stories about his experiences with Mutt back in Saskatchewan. In so doing, he was finding a way to deal with feelings of homesickness; in revisiting his happy childhood, he was trying to put some distance between himself and the bleak prospect of annihilation now confronting him.

There was the occasional trip on leave to London, and another series of love affairs. The most important was with Hughie, whom he met at the Overseas League in March 1943. She was a married British army corporal, her husband a tanker with Montgomery's Eighth Army in North Africa. In falling in love with a local girl, Farley was like many Canadian soldiers stationed in England. Such romances, flourishing in defiance of death, were often as intense as they were short-lived. Two years later, Farley told his parents of this affair, of which he was sure they would not approve: "I didn't approve of it myself. But when you fall in love, and we did. . . . We never actually made love. Neither Hughie nor I could do that. Too much of the betrayal of a serving soldier sort of thing." In London, Farley was also introduced to a hefty British land army girl named Philippa, who, clad in manure-stained jodhpurs, invited him to take a walk along a riverbank. According to Farley, she "stripped" him of his virginity at the behest of one of Farley's senior officers, who had told her the young man "needed doing . . . and there's nothink I wouldn't do for a Canuck!" The story is a good one, but the available evidence suggests Farley is forgetting several other earlier encounters.

"Three years ago in Yellowstone Park, when war was just a rumour, I was probably happy in the sense of the word, that my mind and soul were at peace with each other. I never realized the constant war that has been raging inside me since then, until today, that frustration, impotence, impatience and a consuming haste that had no meaning, would become my only emotions. These last three years have no emotional value for me, call them a coma, they left few memories, and few lasting effects."[2] Farley made this confession in a letter to his mother in July 1942. In part, he was telling her of the turmoil he had gone through since the beginning of the war, before he went to Sicily and then to Italy as a combatant. More than that, he was trying to find some way of describing the painful journey he had taken from boyhood innocence to adult experience. He had thought he was "at peace" during his early Army years, but really he had been in some sort of suspended emotional state.

For Farley and many young men of his generation, war extorted a heavy price. The past—whether happy or sad—was not only forbidden territory but also the gateway to self-deceit; the reality of the present was the ritualized murder of men by other men in the publicly sanctioned exercise known as war. In order to take up arms, Farley felt, he had to both deny and denigrate his young manhood. Only in that way could he hope to participate in the war against Nazism.

Unlike his son, Angus—although he was bitterly aware first-hand of the toll that war can exact—experienced no conflicts about the nature of war, which was for him a holy crusade in which men discovered their full selves. If a man was brave, war allowed him to enter into the fullness of his manhood, a sort of purging away of all the baser parts of the soul. If a man was a coward, he soon discovered just how ill-made he was. Angus was of a generation that still emphasized the Victorian ideal of manliness; no such comfort was available to Farley, soon to experience the stomach-wrenching reality of combat.

At long last, three gruesome years of waiting were over. On June 13, 1943, an excited Farley embarked with the Regiment at Greenock, Scotland, on a combined operation exercise leading to sailing from Greenock through the Strait of Gibraltar to the Mediterranean to join Montgomery's Eighth Army, which, with the invasion of Sicily, would begin the process of driving the Germans out of southern Europe. This military strategy was known as "Operation Husky."

Farley was assigned to the *Derbyshire*, one of a convoy of seven large troopships escorted by cruisers, destroyers and corvettes. Off the coast of Gibraltar, the real war was brought home to them when they witnessed the sinking by depth charges of an enemy submarine.

Now that he was to be a part of the real thing, Farley was certain his soul would be both purged and cleansed. To a friend back in Canada, he wrote, "I'm like a kid who's been anticipating a birthday party for years and years and finally sees his mother lighting up the candles. We are about to quit the play acting. . . . Oddly, I don't feel the least bit scared."

Aboard the *Derbyshire*, Farley and an English sapper lieutenant got into serious mischief when the lieutenant offered to show his Canadian colleague how the newly invented electric mine detectors worked. Since the entire ship was made of metal, the detector responded enthusiastically wherever they pointed it. Then Farley had a bright idea: what about using the hardwood floor in the saloon lounge of the ship, a former luxury passenger vessel? After the Englishman deposited some metal objects on the floor, Farley—the amplifier strapped on his back—put the earphones on his head and proceeded to sweep the floor. Then he changed the nature of the game when, having become thirsty, he started to detect the "highly dangerous liquid mines" in the room. Things proceeded apace until Farley turned his attention to a "Limey brigadier" leaning forward on the grand piano in the middle of the room:

When I looked up from a table I had just swept clear of mines and saw his large posterior directly ahead of me, I got carried away. Yes, I did. I slowly brought the detector head up to waist level and pushed it gently forward, unaware that a hush had descended on the mess and that all eyes were now upon the little tableau by the piano. The hush was shattered as the sapper reached forward and turned up the volume to max. The resultant squeal was like that of a stuck pig. The brigadier stiffened as if shot but before he could turn around to see what we were doing, my pal touched him on the shoulder and in a loud voice said: "Excuse me, sir, but I think you should know there seems to be a booby trap up your behind."

The brigadier was not amused, and the two culprits found themselves in real trouble when they were arrested to await court martial. But the troublemakers were sprung by the commanding officer of the 48th Highlanders because the assault landing in Italy was only three days away.

When Farley told his parents of this incident two years after it happened, he treated it as an enormous joke suddenly gone wrong, not seeing that his conduct might in part have been motivated by trepidation of what was about to come. Yet it seems obvious that he was apprehensive and sought to dissipate that discomfort through comic relief. Throughout his life, Farley would revert to such behaviour on many occasions: unable to confront feelings of anxiety in public forums, he would play the role of jester. He would give the impression of being some sort of demented exhibitionist-cum-clown, when the simple truth was that he was really trying to deal with feelings of inadequacy and shyness. For Farley, a good offence remained the best defence.

A whole series of new, unexpected emotions invaded Farley as he sailed for Sicily. The Germans were the adversary, but there was an even more potentially deadly opponent: The Worm That Never Dies. Farley had to face the fact that his most potent enemy lived within his own breast: he—like many other fighting men—was filled with fear for his own life. So powerful was this feeling, and so ashamed was he of it, that he could not confess its existence to Angus, who apparently knew no fear, neither during the war nor ever afterwards. He was apprehensive that his father would reject a son who harboured such conflicts.

But no escapes were left. And when the moment for battle was finally upon him, Farley felt ready: "This was the moment toward which all my years of army training had been building. It was *my* moment—and if I seized it with somewhat palsied hands, at least I did my best." This was the reflection uppermost in Farley's mind when he and the other men were ordered to disembark at Pachino, Sicily, on July 10, 1943.

Since four hundred vessels were involved in this major invasion, there was a great deal of confusion in the scheduling of such a vast enterprise. Darkness and sirocco winds made landing conditions treacherous. Many of the men in Farley's assault landing craft became seasick, and the vessel wandered far off course. Finally, as dawn was breaking, they got stuck on a sandbar. Farley decided it was time for action.

> Revolver in hand, Tommy gun slung over my shoulder, web
> equipment bulging with grenades and ammo, tin hat pulled
> firmly down around my ears, I sprinted to the edge of the ramp
> shouting, "Follow me, men!" . . . and leapt off into eight feet of
> water. Weighed as I was, I went down like a stone, striking the
> bottom feet-first. So astounded was I by this unexpected descent
> into the depths that I made no attempt to thrash my way back to
> the surface. I simply walked straight on until my head emerged.

Quasi-farce rapidly gave way to tragedy when the sergeant-major—within arm's reach of Farley—was killed by a bullet through his throat.

After reaching safety that first day, Farley fumbled through his duties, "slumped in a state of mindless exhaustion." The landscape that confronted him and his men was as strange as if they had landed on the moon: "The arid hills loomed desolate on every side, while to the north the white cone of Etna shimmered in distant splendour. The road looped and laboured over a wild landscape. Villages of prehistoric origin hung on their pinnacles of sunblasted rock."

As soon as the beachhead was established, Farley and his men marched north. The conditions were horrific: little food and water, heavy packs and intense heat. They advanced fifty miles before clambering aboard tanks which took them to Giarratana, where they established a defence perimeter. Quite soon, death and violence were daily companions. The death of his commanding officer, mild-mannered Lieutenant-Colonel Bruce Sutcliffe, on reconnaissance awakened Farley even more to the grim realities confronting him:

> The loss of those who had been killed in the tumult and confusion of earlier actions had not yet been deeply perceived by us, but this new stroke of death was something else. It shredded the pale remnants of the illusion that real war was not much more than an exciting extension of battle games, and it fired us with rage against the enemy. This killing, before battle had been joined, seemed singularly vicious, almost obscene.

Such atrocities soon became commonplace in the nightmare world into which Farley was plunged.

In mid-July, members of his regiment rode into an enemy trap in the town of Grammichele, overlooking the plains of Catania, which was defended by two infantry battalions of the elite Hermann Goering Division. Farley, standing in the gunner's compartment of an armoured Bren gun carrier, strayed a bit from his duties one afternoon to focus his binoculars on a pair of red-tailed kites soaring on the updrafts from the escarpment. Suddenly, the birds dived out of sight. "I heard a distant snarling bark, a whining scream, and then a stunning crash as a shell burst a few yards away." As the carrier slid sideways into a ditch, Farley remained frozen until one of his mates yelled to bail out. Seconds later, two of the carriers exploded.

Sometimes Farley's past and present conjoined in the most unexpected ways. One day on reconnaissance, the "air was filled with a pungent odour that nagged at my memory until I realized it was the tang of sage—a scent I had last smelled in the summer of 1939 on the arid plains of southwestern Saskatchewan."

As a soldier, Farley saw himself as an Everyman, someone who was simply competent and mildly brave. He could not understand why his commanding officer chose him and his men for a particularly difficult mission: "He must have been aware since early in my tenure with Seven Platoon that I was not the stuff of which heroes are made. Perhaps he wanted to give me an opportunity which, if I could manage to live up to it, would confer on me a tiny touch of what the French call *la gloire* and so turn me into a real fighting soldier." Having put himself down slightly, he completed his own character assassination with considerable dexterity: "On the other hand, since we chosen officers were each to pick our own twenty men, he may have felt he *had* to take me in order to ensure that the best of Seven Platoon's unmannered but hard-fighting toughs joined the assault company."

In the mountain town of Assoro, the Germans were entrenched well above the Canadians. The only realistic way to defeat them was to scale their perch under cover of darkness and then launch surprise attacks at dawn. Farley and the Hasty Pees were given the job of scrambling up the mountain, clearing out sentries and cutting off the road. Once at the summit they had to defend it against counter-attacks. The action was relentless: night reconnaissances, patrols into villages hiding enemy snipers, and expeditions to reclaim the dead.

On July 22, after one rocket had killed four men in Farley's platoon, the Germans pulled out of Assoro. Farley, suffering from dysentery, was evacuated to a field hospital. Upon his return he was reassigned as battalion intelligence officer. At that point, the Worm fully asserted itself: "The truth was that I did not ever again want to have to taste the terror which had overwhelmed me at Assoro. The urge to action which had been my ruling passion since enlistment had collapsed like a pricked balloon—to be replaced by a swelling sense of dread."

Farley was also forced to re-evaluate his sense of connection to the men with whom he was serving.

Leaving Seven Platoon in order to return to the intelligence officer's job was a considerable wrench . . . but I was to discover that after a brief separation they would become almost as irrelevant to my continuing existence as if I had known them only in some distant moment of illusion. This was a startling discovery, and for a time I thought it must indicate a singular lack of emotional depth in me. I was deluded by the conventional wisdom which maintains that it is personal linkages that give a group its unity. I was slow to comprehend the truth, that comrades-in-arms unconsciously create from their particular selves an imponderable eternity which goes its own way and has its own existence, regardless of the comings and goings of the individuals who are its constituent parts. Individuals are of no more import to it than they were in the days of our beginnings when the band, the tribe, was the vehicle of human survival. Once out of it, it ceases to exist for you—and you for it.

He might have added that it becomes almost impossible to establish deep personal connections with others when you know you might be deprived of those friendships without notice. If a soldier died, he was quickly replaced. If he was to die, Farley clearly discerned, no one could afford to miss him.

The Regiment went back to the front line at Nissoria, where it was badly mauled, suffering more than two hundred casualties. Eventually, after the Germans in Sicily had been defeated, the Canadians rested near the hill town of Grammichele. There, staff officers insisted that enlisted men polish buttons, line up for inspections and, in general, keep busy. "Only the Canadian forces," Farley reflected angrily, "were treated like inmates of a reform school." The men lost all respect for officers who treated them like children: "It was inevitable that we would begin to feel a festering contempt for the pompous paper-pushers of our behind-the-lines bureaucracy."

On the first of September, the Canadians were moved to the Strait of Messina for the invasion of Italy, which began two days later. For the next four months, Farley moved with the regiment in the thick of the fighting. He temporarily lost his hearing when a land mine exploded under a truck he was directing, killing two men and wounding seven more. At Ferrazzano, he was shot in the back, but a tin of bully beef in his pack took the hit. As the regiment moved slowly towards the German defence line, the fighting increased savagely. There were 150 fatalities. Farley witnessed much of this butchery.

During one particularly brutal battle, he crawled into a stone hut that held four German soldiers, three of them dead, one dying.

> The fourth man—dimly seen in that dim place—was sitting upright in a corner of the little unroofed room and his eyes met mine as I struggled to my hands and knees.
>
> In that instant I was so convinced that this was death—that he would shoot me where I knelt—that I did not even try to reach for the carbine slung across my back. I remained transfixed for what seemed an interminable time, then in an unconscious reflex effort I flung myself sideways and rolled to my feet. I was lurching through the doorway when his thin voice reached me. "Wasser. . . . Wasser?"
>
> His left hand was clasping the shattered stump where his right arm had been severed just below the elbow. Dark gore was still gouting between his fingers and spreading in a black pool about his outthrust legs. Most dreadful was a great gash in his side from which protruded a glistening dark mass which must have been his liver. Above this wreckage, his eyes were large and luminous in a young man's face, pallid to the point of translucency.

Earlier, on reconnaissance, Farley had looked through his binoculars at some Germans shaving, while "others stood, stripped to the waist, enjoying the first warmth of the sun." "These are men—not Jerrys—just like myself," he had realized. In his confrontation with the dying German, this insight assailed him more sharply, making him poignantly aware that man is the only species of mammal that engages in such vicious internecine warfare. Here is a man just like myself, he sadly understood. The futility of war overwhelmed him in a new way.

Later, when he was sent to lead some reinforcements up to the front from San Vito, the atmosphere of death and horror was heightened. When his friend Al Park was severely wounded and his former company commander, the tough, resourceful, never-say-die Alex Campbell, was killed in the Ortona battles, he felt a complete "withdrawal of sensation." He wept uncontrollably. "I wonder now . . . were my tears for Alex and Al and all the others who had gone and who were yet to go? Or was I weeping for myself . . . and those who would remain?"

By January 1944, he had reached complete burnout. He was ordered to a job at First Brigade Headquarters as a liaison officer, eventually becoming brigade intelligence officer. He took part in the battles of San Nicola, and eventually, in May, the terrible battle for Monte Cassino. In the late summer, he was present at the assaults on the Gothic Line near Pesaro and Rimini as well as in the pursuit of the Germans through the Po valley. By now an acting captain, he kept track of the whereabouts of the Germans, kept battle maps and the official war diary up to date and questioned prisoners and refugees.

The days were exhausting. Yet he had plenty of time to experience a gruesome alienation from himself. He told his parents in April 1944, "We concluded that one thing is certain: any guy who goes home with any expectation of returning to the past is in for a hell of a shock. The ground he used to stand on was in fact a sandbar. It ain't there any more, and the waters over it are deep and cold. We're tough buggers, and we can cope with material changes, but the other side of it looks like being more than we can handle. Truth is, we don't know you—you Canadians. And we don't know ourselves." At one point Helen wrote her son, "I really shouldn't give you advice. But my whole instinct is to put you in a pouch and carry you around like a kangaroo." On another occasion she confided to him, "Don't get blue and despondent, my lamb, over your future. Angus went through very much the same thing after his war and was ages trying to recover his health and his cheerfulness."

When Farley criticized the high-handed actions of some staff officers, his father replied, "Well, what do you expect?" Such harshness had its corresponding softness, however. "Your job, and I mean

Farley, Ortona, 1944

your duty to yourself," Angus patiently explained, "is to continue keeping that little spark of something or other that's in you inviolable from war." More and more convinced that his son's life after the war should be devoted to writing, he told him about a book on the Hasty Pees he was hoping to write; he confided to him the obstacles he was confronting in finishing and publishing his second novel, *Carrying Place*; he encouraged his son to write and to send the results back to him. At a conscious level, Angus knew that putting words on paper was the only therapy that could assist his son in his desperate mental straits. He even forwarded three of the poems Farley sent to him to the *Atlantic Monthly*, which did not accept them.

Writing letters home provided Farley with moral support, knowing as he did how fully his parents loved and cherished him. The Mowats—son, father and mother—were, and remained, compulsive letter writers, often putting into words strong feelings that they probably could not have expressed face to face.

Farley resumed work on the Mutt stories (now becoming a collection called "It's a Dog's Life"), and Angus sent this material to Reg Saunders, his own publisher. Farley was appalled: "That is high school stuff! For the Lord's sake, take it away from him. I may *want* him to publish a book some day and don't want him turned off too soon." In March 1944, Angus retired from the service and returned to his job as Inspector of Public Libraries for Ontario. His war now over, Angus had more time to be concerned about Farley's.

On leave in Naples in 1944, Farley renewed a brief acquaintanceship with Ellen (Betty) Brown, a Canadian nurse from Winnipeg who had worked in Churchill with his great-uncle Frank. She was an "older woman"—she was twenty-nine, six years older than him—and they were not in love, but they gave each other the illusion of romance. Their favourite hangout was the Orange Grove (the Naples' Allied Officers Club), which clung to the cliffs above the city. The flagstone paths through the gardens were ideal for dancing, and the heady smell of jasmine pervaded the place. Sikhs, Soviets, Moroccan Goums, Polish parachutists and Norwegian frogmen were among the regulars there, together with countless "Limey and Yankee" sailors and soldiers. *Vino rosso* and Lacryma Christi were among the drinks.

There was a standing joke in Farley's circle that when Rome fell to the Allied forces he and Betty must celebrate by getting married. A mock ceremony was duly held that June with Mendelssohn's "Wedding March" rendered by two pipers, a harmonica and a two-toned Italian trumpet. Betty wore a mosquito-net bridal veil, and the marriage itself was performed by the brigadier: "It was all quite touching. We were then escorted to a distant grove where a nuptial hammock had been stretched between two fig trees and sternly ordered not to reappear before breakfast time. Well, you know what an obedient servant of the King am I!" Lest Helen become upset, Farley assured her that the entire ceremony had been "definitely unorthodox, although about as close to the real thing as I ever hope to come."

In June, Farley was still at First Brigade as brigade intelligence officer. The following month Betty was sent back to England. More

and more, Farley became convinced that humanity would never elim-
inate the "twin cancers of greed and war." A visit to Rome depressed
him, convincing him more than ever that he despised cities.

Angus, who continued to send Farley books, interested *Maclean's* in
one of his son's short stories, called "Stephen Bates"—a scathing
account of the exploitation of Cape Breton miners—but the Army
refused to allow it to be published under Farley's name. Then the
editor at *Maclean's* decided the story was too bitter and chose another
called "Liaison Officer" in its place (published as "Battle Close-Up"
by "Bunje").

During the winter of 1945, Farley returned to the world of the
Others to find a semblance of solace; his new menagerie consisted of
a linnet, a stuffed ostrich, a stuffed oriole, a stray dog and a guinea pig
named Desdemona.

Back home, Angus and Helen were deeply worried about their
son. He had matured considerably since the outset of the war, but
they felt that he had paid too high a psychic price for the change.
Angus, remembering the difficulties he had himself experienced after
the First World War, reached out to his son as never before, speaking
to him as an equal:

> And I can say this to you, my brother, that the moment of
> elation [at being part of a group of fighting men], which goes
> deeper than any man could express, and that feeling of oneness
> with the finest of mankind will live with you forever—to your
> death and, I have some hope, beyond. Of course, life being what
> it is, some let-down will follow and there will be moments of
> bitterness and disillusion and resentment but beneath it all noth-
> ing can ever take that moment of insight and understanding
> from you. And this is a gift reserved for the infantrymen.

It is an eloquent and moving letter celebrating the triumph of men
who know they have achieved the fullness of their manhood in
battle.

Farley was touched that his father could speak to him so directly
and so intimately, but at the same time, he had become painfully

aware that he was no longer capable of such idealistic feelings. For him, the future remained bleak and empty. He knew he had not found his true self on the battlefield. He was convinced that he wanted to remove himself from the human world and return to the world of the birds and the animals that had been his comfort as a child and adolescent:

> I am becoming more than ever determined to do the hermit stunt *après la guerre*. . . . Having overcome my fear that a corrosive bitterness might be my heritage from *la guerre*. I know my point of view has changed dramatically from the dewy-eyed visions of earlier years, but I don't think the way I see things now is necessarily all bad. Caution, suspicion and selective intolerance are not evil of themselves, as long as they are not directed at the true beliefs and honest actions of others. A blindly benevolent "love thy neighbour" attitude, as prescribed in the best circles, is too much like living on a surfeit of sugarplums.

The world that Farley had witnessed in Europe was corrosive and self-destructive; he did not wish to bind himself to that reality. The only solution that presented itself to him was escape. Farley became convinced—as many soldiers had during the Great War—that the highest echelons of politicians and of the military were completely cynical in the way they managed those under their command; men were numbers, to be moved, manipulated and crunched as their masters saw fit. Although he had always had a healthy contempt for authority, Farley now saw the essential evil and immorality of the way the war was managed. This point was driven home to him by Operation Chuckle, which began in early December 1944. On the second day of that engagement at a high-dyked river called the Lamone, near Ravenna, the divisional commander ordered what became a slaughter when First Brigade crossed the heavily defended barrier in darkness and without a reconnaissance. After that, winter brought an end to most of the fighting. "There was nothing to be done," Farley recalled, "except endure."

In March 1945, the remnants of the Regiment boarded American landing ships at Livorno and headed for Marseilles. From there, they went to Belgium, where they were stationed at Oostmalle, near Antwerp. On leave, Farley took a short trip to Scotland and then journeyed to Shoreham in England to meet up with Hughie, whose husband was due back from Italy that May: "After a couple of hours, Hughie and I said goodbye." Back in London, Farley visited his friend Al Park in hospital and then got together with a group of Hasties on leave at the Kit Kat Club.

In April, Farley was posted to Canadian Army Headquarters in Holland with the rank of captain as technical intelligence officer, a job that involved searching for high-tech German weaponry. Surrounded both by devastation and by thousands of refugees, he witnessed one of war's other faces.

After the surrender of the German forces and in war's aftermath, life seemed even more chaotic to him: he knew he was going to have to make some decisions about his future. He confided to his parents, "But now the race is done. You'll be relieved to know I have dumped most of my repressions, suicidal and homicidal inclinations, inhibitions and rage. Most of them, I say. And I'm sure of one thing: it was a damned sight better that I did it here than back in Richmond Hill."

He spent some time working with the Dutch underground and even took command of a captured German E-boat sailing from Den Helder to Amsterdam to be surrendered. At a nightclub, he met Rita, who claimed to be the daughter of a Dutch foreign office official; if he had been more himself, he might have realized she was prepared to be a "comfort" to anyone in power. When he contracted the clap from her, he was filled with an acute sense of self-loathing.

Help in wresting some sort of meaning from the meaninglessness that he had witnessed came to Farley from Tyce Michels, an officer in the Dutch underground. After the war, Michels reasoned, the British, the Americans and the Soviets would try to grab the best of the German weapons, and each would try to keep what it found from the others in order to obtain military supremacy. But the small countries would be left out in the cold. What if, Farley wondered, a small nation, such as Canada, amassed such a collection? If successful, such an undertaking might give Canada some clout in dealing with the major powers.

That June, Farley and the members of "Mowat's Private Army"—including Canadians Mike Donovan and Jimmy Hood, and Butch Schoone of the Dutch underground army—collected over nine hundred tons of equipment, including all sorts of guns, experimental ammunition and tanks and two V-1 flying bombs—one a manned model for suicide missions. Donovan and Hood even stole a V-2 rocket, which Farley had painted blue and disguised as a one-man submarine. When Farley took a genuine one-man submarine for a test in Amsterdam's Amstel Canal, he almost sank it.

Through a wide variety of subterfuges, Farley managed to get his complete collection of armaments past a labyrinthine bureaucracy and aboard the Dutch ship *Blommersdyk* bound for Canada that autumn. On November 15, the ship and Farley arrived in Montreal after a rough crossing, during which some of the tanks and rockets almost fell into the ocean.

A despondent Farley then spent the next five months in Ottawa

Members of "Mowat's Private Army"

trying to interest the authorities in his collection, even as material for a war museum. Eventually, he had the V-2 delivered to the defence research establishment at Val Cartier, where it was dismantled and studied. Almost everything else in the collection was subsequently lost, damaged by fire or water, junked or sold for scrap.★

In April 1946, Farley made arrangements to have himself discharged. As he recalled, "I got out of the army—the perfect retreat where I could sit and sneer and wait for the inevitable cessation of things to wipe me out like the memory of a bad dream."[3] Farley was suffering from what was called from the time of the First World War "battle fatigue" or "shell shock"; today, the term has been changed to "post-traumatic stress disorder," a designation which encompasses a wide variety of responses to horrible events that irrevocably change a person's life. In the short term, Farley felt shattered, completely incapable of making any kind of realistic decision about his future; in the long run, many aspects of his life would be poisoned by his war trauma.

He had not wished to return to Canada, to be among people with whom he no longer felt he had anything in common. The only glimmer of hope he could see was the prospect of finding a measure of happiness by becoming a writer. Overall, he reflected, "limbo is the place to be right now, and I seem to be in a kind of limbo." The previous June, the distraught son had sought his father's advice in a letter from Europe:

> I am getting scared.
> It is now the second month since the war ended, taking with it my excuse for carting around an empty skull. It is time I snapped out of it. But I can't seem to "snap."
> With considerable effort I've established myself in a physical and psychic spot where there should be no obstacles to mental rehabilitation. Yet, damn me, I can't rehabilitate.
> I sit down to write. I believe I *can* write. A paragraph or so of

★ The manned V-1 is in the Canadian War Museum's Vimy House in Ottawa.

reasonably good descriptive material comes out without much trouble. I stare at it. But no more comes. No *story* comes. In fury I rip the paper up. . . . But the writing block is not the worst. The worst is that I am turning more and more to total immersion in mechanical activities. This seems to be becoming all that I can will myself to do.

Very much aware that even the war collection project was a makeshift way of keeping despair at bay, Farley wanted to break this cycle. Yet any real sense of purpose evaded him. "So I ask you, Pop," he questioned Angus, "how did you get into the swing of living once again?"

5

Raging Boy

1946–1948

UNCERTAINTY now overwhelmed Farley. In an autobiographical sketch from 1948, he tried to put his post-war existence into perspective:

> Before the war (which has been the pivot point of my life), I was a cocksure youth and I knew what I wanted— though I was still too imma-ture to be able to interpret my desires in practical terms. I *had* that intangible, and often mis-represented, quality that can be

called "faith." My life did not appear as an end in itself but as something that could have been—and would have been—directed purposefully towards that queer, illusive goal that draws all life towards it. . . . So I grew up, developing an adequate mind that was not too overgrown in the rank undergrowth of prejudice and intellectual stagnation. I knew that most important thing—how to ask questions; and I knew enough to take noth-ing for granted until my own reason was satisfied that truth might be there. I was not cursed—or blessed—with unreasoned credulity and was not to be gulled by the fascinating simplicity and ready security that was offered in neat little watertight packages, done up in gaudy ribbons, by Religion.

The young man's idealism had been destroyed by the war; any belief he had possessed in moral or ethical goodness in human existence had been shattered. He now became convinced that, in the final analysis, there was no goal worth striving for. Although he had survived when many others had perished, he did not have a wife or children to return to. Since he no longer had any aspirations, he made what he called a non-decision: "I stayed overseas after the war as long as possible, and in an unenviable state of mind. I had nothing to come back for so it was pretty obvious to me that I had damn well better find something. I tried looking for something to replace my lost faith." Much later, Farley—in more explicit, cruder terms—analyzed his dilemma: "Since everything that supported my fat ass turned out to be lies, I had nothing to sit on, and had perforce to build my own chair. Being lazy and confused, and of a suicidal tendency anyway, I resisted the building thereof until desperation forced me into action. What action? Wrong ones, first. Marriage. Children. House. Money. All the usual anodynes that never work."[1]

When the search for substitutes led nowhere, Farley became certain he was an emotional coward:

> After a while my cowardice grew stronger and began to emerge from the back into the front of my mind and I stopped trying.
> . . . I took refuge in that mental dead-end that eventually leads to self-death or madness. I became completely cynical about my life, its values and its dead hopes and dreams. . . . My disgust and revulsion from man was only exceeded by my disgust and revulsion from myself. . . . Finally I came back to [Canada] because it was as easy to come back as it was to stay away.[2]

Farley wanted the sense of certainty that had guided him as a young man to be restored, "[so] I went to Saskatchewan and shot little birds till I grew sick of that slaughter, then I sat in a lot of taverns and talked

Farley, 1946

to a lot of people until I grew sick of that futility—and then I quit again."³ Although he later recalled the summer of 1946 in negative terms, he spent it roaming in his newly acquired jeep through the northern part of Saskatchewan near Lac La Ronge collecting birds for the Royal Ontario Museum. He also stayed in a remote Native settlement and learned more about caribou, animals that had fascinated him during his first northern trip. Yet Farley remained adrift.

Angus, concerned about the nihilistic feelings that had taken over his son, suggested Farley needed the regular routine that being a university student could bestow. Farley enrolled at the University of Toronto in September 1946. Although he later described his attendance at university as fitful, he was an excellent student who achieved first-class marks. His time at the university was made a little more acceptable by the sixty dollars a month in veteran's pay provided by the Army.

The young man's charm certainly did not fail him. He persuaded William Wallace, his professor of ancient history, to give his imagination free rein in recreating the classical past: in Farley's essay on the battle of Marathon, the Persians won. His English professor, Vincent Teller, allowed him to rewrite the plot of a Hardy novel; he also accepted short stories in lieu of essays. If I entertain my professors, Farley reasoned, they will give me good grades. His teachers were seduced. In retrospect, however, Farley sees his three years in pursuit of a Pass Bachelor's degree as "the least important experience in my entire life."

In the winter of 1946, when it seemed that university was not answering his son's emotional needs, Angus intervened. He contacted a friend, John Gray, the publishing director of Macmillan of Canada, and requested that he consider giving his son a position. Gray invited Farley to his office, plied him with a large quantity of sherry and offered him a job. Farley declined. Then Angus suggested his son follow in his footsteps and become a professional librarian. Farley decided against that path and continued on at university.

Early in 1947, Farley determined that he would run away that summer to the Arctic, which seemed "like a good place to run" to in an attempt to escape uncomfortable realities. "But," as he later put it, "something interfered with my plans." And that "something" was Frances Thornhill, a fellow student.

Frances Elizabeth Thornhill, two years younger than Farley, was born in 1923 in Toronto to Herbert Reuben (Reub) Thornhill, a sales manager at Aikenhead Hardware, and Florence Adelaide, née Roos. Reub was Scots Presbyterian, Florence of Alsace-Lorraine and German Swiss extraction. Fran had an older brother, Jack, her senior by six years. The Thornhills, who lived at 81 Balmoral Avenue, were loving, carefree, but decidedly traditional parents. Reub was a championship-quality curler and lawn bowler; like many middle-class women of the time, Florence, who was thirty-seven when Fran was born and had a "tricky heart," took pleasure in making most of her daughter's clothing. The family was sufficiently well off to have a car when most people did not.

Small, lithe and pretty in a refined, delicate way, Fran attended Bishop Strachan School in Toronto. When she graduated, the war

Fran Mowat, 1948

was in progress and all her friends were working on farms or in munitions factories. Deciding on a different course, she trained as a blood technician at Central Tech high school before enlisting in the Wrens (Women's Royal Naval Service) in Galt. Her first posting was to Cornwallis on the Bay of Fundy. Despite her specialty, she was assigned to Physical and Recreational Training and was stationed in Halifax, Ottawa and Toronto. After her discharge, she enrolled in September 1946 at Victoria College in the University of Toronto. She had wanted to attend McMaster University in Hamilton, fifty miles away, in order to put some distance between herself and her parents, but they were determined that after a long absence, their daughter would live at home with them. Like Farley, Fran decided to get a quick three-year degree. She had two or three boyfriends "lined up" when Farley came along.

Fran and Farley were in some of the same classes, and at first they were simply pals. During chemistry and botany labs, Farley, in a series of comic turns, continually stole her seat. When Fran could not get her microscope to focus on specimen slides, he gallantly came to her assistance. Since there were several blocks between their classroom at the ROM and the old zoology building on College Street, she began to accept his offers to drive her in his jeep between the two buildings. What became a casual "spring love" in April 1947 was, by July, transformed into a "raging flame." She told him, "I find that I compare and value people in terms of you. No one measures up to your standards. No one says what you say and in the way you say it." Farley, by his sheer force of personality, "disturbed" her far more than she wanted to be disturbed.[4]

Farley and Fran had a lot in common. They were both loners, quite content to be solitary for long periods of time. They shared the same backgrounds and values; both had served in the war. But they were really too much alike, often underscoring each other's vulnerabilities rather than their strengths. Although Farley reciprocated Fran's feelings, his natural inclination was to find a loophole that would magically and painlessly allow him to escape her charms.

Even more than Farley, Fran was prone to long periods of intense depression. Her melancholia was deeper and went back farther, whereas Farley's was war-related. One day not too long after they met, Farley visited Fran on Balmoral Avenue and was told by Florence—who had a soft spot for Farley—that her daughter was confined to bed with a severe headache. When he visited Fran in her room, Farley could see the extent of her unhappiness in the "black" pallor of her complexion. He became frightened, realizing that maybe he did not wish to become involved with a woman who was so vulnerable. Although he was "blindly" in love, he decided in the spring of 1947 to follow his original plan to escape—at least temporarily—to the Arctic.

During the previous winter, an Army friend had given Farley a copy of Joseph Burr Tyrrell's *Report on the Doobaunt, Kazan and Ferguson Rivers and the North-west Coast of Hudson Bay* (1896), which described the Barrenlands of Keewatin and marvelled at the "greatest single caribou herd ever seen by a white man—a herd so vast that for many

(top) *Farley and Ohoto, 1948*
(above) *Ootek, Yaha, Farley, Hekwpw and Ohoto II at Nueltin Lake, 1948*

miles the surface of the land was obscured beneath the blanket of living beasts!" Tyrrell also spoke, in a fragmentary but tantalizing way, of the "People of the Deer" who lived there. At about this time, Farley's imagination was captured by another acquaintance's description of the Barrens as "that damn and bloody space, which just goes on and on and on until it makes you want to cry, or scream—or cut your own damn throat!"

Curious about people who struggled to exist in primitive conditions, eager to be alone in a vast, uncharted wilderness and anxious to put aside some of the conflicted feelings that were bothering him, Farley accepted an opportunity to go north with Francis Harper, a much older American field biologist then living in Moylan, Pennsylvania. Harper had received a grant from the Arctic Institute of North America, headquartered in Montreal.

On April 7, 1947, Harper extended a cordial invitation to join what he grandly called the First Nueltin Lake Zoological Exploratory Expedition, which might include several other Americans—or, as it turned out, only himself. Since Farley was interested mainly in birds, he anticipated no conflict between them; yet, Harper realized, there was "always a possibility of minor frictions developing; but devotion to a common scientific cause should minimize such a possibility."[5] Although he was intrigued, Farley hesitated because of financial considerations. Those objections were overcome when the Arctic Institute gave him a grant of three hundred dollars.

The first half of *People of the Deer*, Farley's first and most controversial book, tells of his six-month expedition north to, among other places, Nueltin Lake and Brochet. He tells of arriving by train in Churchill, a grim and desolate place, where he chanced upon a man whom he had met there years earlier with his great-uncle Frank. That acquaintance put Farley in touch with Johnny Bourasso, the owner of a twin-engine Anson. Farley's interest was piqued by what he had learned about a German immigrant trader who had a trading post he had run with his Indian wife and five children but which was now occupied only by his three sons. Since the family's cabin, situated at the mouth of Windy River at Nueltin Lake in south-central Keewatin territory, seemed an ideal base, Farley hired Johnny to fly him and five hundred pounds of supplies there, three hundred miles northwest. The "spot" was difficult to find: eventually they saw "the land gape wide beneath to expose a great valley walled in by rocky cliffs and snow-free hills." Suddenly, Farley caught a glimpse of "something" that proved to be the cabin:

> Johnny wasted no precious gas on a preliminary circuit. The sound of the engines dulled abruptly as we sank heavily between the valley walls. Before us stood a twisted, stunted little stand of spruce; a river mouth, still frozen; and the top foot or so of what was certainly a shanty roof, protruding slyly from the drifts.

After the two men quickly said their goodbyes, Farley made his way to the cabin:

> The doorway was snowed-in to a depth of several feet, and when I had dug my way through, I found only a log cabin in the drifts—dank and murky and foul-smelling. The dank was the stinking damp of long disuse, and I could trace the smell easily enough to the floor that was buried under the dirt of years and the accumulated refuse of a winter's meals. . . .
>
> The walls of the cabin were furnished in fur. Wolf and arctic fox pelts, all as white as the snows of early winter, were spread over the log walls to dry, and by their simple presence showed that the place was not completely deserted after all. During the next week I came to regard them with affection, for they were the link with the unknown man who had brought them in and who, I sincerely hoped, would come himself before too long.

After a week at the camp, Farley finally encountered Charles Schweder—called "Franz" in *People of the Deer*—one of the German trader's half-native sons. He told Farley that he was in the midst of carrying food to the starving Ihalmiut (People of the Little Hills) who were camped along three small lakes some sixty miles away. Farley met members of the band of forty-nine Inuit and quickly made friends with two of them, Ohoto and Hekwpw:

> Both were dressed in *holiktuk*—parkas—of autumn deerskin with the fur side turned out. The parka of Hekwpw was decorated with inserts of pure white fur about the shoulders and by a fringe of thin strips of hide around the bottom edge. Ohoto's was even more dressy. . . . But despite the beads and insets, the general appearance of both men was positively scruffy. Great patches of hair were worn off the garments and rents and tears had been imperfectly mended, evidently by an unpractised hand. Food juice and food drippings had matted the thick hair that remained, and dirt from unidentifiable sources had caked broad patches of the fur.

Farley's romantic notions about the existence led by these primitive people were destroyed in a flash: "My first reaction as I saw and smelled these men was one of revulsion. They seemed foul to me and I felt the instinctive surge of a white man's ego as I wondered why the devil they couldn't find clean clothes to wear." Under Charles's guidance, his abhorrence was quickly replaced by understanding and compassion: understanding that the Inuit were essentially different from himself, compassion for the ways in which their lives had been irrevocably altered by the settlers. Trapping, once peripheral to their way of life, had become for them the means of acquiring guns, food and manufactured goods, including alcohol. When the value of furs plummeted, the settlers abandoned the Inuit, having destabilized their once stable existence.

The more time he spent with the Inuit, the more Farley came to admire and celebrate their differences. Rather than expecting the Inuit to adapt to him, he moved towards them: "The unadorned fact that I, a white man and a stranger, should voluntarily wish to step across the barriers of blood that lay between us, and ask the People to teach me their tongue, instead of expecting them to learn mine—this was the key to their hearts." The landscape and peoples of the Barrenlands spoke to Farley's heart. In the land's majestic, austere loneliness and in the simple friendliness of its inhabitants, he discovered again—as he had in childhood—the verities of the natural world. During his time in Europe, after witnessing wholesale pillage and destruction, he had come to see a world both unworthy and incapable of redemption. Although well aware of the degradation to which the Inuit had been subjected, he wondered if the clock could somehow be turned back.

Later, in the middle of that summer, Farley joined Charles for a six-hundred-mile round trip journey by canoe south to Brochet, in northwestern Manitoba on Reindeer Lake near the border with northeastern Saskatchewan, in order to replenish supplies that had been used to assist starving Inuit the previous winter. While there, he learned that Johnny Bourasso had gone missing and was presumed dead. Later, in September, Farley and Charles travelled for six weeks by canoe from Nueltin Lake to Churchill.

When he returned to Toronto that autumn, Farley wrote an account of his experiences, which he sent to the Department of Mines and Resources, the federal agency responsible for the Inuit at that time. He also wrote to R.A. Gibson, the deputy commissioner of the Northwest Territories, describing the starvation among the "Ihalmiut of the Upper Kazan River"; in that account, he was careful to mention that his information was mainly based on two sources in addition to Charles Schweder: Ohoto and his friend Ootek. Since he considered the testimony of these two men to be accurate, he made their observations his own in his subsequent writings about the plight of the Inuit.

At the beginning of chapter 2 of *People of the Deer*, Farley wrote: "On a morning in May of 1947 I boarded the train and gave myself up to the demands of the fever that was in me." Throughout the rest of his account of that trip, he gives the reader the impression that he travelled north by himself. Completely excised from *People of the Deer* is Francis Harper.

A veteran of the Great War, in which he had served as a Rodentological Control Officer (rat catcher), Harper, in his late sixties in

1947, was characterized by Farley as a Southerner and a racist who sometimes referred to the Indians they encountered as "niggers." Harper had absolutely no reluctance about sharing these views with Farley, whom he labelled a "young buck." His health was debilitated by diabetes; he was often irascible and irrational; he treated his much younger companion as if he were a servant.

In The Pas, Manitoba, Mowat and Harper met Fred Schweder, Charles's father, and arrangements were made to use the Schweder cabin at Nueltin Lake. At that meeting, Schweder gave the two men information about the three sons who were still living near there (in addition to Charles, there were Franz and Mike).

Despite the fact that he and Farley were the guests of the brothers at the Nueltin cabin, Harper, after arriving, scorned them. When the cabin flooded, one of the brothers put on Harper's rubber boots while cleaning up the resulting mess. Furious at what he considered an unsanitary invasion of his private property, Harper burned the boots. In order not to worry his parents, Farley wrote to Angus and Helen on June 30 that he and Harper were "getting on and that's all. No doubt there are mutual faults, but we are about as incompatible a pair as it would be possible to find and we recognize it."[6]

Farley did carry out some of the planned research at Windy Lake, but his motivation to undertake various trips (beginning on July 8 in an eighteen-foot freighter canoe) was enhanced by the prospect of escaping from Harper and the poisonous atmosphere he had engendered at the cabin. The American was furious at Farley's departure; when Farley and Charles returned on August 5, Harper was still so angry that he informed Farley he would not be allowed to board the plane to Churchill in the autumn. So on August 15, Farley and Charles set off again by canoe heading east. The two men canoed to Eskimo Point on Hudson Bay and then hitched a ride to Churchill on a military plane.

In February 1948—six months or so after both men had made their separate ways back south—Harper wrote to his former colleague, ordering him to refrain "from mentioning in print my name."[7] Farley shot back, "You flatter yourself unduly,"[8] but he was happy to obey Harper's injunction quite literally.

Francis Harper may not be present in *People of the Deer*, but Charles Schweder is. He talked "as if his voice had been denied to him since childhood days. His story was the tale of the intruders in the land, and of their struggles to make the land their own. And his tale gave me," Farley recalled, "a chilling insight into the manner in which the Barrenlands had kept themselves inviolate from us."

At the same time as he was struggling with Harper and beginning, with the assistance of Charles Schweder, to identify the wellspring of much of his subsequent writing, Farley desperately missed Fran:

> God knows I hadn't intended that you would be able to reach
> my emotions. I had firmly decided that those emotions which
> had been curdling inside of me should never be dragged out into
> the open again. But, oddly enough, I didn't seem to have any
> choice—I was in love. . . . I discovered that I was ashamed of
> myself. I hadn't been before, hadn't cared enough to be, but
> now I was in love, though without yet realizing it, and I was
> ashamed of myself and of my cowardice.[9]

Throwing caution to the winds, Fran, desolate back in Toronto, wrote to Farley: "I find that you are entirely too vivid before me when I am talking to people and thinking when alone. You appear too realistically in everything I do to be so far away. It frightens me very much to discover that you have become so closely connected with even my intimate life."[10] Fear was always a part of love for Fran.

Ten weeks after his return to Toronto—on December 1, 1947, at Christ Church, Deer Park—Farley and Fran were married. Fran's parents liked Farley and were happy to have Fran marry him. Helen disapproved but said nothing to Farley. Angus was blunt: he told his son he objected to Fran. Although Angus did not say so, Farley was certain that his father, always a bit of a snob, felt her background was not good enough for a Mowat. The wedding party was small: both sets of parents were there as well as Andrew Lawrie and a friend of Fran's from the Wrens. The honeymoon, as far as Fran was concerned, was not a success. After they had spent five days in a log cabin north of Toronto with inadequate heat, she told Farley, "If you're not going home, I am!"

The newlyweds briefly lived with the Mowats in Richmond Hill, where Fran considered her mother-in-law to be both cold and hostile. One day Helen called her daughter-in-law aside and informed her she should quit university. When a very startled Fran was not sure how to respond, Helen simply observed: "You've got Farley." The implication was clear: Fran's role was to assist her husband; a good wife did not have overriding needs of her own. Helen, her daughter-in-law sadly remembered later, never once gave her a birthday or Christmas present. According to Fran, when she told Farley about Helen's behaviour, he took his mother's side. Later, when Fran suggested a move back to Balmoral Avenue in Toronto, where she would be treated more fairly, Farley reluctantly agreed.

In a way that he himself recognized was unorthodox, Farley had managed to get through his second year of university quite success-fully. But the call of the wild beckoned him north yet again in 1948, this time to concentrate on the caribou. And he had to face a horrible realization about himself: not only had marriage solved none of his major problems, it had intensified them. Although he did not broach the topic directly with Fran, he was, as he later told her, certain she "assumed that I was putting the trip ahead of my love for you either on purely selfish grounds or that I was just thoughtless enough to believe that I could have my cake and eat it too."[11]

Even to himself Farley did not wish to admit that although Fran had awakened him to a new sense of purpose, he still intended to live life his way. Fran, in turn, was well aware of the issues dividing her from her spouse. She told him, "You must remember, dear, that a woman's world is much narrower than a man's. You can forget a large number of trifles, worries, etc. by concentrating your full forces on your work. Whereas a woman hasn't that faculty."[12] But initially, Fran's own independent streak led her to be uncomplaining about the proposed seven-month absence of her five-months' husband.

Farley's new trip to the Arctic was undertaken in cooperation with his good friend Andrew Lawrie, who had graduated that spring with a master's degree in biology. The two solicited funds to study caribou, wolves and the inland Inuit and were initially accepted for funding by the Arctic Institute. However, the Dominion Wildlife Service (DWS) had a caribou study in mind, and the two young naturalists were absorbed into it. The DWS was conducting studies in three regions simultaneously (the Back River region in the north-central Northwest Territories, the Great Slave region in the southwest and the Keewatin region in the south-central). Lawrie was named leader of the Keewatin party, and Mowat his assistant. Arrangements were made to use the Schweder cabin once again, and the two men were given the specific job of collecting statistics on the number, migration routes, reproduction rates and state of health of the caribou. When Farley's exams were over in the spring of 1948, the two friends left by government plane for Churchill and then flew to Nueltin Lake on May 23 in a chartered bush plane.

In Churchill, Farley met again with Charles Schweder, who told him that caribou had been in such short supply the previous winter that the Inuit were starving again. Since some supplies sent by the government for these people were still in Churchill, Farley and Andrew arranged to have them loaded aboard the aircraft that took them to the cabin on Windy River. By June, Farley had made contact with Ootek and Ohoto and heard from them the bleak details of the sufferings of the past winter. Farley and Andrew used their radio transmitter to contact their employer for emergency supplies of food and ammunition, but no action resulted. By mid-June, the two researchers had handed over some of their own supplies and radioed Ottawa again. In reply, they were instructed not to interfere in matters concerning the Inuit since this was the responsibility of a different branch of government.

In his subsequent published accounts of his experiences with the Inuit, Farley, for the most part, ignored the impatience and frustration that he sometimes experienced in dealing with them. On June 24 he recorded in his diary, "Gave Halo a going over and made it quite clear that from now on we give our tea, etc. only when the

Inuit produce something in return—be it only a ground squirrel tail. The happy days of milking the Kabluna [white people] are over."[13] He became furious at the waste when Ohoto killed a deer but took only a few pounds of meat from the carcass. However, as far as Farley was concerned, the failings of the Inuit were slight in comparison to their virtues, and the largesse of the government was minuscule when seen in the context of the real needs of the starving Native population.

While travelling to Inuit camps near Nueltin and Angikuni lakes, Farley, in addition to continuing to learn the language of the Ihalmiut, collected information about the flora and fauna of the region; he also recorded the real-life histories and the mythological accounts of the Inuit with whom he came into contact. In July, in response to yet another request for assistance, officials in Ottawa sent more supplies for the two men but ignored the Inuit. The pair flew north to study caribou on the Kazan River for a month; when they returned to Windy River in August, they found that nothing further had been done to help the local population.

At the same time that he was a hapless witness to the plight of the Inuit and an unsuccessful proponent of their cause, a very lonely and confused young husband was trying to sort out his emotional needs. He asked himself, what did I hope to gain by leaving Fran alone after only five months of marriage? He confessed to her, "Primarily I wanted time, and I wanted to be placed in such a position that I would have no alternative but to face the thing out. . . . I could only get what I needed by going away from you and filling in the love I need from my imagination." Realizing the absurdity of trying to have a relationship *in absentia*, he added: "So here I am. Between now and fall I shall have fought the battle and shall have won or lost it. If I win, you will get back a man who has found himself—or you will get back nothing." Confident of winning the difficult struggle to find his lost self, Farley requested Fran's "clear and unquestioning love."

Rightly, he saw his twelve-page typed letter of July 17 to Fran as an attempt to establish "the unity of minds as well as hearts, the lack of secrets between us" that constituted a good marriage. Yet the situation remained hazardous:

> Have faith in me and keep that faith alive—by fall I shall deserve it, if I haven't deserved it before. I lost ground, and for a while was a coward again after getting your last letters—but that's over and the loss re-gained. I *do* understand that I am not alone in having battles to fight. I *do* understand that you are fighting yours and that they must be as hard for you as mine. I know you will win them as I am winning—and if we keep our love clear and fresh, we will extract a very great prize from the winning of our mutual struggles—if we let our love grow faint and doubting, the struggles will be fruitless and empty mockeries.[14]

Fran's surviving letters to her spouse are not as melodramatic as his. For instance, she told him—more than a month before his long letter—"Your letter regarding our marriage was one reason I haven't written before now because I have been giving it more than due consideration. I am very pleased and satisfied that you have gained one important factor. I shall say no more until I have got my mind out of the confused state it is in at the moment or at least I have reached a decision of some kind. However, dear, I still love you and miss you. Perhaps I wouldn't be so confused if I could see you."[15] Five days later she added, "Have come to no conclusions about anything this past week. Manage to exist by eating, sleeping and working, and it is sordid to the point of exhaustion."[16]

To his parents Farley confided his low spirits on July 12: "I miss my wife more than I thought it possible to miss anyone. Also, it is a very poor show, on my part, to dash off for so long after a brief five months of marriage leaving Fran with neither husband, house nor offspring. This being the case, I shall either come out this fall and give up the caribou job—or persuade Fran to join me here in August—I really don't care which it is as long as I am with her again." He added, "Better see what jobs are going, Pa."[17] He was, he was now fully aware, "smitten with desire for the company of my girl." He missed her "like the devil" and was reduced to misery over parting from her.

Fran's letters of June 13 and 18 were delivered to Farley on July 20 by the pilot of the plane flying him and Lawrie north to the Kazan region. He was plunged into an even deeper sense of despair. In his entry in the journal he kept for finances, he asked: "Is it all over? Looks that way. It's your marriage as much as mine, darling, and if you want to jettison it, I doubt if I can, or would, stop you." The love-sick husband was obviously overreacting to what his unhappy wife was telling him.

On August 15, when their bush plane picked them up again and flew them back to Nueltin Lake, Lawrie disembarked, but Farley—now sporting a beard—accompanied the plane to Churchill, where he intended to take direct action on behalf of the Inuit. First he confronted the agent responsible for the Inuit and extracted a promise from him that something would be done immediately to alleviate the wretched conditions in which his charges existed; he also visited Lieutenant-Colonel D.C. Cameron, commander of the military base at Churchill, who donated a number of army rifles and some ammunition for the Inuit. Then—in a quixotic gesture—Farley flew south to Toronto, where he picked up Fran and returned with her to Nueltin Lake on September 9, having been "outside" on an unauthorized leave for over three weeks.

Farley went to Toronto partly because of a letter Angus had written to him. Before leaving with Lawrie to go to the Kazan on July 20, Farley had written his father, asking him—without informing Helen—to meet with Fran to discuss the problems resulting from his prolonged absence.

Angus and Fran met for lunch on August 12. Although Fran was perfectly amiable to her father-in-law, she was understandably not willing to discuss her intimate feelings about Farley with him. She did admit that Farley seemed "uneven" in his letters to her. Angus reported to Farley, "One time everything is O.K. and the next everything is blue, and that makes Fran also uncertain about the whole show. I did come out plainly and say that if you failed in this job and came out leaving it unfinished . . . you would cook your goose not only with the government but with all the other biologists and arcticers." He suggested that Fran leave her job at the ROM library and join her husband at the earliest opportunity and then outlined a course of action to his son: "It seems to me that if you could say to her, 'I'll be at such and such a place on such and such a date, come' then she'd probably make up her mind in a hurry and go." He suggested Farley deliver this invitation in person. Angus also offered a gratuitous piece of advice; during his conversation with Fran, he had become aware of the "direction in which her mind" was working: "She needs to reproduce, I am sure. All healthy women do. It's basic."[18]

The condescension towards women voiced here was something many men of Angus's generation practised without really thinking about it. In Angus's view, women may have been very necessary to men, but they were also ancillary, not really on the same plane of existence as males. Many of the sons of the men of Angus's generation inherited their fathers' attitudes, possessing a sense of noblesse oblige towards members of what they considered the second sex. This was true of Farley at the time. He could passionately love women, but he was also distrustful of them. As a child, Farley had witnessed Angus's betrayal of Helen and beheld Helen's willingness to accept that betrayal. At some level, he learned that that is what men are like, how they conduct themselves.

As soon as he and Fran arrived at the cabin, where a surprised Andrew Lawrie greeted them, Farley had to make the previously messy living conditions more suitable. He cleaned out a back room to make it into a bedroom. He patched the roof. He kept a stove burning all day to remove the dampness from their living quarters. He even constructed a makeshift bathroom for Fran out of an old canoe. Fran would later have vivid memories of Farley repairing the roof with caribou skins, as a result of which procedure their living quarters were infested with thousands of moths. In Toronto, Fran might have been lonely and miserable without her partner, but, city born and bred, she had no real desire to live in the wilderness.

During their brief courtship, Farley had intermittently witnessed his future wife's black depressions; now, as his diary reveals, he had to confront them on a regular basis:

SEPTEMBER 30: Fran rises not but lies in death-like silence.
OCTOBER 8: Fran low all day.
OCTOBER 10: Fran took another dive into the dumps today.
OCTOBER 11–12: Fran extremely low.

Without doubt, Fran had a melancholic streak, but more significantly, she had a tendency—like her husband—to run away from intimacy when it required day-to-day contact. Although very much in love, Farley and Fran were never comfortable with each other on a daily basis.

On October 13, a plane landed at Nueltin Lake to take the researchers south to winter headquarters at Brochet, a Cree and Dene community with a Hudson's Bay Company trading post and a Roman Catholic mission. However, since the fall caribou migration was still in progress, Lawrie decided to stay behind until December. Because of Fran's worsening mental condition, the Mowats took the flight. When they reached Brochet, Farley found a derelict Indian shack—"bummed from the Roman Catholic mission"[19]—which he and Fran made habitable (his assigned quarters were a bunk in the Army's Signal Corps station). When finished, the single twenty-five-foot square room had whitewashed log walls with blue trim and a cream-coloured roof with wooden beams across it. A built-in bed in one corner served as a chesterfield during the day and was covered with red Hudson's Bay blankets. A large oil stove stood in the middle of the room and the other three corners of the room were occupied by a kitchen with a wood stove, a dining nook and a work space for Farley and his typewriter. In the attic—reached by a ladder and a trap door—the indoor john, consisting of a ten-gallon pail and a lid with a hole in it, was "resplendent in cream enamel and shit-brindle brown floor paint."

When the caribou arrived at Brochet on November 20, they swarmed about the town, as Farley recollected: "Everywhere little strings of deer meander eastward while around and amongst them are dog teams and men, women and children on foot. Looks like a giant rodeo." Fran's depression seemed to lift: "She seems to take to this life like a duck to water and bustles and scurries from dawn till dark, occasionally stopping to admonish me to get back to my typewriter. Her idea is that we stay for a year. Both of us fat and healthy, could hardly be otherwise of course."[20] Quickly, though, Fran got tired of the canned goods that were the staple of their diet. "For God's sake," she ordered him one day, "go out and kill a caribou!" Farley did shoot deer, ptarmigan, spruce grouse and sharp-tailed grouse.

The graveyard at Brochet provided Fran with testimony to the white man's indifference to the indigenous peoples. A year or two before, a government official had taken his young son with him by plane on a visit to the village. Although the boy had recently recovered from measles, he remained infectious. The subsequent outbreak of the disease killed dozens of people in the area.

Even in the relatively comfortable confines of Brochet, some basic differences between Farley and Fran asserted themselves. He was a morning person, she an evening one. If Farley came up with an idea, Fran observed, it was a good one; if she made a suggestion, he often vetoed it unless she could somehow convince him it was really *his*. They were very young, very inexperienced with members of the opposite sex. During an argument, Farley once sought refuge in a strange defence: "I'm an only child!" Fran replied, "That's the problem!"

As far as the government was concerned, Farley had made himself a nuisance by poking his nose into matters which were none of his business. He had compounded his offences by absenting himself without permission, travelling to Churchill and Toronto and returning with his wife. When Frank Banfield, the chief government mammalogist for the caribou survey, gave him an ultimatum to abandon the shack and move into the "Met station," which had one single bed available for him and none for Fran, Farley balked since this would have meant Fran's banishment back to Toronto.

Within two weeks of the Mowats' arrival in Brochet, R.A. Gibson, the deputy commissioner of the Northwest Territories—to whom

Farley had earlier complained about the treatment of the Inuit—
expressed his displeasure with Farley's behaviour to the head of the
Wildlife Service:

> We have had employed since May on the caribou survey a chap
> named Mowatt [*sic*] who, while greatly interested in wildlife
> problems, does not possess the full academic qualifications for
> the work that he has to do. . . . We were not much impressed
> with Mr. Mowatt when we met him, but in view of his evident
> enthusiasm, and because there was no one else in sight, we took
> him on. This man has cost the Northwest Territories Adminis-
> tration a considerable amount of money because he made erro-
> neous reports about the Eskimos in the district. It is now evident
> that these reports were based on insufficient investigation. I am
> told that he left the area where the caribou were congregating in
> order that he might bed himself down in winter quarters. His
> associate remained on the job. Moreover, without notifying
> your office, he brought his wife from Toronto to the winter
> quarters and is now asking us to pay rental on a building because
> he cannot bunk with the Signal Corps on account of his having
> a wife with him. While I have reasonable sympathy for those
> who undertake tasks of this kind in remote areas, it is evident
> that we should replace Mr. Mowatt.[21]

Farley's "erroneous reports" and "insufficient investigation" about
the Inuit were the real reasons that he was fired; his unauthorized
leave to collect Fran and her presence at Nueltin and Brochet merely
provided the necessary excuse.

Farley knew his defiance of a direct order would lead to the three-
word telegram—"YOU ARE FIRED"—that reached him on December 1. For some weeks he and Fran had been prepared for such an
event and had already decided to stay in Brochet until the spring of
1949. Farley, who had begun to spend part of each day writing, was
going to "work up the Eskimo material" he had gathered. The first
project was, as Farley told his anthropology professor at the University of Toronto, "a story, presented as fiction, but true for all of that,

which graphically illustrates the gross stupidity and criminal negligence of the Proper Authorities in connection with the Ihalmiut."

In fact, on the very day he was fired, Farley sent a short story, "Eskimo Spring," to the *Atlantic Monthly* in Boston. In a covering letter, he explained the genesis of the piece:

> While on the Barrens in 1947, I came across the remnants of the interior Eskimo group that at one time occupied the whole interior of Keewatin. It was my bad luck to meet these people at a time when their sands were about to run out—but I saw enough of them to want to see a good deal more. In 1948 . . . I went back to the Barrens as a biologist. . . . From May until October I lived with the Eskimos and travelled—in company with another young biologist—over much of the land that had once been inhabited by the Ihalmiut. I saw my fill of graves and of deserted campsites. I learned the language of the people, since they understand no English, and eventually I began to piece together the history of the people and to discover something of the magnitude of their tragedy. . . . I was very deeply disturbed by seeing the havoc that can be wreaked on the interior peoples by the passive stupidity of an avowed friend—the white man. It wasn't the sort of picture I expected to find in my own land; it is a damned ugly picture, and rightly or wrongly, I feel impelled to do quite a lot of talking about it.[22]

Having witnessed on the battlefield in Europe the evil that can be unleashed "by the active malice" of a country such as Germany, he was both surprised and appalled to see what he deemed to be similar conduct on the part of the Canadian government. His emotions came back to life; the dam of despair had been broken. Farley had discovered a cause worth living for. A man who always considered himself an outsider, he would defend the rights of the Inuit, outsiders to the Canadian government's political agenda.

He had also stumbled upon his vocation. Two years earlier, at the end of the war, the distraught son had asked his father how he had coped after his experiences in the Great War. The obvious answer to his own dilemma finally made itself known to him: "Only one thing has ever given me complete satisfaction and peace of mind or soul— that is writing. I have known this for years. Why then, didn't I go to it for help long ago, instead of wasting my energy and my self respect on wild goose chases?"[23]

6

Saga-Man

1949–1953

"Squib and Fran come home this month," Angus told a friend in January 1949. "They have been in a shack at a Hudson's Bay post on Reindeer Lake and loving it, but the job is through and the university insists that Squib come home and attend a few lectures if he wants to take his degree next spring."[1] With two professors— J.R. Dymond in Biology and T.F. McIlwraith in Anthropology— Farley had made arrangements to submit reports based on his experiences in the Barrenlands in lieu of class attendance, essays and exams. He had to return in order to complete the more usual academic requirements, and received his bachelor's degree in May 1949.

There was another reason for returning south. Although Dudley Cloud at the *Atlantic Monthly* had sent his short story back to him, he encouraged Farley to write a book about the Inuit and the Barrenlands.★

★ After serving as managing editor of the magazine, Dudley Cloud became director of the Atlantic Monthly Press. In the latter capacity, he became Farley's first editor and publisher.

In response, Farley drew up an outline with the working title "River of Men," to which Cloud enthusiastically responded by taking an option on it. Now more certain of where he was heading, Farley decided to write his book in the relative comfort of Ontario.

Soon after returning, Farley—now committed to the writing life—was determined to find a home base which would allow him to pursue his profession at a safe distance from anything that resembled an urban environment. His first choice was to buy land at Sapawe near the head of Lake Superior and Lake of the Woods, but then a ten-acre parcel of somewhat swampy land in the Albion Hills thirty miles north of Toronto was offered to him. Years earlier in Richmond Hill, Farley had been a good friend of Bette Campbell; at university, he had introduced her to the sculptor E.B. Cox, whom she married. In 1947 or 1948, the Coxes had bought one hundred acres of land in Palgrave, and when they learned that the Mowats were looking, they proposed severing ten acres of their own property to them for five hundred dollars. The offer was quickly accepted.

That summer, the Mowats—assisted from time to time by the Coxes—dug the foundation for and constructed their three-room log cabin. Fran and Farley lived in tents for six months until all the prefabricated logs could be fitted into place, bonfires providing much-needed heating at night. The house cost about three thousand dollars, most of the funding coming from Farley's Army pay, which had been placed in Helen's safekeeping. Fran cashed in her life insurance to pay for the roof and redeemed her war bonds to pay some other expenses.

During the building of the cabin, Fran formed the decided impression that Farley did everything in the most rigorous and punishing way possible; she attributed this stubborn determination to her father-in-law's influence. The simple or more uncomplicated way was always to be avoided or denigrated in favour of the more authentic or primitive. In September 1949, the couple moved into their new home, which was still without water or electricity. When after two years the house still did not have running water, Fran gave her husband an ultimatum: if he did not install it, she was leaving.

Their neighbours were a diverse group. They included Edith and

Palgrave, 1949

Keith McKeiver, early patrons of the Group of Seven; the painter A.Y. Jackson was a frequent visitor to the McKeivers' home. Ross and Vicky Taylor, associated with Eaton's, had a summer home in the vicinity. The Mowats were also friendly with painter Will Ogilvie and a physician by the name of Tweedie.

Fran and Farley were a couple who did everything together, although she was quite candid in telling the neighbours that she considered her husband a bit on the outlandish side. She also confessed her dislike of their two husky dogs, Kip and Ohoto, who could be demanding. One day, they arrived home looking like "animated" pin cushions. "Taking porky quills out of dogs," Farley told his father, "is not an amusement for those with weak stomachs but the beasts were very good about it. . . . Poor buggers! But this may learn 'em that all beasts what romp the woods aren't woodchucks and squirrels."[2] The neighbours viewed Fran as prim and proper, whereas Farley's arrival in his jeep, *Lulu-Belle*, was gleefully anticipated by many. Farley's anti-establishment turn of mind provided them with many humorous moments—and anecdotes.

Shortly after completing work on the cabin, he placed a large sign on the boundary of his property:

Property of the Keewatin Research Project
WARNING!
Radiation Hazard
dangerous to all
unprotected personnel.

When provincial health authorities came calling to inquire about nuclear contamination, Farley explained that anyone coming onto his property naked risked being sunburned. Farley adopted a motto: "My dogs, my jeep, my house!" Fran was a bit affronted not to have made it into her husband's top-three list. She also soon became sick of his "five-year plans," wherein their future goals were mapped out.

During 1949, Angus never offered his son any kind of financial assistance, although he was well aware that Farley and Fran were desperately poor. He would provide the couple with boxes of books from the Ontario Travelling Library, but no other kind of help was forthcoming. From time to time, he would mumble something about Farley becoming a librarian. Farley was distressed by the lack of assistance proffered by his father but was damned if he would ask outright for financial aid. The lack of it at this juncture made life more difficult for the young couple.

Farley, Fran later recalled, was particularly insecure about becoming a writer on two scores: he had witnessed Angus's lack of success with two novels, and he knew that his father would have high—if not unrealistic—expectations of any writing his son undertook. Farley's own reading was—and remained—eclectic. Good storytelling remained his chief criterion for his own work, both fiction and non-fiction, and for the work of others. He did, however, have a special affection for travel literature and was building a collection of works devoted to the Arctic.

During the latter part of 1949, in a quasi-military manner, Farley put "Operation Eskimo" into full swing. This manoeuvre was an attempt to bring the dire situation of the Inuit to public attention while transforming his experiences in the North in 1947 and 1948 into saleable writing. In a facetious and ironical vein he told a friend, "It is my firm conviction that one should exploit the Eskimos in all possible ways. If I was a missionary, I would exploit them spiritually for my own great good when I reached heaven. If I was a trader, it would be straight financial blood-sucking. As a writer, I can only exploit their tragedy—and this I am doing to the best of my ability."[3]

His first success was to sell six talks on the Inuit by way of Robert Weaver to CBC Radio; he himself read them on the air. The latter activity earned him the enmity of some announcers, who felt he was taking work away from them. Hoping that W.O. Mitchell, editor of *Maclean's* and author of the classic *Who Has Seen the Wind*, might be sympathetic to the directions he was taking, Farley sent the piece called "Eskimo Spring," which he had previously shown to the *Atlantic Monthly*. Farley was summoned to Mitchell's office, where he was told that if he wanted to survive financially, he should write boy-meets-girl–happy-ending stories in five thousand words. Insulted and angry, Farley stormed out of Mitchell's office. Fran later remembered this incident differently. She was sure it took place at Mitchell's home, where she and Farley were invited to dinner, after which their host "entertained" them by reading aloud from his work for more than an hour. After that, she recalled, Mitchell offered his advice, at which point Farley—accompanied by Fran—stormed out. Either way, Farley would not be writing for *Maclean's*, at least not for several years.

Ever on the lookout for ways to help his son's career, Angus came across a reference to Littauer and Wilkinson, a literary agency on Madison Avenue in New York City, and urged his son to get in touch with them. Kenneth Littauer handled books, and Max Wilkinson specialized in magazine articles. Very soon after Farley sent "Eskimo Spring" to him, Wilkinson placed it (as "The Desperate People") with the *Saturday Evening Post*, where it was published on July 29, 1950, for $750, a fee much higher than anything Farley would have received in Canada. During 1951 and 1952, Farley submitted seven short stories to Canadian magazines, five of which were sent back. All five were accepted by American periodicals, which paid about six times the going rate in Canada.

Hard-boiled, snappish and wisecracking, Max Wilkinson was immediately convinced of Farley's talent and marketability. Since he felt that Farley was a young man in need of sober fatherly advice, he was quite willing to be blunt with him: "Alas and alack, this story is a dud. It ain't got no character, or feeling, or organization, and it is too long into the bargain."[4] He also poked fun at Farley: "Soon you will be so famous the public will demand you be stuffed and placed on permanent exhibition!"[5] Max cheerfully assumed the role of the avuncular American backwoodsman amused by the quaint customs in even more backwater Canada; when Farley was preparing to visit him in the United States, Wilkinson gave him some tips in anticipation of their encounter: "Our ways are simple. Mukluks for social events, calked boots for business ones. Shave twice a week and on Easter, Christmas and General Lee's birthday. This far south the women eat with the men. You'll get used to it quickly."[6] Once when Farley asked Wilkinson's advice about "slanting" his work in order to win public acceptance, the older man testily replied, "Write what you *must* write and don't even bother to send me 'slanted' work. Write the best stuff you can produce, and if it's good enough—I'll find a home for it."[7] And although he did not like to show it too often, Wilkinson also had a tender side, which can be seen in this aside in a letter to his client: "If you get scared, or depressed, let me hear."[8]

Angus, who had taken a wait-and-see attitude to his son's fledgling writing career, told a friend in April 1950, "I don't know whether Squib is booming along or not, or whether he will be a credit to the family or not. So far [he and Fran] have managed to keep eating. That in itself is a relief to my mind. His agent in New York keeps selling stories for him every now and then."[9] "Every now and then" included acceptances in the early and mid-fifties from *Bluebook, Argosy, True Magazine, Saga Magazine, Canadian Forum, Atlantic Monthly, Maclean's,* and *Saturday Night.* "Lost in the Barrenlands," published in the *Saturday Evening Post* in October 1951, was awarded the 1952 President's Medal by the University of Western Ontario for the best Canadian short story of the year.

At the *Atlantic Monthly*, Dudley Cloud was more sedate than Wilkinson, but he too was quite willing to provide candid opinions. Cloud's role as a publisher was an unusual one. He was the head of the publishing arm of the distinguished Boston-based magazine which, in cooperation with the Boston publishing firm of Little, Brown, published books under the Atlantic imprint; the editing, design and printing of such books were Cloud's responsibility, but advertising, marketing and accounting were done by Little, Brown, which sometimes tried to interfere in editorial matters.

During the first nine months of 1951, Farley worked an average of ten hours a day writing and revising his book, for which Wilkinson had negotiated an advance of eight hundred dollars. Since the Atlantic Monthly Press seemed to be dragging its feet in publishing the book, Farley spent a lot of time preparing stories for his agent to sell. He told his mother, "The excitement and confusion of the book nearing its birth occupies all my time. Pregnancy plays the devil with you, doesn't it?"[10] He was often exhausted, but happy: "Didn't believe I could work so hard." He asked his parents, "Don't go cluck–cluck and mutter about the quality of my output. The quality is OK, though not what it might be if I had longer to work on the book. As it is, we simply have to get the thing done or learn how to starve."[11]

While Farley was struggling to stay afloat financially and to finish his first book, there was a dramatic turn in the lives of his parents, as indicated in a letter Angus wrote to a friend in November 1951:

> Farley, by the way, keeps me in a state of partial (more than usual) stupefaction. He has sold another story to the *Saturday Evening Post*, this time at their top price, and I think I told you that the *Atlantic Monthly* is going to serialize his book (with his stupid face on the cover) and are considering bringing out his journals.

And then just to add a little spice to life, Helen and I are negotiating for a foster child. . . . It is some years since I used to spend
most of my time leaping overboard to haul out fallen-overboard
children. Maybe I have slowed up during those years. . . . Helen
is being a bit obdurate about one detail. I wanted a little
coloured boy because I like the coloured people; and the county
welfare officer is keen for us to take an Indian but Helen is
standing firmly for a white child. What's the matter with her?
Hasn't she got any imagination?[12]

The negotiations with the welfare officials eventually led to the adoption of John, a five-year-old Ojibway boy.

Since Helen was not even certain she wanted to adopt a child,
Angus enlisted Farley's help to turn the tricky situation in his favour:

I pick up the little boy this afternoon and take him home. He
is 5½ and Helen and I both fell for him like a roof falling in. He
is an Indian, but I don't know yet from what tribe. Farley turned
the tables in his favour. Helen said it was enough to ask her to
take just a little white boy, even though they have been unable
to place this one because of his colour, but when Farley was told
all, he flew into a wild excitement and said take him and if we
die or get paralysed he will take on the job for us. That did it. I
am very pleased. One of Helen's friends fainted at the telephone
when she heard, and when they brought her round, her first
question was, "But *what* do the idiots propose to do when it
comes time for him to marry?" Naturally, I replied, "Nothing
. . . he'll probably know what to do himself by that time."[13]

In 1951, Helen was in her mid-fifties, Angus fifty-eight. She did
not want to raise a young child. Over the years, she had grown away
from her husband emotionally and certainly did not share his enthusiasm for this new project. Yet in order to keep the peace, she allowed
herself to be carried along.

Angus's motives are more difficult to decipher. He missed Farley and
wanted the pleasure of the company of a youngster; like his son, he also

held strong convictions about the inappropriate and callous ways in which the indigenous peoples had been treated by white men. By adopting an Ojibway child, he was trying in a small way to right one of society's wrongs. But there may have been a more selfish force at work. For many years, Angus had been a philanderer. His job required him to travel a great deal to rural locations, where he often bedded local librarians. During the war years, Helen had obviously been deeply worried about Farley; after her son returned home, went north and married, she was less involved with him. There is the strong possibility that Angus may have wanted to find a way to keep his sexual arrangements intact by keeping Helen preoccupied with raising a child.

Helen immediately found dealing with the young boy exhausting; Angus, however, remained oblivious to her tiredness. On December 18, he told Farley the biggest obstacle was "Helen's physical ability to stand up under pressure. . . . I observed very carefully for the first week, when the pressure was strongest, and saw no sign at all of what I had feared. In fact, she is better physically than she has been for years." She no longer had as much time as before "for the mystic brooding. No time for it. She really is very good indeed."[14]

As spring arrived in 1951, Farley's once molasses-slow American publisher started to move "like greased lightning." Airmail letters and telegrams "buzzed" between Palgrave and Boston to the extent that the antiquated post office in Palgrave was in a "complete flap." At about this time, Farley received two letters from John Gray at Macmillan in Toronto asking to purchase Canadian rights to what would become *People of the Deer*. As it turned out, though, there was nothing to negotiate. McClelland & Stewart acted as the agent for Atlantic–Little, Brown in Canada, and the Boston firm wanted that arrangement kept intact.

In November 1951, when the page proofs of the book arrived, work on them reduced Farley to a nervous wreck and—what was for him a new and extremely rare phenomenon—to speechlessness.[15] He was, he observed, in a "tizzy" and "sweating blood over the chore," for which his publisher had given him ten days.[16]

The book was duly published early in 1952. The young author's anxieties about it soon came to be centred on the inefficiency of McClelland & Stewart in distributing and publicizing the book in Canada. In April 1952, Farley told his father just how distraught he was:

> In effect I accuse them [in a letter] of deliberately dragging their feet, and I cite enough evidence to damn well prove it. I have asked Max to see if publication by M&S can be discontinued and I am writing to Gray at Macmillan telling him the general outline and asking whether he will be willing to take over this book, and all future books by me, for Canadian publication. . . . Would you call him and have a chat, explaining as best you can how I feel about it, and why?[17]

When, with some difficulty, Angus got in touch with Gray, the publisher told him that after he had read the portions serialized in the *Atlantic Monthly*, he had offered to publish the book; he would not, though, be interested in "taking over" late in the day. First, Little, Brown had already decided that it would not remove a previously published book from McClelland & Stewart. Second, Gray considered M&S a good firm, although he agreed that their advertising campaign for *People of the Deer* was lethargic. Gray would be delighted, though, to meet with Farley in order to have the chance of considering future books. On this point, Angus commented, "My own feeling about Gray is that he is the best book man in the Toronto trade. Also I like him personally." Farley promptly submitted the manuscript of a young adult novel, "Phantom in the Wilderness" (as *Lost in the Barrens* was called at this time), to Macmillan.

Angus proceeded to give his overwrought son some no-nonsense advice. First he tried to put things into perspective:

> You know, Farley, I am not greatly concerned with [M&S's] handling or mis-handling of the Canadian sales. As far as sales and notice are concerned, I am inclined to feel that your success

has been substantial, would be considered substantial by any writer, and that for a beginning one and for a first book gratifying and encouraging very, very far beyond expectations—or rather the most hopeful dreams.

Having suggested that Farley was overreacting to adversity, he then told him to take the long view and to conduct himself stoically:

> My concern is for the future and for you. For your life. I look at it this way. For the creative artist the only thing that is of significance is his stature. I am not talking about a mere writer. There are too many of them. They babble incessantly. The true creative artist in contemporary letters is becoming rare and is being shouted (or babbled) down. But I believe it is the only thing worth striving for—to *be* a creative artist—and I firmly believe you have it in you. I have no doubts. But it is a long road and a consistently hard one, and success or failure along that road depends, I believe, absolutely and entirely upon the stature of the man. In *People of the Deer* you showed stature. Not full growth, not by any means, but sure evidence that stature is there. It is the work, in many parts at least, of a man of vision and understanding and the dignity and humility that go with strength.

Angus's message was clear: a person of stature rises above bad reviews and incompetent publishers. Such a man can be indignant, but he does not display his temper. "I know this to be true," Angus added. "I've had a bad temper all my life."

He ended his letter with uncharacteristic humility, saying how hard it had been to pen it: "I am not much on advising people and I'm not advising you but I have spoken my mind—and have every right to—because the growth of the size of you is my most important" consideration.[18] There are other reasons that would have made this letter a particularly difficult one for Angus to write: his own efforts as a novelist had not borne much fruit. And as with much of Angus's wisdom, there was a catch. Without being aware of it, Angus was also, by speaking of the profession of writer as an almost sacred call-ing, raising an exceedingly high bar.

Farley's anxiety about the distribution of his first book in Canada shows how much he had riding on the book's success. First, he was certain from the outset that the Hudson's Bay Company and the federal government in Ottawa would be outraged. In order to launch his career properly, he knew that he needed to bypass those two insti-tutions and to appeal to the general reading public. Second, he wanted the book to sell well so that he could obtain a measure of financial freedom. Third, he realized that financial success in writing was very chancy, something that few authors ever attain, especially in a country with a relatively small population—Farley wanted to be one of the chosen few.

In retrospect, publisher Jack McClelland recalled that Farley was "not easy to get to know in the early days. Scarred by his role in World War II, he was brash and abrasive. . . . The so-called northern experts claimed there were many fallacies in the book. Farley was not intimidated. He responded with fervour and brilliance."[19] In those remarks, McClelland papered over the fact that his relationship with Farley was almost derailed before it began. Although the two men eventually became personal as well as professional friends, their early days together were not easy.★

Like Farley, publisher Jack McClelland in the early fifties was a maver-ick young man very much on the make. Tall, handsome, flamboyant, a year younger than Farley, he had served in the Navy during the

---

★ The extant correspondence between Jack McClelland and Farley Mowat in the McClelland & Stewart archive at McMaster University begins in 1955. When I researched and wrote my biography of Jack McClelland, I did not know about the dispute which lasted from 1952 to 1954. Documentary evidence regarding this early fight between author and publisher exists only in the Angus Mowat papers at the University of Western Ontario Library, although there are detailed readers' reports in the "rejected manuscripts" portion of the Macmillan Canada archive at Mc-Master. When I apprised Farley of my discovery, the information with which I supplied him triggered his memory of the dispute.

Second World War before joining his father's firm in 1946. From the outset, he disliked the agency system, whereby his firm made most of its money distributing titles from foreign publishers. He did not wish to pursue what he considered a relatively easy way of doing business; instead, he wanted to promote and publish Canadian authors.

Jack's early relationship with Farley quickly reached a crisis point because of the shortsighted way in which M&S did business. Since M&S had no direct investment in *People of the Deer*, having imported finished books, it had no good reason to be overly concerned whether the book sold five hundred or five thousand copies. As far as Farley was concerned, this was totally unacceptable. He knew his book could be selling better in Canada. So angry was he with M&S that he might have broken away from the company in 1954 had it not been for the English-born editor of juvenile texts at Macmillan to whom the manuscript of his novel for young people was assigned. Despite glowing evaluations from others in the firm for what would become *Lost in the Barrens*, that person wrote a contemptuous letter to John Gray claiming that Farley knew nothing of the North, particularly about paddling a canoe (Farley's description of that activity was based on what he had learned from the Dene). In part, this evaluation dissuaded Farley from switching publishers; there was also Jack McClelland's infectious charm, which, when it suited him to use it, could seduce almost any author.

Although Jack was concerned to keep Farley as an author, social niceties never hindered him from being brutally honest when he felt it necessary. In 1958, for example, he did not like the foreword Farley supplied to a book:

I don't know why you gave it to me. I don't want to be a bloody editor. However, since you have done so you will reap the reward. In general outline and in scope I like it. I think it is entirely suitable for the book and probably just what is needed. There are two things I would like to see you do to it. Firstly, I think it's a little too long. And secondly, I think it is badly over-written. Some of the phrases and some of the pictures that are conveyed are extremely good, but it's a bit too contrived and a bit too purple for my liking, and I think you should tone it down so that it will read more smoothly. To return to your own immortal words: "I don't think, Mr. Mowat, that this is up to your best standard." It's far better than I would expect to see from another author. It's terrific, fabulous and fantastic, but it isn't your best work and needs further effort. In short, it's none too good.[20]

One of Jack's most idiosyncratic tendencies as a publisher-editor was to mouth seemingly contradictory statements in the same breath. So Mowat's writing could be simultaneously "a bit too purple" and "fantastic." But his star authors loved the way he engaged with them personally instead of passing them off to more junior editors.

One bond shared by Jack and Farley was a love of pranks. In late November 1956, the publisher asked the author to make an impromptu appearance at a staff Christmas dinner at a Toronto restaurant, Fantasy Farm. Farley was to announce himself as a delegate of the authors, who had been excluded from the event. He was to begin in a laudatory manner and then to refer to "the beautifully designed [dust] jacket with" his name misspelled; he was to mention the autograph party at which nobody turned up. In short, he was to recite a litany of complaints. Farley was game: "All right, you bastard. . . . I shall be guided by that invidious document you sent me, and will embellish upon it as the mood strikes me."[21] The ploy succeeded admirably. Jack, who was well aware that there was a melancholic, reclusive side to Farley's character, encouraged him to assume a devil-may-care persona. "Playing the fool" was the way Farley dealt with his uncomfortableness in public situations, and once begun, it was impossible to discard—either for himself or for his public.

Within four years, a companionable, semi-acrimonious, comically competitive friendship had been established between publisher and author. When Jack learned that Farley had spoken out against his supposed overzealousness in publicizing books, he told him, "I was only sorry that I learned far too late that you had been saying all sorts of shocking things about me on the television show. I say far too late because I lost the opportunity to beat you over the head."[22] When he felt it necessary, Jack could tap into Farley's insecurities, assuring him that one of his books was "selling but setting no record. It's still slightly ahead of [a book by Pierre Berton], if that makes you feel better."[23] Jack was deliberately fuelling the competition between the best-selling popular historian Pierre Berton and Farley, obviously feeling that M&S would obtain better books in the process. In turn, Farley told Jack, "You're such a depressing son of a bitch. There are times when I darkly suspect that you are too interested in making money."[24]

Fifty years after its original publication, *People of the Deer* remains Farley's most controversial book. The outline optioned by Dudley Cloud envisioned "a semi-novel based on the lives of several Ihalmiut men. Covers the period from 1885 till the present and will be anthropologically accurate in all details that I have knowledge of. It will show clearly, without tirades or innuendo, the history of the inland people."

At the same time as he imagined his book as having a strong fictional component, Farley knew that he was flying in the face of previously published research by some prominent Arctic scholars, most of whom were unaware that the Ihalmiut even existed. Farley told McIlwraith, his anthropology professor at the University of Toronto, that the Ihalmiut "are at least twice as primitive as the so-called Caribou Eskimos of [the scientific] literature who evidently AREN'T the real caribou people at all." In attempting to substantiate these observations, Farley, after returning to Ontario, turned to the federal government, the Royal Canadian Mounted Police and the Hudson's Bay Company. All refused to assist him.

Realizing he could not in such circumstances write in a scholarly fashion about the inland Inuit, Farley decided to write a book that would have popular appeal. He was, he knew, a "head-banger," but this time "the banging is going to be altruistic in one sense, and selfish in another. I will get paid for it, and I will eat."[25] Farley, a meticulous keeper of diaries and field notes, quickly abandoned the idea of either quasi-fiction or pure scholarship in favour of writing a semi-fictional-ized narrative in which he attempted to provide both an accurate account and a good story. He decided to write a narrative in which the essential truthfulness of the history, daily existence and tribulations of the Ihalmiut could emerge.

People of the Deer is best seen as a fictionalized autobiography in which the protagonist, intrigued by the Barrenlands since his teenage years, returns there and encounters a group of inland Inuit who call themselves Ihalmiut. On the one hand, he admires the tribe for their primitiveness. On the other, he is frequently impatient with them and becomes, at times, quite angry with them; he even openly declares some racist sentiments. Yet as the book progresses, he shows a deep sympathy with the tribe and discovers that they are obsessed with their past and have customs and habits that he simply does not fully comprehend. For instance, their "unusual approach to the problem of ownership was a source of annoyance to me until I grasped its significance. When I first came among the Ihalmiut, they, with their limited knowledge of white men, treated me as they would treat one another. They were not aware of the gap in law and usage which separated us." Wife-sharing, infanticide and mercy killing among this group of Inuit are described not as crimes or sins but as elements in their culture which are different from the white man's.

In vivid and forceful language, *People of the Deer* tells of its author's encounters with the Ihalmiut, once a prosperous, self-sufficient tribe of two thousand, who become victims of technological and economic "advances" introduced by the white man. In 1950, they were reduced to forty-seven destitute people. Without doubt, the book would not have been as interesting if its early part were told as a two-man expedition or if some passages were merely reproduced as stories or experiences told to the author by others. Farley, who renders his story about the summer of 1947 with artistic licence, does so in order to make his material vivid, immediate and enticing. The most significant information concealed from the reader is the venomous nature of the relationship that developed between Mowat and Harper.

Farley identifies with Franz (Charles Schweder), an outsider who, in part because of his half-native status, attempts to better the living conditions of both the Indians and the Ihalmiut. During the course of the book, Farley becomes more and more in tune with the surviving members of the tribe, who recount for him their history and traditions. Although there are many hints early in *People*, the real villains of the book—the missionaries, the Canadian federal government in Ottawa and the Hudson's Bay Company—surface only in the last two chapters, the portion of the narrative that caused the heavens to fall upon the head of its author. In fact, in his catalogue of government, religious and mercantile corruption and ineptitude originating in Canada, another country emerges unscathed:

> I can tell you of a place where all I have asked for the natives of the arctic has already been granted to an Eskimo people. The place is Greenland, the far eastern outpost of the Inuit, where the Danish government has for many years followed an enlightened policy of native administration, a policy which pitilessly exposes *our* blundering efforts for the thin shams they are.★

The review of *People of the Deer* in the *New York Times* was both positive and congratulatory, as was the declaration of Montreal-based novelist Hugh MacLennan: "the finest thing of its sort to come out of Canada." Most of the notices in Canada were positive, although a few reviewers chided the author for small inaccuracies.

In *The Beaver*, a magazine owned by the Hudson's Bay Company, Dr. A.E. Porsild, who took umbrage at MacLennan's words of praise, launched a bitter invective against the book. Porsild, a civil servant in the Department of Resources and Development, had several key points: "An examination of official reports shows that Farley Mowat was in the Barrenlands no more than 47 days altogether and that, during 1947 and 1948, he spent no more than six months all told in

★ When I visited Inuit communities in Greenland and Nunavut in July 1999, I observed a vast difference in the lifestyles of the indigenous peoples in the two places. For instance, the communities in Canada had generally abandoned the use of dogs in ice fishing; dogs in Nunavut are pets. In contrast, a number of Greenland Inuit communities continue to use dogs and, in some cases, have banned the use of snowmobiles entirely.

the Northwestern Territories." He also attempted to attack the very foundation of the book: "Nor has Mowat explained that mysterious tribe—the Ihalmiut—that, as far as I can see, was created solely as a vehicle for his attack on government administration and on the wicked traders. There never was such a tribe."[26] Porsild did not bother to inform his readers that it would be highly unusual for Mowat to have spent the winter in the Barrenlands since he would not be able to conduct any research during that time of year. In making the absurd claim that there was never such a tribe as the Ihalmiut, Porsild bordered on the ridiculous; what he meant was that respected Arctic explorers and scholars, such as Knud Rasmussen, had never classified such a group.

Having spent a considerable part of his boyhood in Greenland and having visited many communities of Inuit, Porsild also asserted that no one could have learned the language of the Inuit as easily as Mowat claimed. And he also sneered at the assertion that contact with the white man had been disastrous to the Inuit. In the same issue of *The Beaver* in which *People of the Deer* was demolished, two other books on similar topics by writers not associated with the Hudson's Bay Company were also blasted.

D. Leechman, in the *Canadian Geographical Journal*, admitted that the book had some virtues, but he also attempted to dismiss the book by questioning its accuracy. He was scathing about a reference to the Hudson's Bay Company's request that the Inuit bring them the tongues of dead deer to trade for ammunition. Mowat did not know, he claimed, that "deer tongue" was a plant used for flavouring tobacco. Yet, seemingly unknown to Leechman, research published years earlier in *The Beaver* had revealed that the Indians and Inuit frequently took only the tongues of dead caribou for food.

Lost in Porsild's and Leechman's hostile notices was the fact that the indigenous people had suffered from the great cruelty of the white man. In an article in *Saturday Night*, Scott Young offered a rebuttal: "Mowat does admit to errors of treatment and fact, but the basic premise—which *The Beaver* does not attempt to refute—that the Inuit have been badly treated and will become extinct is accepted by most authorities. *The Beaver* attempts to refute the book by attacking niggling details."[27] The methodology of Mowat's detractors was, according to Young, as plausible as attacking Albert Einstein's theories by making fun of his haircut. Since *The Beaver* had refused to print Mowat's refutation of Porsild's review, Young's article was a crucial defence of an author who was not allowed to speak for himself.[28]

Two years later, on January 19, 1954, the debate between Mowat and Porsild about the Ihalmiut found its way into Parliament when the opposition decided to use it against the government. Minister of Northern Affairs and National Resources Jean Lesage, placed in the embarrassing situation of having to defend policies and practices he knew little about, waved Porsild's review around and offered to make it available to any interested party.

When *People of the Deer* was awarded the Anisfield-Wolf award in the United States for the book published in 1952 that contributed most to bettering race relations, Porsild wrote a condemnatory letter to the awards committee. But his became essentially the lone voice of dissent. *People of the Deer* was published in England, France and Sweden in 1953; a year later in Germany, Italy and Norway; and within the decade in Japan, Yugoslavia, the Soviet Union, Romania, Finland and Poland. Although Porsild did not intend to do so, he helped to establish Mowat's reputation as a fierce, controversial champion of Native and ecological issues.

In the late autumn of 1952, after the excitement surrounding the publication of his first book died down, Farley completed the cement basement to the cabin at Palgrave, shingled the roof, built an addition, gathered wood and prepared the garden for the winter. He had by then also completed a first draft of the "boy's book" (*Lost in the Barrens*), which ran to seventy-five thousand words and which, upon completion, seemed better to him that he had first thought.[29] His work schedule had settled into a comfortable routine: he wrote from eight to ten in the morning, worked at his various household chores until seven and then wrote again for three hours in the evening.[30] To this heady mix was added a commission in 1952 to write the history of the Hastings and Prince Edward Regiment for three thousand dollars, a task Angus very much wanted his son to undertake.

Sometimes Max Wilkinson, like Jack McClelland, could offer conflicting advice. At first he was very negative about *The Regiment*: "I don't think your little war memoir will sell. It is entertaining but blasé Yanks are apt to say so what. I'll try it around in a few chosen spots and if we have no luck perhaps you can turn it to good account there in the wilderness. In general stories about the war do not readily sell."[31] Having offered that pronouncement, he then backtracked: "I think this is a good sort of book to do, because it will make you a beloved author to many Canadians who know you now only as a ferocious soldier and assaulter of the Hudson's Bay Company. This latter history, by the way, is the one you should strive for. What a big wonderful book this could be!"[32] Very much a man looking for the main chance for himself and his authors, Wilkinson, who claimed Farley had no instinct for making money, could even with calculated irony accuse Farley of being overzealous to make some: "What an instinct for venality [you have]! I expect you will die the richest man in Palgrave."[33]

Angus, who had collected a great deal of information about the Hasty Pees, made his research available to his son. However, at the outset, Farley saw his new book as the "inevitable war book that all feel impelled to write. But I shall be different, for this will be a war novel that is of war, but not of battle. Relegate the blood and guts of our prolific American brethren to its proper—and minor—place in the scheme of things and write, instead, of that ephemeral mood that itched as badly as blue balls, and that was as quickly cured and as urgently relegated to the forgotten limbo of the subconscious with our return to normalcy." At that point, the book had the working title "Mood of Battle." Farley considered this a good title but observed that it "remains to be seen whether the book will have the mood."[34]

Very soon after beginning *The Regiment*, Farley knew he could not write the book he had first imagined. Emotionally, he was not ready to revisit the complicated feelings that he had experienced at the front: "Although the guns were silent over the fields and hills of Europe, they still rumbled in my head, giving rise to a bedlam of grotesqueries where nothing was as it might seem or ought to be.

Dark memories still shuffled in kaleidoscope confusion." But since he did not wish to disappoint his father, he wrote a factual account of their regiment.

The resulting book, which begins with a brief history of the Regiment but then concentrates most of its attention on its history in the Second World War, is very much the work of Farley Mowat the historian, exactly the type of narrative that Porsild and others might have wanted *People of the Deer* to be. But it was not the kind of book Farley wanted to write: his first book highlights all his strengths, the second, his weaknesses. Although it is a perfectly competent and interesting book, it simply lacks the liveliness and human interest of *People of the Deer*.

The more he considered the offer to write the history of the Hasty Pees, the more Farley thought a return journey to the places he had known in wartime might assist him to "make sense (if sense could be made) of what had taken place. Might help to mute or even still the echoes of the guns." In a much later book, *Aftermath: Travels in a Post-War World* (1995), Farley provides an account of the trip he and Fran made to England, France and Italy in the spring of 1953. Instead of exercising prudence, they decided to "blow the whole three grand" of Farley's commission. Sixteen hundred went towards the purchase of a Hillman Minx convertible (christened *Elizabeth*, or *Liz*, in honour of the young queen whose coronation took place while they were in England), which they took delivery of in England. The remaining fourteen hundred paid for the actual expenses of the trip.

Fran is an occasional presence in *Aftermath*, but purposely omitted is the fact that she suffered a severe nervous breakdown in Grenoble when the couple, after having gone as far south as Sorrento, Salerno, Capri and Positano, were returning to England by way of France. Deeply worried, Farley drove her back to England as quickly as he could. Upon her return to Canada, she quickly recovered. Once again, Farley had been startled by a sudden turn in Fran's state of mind.

The Europe that Farley travelled through in the spring of 1953 was busily restoring itself to at least the appearance of normality. At the end of *Aftermath*, Farley tells of an encounter with Peter Scott, the son of the Antarctic explorer Robert Falcon Scott, at Slimbridge near the River Severn in Gloucester. While they chatted about the possibility of swords—military hardware—being transformed into ploughshares, three Meteor jet fighters shrieked low overhead. Farley was convinced that a permanent peace would never occur. Scott, looking up into the sky, reflected: "P'raps you're right. It may *not* come to pass . . . but you know, Mowat, if it doesn't . . . and if we don't stop mucking things up other ways as well . . . one day the old Proprietor up in the sky is going to shout: 'Time, gentlemen!' and turn the lot of us into the night. . . . And where will we go then, poor things?" For Farley, the visit to Europe was unsettling. Although his writing career seemed on track, he was still deeply worried about the fate of the human race—and the future of his marriage.

PART TWO

The Man Who Couldn't Be

7

Nomad

1953–1959

FARLEY'S sense of isolation and malaise was underscored by the political climate of the time. The Cold War between the United States and the Soviet Union was in full swing in the early fifties. The Canadian government, following the lead of Dwight D. Eisenhower's Republican administration, was deeply suspicious of all things Russian, as well as anything that smacked of socialism. In addition to making Farley deeply concerned about the future of the human race, the trip to Europe helped push his anti-American sentiments to the fore, allowing him to understand the Soviet point of view. In the immediate wake of the war, Farley had been decidedly apolitical. He now became associated with left-wing causes, through support first of the CCF and then, in 1961, of its successor, the NDP. In 1955 he took an active part in helping to unseat his complacent municipal government; he later participated in the anti-nuclear protests in Ontario and Saskatchewan spearheaded by Tommy Douglas, leader of the NDP.

Upon his return to Palgrave in the summer of 1953, Farley had many projects on the go. He was completing work on *Lost in the Barrens*, starting to write *The Regiment* and feverishly composing stories and articles to support himself and Fran. Although the bread-and-butter jobs consumed most of his working days, he also devoted much time and effort to his new books. Farley and Fran also had to work many long hours to maintain Palgrave. Since his home and its needs distracted him, Farley rented land in nearby North Albion, where he wrote in a trailer. When within a few months following their return to Ontario Fran became pregnant, many of the tensions between her and Farley were neutralized as they prepared for the birth of their child.

At that time, another new Mowat also arrived. In 1953, Angus and Helen adopted Rosemary (called Mary as a child), a six-year-old Oneida girl from an orphanage in London, Ontario. Like John, Rosemary had been in a number of foster homes before joining the

John, Angus, Helen and Rosemary Mowat, circa 1957

Mowats in Richmond Hill. A 1957 article by Florence Schill in the *Globe and Mail* ("Adoption a Success: Parents Proud of Indian Children") provided a glowing account of their family life:

> The Mowats, Mr. and Mrs., both in their sixties, may be sitting before the fireplace, he with his pipe, she with her knitting. The Mowats, John and Mary, may be in any one of a number of poses—John pasting pictures in his photograph album, pictures taken last summer with his father on his sailboat, Mary pecking away at her typewriter; John reading and Mary playing with her doll.
>
> Or, if it's later in the evening, John and Mary may not be in sight at all. But the chances are that, sooner or later, you will hear suppressed giggles from the stairway and catch a glimpse of two faces peering bright-eyed over the railing.

Although Helen admitted to being concerned at the outset that "we would have all sorts of problems [in adopting Native children]," she and her husband had experienced "none to speak of." The article concludes with an amicable exchange between husband and wife:

> "You could keep us talking about [the two children] all night," says Mr. Mowat.
>
> "If I were only 10 years younger, I'd take 10 more," adds Mrs. Mowat.
>
> His comeback to this is: "Well, mother, I'll gladly give up any idea of retiring if that's the way you feel about it."[1]

But behind the scenes, the situation was not so rosy. Helen had not wanted to adopt any children and now she had two to look after. Husband and wife demarcated their parental responsibilities along gender lines: Angus—when he was home—was responsible for John, Helen for Mary. John remembers Angus as a disciplinarian and a taskmaster but an extremely charming one, a person who knew how to state his expectations with gentle force. Rosemary recalls Helen as a parent with whom she had nothing in common. When almost immediately after her arrival Rosemary started to rebel against her adoptive mother in small ways, she found Helen completely rejecting: "There could not have been two people less suited to each other."

Another significant change came six years later in 1959 when Angus retired and he, Helen, John and Rosemary moved from Richmond Hill to Port Hope. Their new home, at 18 King Street, was a wooden 1840s Ontario cottage originally built for farm workers.

The Mowat family was reconstituted at two significant turning points in Farley's life—shortly after he had married and moved away and then just as he was about to become a father. When Rosemary arrived at Richmond Hill in 1953, Fran was pregnant with Angus and Helen's first grandchild. At an unconscious level, Angus may have seen the fresh directions in Farley's life as some sort of breaking of the bond that had existed between them and he forged the new family ties as a result.

When Robert Alexander—always called Sandy because of his light-coloured hair—was born on April 4, 1954, Helen, who had never gotten along with Fran and who was overwhelmed by her own domestic concerns, told her daughter-in-law, "I hope he won't be a tiny little runt like his father."★ The young mother, who had hoped Sandy would help her establish a bond with her remote mother-in-law, was both saddened and dismayed.

Two months after Sandy's birth, Farley, Angus and a young friend of Farley's, Murray Biloki, sailed on Angus's ketch *Scotch Bonnet* from Montreal downriver into the Gulf of St. Lawrence, heading towards the Atlantic through the narrow Strait (or Gut) of Canso. During a storm, the crew of three tied their boat alongside a tugboat belonging to the Foundation Company, a salvage company that rescued distressed vessels caught in the often ferocious weather conditions in the North Atlantic. The young storyteller, treated to some spellbinding accounts of the hair-raising exploits of the Foundation's fleet, began to imagine the book he could write about one such salvage tug, the *Foundation Franklin*.

★ Here I am quoting Fran in conversation with me. Farley's response: "This is Fran. Helen would *never* have used a word like 'runt.'"

Soon after his return to Palgrave, Farley was itching to get away again. Intrigued by what he had heard of the ruggedness of Newfoundland—especially the outport communities—he wanted to journey there. There were other incentives. Many of the men whose stories had been told to him on the tugboat were natives of that province, especially the captains. They seemed to be blessed with a unique kind of heroic endurance. Farley saw immediately that the lives of many people on the Rock, people whose existences had been relatively untouched by progress and by many of the comforts of civilization, might make a similar story to that of the Ihalmiut. Then, too, there was the mysterious call of the sea. Farley had previously been devoted to the study of birds, wolves and caribou. Now his imagination was enlivened by whales, porpoises and seals.

In the early fifties, Farley remained uncertain where he was heading with his writing. After a good meeting with Dudley Cloud in Boston, at which the publisher urged him, in the wake of the enormous commercial success of his first book, to take careful, measured steps for the future, he deluged Cloud with ideas for a number of book-length projects. In March 1954, Cloud was exasperated:

What's eating you? We're puzzled.
    What we want from Mowat is a book that will be a smashing success, both critically and commercially, a second book that is a worthy successor to POD, written with the eloquence and assurance and clear purpose that will establish you as a writer. At this stage you can't afford an anti-climax. Maybe you have that book in the works, but your letter certainly doesn't give us an indication of it. You seem to be pecking away at too many scattered ideas.

Cloud, worried about what he considered Farley's scattershot approach, was sounding a warning: be careful of what you are doing or risk being badly burnt. Although he did not decide until September 1955 to reject *The Regiment* as unsuitable for the American market, Cloud considered that book a mistake all along. He also was worried about two collections of essays Farley was preparing, a proposed novel and the almost completed juvenile novel *Lost in the Barrens*. When Farley sent Max Wilkinson "Valley of Dead Dreams," a collection of essays based on his 1953 trip to Europe, Max was sympathetic but frank: "I'm awfully sorry, kid, but I don't believe there's a place" for this book in the United States.

But in the midst of all this bad news was Jack McClelland's unswerving eagerness to publish *The Regiment*. Since Farley—despite the appearance of bravado—was also, in the wake of *People of the Deer*, understandably sensitive to criticism, he was heartened when he received Jack's endorsement, even though it was qualified: "I think the book is slightly terrific, that it is one of the most interesting reading experiences I have had in a long time, and that its publication will undoubtedly enhance the not inconsiderable reputation that you have already achieved."[2] The relieved author confessed, "That's the first professional opinion I've had [of this completed book], and despite my heavy armoury, my body-armour is light and subject to rust holes. I feel much happier about the book."[3] A bit later, Jack had to tell Farley he could not discard the title just because the author was fearful that it might give book buyers the (correct) impression that they were being asked to purchase a book about military history: "The only effective way of hiding the fact that it is a regimental history is for you to rewrite the book completely, using an entirely different topic, say Girl's Basketball."[4]

Despite Farley's difficulties with Cloud, the manuscript *Lost in the Barrens* quickly found great favour with one of Atlantic's senior editors, Jeannette T. Cloud, Dudley's wife. Although she proved to be rigorous in her demands for changes, she responded enthusiastically to the two main characters: Jamie, the white boy, and Awasin, the Cree boy: "I like their self-reliance, their ingenuity, their courage. They seem to me well-differentiated, good foils for each other."[5]

Having placed his juvenile novel with Atlantic–Little, Brown, Farley tried to interest them in a book on the exploits of the Foundation Company ships. Then he presented them with something unexpected: a book about Mutt. This narrative, some of it written during

Peter Davison, circa 1965

the war, showed a talent for comic invention that had been absent from his other work. All of a sudden, both agent and publisher were forced to recognize that although the young Canadian author might be too big for his britches, those britches were very large and varied.

The Mutt typescript found immediate favour with both Wilkinson and Cloud, although both felt that it did not hold together well and should be divided into "short crisp magazine pieces."[6] If Farley was determined to leave it as a book, they urged him to tie the various strands together. When, in February 1956, Farley had revised as much as he could, Cloud was still dissatisfied and Wilkinson considered the results far too "poetical." The book sat in limbo for six months until Cloud left Atlantic to take up a teaching post at Wilbraham Academy.

When Cloud's replacement, Peter Davison, read the revised Mutt manuscript that autumn, he proposed—in complete disagreement with the advice offered by Cloud and Wilkinson—restoring the original version of the book, in which a slew of subsidiary characters, such as the owls Wol and Weeps, wander in and out of Mutt's adventures. For Davison, the real problem was the book's title, which changed in short order from *Mutt's Time and Mine* to *Whither Mutt?* to *Mutt in My Life* to *Animal Spirits: A Prairie Boyhood* to *They Bark at Me* to *Animal Caravan* to *On Wings of Dog* to *Mutt: A Prairie Boyhood* to *Mutt: The Dog Who Wouldn't Be* to, with some genuine hesitation, *The Dog Who Wouldn't Be*. Along the way, Davison, in moments of exasperation, even considered two other titles: *A Bestial Boyhood* and *Puberty on the Prairie*.

In Peter Davison, Farley found his ideal editor, one convinced of his genius but equally determined that he needed rigorous editing. However unstinting and unconditional his support for Farley, Davison was always more than willing to call his author's attention to shortcomings. At the age of twenty-eight, in 1956, Davison, darkly handsome, New York City–born and Harvard-educated, had been a Fulbright Scholar at Cambridge University; eight years later, in 1964, he won the Yale Series of Younger Poets award for his first collection of verse, *The Breaking of the Day*. On the surface, Farley and Peter seemed vastly different. Farley hated cities, whereas Peter thrived in them. Davison's imagination as a poet is subtle, psychological and deeply interior; Mowat's work may be autobiographical and reflective, but it is very much concerned with survival in the physical world. Peter is a cultivated, worldly man, whereas Farley maintains a more down-to-earth, homespun persona. What brought them together was a deep pleasure in the art of storytelling, a common intrigue with the right ways to bend and manipulate words.

By January 1956, Farley had published two books (*People of the Deer* and *The Regiment*) and had taken giant strides forward on three others (*Lost in the Barrens*, *The Dog Who Wouldn't Be* and *The Grey Seas Under*, his book about the *Foundation Franklin*). Sandy was a thriving twenty-one-month-old toddler, Fran was seven months pregnant, and Palgrave, with the addition of several small buildings, was growing into a small estate. Then the family's stability was suddenly jeopardized when Fran became gravely ill.

The specialists the Mowats consulted told them that two dismal choices confronted them: Fran could have a Caesarean section to abort the foetus and possibly save her life, or she could carry on with the pregnancy with the strong possibility that the placenta had been torn away, causing great harm to the foetus and possibly endangering her own life. In addition, Fran and Farley were informed that if the baby survived, he or she would be seriously impaired. It was a highly distressing time for both. As Fran vividly recalled later, she was reluctant to have the operation but Farley insisted: "I don't want a moron for a child!" he told her. Farley does not recollect making any such statement. He may not have wanted to have a deficient child, but he also did not wish to risk his wife's life.

The abortion was performed at a hospital, where the nurse in attendance was a Roman Catholic who let Fran know in no uncertain terms that she thoroughly disapproved of her conduct. Fran did not suffer a depression as a result of the procedure, but she now became convinced that other people (the nurse, the doctors and Farley) were either making decisions on her behalf or condemning her for her decisions.

Soon after the loss of the baby, Farley suggested they consider adoption. Fran was not completely convinced that path was the right one, but she went along with it. The couple arranged to adopt from a pregnant woman from Orangeville, but she decided after giving birth not to give up the baby. Then, in 1957, Fran and Farley turned to the Children's Aid Society, from which they obtained fourteen-month-old David, who had been in five foster homes before he came to them.

Fran now became certain of two things: that Farley's championing of adoption was inspired by Angus and Helen's earlier adoptions of John and Rosemary and that he was trying to find some way of distracting her from the physical and psychological suffering she had endured. The abortion had driven the couple further apart. Although Fran could see and sympathize with Farley's point of view, she felt

Sandy and David Mowat, circa 1958

violated by what had taken place. Fran saw her life with her husband as life on a roller coaster—she was no longer certain she could cope with the abrupt ups and downs. More than before, she retreated into herself. Earlier in their relationship, Farley had witnessed black depressions take Fran over. Such incidents increased markedly after 1956.

When Arnold and Vi Warren moved to Palgrave in about 1957, they were immediately struck by Farley's eager friendliness and by Fran's quiet reserve. Both Arnold and Vi were commercial pilots and had worked in Indonesia before settling in Palgrave, which was within fairly easy driving distance of Malton Airport (now Toronto's Pearson Airport), where they worked. Vi clearly recalls the day Farley drove over to their place in his little red jeep: "I've come over to say hello. I've left it long enough." At that first meeting, Farley told the Warrens about his various exploits in the North, and they responded with tales of their adventures in the Far East.

Although Arnold was about fifteen years older than Farley, the two men quickly formed a close friendship based on their love of far-flung exploits. They also had similar political views, both taking pleasure in poking fun at figures in authority. These strands came together in the formation of Trans-Polar Aviation, which would offer dirigible service to Moscow from North America by way of the North Pole. Stationery was printed with the company name and logo; the two men applied to the transport ministry in Ottawa for a licence to start an airline; they made inquiries about the availability of Goodyear and Navy surplus dirigibles. Trans-Polar may have been an elaborate practical joke on bureaucracy, but it led to the beginning of Farley's extensive RCMP file, wherein his many supposedly left-wing activities were duly entered.

On a more serious note, the two men formed the Committee for Canadian Independence, a group that promoted journalist and pundit James M. Minifie's philosophy that Canada should take an active anti-American stance in world affairs and economist Walter Gordon's notion that Canada should be economically separate from the United States. Farley even ran, unsuccessfully, in a municipal election. In its circular letter, the group admitted that it could not "cope with the many problems inherent in the organization of a movement which" reflected widespread concern by Canadians about their future. "We feel, in a word, rather like the man who caught a tiger by the tail."

When the Warrens saw Farley for the second time, he was accompanied by Fran. Vi immediately saw a woman very much in need of a friend, someone trying to get her life back to "normal." On several occasions, the two couples went into Toronto for supper and a movie. When the four got together at the Warrens', Fran seemed overly dependent on Farley. She could also become whiny. Fran had little patience if these get-togethers lasted too long: "Farley, it's your second drink. It's time to go home!"

Farley asked Vi to cheer Fran up, but that proved to be a difficult task. One day Fran told Vi that Farley wanted to have sex too often for her liking. When Vi noticed that Fran was letting her physical appearance go, she persuaded her to buy a pair of red pants; on another occasion, she insisted Fran spruce herself up by borrowing her black suit.

Farley increasingly saw himself as a bystander within his own marriage, unable to make things better between himself and his wife. Fran withdrew more and more, and he became frightened. It was reminiscent of an earlier time, just two years previously, when Farley wrote to his parents about Fran's always perilous health: "Much silence from Palgrave recently due to much sickness. After Angus's visit, Fran got 'wuss and wuss' and finally spent two and a half weeks in bed. She is still a convalescent and must go to bed at 8:00 P.M. each night and will continue to be house-bound until the end of the month. Gad, what a winter. First, she had pneumonia, then bronchitis, and finally this bloody flu. She is about done, all pale skin and brittle bones."[7] Once, on a three-day working visit to Palgrave, Peter Davison saw almost nothing of Fran. She was in bed, too sick to see anyone. Farley soldiered on with the two children and the two dogs, all four of whom he cheerfully and zestfully and solicitously treated like mischievous puppies.

Although the mid-fifties were disastrous at Palgrave, they also saw the publication of Farley's first novel, *Lost in the Barrens*, his only book ever to win a Governor General's Award (in the category of Juvenile Literature); it was also awarded the 1956 Book of the Year Medal (by the Canadian Association of Children's Librarians) and the Boys' Club of America Junior Book Award.

The contrast between the raw eagerness of Farley Mowat and the laid-back shrewdness of Franz (Charles Schweder) in *People of the Deer* is given a completely fictional reworking in the depiction of the friendship between Jamie, a white boy, and Awasin, a young Cree boy, in *Lost in the Barrens*. Stranded in the Barrens during the winter, the two friends survive because Jamie's inventiveness and Awasin's experience perfectly complement each other. Moreover, during the course of their adventures, Jamie gains an appreciation of Awasin's intuitive understanding of the forces of nature, an area of experience where white man's knowledge is negligible and often meaningless. At one point, Jamie is outraged when wolves kill a fawn, but Awasin tells him that the fawn is a natural prey for the wolves, which must eat to survive.

Towards the end of the book, the two boys are befriended by Peetyuk, an Inuit lad, who offers them hospitality and assistance: "A year earlier neither Jamie nor Awasin would have believed that one day they would be sitting in a huge snowhouse surrounded by at least thirty of the fur-clad people who, for centuries, the Indians had considered to be no better than bloodthirsty savages. But this is what the boys were doing the day after their meeting with Peetyuk." Although brief, the friendly encounter with the Inuit in this book mirrors the adventures of Farley and Franz in *People of the Deer*, but in the world of fiction the Inuit assist the white man and his companion rather than the other way around.

The quest is a traditional literary form, one used over and over again in children's literature, but Farley skilfully embellishes his narrative with information about the flora, fauna, anthropology and history of the Barrenlands. The boys' initiation rite in the North may be one common to Canadian literature (such as Susanna Moodie's *Roughing It in the Bush*) and in classic writing for young boys (such as Robert Michael Ballantyne's *Silver Lake, or, Lost in the Snow* and Egerton Ryerson Young's *Winter Adventures of Three Boys in the Great Lone Land*), but Mowat's adaptation of his own experience in the

Keewatin district is startlingly original and bold in its dramatic story-telling, in its colourful use of factual details and in its subtle depiction of the possibility of accord between white and Native men.

Although obviously not as directly propagandistic as *People of the Deer*, *Lost in the Barrens* displays a side of Farley Mowat that had been already visible. *The Dog Who Wouldn't Be*, published the following year, is the first piece of writing in which his comical and fantastical skills are fully displayed. The real Mutt had been an amazingly intelligent and affectionate canine; the book version of Mutt is in essence a fictional alter ego of the comical, mischievous and rambunctious sides of his owner-creator. Mutt's appeal as a character ultimately resides in his blend of animal and human traits. The fictional Mutt climbs trees, outsmarts Father and Farley Mowat at every turn and, in general, is as canny and charming a creature as ever existed. Often described in quasi-epic and mock-heroic language, he is the very stuff of legends:

> Word of Mutt's phenomenal abilities soon got around, for neither my father nor I was reticent about him. At first the local hunters were sceptical, but after some of them had seen him work, their disbelief began to change into a strong civic pride that, in due time, made Mutt's name a byword for excellence in Saskatchewan hunting circles. Indeed, Mutt became something of a symbol—a truly western symbol, for his feats were sometimes slightly exaggerated by his partisans for the benefit of unwary strangers—particularly if the strangers came out of the east.

In the east, in a strong notice in *Saturday Night*, Samuel Marchbanks (a pseudonym used by Robertson Davies) praised the book in no uncertain terms: "Let those critics who say that wit, style and imagination are lacking in our Canadian books read this one, and change their tune."[8]

When Farley mentioned the possibility of doing a book on the Foundation Company and its vessels, Jack McClelland, Max Wilkinson and Peter Davison unanimously encouraged him to pursue the matter. Through Helen's sister, Frances Thomson (an employee of the Foundation), doors were quickly opened on Farley's behalf. The company warmly supported his desire to write a book on the exploits of their men and ships, and in the spring of 1956, Farley signed a contract with the Foundation.

At Palgrave, he purchased some adjoining land to his property and continued to work on short stories, articles and radio pieces. That winter, he worked on the final draft of *The Dog Who Wouldn't Be*.

But the chasm between husband and wife deepened. Just before and after his marriage in 1947, Farley had escaped to the Arctic. In the mid-fifties, a similar inclination to run away asserted itself. He began to absent himself from Palgrave as much as possible. Although David had barely joined the household, Farley made several week-long excursions in 1957 to Halifax and Montreal to conduct interviews and take more trips on salvage tugs.

That August, anxious to get away for an extended period of time, Farley decided to visit Canada's newest province, which he had hankered to see ever since his trip to the Maritimes on *Scotch Bonnet* in 1954. He travelled to Port aux Basques and then on a coastal boat, the *Bar Haven*, along the island's south coast and so to St. John's, the capital of Newfoundland. Over drinks on board ship, Farley met Jack Courage, the speaker of the House of Assembly. If Farley wanted to get to know the *real* Newfoundland—and its rough, primitive but invigorating way of life—Courage urged him to call on Harold Horwood. Then working as associate editor at the *Evening Telegram*, Horwood was also the editor of the weekly *Examiner*, sponsored by the Newfoundland Federation of Labour and Canadian Labour Congress.

Two years younger than Farley, Horwood was a native of St. John's, where he had attended Prince of Wales College. In 1945, he and his brother Charles had begun the journal *Protocol*, which specialized in experimental writing. A proponent of amalgamation of Newfoundland within Canada and an admirer of the feisty, dynamic leader of the Newfoundland Liberal party, Joey Smallwood, Horwood was elected at the age of twenty-seven to the Newfoundland legislature as the first member to represent Labrador, the mainland section—500 miles

Harold Horwood, circa 1960

south of Greenland—of what had become in 1949 Canada's tenth province.

After he left politics in 1952, Harold continued to support Small-wood, but by 1956 he considered the premier a demagogue and attacked him fiercely and regularly in his *Telegram* column, "Political Notebook." Smallwood's enormous popularity in the mid-fifties meant that Harold was almost alone in his views. He was deliberately eccentric and often irascible, but he could also be a loyal and caring friend.

Harold was not overly impressed by the stranger who "poked his blunt, freckled nose" into his office at the *Telegram*.

> "I'm Farley Mowat," he announced, and when that failed to raise an eyebrow, he added, "the writer."
>
> "Ha!" I said. "Another mainlander here to pick my brains." I'd recently had visits from two non-fiction writers with inflated reputations in Canada, who were now honouring Newfoundland with their attention. I didn't much care for these visits of the great and the near-great. I felt that if anyone was going to write about Newfoundland it ought to be me, not someone from the backwoods of Ontario or the mudslides of British Columbia.
>
> "Actually," he said, "Jack Courage told me I ought to look you up. . . . Do you drink rum?"

"Of course," I said. "You've got a bottle with you?"

"In my rented car."

"Then I'll knock off for the day and we'll go sample it. What kind of stuff do you write?"

"About the Arctic, mainly. And about the sea."

"The Arctic? . . . Did you write a book called *People of the Deer?*"

"That's me."

"Ah, now I place you. I was in the Press Gallery at Ottawa when they had that row about the tribe of Caribou Eskimos the government said didn't exist. A few days later they flew in a load of buffalo meat because the nonexistent Eskimos were starving."

"That's the ones," he said. "The Ihalmiut. I lived with them for a while."

"So we may have something in common. I've travelled a bit with the natives of Labrador as far north as people live along that coast."

Although the friendship that quickly formed between Farley and Harold was a strong one, it had its fair share of acrimony. Harold deemed himself to be the real expert on his place of birth and regarded Farley as a somewhat sentimental interloper. Farley, in turn, considered Harold to be truly knowledgeable about St. John's and distinctly unreliable about what was for him the *real* Newfoundland—the tiny, rugged-living outport communities. Harold appraised Farley as a writer who "speaks directly to a mass audience, as loudly as he can, writing books with mass appeal, and promoting them with numerous TV appearances. I have tried to appeal to a small circle of readers with tastes and interests close to my own, believing that if I can move them, their influence will reach out across the world and help change it." He also claimed, "He and I have never been in competition. The kind of writing he does tries to be personal and emotional; mine tries to be factual and objective." And yet the lure of Farley's name was hard to resist: "I'd like to collaborate with you on a book," he once stated, "if for no better reason than that it would tickle my vanity no end to appear with you on the cover."[9]

Despite his claim that he and Farley were not rivalrous, Harold envied his friend's commercial success: "I soon discovered that Farley was an actor (and acting pretty nearly all the time), a salesman for his writing following the rule that you must sell yourself rather than your books—and at almost any cost, including your own dignity. . . . His style strikes me as a bit florid, his metaphors sometimes extreme, his anecdotes even exaggerated beyond credibility, but the public is obviously in love with his stuff." He once told Farley, "You irritate me no end. We're not very much alike, you know. For one thing, you live on an intense emotional level which I couldn't cope with at all." Having made that declaration, he added: "N B: your irritating me doesn't mean that I'm not fond of you."[10] In an outburst that might have destroyed other friendships, Harold provided Farley with a caustic biographical overview:

You are a very strong personality. You are a reformer. You believe you are right about everything. You have a long period of success behind you, and the events of your career have tended to confirm you in your God-like pose. You were an only child. You shot up to the rank of Captain in the army. Your first book was an international best seller. How could anybody survive this without coming to believe in his own infallibility?

In another sniping moment he observed, "Unlike you, I can't dash off a book with a shrug and sneer."[11] Despite all the drawbacks, Farley nevertheless remained for him "the only living person for whom I have a true feeling of brotherhood."[12]

During that summer, Farley and Harold visited the oldest European settlements in Newfoundland in the great bays of Conception and Trinity, which were settled by West Country fishermen in the sixteenth century. At those places and at Port de Grave and Ferryland, Farley carried a tape recorder, on which he meticulously recorded his interviews. The two men, both eager birdwatchers, searched for migrating shore birds on the tidal flats of the southern shore and St. George's Bay. In between, they diluted their rum with water from wayside streams, lived under tents at night and spent many happy hours chatting with fishermen, masters of trap crews and backwoodsmen. Farley, Harold observed, never spoke about Frances or the children.

When he made his way to Palgrave the following year, Harold noticed a nude department-store mannequin next to the radiation warning sign. In back of the dummy, there was a thick belt of trees, beyond which Farley, Sandy and David were romping about in the nude. "Frances, however, was fully dressed. 'You mustn't mind Farley,' she said, 'It's just his way. I've given up trying to civilize him.'"

In the winter of 1957, Farley began *Coppermine Journey*, an edition of the journals of the great Arctic explorer Samuel Hearne (1745–92). In 1766, Hearne was commissioned by the Hudson's Bay Company to search for a western passage, by water, across the Barrenlands; he was also on the lookout for copper. With Matonabbee, a Dene leader, he traversed trackless wastes, patiently following the migration of the caribou. Hearne fell out with his Indian companions when he refused to take part in the massacre of a helpless party of Inuit at a place later called Bloody Falls. Farley, still feeling badly stung by the attacks on *People of the Deer*, was attempting to make a significant contribution to Arctic studies by preparing an edition of the writings of a man whose love of the North was similar to his own.

During the summer of 1958, Farley made two major trips, first back to Newfoundland and then to the Arctic. He and Harold travelled from Stephenville to St. John's, their longest stop being two weeks in Ferryland. In his personal chronology, Farley wrote, "Becoming extremely enamoured of Newfoundland in direct proportion as becoming un-enamoured with marital arrangements at home."

The two men tried—in the spirit of the Committee for Canadian Independence—to find out if nuclear bombs were stored at Ernest Harmon Air Force Base, an American base at Stephenville. This investigation eventually led to an article by Horwood in the December 3, 1960, *Examiner*, wherein he charged that, contrary to Prime Minister Diefenbaker's assertion, there was "proof beyond all reasonable doubt" that such bombs were kept at the American base:

I would be willing to bet that Stephenville has been marked out by Russia as a prime target for instant destruction in case of war, that a Russian missile armed with a hydrogen warhead is sitting on a pad in the Arctic right at this minute pointed at Stephenville, with its trajectory figured out to the billionth part of a degree, just waiting for someone to press a button in order to turn Stephenville into a pool of red-hot lava twenty minutes later.

While Horwood had no way of proving that bombs were stored at the base, he observed that "any taxi driver [in the area] can point out the location of the 'top secret' weapons dump . . . and tell you exactly when the first atom bombs were stored there."

William H. Christensen, the U.S. consul general in St. John's, wrote to the State Department in Washington, D.C., that Horwood's "insinuation that the United States is hoodwinking the Government of Canada about the storage of nuclear weapons . . . reveals his almost psychopathic antipathy towards us. Despite the fact that Horwood is looked upon by many people here as a crackpot, he has a certain nuisance value to people like Farley Mowat."

To Christensen's chagrin, Horwood boasted that Farley was quite "capable of stealing an atom bomb and taking it to Ottawa." Horwood, the American consul added, had bragged that he could lead "Mowat's commandos to the Stephenville stockpile with my eyes shut."* Christensen was particularly irked because Farley had been making allegations about the bombs in "a buffoon-like" manner on CBC Radio broadcasts.[13]

What Christensen did not know was that Farley, Harold and a few others had founded the Newfoundland Revolutionary Society, dedicated to "ridding the island of foreign military forces, and then to

---

* Harold Horwood wrote jubilantly to Farley on December 16, 1960, about Goose Bay in Labrador, "We've really got the dope on Goose: underground bunkers, special nuclear-weapons loading gear installed there; armed jeeps with machine guns flanking the planes as they load and unload their motorized bomb-carriers, etc., etc. All eye-witness stuff, and can get any number of additional eye-witnesses prepared to swear to what they see there. Dear John [Diefenbaker] will have his paws full explaining it away" (Harold Horwood to Farley Mowat; ms: McMaster).

freeing the world from the looming threat of nuclear dissolution." Their plan of action was simplicity itself:

> We would drive across the island to Stephenville . . . carrying a gallon or two of that singularly ferocious Newfoundland rum called Screech. We would approach the secret SAC bomb arsenal in a carefree way and offer to share our grog with what our informant assured us would be a bored and merely token guard detachment. When the Screech had done its stuff, we would tenderly remove one of the smaller bombs, transport it to Red Indian Lake in the interior, and drop it gingerly into the almost bottomless depths of that great body of water.

After issuing its manifesto, the group—having consumed two or three bottles of rum—made their way to bed. In the morning, clearer heads prevailed.

In the spring of 1958, Farley heard rumours that the Ihalmiut were again in serious trouble. In the years since *People of the Deer*, officials in Ottawa had taken steps to assist members of the previously "non-existent" band. In fact, it was a government employee who alerted Farley to a particularly tragic story concerning two families living next to each other at Henik Lake.

When his family was starving to death, Halo resolved to travel with them south in search of assistance; that decision did not sit well with Ootek, his closest friend, who was in too ravaged a state to make such a trek with his own family. Borrowing a rifle from Halo's wife, Kikkik, Ootek shot Halo dead near a fishing hole. The crime was discovered by one of Halo's daughters, who told her mother what had happened. Realizing that Ootek would prevent her and her children from setting out, Kikkik killed him with a knife and then set off with her five children, two of whom she was forced to abandon along the way. One daughter, Nesha, perished, and Kikkik was charged with not only the murder of Ootek but also the wilful abandonment of her daughter, resulting in her death. Although the judge, Jack

Sissons—well aware of the dire situation in which she had been involved—directed the jury to find her not guilty, Kikkik endured not only tragic loss but also public ignominy.

Desperate to return to the Arctic but short of money, Farley was delighted when Frank Walker, an executive of the Hudson's Bay Company, invited him—all expenses paid—to accompany Norman Ross, the head of the Arctic Division, on his annual inspection of trading posts in the central Arctic. Why, Farley asked, was an olive branch suddenly being extended to him—"Unless the plan is to dump me into the Arctic Ocean somewhere. What's all this in aid of, anyway?" Unruffled, Walker responded, "Nothing special. Call it a goodwill gesture. You and the Company have been at odds too long."

During this trip Farley investigated the circumstances surrounding the misfortunes of Kikkik and her subsequent trial. He also met tall, powerfully built, soft-spoken, no-nonsense Doug Wilkinson, the northern service officer (NSO) in Baker Lake: "Would you be Hardly Knowit? . . . if you'll pardon me using the tag some of the old Arctic hands have pinned on you." From that inauspicious start, a good working relationship between the two was quickly established. With Wilkinson's assistance, Farley learned of the mysterious disappearance of Father Joseph Buliard, an Oblate priest who had established a settlement near Garry Lake, of the deaths by starvation of seventeen Inuit once in Buliard's charge and of the sexual molestation of Inuit children by Ernie Caygill, a nurse. In addition, Farley once again confronted the condescension and racism that inhibited all the white man's so-called efforts to assist the Inuit. Of his parishioners, Buliard wrote, "They do not have a pleasant appearance and at times are even repulsive." In such circumstances, the priest claimed the Inuit "sorely need the missionary to drive away the dark clouds of paganism and show them the way to Heaven."

Farley spent considerable time travelling with another Oblate priest, Father Charles Choque, a man whose courage and dedication he greatly admired despite the fact that they held very different opinions. And then there was Major D.W. Grant, the NSO for Term Point on Hudson Bay—where Kikkik and some other Ihalmiut were being moved in order to be "rehabilitated." When Farley asked for permission to go there to meet with Kikkik, the major immediately extolled the "revolutionary project" whereby "a lot of the problems of the natives" were going to be solved: "There will be remunerative work for everybody. The natural resources up here are absolutely unbelievable! We'll have native tradesmen skilled at cooking and canning Arctic foods; trophy hunting of seals, walrus, polar bears, and whales by wealthy sportsmen!" He was not pleased when Farley interrupted with a question: "Might there be a bit of difficulty getting the inland Eskimos to adapt to such a changed way of life?" Grant responded decisively: "Not a bit of it! They can be taught. They *will* be taught!" Farley attempted to turn the conversation back to a possible visit with Kikkik:

"It all sounds very promising, Major. So, can I go along and see for myself?"

"I don't believe so, Mr. Mowat. Not quite the right time, eh? Come back in a year or two, then we'll see."

Well before this, his third trip to the Arctic, Farley had been in touch with several officials in Ottawa, men who were well aware of the plight of the Inuit and wanted to assist them in meaningful ways vastly different from the Term Point scheme. Earlier, in April 1957, in an effort to make sure that a second book on the Arctic would escape the kind of condemnation visited upon his first one by people such as Porsild, Farley contacted his one-time opponent, Jean Lesage, the minister of Northern Affairs and National Resources, who extended an offer of assistance: "There are few northern books having wide attention which do not receive some criticism, but I can fully sympathize with your desire to reduce the criticism to a minimum by the most careful checking of background information." Although Lesage did not wish to "influence" Farley's work, he was "conscious of the value of a public understanding of the north . . . and the part which may be played by competent writers in achieving this end."[14]

Soon afterwards, Farley was obtaining information from Ben Sivertz, the director of the Northern Administration and Lands Branch, who as a young man had worked as a third mate on a salvage boat, and later from Bob Phillips, assistant director of plans and policy in the Northern Administration Branch. These men were in almost total agreement with Farley about the execrable conditions in which the Inuit lived; in fact, some of Phillips's published statements about the Inuit read as if they could have been written by Farley: "Some Canadians believe the Eskimos are happy. If ignorance, disease and economic serfdom are definitions of happiness, this may be true."

That winter of 1958—when *The Grey Seas Under* and *Coppermine Journey* were published—Farley wrote *The Desperate People*, which was published the following year. In contrast to the intimacy of the first-person voice used in *People of the Deer*, Farley's second nonfiction Arctic book is written in omniscient third person. The book begins with an overview of the majestic Arctic landscape in language both lyrical and epic:

> Across the northern reaches of this continent there lies a mighty wedge of treeless plain, scarred by the primordial ice, inundated beneath a myriad of lakes, cross-checked by innumerable rivers, and riven by the rock bones of an elder earth. . . . It is a naked land, bearing the deep excoriations which are the legacy of a glacial incubus of ice a mile in thickness. . . . It is a land uncircumscribed, for it has no limits that the eye can find. It seems to reach beyond the finite boundaries of this earth. Brooding, immutable, given over to its own essential mood of desolation.

The inhabitants of this terrain were in every way appreciative of it:

> They were a rich people, as richness is measured in their world, for they seldom knew hunger; they had an abundance of the warmest clothing a man could want—caribou skins. . . . They had no effective enemies amongst men. The deer were incredibly numerous. . . . They had time to dream, and time to work with words and thought. . . . Such was the hidden world of the Ihalmiut as the second decade of the present century began.

The "hidden world" of the inland Inuit was exploited comparatively late by the white man, but when this devastation finally occurred, it had horrible consequences. Farley goes on to describe his earlier visits to the Arctic, discuss his recent visit, tell of the ordeals of Kikkik, outline the progressive steps being undertaken to assist the Ihalmiut and provide a poignant epilogue; he ends with an appendix which gives biographical information on 111 Ihalmiut—the group Porsild claimed did not exist—from 1946 to 1958.

By 1959, Farley's barely ten-year-old writing career had moved into high gear: he had published six books and scores of magazine stories and articles. Although Atlantic–Little, Brown had been the most effective of his publishers, they seemed miserly in what they would pay. Max Wilkinson told Farley in November 1958, "You know, I rather like young Peter too. But I cannot warm to the spirit of the house he represents. A thin, mean streak of parsimony is evident in their thinking. . . . Fellow name of Mowat, for instance, can get a $5000 guarantee and a straight 15% royalty on the strength of a post-card from any top publisher in town. Can he get it from his publisher, for whom he has made a packet?"

Max devised a plan: "I share your feelings about young Peter. I sure don't want to hurt him either. Therefore, let us do this: Let us give Atlantic *this* book, which is a sort of sequel to POD anyway. And, instead of permitting ourselves to get in their pocket on the next one, let us instead tell them you are going to do a book for Harper, which is your right under the terms of the contract. . . . Try to think of an idea for a book that *might* have been stimulated by Harper. Don't you think this is the most painless way? Eh?"[15]

Farley had mixed feelings about such a move, not only because of Peter Davison's extraordinary efforts on his behalf but also because of his editor's congeniality and honesty in dealing with his author's often perplexed state of mind. Once again Farley was not certain exactly what projects he wanted to work on next.

Late in 1958 and throughout 1959, Farley started to spend a great deal of time in the hard-rock country, replete with magnificent shards of Precambrian rock, around Bancroft—one hundred miles northeast of Palgrave at the foot of the Haliburton Highlands and within striking distance of Algonquin Park—with the purpose of collecting information on a latter-day Paul Bunyan named Robert Harvey (Harve) Gunter (1866–1951), who had lived at Weslemkoon Lake. While in the Army, Farley had become friends with Clifford Broad, Harve's grandson, who told him of his grandfather's life as lumberjack, backwoodsman, subsistence farmer and storyteller. In his visits to Bancroft and nearby Marmora, Harve had "spent much time . . . consorting with hard-drinking, hard-living, story-telling eccentrics who would have done justice to a novel by Faulkner."[16]

Farley also wanted to write a book exclusively about Newfoundland. He admitted to Peter Davison that he was in some ways displeased with *The Desperate People* because it was more impersonal than *People of the Deer*. Davison understood those feelings perfectly:

> I know you had some doubts about this book when I saw you last summer [1959], and I fear they were justified. Your next book should, as I have said before, be something far more personal and closer to your firsthand feelings and experience. If you can in due course turn your attention to Newfoundland and Harve Gunter, I think that you will get greater satisfaction from the writing, and that the book will do more complete justice to your talent than have either of these last two volumes. They were in a sense journalistic, weren't they? They dealt with subjects which you wanted other people to feel strongly about, but which perhaps did not move you as deeply as you hoped they would.[17]

Although Farley did collect information on Gunter and his life in the lumber camps, his existence as a subsistence farmer and his tales of wolves at his door, he eventually lost interest in the project. Newfoundland, however, would remain a consuming interest.

There were many tense times between editor and author. When Farley travelled to New York City in the autumn of 1959 to promote *The Desperate People*, he became incensed by what he considered to be the ineffective and sloppy way in which the Little, Brown publicity people dealt with him. Peter replied in his best no-nonsense manner: "Boyohboy, you don't give a man a moment's peace. I do think you are being damned unfair to the New York office of Little, Brown. . . . I would be glad to pass on your blast if I thought it were justified."[18] After this incident, Peter, convinced that Farley's temperament was completely unsuited both to the United States and to the way book promotion was handled there, refrained for many years from suggesting Farley travel south on an author tour.

When Peter discovered in January 1960 that Farley—who had begun work on an anthology of Arctic writings—was jumping ship with that book, he was equally forthright:

> What is all this about your offering the Arctic Anthology to Harper? I don't, frankly, understand where you got the idea that we were not enthusiastic about the project. . . . In any case, I take it a little badly that you are offering this to Harper. The Atlantic and Little, Brown think of themselves as your publishers, which means that we want to publish everything you write; and we hope that you will look on us in the same light. . . . You must, of course, do what you feel is in your best interest; but I am somewhat surprised to hear that I have shown "less than enthusiasm" for a book I have been told next to nothing about. I am not telepathic.[19]

Peter's honesty elicited a corresponding loyalty on Farley's part. After all, he concluded, it was impossible—and decidedly foolish—to part company with a man who could be both completely supportive and rigorously critical. For instance, the original manuscript of *The Desperate People* contained a long section on the incidents that had taken place at Garry Lake. Peter was adamant that this material should be removed and used in another book or article: "Give some thought to dropping the Garry Lake chapter. I think the book will be far more moving and dramatic if it focuses exclusively on the Ihalmiut. In the Garry Lake episode . . . you have a tendency to over-write, simply because you don't know the people personally. I would far rather see the body of the book end with the tragedy of Kikkik. . . . Doing this would make your case far stronger than adding on Garry Lake like a tail to a kite."[20]★

Farley also found it difficult to jettison someone who made this reply in response to Farley's offer to him of the post of "Chief Inspector of Sperm Whales": "Might I point out that the whale-oil market is low? I suggest that a post for which I might well be better qualified would be Chief Collector of Cod. . . . Think it over and let me know. I would also be interested in the job of Director of the National Bank or Treasurer of Anything Else."[21]

At the same time that Farley came more and more under Davison's editorial sway, he was moving more closely into the orbit of Jack McClelland, whose penchant for attention-getting stunts originally placed him on a collision course with his publicity-shy author. Jack had come to realize that Farley was a very different type of person from Pierre Berton, who had a strong yen for public attention of any kind; in 1958, when *The Grey Seas Under* was published, Jack instructed the publicist, "The party can be much less ambitious than the one for Pierre. I think we can justify this on the grounds that we will get more mileage out of Farley because of his nature at a small, less formal group. . . . Mowat is at least as important to us as Berton and has to be treated as such. We know, however, that he doesn't react well to the same sort of things as Pierre. He's much less formal and he despises expensive, showy places." He added, "Keep Mowat as busy as possible. If he's allowed to sit around, he'll drink and get depressed."[22]

Hugh Kane, second-in-command at McClelland & Stewart, was not as enamoured of Farley as his boss, whom he warned, "I think Farley is becoming a 'money-grubber' and I think you're partly to blame. My advice to him at the moment would be to stop trying to turn out a book each season; stop anthologizing other people's writing; stop thinking that he's an authority on the Arctic, which he's not; stop writing immature & superficial articles for popular

★ The story of Garry Lake was finally published in 2000 in *Walking on the Land*.

magazines and settle down and sweat out a good book of imaginative or creative writing—which is something he can do superbly—
possibly as well as anyone now alive."[23] Kane was convinced that
Farley's proposal for a three-volume anthology of Arctic writings
would be not only a commercial disaster but also a waste of his
time. He wanted Jack to be tough with Farley—but that was something Jack was always reluctant to be, with any author.

Angus remained a crucial literary confidant. In December 1959,
Farley was upset when the American *Library Journal* recommended
against *The Desperate People*: "Here is a gloomy account of ravages
visiting the Eskimo of Canada's barren grounds. The author
published a book in 1952 called *People of the Deer* in which he
attracted attention to the desperate plight of these people. He stirred
up considerable controversy, but out of the turmoil some, though not
enough, help came to the Ihalmiut. So the first book, written in
anger, served a purpose. The anger is here, but the purpose is fading
and the general reader is faced with a sometimes boring account of
people dying one by one."[24] To his father, Farley wrote, "I don't
know what, if anything, you can do about it. Maybe someone in our
library system could take exception to this review by means of a letter
or something to the Library Journal?"[25]

In June 1959, Farley had a harrowing scare when a lump at the back
of his neck proved to be skin cancer. After the tumour was removed,
however, he had no further problems. The event called forth a
comic, but not very sympathetic, response from Harold Horwood,
who concentrated on the marketability of the event: "Cancer is a
very fashionable disease, but I'm afraid skin cancer doesn't fill the bill
for literary purposes—too easy to cure. You could never jerk many
tears with an opus called 'My six-month battle against skin cancer.'
What you want to get is some incurable internal cancer that will take
you off very slowly, giving you plenty of time to write about it,
describing each spasm in detail . . . converting the whole thing into a
glorious, prolonged religious orgasm. . . . Then as you die, inch by

inch, you have the satisfaction of watching the royalties mount up, yard by yard."[26]

But Farley's real depression centred on the state of his marriage. He drank heavily on occasion, feeling himself very much a lost soul in his relationship with Fran. And he became infatuated with the journalist June Callwood, who was happily married to the sportswriter Trent Frayne. So insistent was Farley in proclaiming his love that she asked a mutual friend to call Farley off. Then in July 1960 Farley wrote to Jack from St. John's, "Have met most lovely woman in world (as opposed to most lovely woman in Newfoundland) and know you will feel the same. She is somewhat hampered by husband and offspring. But this should present no problem. For God's sake, bring some rum [when you come down from Ontario]. In the past three days Horwood and I have totally exhausted supplies in the local liquor store."[27]

Farley's friendship with McClelland was augmented at this time, as he began to spend a great deal of time with him in Toronto. Jack was a heavy smoker and drinker and, although married, a womanizer.

Mostly alone at Palgrave with the children, Fran was despondent. She saw a psychiatrist twice before deciding not to return to her consulting room; Fran told her husband, "She thinks I'm crazy!" She also became impatient with what she calls Farley's "patter"; once, when Farley was out driving with Fran and four-year-old Sandy, they drove alongside a speeding train, which Farley called to his son's attention by using the expression "choo-choo." Matter-of-factly, Sandy told him, "It's a train, Dad."

The more Fran and Farley drifted apart, the more she clung to him. Paradoxically, she became aware of how much she loved her husband at the very time that new crevasses were threatening the already precarious stability of their marriage. She wrote him in desperation:

My darling Farley,
I can't bear it without you. Please, please give me a little hope that we can go on together under any conditions.
  If separation is necessary I can carry on if only you can indicate

in some way that it isn't forever. I'm beginning to lose control. I don't think I can go on living with the thought this is final. I need you, Farley. Oh Farley, I need your love more than anything in the world—more than I need Sandy or David.

Whatever it is you want I will do—anything.

This is a cry from a soul in agony. Don't please, please ignore me, Farley.

I know you are a great writer. I believe so much in you and want to give you so much. I love you, my darling Farley. I have never, never wanted anyone or anything but you. I can't bear it. I can't go on living now.

I've always believed in you so desperately and knowing you were so unhappy I didn't know what to do.

I've been hurt deeply, Farley, and if I thought it served any definite purpose I could go on but it doesn't make any sense.

I know you have been terribly unhappy about so many things and a sense of frustration on my part in regard to your problems has made me unreasonable.

Forgive me, please. Please forgive me and I beg and plead with you from the depths of my soul.

In agony and a feeling of utter despair I cry out to you to come. Oh please come before I lose control completely.

My love forever

Fran[28]

Torn and guilt-ridden—so Farley felt as he withdrew from Fran. In many ways, Farley remained in love with his wife, but he also found it impossible to live with a chronically depressed person. He realized sadly that he and Fran were very much alike in ways that did not help each other. He also had the tendency—exacerbated by the war—to retreat in the face of anxiety-provoking situations. Since his marriage and children did not allow him to find himself, he sought freedom in order to continue with his writing career and to discover himself—somehow—as a person.

While he was making preparations to separate from Fran, Farley was surprised to learn that his father, after countless affairs, had fallen madly in love with a woman many years his junior. Once again—just when he was trying to forge his own identity—his life and Angus's were inextricably and uncomfortably intertwined. Neither man, it seemed, had discovered a settled way to live, and the son wondered if he had inherited his father's tendency to be dissatisfied with any semblance of tranquility.

8

Happy Adventurer

1960–1962

IN mid-April 1960, Fran's health was again bad, and much of the housekeeping at Palgrave had to be handled by Farley, who was finishing work on the first volume of his Arctic anthology. Within two weeks, he planned to complete work on that book and leap on board a plane to Newfoundland to purchase a boat, to be owned jointly with Jack McClelland. He expected to be there for ten days, fly home—leaving the chosen boat to have her holes caulked and other repairs attended to—and then, on June 15, return by jeep to Newfoundland, where he expected to find a seaworthy vessel awaiting him.

The friendship between Farley and Jack had accelerated to the extent that they purchased the *Happy Adventure*, a schooner—a particular type called, appropriately enough, a Jack boat—with the ambition of refitting it and putting it to sea for cruising around Newfoundland and the north shore of the Gulf of St. Lawrence. *The Boat Who Wouldn't Float*, the book based on their co-ownership, is a piece of fiction very tenuously attached to fact. It does, however, pay an affectionate, comical and sometimes satirical tribute to Jack McClelland.

The thirty-one-foot boat Farley purchased that February from two fishermen in Admiral's Cove was not—as in *The Boat Who Wouldn't Float*—originally called *Passion Flower*. And it was Ned Power, the original builder, who refitted the vessel with a massive 1920s seven-horsepower, single-cylinder engine that caused many problems; in the book, Power became the magnificently Dickensian eccentric Enos Coffin.

Jack's attempt to take charge of a capricious situation from the wily Enos is wonderfully exaggerated in *The Boat Who Wouldn't Float*. Not realizing that it is impossible to organize the chaotic, the heroic publisher tries to give orders to Enos, Obie and a host of would-be helpers who are assisting him and Farley to make the increasingly recalcitrant boat seaworthy:

> Jack concluded that our major problem was our lack of organization and the first thing he did was hold a conference in Enos's kitchen. . . . In his best boardroom manner Jack explained that we had been wasting too much time. The almost daily trips to St. John's were not necessary, he said. Instead, we would make up a detailed list of every item of gear and equipment needed to complete the boat, then he and I would go to the city and in one day of intensive shopping would obtain everything we required.
>
> Upon our return, the four of us, working to a carefully scheduled list of priorities, would pitch in and complete the vessel in a hurry.

Of course, everything goes wrong.

Not surprisingly, there is a marked discrepancy between Farley's account and Jack's recollections. The publisher's first appearance in a small, remote fishing village in Newfoundland was rendered comically by Farley. Here is Farley's version:

> Jack McClelland's magnificent elan even in dire adversity is legendary. How well do I remember his arrival . . . to join me

Jack McClelland aboard
Happy Adventure, *circa 1961*

and the little schooner we had bought to make a voyage around the world.

True to form Jack arrived at Muddy Hole in a huge, red Buick convertible, the like of which had never before been seen in Newfoundland. The fish plant had just let out and scores of workers were pouring out of the building. They were transfixed by the raucous blare of the Buick's horn. Looking up in astonishment, they beheld a mass of gleaming chrome poised on the lip of the steep, rocky slope behind the plant. A hundred arms began to wave, and as many voices were raised in a great shout.

Jack, serene behind the wheel, was delighted. He thought the admiring villagers were welcoming him. He did not realize there was no road beyond the point that he had reached; and that the fisherfolk were frantically trying to warn him of that salient fact.

Jack started down; realized that all was not well and tramped on the brakes. Too late. The red behemoth lunged down the slope leaping and bounding like an insane hippopotamus. The trunk flew open and Jack's modest assortment of sea going clothing, contained in five pigskin cases, was flung high into the air.

Then it was over. The car stood still, its shiny face buried in a sheep shed. Before anyone could run to the rescue, Jack emerged in a pungent dust cloud. He had lost nothing of his fabled cool. With a casual wave at the stunned onlookers he strode blithely down the remainder of the slope toward our tattered little vessel—as nonchalantly as if about to board the Royal Yacht at Cowes.[1]

Jack's prosaic account in a letter to his wife, Elizabeth, is perhaps a trifle more accurate as to details:

> I left about 3 pm for where the boat is located, still with the rented car which by now was packed full of gear of every description. The drive is about 60 miles over very rocky, hilly dirt road. You pass through some of the most majestic scenery one would find anywhere. . . . It was a beautiful drive on a lovely sunny day. The dust was incredible and I wouldn't have wanted to drive my own car here. . . . I followed directions and found myself driving up the face of a precipitous cliff on one of the worst roads I have ever seen in my life. When I got to the top I found the road led to a sheep pasture of sorts. Obviously, I had taken the wrong fork so I turned around and went back down. All this was a good start for me here—I found out later the road had been condemned. However, I got down safely— losing, I think, the bottom out of the car and could see our little vessel. . . . I parked the car and got to the ship by walking about 200 yards through dead codfish, sheep dung, tin cans, flotsam & jetsam of every description.[2]

In 1961, Farley had jokingly threatened his publisher by informing him he would write a book in which he would be a major character: "You're a stupid old bastard at best, but thank the Old Gods for you." The book would be "part repayment for your forbearance, understanding, and damned practical aid."[3] Farley's portrait of Jack in *The Boat Who Wouldn't Float* is a splendid one, especially of the bossy side of his personality. However, the remarkably quixotic makeup of the book's main protagonist—the *Happy Adventure*—is a reflection of Farley Mowat, just as are the endearing, quixotic sides of Mutt in *The Dog Who Wouldn't Be.*

Even before he purchased the boat, Farley had spoken of writing a comical book about his adventures at sea. On January 20, 1960, he had sent his publisher a memorandum:

> Memo to Mr. Liquid-Lunch McClelland, Further to our conversation of recent wetness, and to confirm the decision made at that time, I hereby commit to paper (and probably to damnation) the gist of what was then decided. 1. With the financial assistance of said Wet-Back McClelland we shall purchase a small auxiliary Newfoundland fishing schooner . . . in the early spring of 1960 . . . Said vessel to be delivered to me on or about the end of May, and to be manned by one able fellow, preferably a retired Newfoundland skipper . . . 2. At some time during the summer you are to give up your pretensions at being a book publisher and are to join said vessel in Newfoundland. 3. At the termination of the navigation season . . . I will . . . bring the vessel up-river . . . where she will then become your sole personal property . . . 4. There will be no guarantee of a book out of all this.[4]

By April, though, the book was taking shape in Farley's imagination: "Have been cogitating on our sea-borne venture and, vaguely, thinking about the possibility of a book in connection with it. Since a book from this adventure would be to both our benefits (maybe) I am inclined to give the possibility due deference."[5]

Even if the *Happy Adventure* had not been prone to sinking and all kinds of other maritime incivilities, its personality would probably have been preordained in the service of literature. The fog, the leaky hull, the defective water pump and a host of other casualties may all have been part of the story of the real *Happy Adventure*, but in the book they are magnificently exaggerated. One embellishment is false, according to Harold Horwood, who claimed he did not assist Farley in his purchase of the boat, and deeply resented the implication that he—a native Newfoundlander—had aided in the acquisition of such a dud. Farley has a different memory: "Harold actually took me to Admiral's Cove to see the boat. True, he didn't push me to buy it, but he didn't try to stop me either!"

In the spring of 1960, Farley's mood swings were erratic, but they were not droll. He longed to escape from Palgrave, was determined to make a new start, and yet he felt stymied. He had many conflicted feelings about Fran. He did not blame or castigate her for the failure of their marriage, being more than willing to shoulder his share of responsibility for what had gone wrong between them, but he could no longer live with her. In addition, he felt deeply guilty about depriving his two sons of a full-time father.

In April 1960 another separation was in the offing. Despite Peter Davison's objections, Max Wilkinson and Farley had, late in 1959, contracted *Ordeal by Ice*—the first volume of a trilogy (*The Top of the World*) devoted to the writings of Arctic explorers—to Evan Thomas at Harper & Row. From the outset, this book caused all kinds of trouble. For one thing, Farley could not get along with Thomas (nor with the editor at McClelland & Stewart assigned to the project), and he alerted Jack McClelland to this fact. In turn, Thomas became extremely angry with both Farley and McClelland: "I have twice offered to fly to Canada to discuss the manuscripts," he wrote Farley that April. "This scarcely constitutes vagueness or lack of willingness to make an effort as charged by McClelland. If we cannot communicate better directly, we will with regret accept cancellation of the contract."[6]

Thomas was very displeased with the book Farley had finally offered him. He found many of the excerpts too similar, and he felt that it had extremely limited market potential for the great deal of money he had paid for it. But even prior to Thomas's rejoinder, Max Wilkinson, in an effort to save the book, on March 23 did something uncharacteristic—he offered detailed editorial advice to an author:

> I think the narrative should be severely edited, but with the most selective and calculated touch. You can, by bridging within the framework of the narrative itself, eliminate a good deal that is repetitive. And you can, by using your deductive powers a bit, interpret (in these bridges) the character of the narrator. In my opinion, one of the shortcomings in the tales is

the lack of a personal sense of the teller of the tale. . . . I don't think this book should run much over 100,000 words. And I should like to see about a quarter of it your own enlightened comment. We want the book to sell, and when you consider the cost of manufacturing such a work . . . we should be obliged to price it out of the reach of most readers if the deadweight of type is backbreaking.[7]

Farley was unresponsive. He obviously considered Thomas a difficult editor and probably missed the calm guiding hand of Peter Davison, who told his capricious author, "I'm sorry about the final decision for Harper, of course; but you have made your decision, and we respect it, without recriminations or backward looks. . . . It will feel queer, of course, not to be working on it for you; but why not let Harper have a headache or two?"[8]

When, in response to Farley's irritation with Thomas, McClelland—who bluntly accused Farley of compiling the anthology to "carry on your personal vendetta regarding historians, the Hudson's Bay Company, the Royal Canadian Mounted Police and Canadian lack of initiative"[9]—considered offering the book to another publisher in the United States, an indignant Wilkinson told the Canadian publisher to mind his own business: "For your information, my dear Jack, Farley asked me to arrange this contract with Harper. For better or worse, I am the agent of record for the book, and the first submission you make of it in the States (if Farley chooses not to offer the revised script to Harper) will end my relationship with him." Max would regretfully do this, even though they had maintained a "warm and affectionate relationship for ten years." He admitted that the entire matter puzzled him: "If this work were a collection of sonnets, or an original work of fiction, or non-fiction, such as *People of the Deer* or *The Grey Seas Under*, I could understand the rigidity of Farley's posture. But the anthology is none of these. Farley once referred to it as a piece of journalistic hack work, and if this is his true feeling about it, I should think he would want to talk about it with a first-class editor."[10] By June, the matter was resolved; Harper's advance was returned and Peter Davison bought the book on behalf of Atlantic–Little, Brown. Davison wrote a pleasant "I told you so" letter to Farley: "I'm truly sorry about the contretemps with Harper, but that sort of thing will happen if you go playing footsy, you know. Some people eat toes as a steady diet."[11]

On the surface it appeared that any bad feelings between author and agent had been resolved. Unfortunately, this was not the case. In November 1960, Wilkinson was furious when he learned that Farley had—using an agent in Toronto—entered into negotiations with a publisher in East Germany for the sale of paperback rights to *People of the Deer*: "I'm afraid, Farley, this is where I get off. You do what you will with your stuff in the future. I will continue to service those contracts on which my name appears. Try not to foul up contracts which are in existence."[12]

Farley's recollection of his split with Wilkinson is somewhat different: "As our relationship grew older we both changed. For reasons unknown to me, Max began to lose his grip. Always a powerful drinker, he became an alcoholic. He still tried very hard to serve my best interests but was losing the confidence of editors and other buyers. I, on the other hand, was on the ascendant. I began to become impatient with him. And I no longer needed him much since I was no longer peddling short pieces but mainly writing books, and I felt I could make my own arrangements with Jack and Peter. In short, I cut him out." He adds, "I still feel badly about" what happened.[13]

His regret is tinged with the conviction that Wilkinson had failed him by introducing him to Thomas, with whom he had an incompatible and combative relationship. On the other hand, both Farley and Wilkinson had been dissatisfied with the amount of money Davison was able to offer (the Harper advance had been $1750, whereas Atlantic–Little, Brown paid $1500). On November 18 Farley told McClelland, "You will be delighted to know that Max Wilkinson and I have, at long belated last, parted company. . . . Old loyalties die hard, but he is really becoming impossible."[14] A year later, in November 1961, when Farley interfered with the contract for yet another book under the control of Littauer and Wilkinson, Ken Littauer told him he was "angry" at his behaviour: "Max has deserved better treatment than this."[15]

* * *

At the end of the summer of 1960, Davison lamented that he had not heard in months from his wayward author, who was known for his fondness for spirits: "I can only assume that this is because you have seldom been sober enough to write. With a bottle in one hand and a tiller in the other, who wants to write anyway?"[16] Taking poetic hand to paper, he sent him a "charming moralistic ballad" celebrating the ship and her captain:

> When salty Mowat walked the plank,
>   drinking anarchistic rum,
> His enterprise turned foul and dank,
>   drinking anarchistic rum.
>
> Naked on the quarter-deck,
>   drinking anarchistic rum,
> But covered up above the neck,
>   drinking anarchistic rum.
>
> He took his publisher to school,
>   drinking anarchistic rum,
> And acted like a bloody fool,
>   drinking anarchistic rum.[17]

Not to be outdone, Farley sent the recently married Peter a riposte:

> When passionate Peter took a bride
>   (up to his ass in printer's ink)
> He had no condoms by his side
>   (up to his ass in printer's ink)
>
> The net result of course is that
>   (up to his ass in printer's ink)
> He'll soon be father to a brat
>   (up to its ass in printer's ink).[18]

As the poem hints, Farley's spirits had soared during the summer of 1960.

That June, Farley and Jack sailed the *Happy Adventure* to Burin, Newfoundland. When Jack left to go back to Toronto, his place was taken by an army friend of Farley's, Mike Donovan, who by then was the director of public libraries for Newfoundland. The *Happy Adventure* set sail for the French overseas department of St-Pierre and Miquelon, a small group of islands in the Atlantic about fifteen miles southwest of the Burin Peninsula. Rocky, covered with a thin volcanic soil and barren except for scrubby yews and junipers, the islands allowed France a toehold in the fishing grounds of North America. During Prohibition, they had been used by Canadian liquor companies to store contraband being smuggled into the United States. The waters between the islands of St-Pierre and Langlade, once known as *la Gueule d'Enfer* (the Mouth of Hell), accounted for many shipwrecks in the nineteenth century and bestow upon the cliffs and waters of the islands a romantic glow associated with isolated coves, pirates and buried treasure. As Farley told Angus, he had encountered only minor problems en route, "apart from being lost in the middle of Placentia Bay with a hurricane coming, no compass, a defective log, and the thickest fog in living memory."

Most of the French colony's population of six thousand was concentrated in the town of St-Pierre on the island of that name. There, Donovan and Farley undertook some much-needed repair work on the *Happy Adventure* and hauled it ashore on the slipway. In an attempt to reform the wayward character of his vessel, Farley agreed to have it baptized by a priest and, in accordance with local custom, changed its name. However, its new appellation in Basque— *Itchatchozale Alai*, mercifully shortened on most occasions to just plain *Itchy*, sometimes to "Itchy-ass-sally" by Farley—sounded a trifle more pagan than Christian. *Itchy* now flew the Basque flag, "the only vessel in the world so to do," Farley boasted. "I am an honorary

Claire Wheeler and Farley aboard Happy Adventure, *circa 1962*

Frenchman with an option to make it permanent. No, NOT French-man, St. Pierraise. There is a large difference."[19]

Farley was readying his boat one afternoon when three young women from Toronto, having heard a famous Canadian author was aboard a ship in the harbour, visited the boat in dry dock and were invited aboard. One of them recalled, "He was dressed in the most raggedy old pants imaginable and a shirt that was filthy dirty as well as dotted with green paint."[20] A day or so later, Farley encountered one of the women, Claire Wheeler, sketching the harbour. The boat was to be relaunched that afternoon, he told her. Would she join him for that occasion? She immediately agreed, and the two continued to see each other for the remainder of her stay on the island. The back-ground to their romance was distinctly French—the Café L'Escalle, Le Select and an assortment of other bistros and restaurants.

In 1960, Claire was twenty-seven years old, Farley almost forty. Immediately entranced by the radiant beauty of the "golden-haired young fugitive from Toronto," Farley was aware from the outset that Claire was a kindred spirit, a person with whom he shared many interests and values. Claire and her younger brother, Fred, were the children of a comfortably established Canadian father and an English mother, who lived in Toronto's posh Rosedale area and who had

Claire Wheeler, circa 1966

sent their daughter to Havergal (a private girls' school) and the Ontario College of Art. In 1960, Claire was working in the Simpson-Sears Store Planning Department in pursuit of a career as a graphic designer; she had travelled to St-Pierre to study French at a summer school run by the University of Toronto.

Though she had led a life of some privilege, Claire was dissatisfied with the emotional poverty of the world around her. As a child, she had found family life barren of real joy and feeling; as a young adult, she now questioned many of the commonly accepted values of her contemporaries. Claire quickly established common ground with a man who was a self-proclaimed dissident, a person who railed against many of the conventions and the accepted niceties of modern life— and to whom she was also physically attracted.

After meeting Claire, Farley began to feel transformed, as if all the barriers and impediments that had clogged his existence since the war had miraculously disappeared. Even a year after they met, the rapture remained intact:

Despite my disinclination to envisage a future, I find myself more and more thinking in terms of the frightening prospect of a future without you. It is a terrifying and ghastly prospect. Absence has not diminished my love for you, nor my need of you but has intensified both to an astonishing degree. Astonishing to me, because I had not believed myself still capable of such longings in the inner heart. Bien, such future must not be. It would be unsupportable. We will bloody well have to do something about it, though as yet I cannot see what can be done. We must pour many libations and invoke the intercession of the old Gods on our behalf. Let us make love so magnificently that they will be moved to pity.[21]

After their separate returns to Toronto, Farley felt bereft. Life back at Palgrave was more trying than ever before, even though he and Claire saw each other on a regular basis at Claire's home on Douglas Drive in Toronto and at his trailer workshop in North Albion.

That autumn, after *Ordeal by Ice* was published, Lionel McGowan of the Foundation Company asked Farley to write a second book about the salvage tugs. Farley agreed to write *The Serpent's Coil* about two ships, the hurricane-damaged *Leicester* and the salvage tug *Foundation Josephine*. Meanwhile, poor *Itchy*, moored at St-Pierre for the winter, sank when ice stove in its stern.

Also sinking fast was Farley's marriage. Since his life had begun "a-new" at St-Pierre, he told Angus, "It is in the cards that Palgrave and I are at the parting of the ways."[22] He revealed his affair with Claire to Jack, Harold, and his father. However, the repository of his most intimate feelings about Claire was Angus's girlfriend, Barbara Hutchinson. On September 3, he wrote her from "Palgrave. Death Valley": "Got to Nirvana and fell in love, and drank much cognac and forgot the world. . . . Now however I am back—not home— just back. Frightful. Doubt if I can stand it more than a few more days. Shadow men and shallow women, and the smell of death and dissolution. St. Pierre, for your private information, may be the last stronghold of manhood and womanhood this side of the grey waters." He added, "I have found something for myself after a ten year hiatus."[23] He wrote more to the same correspondent five months later about the "hellish" conditions at Palgrave; he had been trying to write a war novel, but decided it "wasn't bloody good" and tore it up. "I can look forward," he lamented, "to twiddling my thumbs until spring. Trapped like a trap in a trap in a trap in a trap." He concluded by requesting from the thirty-five-year-old Barbara "some sage, matronly advice from our Smiths Fallsian Mother. Before everybody goes berserk."[24]★

The following June he pleaded with Barbara in a letter, "I wish you'd write to Claire in the same vein as your letter to me. She gets pretty depressed with what appears to be the futility and uncertainty of loving a Mowat. Hard for her because she is a loving kind of woman which, as we all do know, are rare beasts, and to be nurtured when found." Although others doubted the permanence of his relationship with Claire, Barbara proved steadfast in believing they would stay together. Farley told her,

> You know I value your maternal advice quite surprisingly.
> Many of my youthful companions around here are making book that C. and I will drift apart in the face of present and continuing strains and that I'll let her go. You, however, seem to have more faith. I hope you are also more prescient. Frankly, I *never* know what the hell *I'm* up to. Continue, please, to be the prophet of an enduring bed.[25]

Pretty, freckled, outspoken, red-haired Barbara Hutchinson— thirty-four years younger than Angus, five years younger than Farley—was born in Windsor, Ontario, on June 22, 1926, the youngest surviving daughter and the second youngest child of seven. Her father, a tall, stately man who was secretary-treasurer of a local

★ In retrospect, Farley has harsh words about Barbara and her conduct at this time: "It was to her advantage to have me leave Frances and run off with Claire, and for her to try and assume my mother's role in my life. It was *her* wish that I call her 'Ma' (hers and Angus's)."

Barbara Hutchinson

factory, and her mother, a well-read, cultivated person, were devout Anglicans. Since both of Barbara's brothers were hemophiliacs, Barbara's parents, who lavished their time and attention on the two boys, were afraid that the four surviving daughters were carriers of the disease.

Left to her own devices as a child, Barbara became extremely introspective. She decided not to attend university, worked in Montreal during the Second World War and then returned home in 1946. About seven years later, Barbara's close friend Beryl Gaspardy, a nurse, persuaded her to move to Toronto, where she obtained work at the public library at Jane Street and Weston Road. A woman who refused to hide her intelligence, she put off many would-be suitors, although she had several serious boyfriends in Toronto.

In the late fifties, Beryl and several other nurses went on holiday to Chapleau in northwestern Ontario. There, on the main street of the town, she and her friends encountered Angus Mowat in his tam-o'-shanter and backpack, looking as if he had just stepped out of the

174

woods. During a chat at a pub, Angus told Beryl he was searching for reliable, committed librarians for the hinterlands. Beryl immediately thought of Barbara and gave Angus her address. When he returned to his office in Toronto, he wrote to Barbara inviting her to lunch. Shortly thereafter, she was on her way to the town of Smiths Falls in eastern Ontario, about forty miles west of Ottawa, as the new librarian.

Once she had settled into her new job, Angus paid Barbara a visit, but unlike in the series of fleeting amours that had been his sexual mainstay for many years, Angus fell deeply in love. From early in 1960, Angus spent even more time away from Port Hope, always in company with Barbara. In order to protect the secrecy of their relationship, they eventually built a small cottage north of Kingston. Angus even assumed a new identity when he was with Barbara: Arthur Urquhart Burgess. (Bob Burgess, the lawyer who would act for Farley in his separation agreement from Fran, was a pal of Angus and Barbara's; the choice of a name was, in part, a joke on Bob.) Once, on the streets of Kingston, an acquaintance accosted the couple: "Aren't you Angus Mowat?" he asked. "Certainly not!" Angus stiffly responded and walked brusquely away.

Farley was impressed by Barbara's intelligence. He also witnessed a remarkable change in his father, whose zest for life seemed doubled. Naturally, Angus swore his confidant Farley to secrecy, it being crucial that Helen not learn of her husband's love affair. Father and son began to refer to Helen as PDH (for "Poor Dear Helen"), a nickname invented by Angus to suggest that although Helen was a sweet, nice enough person, she was not someone in touch with the real facts of life. Barbara also became a confidante for Farley. He was aware, of course, that Helen, although she liked Claire, could not be expected to be sympathetic to his having an affair—he was a married man with two children. Farley loved and respected his mother, but from childhood he had really wanted the sometimes grudging approval of his father, whom he idolized. Although he did not wish to take sides, Farley in essence now conspired with his father against his mother.

There were many secrets, many lies, many complications. Angus, who maintained two homes, was living the life of a bigamist. By virtue of the confidences exchanged by father and son, Farley kept a dangerous secret from his mother. This added weight to the heavy burden of guilt he was already carrying. Angus and Barbara, both fond of Claire, urged Farley to leave Fran. And yet Farley, who knew the vagaries of his often fluctuating heart, was not yet ready to make a complete break with his wife.

Finally, in January 1961, Farley, having told Fran he wanted a separation and having endured visits from both a minister and a lawyer, passed on to Barbara the news that these two officials were certain that Fran "must [in any legal proceedings] act like the wronged woman. So far she is resisting them. But I foresee trouble. For the transgressors. And an upshot of battle and consequent bitterness and lesions."[26]

Farley tried to escape to the McClelland cottage at Foote's Bay, near MacTier on Lake Joseph, but was forced by "Fran's collapse" to return within the week: "Haven't the vaguest idea what happens next and, at the moment, don't give a damn. Mark time until spring, I suppose."[27] A week later, things did not seem as bad as he had at first thought:

> Fran now sees quite clearly (for how long?) that life with me will destroy her, but she is not champing at the bit to try life on her own. As a result I return to the [McClellands' cottage]. I have no illusions that I will be left in peace there, but each departure and return cracks the facade that much deeper. She is now resigned to my eventual departure—on the conscious level—and is even showing signs of emotional acceptance.[28]

That winter and spring, Farley worked at a much slower rate than usual, although he took two trips to Halifax to research the book about the salvage tugs. He completed work on the children's book *Owls in the Family*, about Wol and Weeps. And he earned the further enmity of the RCMP, who hated Fidel Castro's regime, when he joined the Fair Play for Cuba Committee.

*   *   *

Farley introduced Claire to Arnold and Vi Warren, his neighbours at Palgrave. Uneasy eyewitnesses to the disintegration of the relationship between Farley and Fran, the Warrens had some serious reservations about their friend's commitment to any serious long-term alliance. What is more, they were deeply touched by Claire's friendliness and warmth—and by her vulnerability. They knew there was a considerable emotional distance between Claire and her parents and guessed she would have little support there.

Arnold, who had left his first wife to marry Vi, wrote Claire a long letter on May 1, 1961, in which he proffered parental advice. He did not wish to tell Claire what to do, but he wondered how much she really knew about Farley. Was she aware, for example, that Farley was completely single-minded when writing? Did she know that Farley had been unable to write recently? Was she firmly of the persuasion—he hoped she was—that women were *not* put on earth solely for the purpose of ministering to men?

From all I have seen and heard, Farley is not interested in a complement. He is—or seems to believe that he is—sufficient unto himself. He may be right—but I doubt it.

Enthusiastic physical love is a fine thing and pretty essential to a successful union but, by itself, it cannot produce one. The lives of a man and a woman must mesh as perfectly as possible, and this requires a great deal of adjustment by both. In other words, they must give something of themselves to the union. I am sure that Farley has given freely of his physical strength—in bed. I know that he has given freely of his time. . . .

I have neither seen nor heard anything to make me believe that he is prepared to give one iota of himself.

I don't say this critically and I don't mean it critically. I state it merely as a matter of fact.

I believe that Farley wants a girl friend—someone to sleep with, to chum around with, to have fun with—perhaps to cook his meals and keep his quarters tidy from time to time—and one who will make no demands on him whatsoever. Obviously, he has found—or believes that he has found—in you all the qualities he desires.

What would happen, he wondered, if Claire made real demands on Farley? From the outset in any relationship with him, Claire should think of herself as an individual, not as a member in a partnership. Having made this step, she would have to be certain to assert her own individuality or she would be drowned in Farley's. As Arnold saw it, Claire had three options. She could accept the situation with all its drawbacks; she could make modest demands; she could run. All in all, Arnold was deeply conflicted:

> I have a very high regard for Farley as a writer, and we have been good friends—and I hope we will be for a long time to come. For these reasons I want to see him back at work— because he must get back to work. For years I have felt that he would be a greater writer if he gave of himself to the woman who could complete his life—that he would gain both as a writer and as an individual far more than he gave—but I suspect that I am putting dangerous ideas into your head.[29]

Claire was relieved to get this letter. She had found it impossible to discuss the subject with any of her close woman friends, who tended to regard her relationship with Farley as just an affair. Because she had been in a state of turbulence since meeting Farley, she was grateful to Arnold for his intervention:

> The time has come when some demands must be made. I hesitate to do this because I still feel very much the intruder in an established domestic situation. Despite Farley's reassurance that the trouble started long before I came long, I still don't feel that he would have left Palgrave without my entry into the picture.
> Of your three suggestions, the only one with any real future in it is the second. Some demands must be made. Some foundations must be sought after. Despite anything that Farley might believe to the contrary, the situation as it is now just cannot go

on forever. Of course there is the fear that perhaps he doesn't want it to continue forever. The foreverness of marriage seems to have left a bad taste in his mouth and possibly the prospect of a future filled with many successive mistresses appeals to him.

However, she was sure that was not the case. She wanted to see Farley in the throes of writing; she wanted to keep her independence; she wanted to be sure that her love affair with him was not simply an escape for him, or for herself:

> Apart from the tribulations of Farley and of myself, I worry about his family. If we do decide to take up a life together, is the life of his wife going to be completely shattered by his leaving her? And worst of all—how is he going to react to seeing his children only occasionally? Watching them grow up without him. These are the harsh realities that frighten me, for him. Even I would have to leave my own family on a note of distaste, but this is nothing to leaving one's children. Perhaps being a woman, this hits home more intensely, but I am deeply concerned for Farley in this respect.

Of one thing she was reasonably certain: "I do not believe that Farley is sufficient unto himself, even though he gives this impression. Nor do I believe that he himself thinks that he is. Perhaps it is vain of me to think that I might become the complement he needs, but this is what I would strive for."[30] Young and very much in love, Claire was both clear-eyed and tenacious in dealing with Farley. She had an excellent understanding of his faults and was prepared to deal with them; she wanted her relationship with Farley to work.

In late June 1961, Farley returned to St-Pierre to refloat *Itchy*, which was, after an awful winter, in terrible shape. He told the boat's co-owner, "Sweet Fuck All has been done. So it's back to the dungarees and cod guts. With some compensations. When I get fed up (which I do far more easily this year) there is always a bar within shouting distance."[31] This time around Farley became aware of the French colony as a feudal outpost: the governor was a puppet of France, and during the war the island's wealthy families had been pro-Vichy and thus pro-Hitler. They were also "thoroughly cynical and amoral" after years in the smuggling business. The tourists "flitted like shadows" through the scenic spots and then waited "querulously for the fog to lift and for a plane to get them out."[32]

A bereft Farley saw the world in a new way because Claire was not with him: "I miss you with such a devastating and all consuming hunger. It is somewhat disgraceful. When I merely look at an attractive girl who is not you, there is such a total lack of response that I think I must be dead. . . . Come quick, vite, vite, vite."[33] A brief visit from Harold Horwood kept Farley from going round the bend.

In late July, after *Itchy* had been rendered seaworthy, Farley flew to Sydney, Nova Scotia, to meet Claire's train from Toronto, and the couple flew back to St-Pierre. Farley's hostility to the place reasserted itself when he witnessed the ritualized killing of the pilot whales, which had been chased into the harbour by killer whales. Suddenly, he heard a great noise, which

revealed itself as the mass aficionados of blood sports of St. Pierre—most of the population, clustering on every wharf, and all over every boat including ours, to watch the beginning harassment of the school of whales. Harassment it was too, brutal, unjustified and bloody. First came a dory armed with a singularly crude spear which, after several futile throws, was fixed in the back of a big bull—but no preparations had been made to follow through, and the bull swam off, blowing blood from his spout, trailing a length of broken line behind him. The school was now becoming very frightened and they surged back and forth the length of the harbour, but they must have believed the killer whales were still lurking outside, for they would not pass out to freedom and deep water. In any event, they were several times turned back at the end of the mile by someone with a rifle who kept firing into the great black bodies as they surfaced for air.[34]

He was both elated and heartbroken that night when "with heart-stopping suddenness, the entire pod surfaced all around me. A calf blew directly under one upraised oar and my little boat rocked lightly in its wash. It should have been a terrifying moment, but it was not. Inexplicably, I was no longer afraid. . . . Time after time they surfaced all around me and although any one of them, even the smallest calf, could have easily overturned the dinghy, they avoided touching it. I began to experience an indescribable sense of empathy with them . . . and a mounting frustration. How could I help them to escape from what the morrow held?" In an attempt to assist them, he shouted at them, hoping they would move towards the harbour entrance and escape in the darkness. They sounded, diving deep and long. "I had done the wrong thing—the human thing—and my action had brought an end to their acceptance of me."[35]

The next day, a "score of men waded in amongst the heavily thrashing beasts and, being very cautious about it, stabbed them to death with knives, literally slashing them with so many surface wounds that in the end they bled to death." When Farley confronted the ringleader and asked why he was murdering the whales, the man replied "with gusto, that he had just made a thousand dollars since the whales would be sold to" a local mink ranch.[36] Completely unnerved, Farley reflected: "The whole affair was a terrifying example of the savagery and brutality which distinguishes mankind from all other animals, and it completed the reduction of my already much faded respect and regard for the St. Pierraise though, to be honest, I must admit that the tourists from Canada and elsewhere seemed to enjoy the spectacle as much as the natives did themselves."

A few days later, the couple, having sailed into Bay d'Espoir, Newfoundland, were idyllically happy in each other's company, as excerpts from Farley's diary testify:

Sunday, August 13
This became one of our most poignant nights together. We were quite alone, as alone as if the world had ended while only we survived. The wind moaned and whinnied more and more loudly from the high hills. Our rigging sang a nasal refrain. The

ship tugged at her chain anchor like a restive horse tugging at its bit. Yet we were secure within a womb-like security. I lay, naked, on my berth smoking and fiddling with the radio trying to get a weather report—and succeeding, by damn, in getting one at last—but from Moscow, which didn't seem very relevant. Claire sat and sketched, and then we read a little, and we snoozed, and we made love, being very close to one another. Itchy moved under us as if in sympathy with our passion and we were one, my love and I.[37]

Monday, August 14

It had become very warm and the sun was shining through the trees that screened us. And so we stripped and bathed, like a maid and a centaur. It was a fairy place surrounded by giant ferns and green, wet cushions of rank moss. No flies disturbed us, and no sound came to our ears. The water was ice cold and ran down our naked bodies with the touch of ecstasy. My love was lithe and golden in the dappling sunlight, and more beautiful than all the world.[38]

Pushthrough, 1961

At the outports of St. Alban's, Milltown, Pushthrough, Harbour Breton and Bay L'Argent, the couple witnessed the strong communal values of the residents, people who lived simple lives in the face of the most difficult conditions nature could exert. They became aware of how the lives of these people were being destroyed by the resettlement of fishing communities and how, in the process, they were becoming overly dependent on the government to provide welfare and unemployment benefits. In some places, 80 per cent of the able-bodied men were on unemployment insurance.

Farley and Claire heard strange, Gothic stories, the most chilling concerning a thirty-year-old "boy" from Richards Harbour who

> since the age of twelve had been shut away from the world in an upstairs room. Originally he was only a little "simple" but his widowed mother wished to remarry and she was afraid that her son would prove a barrier. So she locked him up. Over the years he went quite mad, and for many years has been barricaded in a lightless room. Here [an official] found him, sitting naked in the remnants of a bed, surrounded by his own filth, overgrown with hair, and filled with animal suspicion at any one who entered. His mother gets fifty odd dollars a month for him now from the Government, and she refuses to give him up for institutional care.[39]

There were other fascinating legends. Once a great blue whale, fifty feet in length, tried to enter a narrow gut in a little community near Great Jervais; it ran aground partway through, unable to retreat or advance. So every able-bodied man, woman and child in the place got behind the whale and pushed it out to sea. This was why the name of the outport was changed to Pushthrough.

Some days, *Itchy* would be tied up so that Claire could take the walks she hankered for. She was especially drawn to churches and graveyards, where she sketched. During the final days of August, the boat headed towards St-Pierre, from which Claire would fly back to Toronto. A profound unhappiness invaded Farley, who still could not make up his mind to leave his wife for good.

Saturday, August 26
A black day, following hard upon [a golden one]. Time draws
on, and both Claire and I are prisoners of our own indecision. I
feel that I have but to muster my resolve and ask her to remain
and she will stay—but it is too late. Too late, this time.

Sunday, August 27
The day fated for Claire's departure, but the fates were mis-
informed. It blew a gale out of the east. . . . There were no
planes flying and so we took the day of grace.

Monday, August 28
Let there be no more partings as sad as this one.

A week before the leave-taking, Farley wrote to Jack McClelland,
"I've written to Fran to tell her I won't be back until the third week
in Sept. She will have conniptions. If you can call her and convince
her of the necessity of my remaining here, it will help. . . . I am
presently taking Claire back to St. Pierre to send her home. She has
been a magnificent shipmate, contrary to all expectations, and I shall
be damned sorry to part with her."[40] Farley knew he wanted to quit
his marriage; he was not absolutely certain he wanted to embark on
another one, no matter how "magnificent" his would-be partner
might be.

The next three months passed by in a blur. Farley and Harold
Horwood spent September taking a month-long cruise in the Bay
d'Espoir. Then, at long last, Farley faced reality. He returned briefly
to Palgrave to inform Fran he was not coming back. Then he went to
Halifax, where he was joined by Angus; they travelled together on
the *Baccalieu* along the south coast of Newfoundland to St. John's.
Fully aware of Farley's unhappiness, the father encouraged his son
to follow through on his plan that he and Claire should make their
way to England and there begin their life together; Angus undertook
to look after Fran and the boys in Farley's absence. Impressed once

again by the transformation of his father under Barbara's influence, Farley wrote her at the end of November:

> Gawd! He IS incredible, no? In three days he has outrun me, out drunk me, out enthused me, and generally left me gasping. All this and no end of good advice as well. What a wellspring you must be!
>
> I have my orders. No turning back. I sail for Blighty December 4th and so fearful am I of your wrath that I shall burn my passport once I'm safely in the nearest Limey pub. OK?[41]

On December 5, Farley sailed alone from St. John's on *Newfoundland*; Claire had promised to meet up with him in January. Farley's crossing was a "stinker": "Three full gales, two of them with winds of Force 12 plus. Hove-to on two occasions, once for thirty hours. I am now ready to write *The Serpent's Coil*." But during the trip he saw within himself the makings of a changed person who could, at long last, make a cool, detached self-evaluation:

> Before Claire (B.C., that is), I looked into a thousand women's faces and saw what I desired to see, the image of a waiting love, and always it was an illusion, and always it disintegrated into cold dust when I reached out my hand towards them and never could I surmount that bitter recognition.

A strong resolve filled him, allowing him to overthrow his previous vacillation. But a new scenario played itself out in his mind: "I've been far too permissive all these months; too negative," he wrote to Claire. "Well, the hell with that. No more bloody nonsense about 'free choice' and your right to make your own decisions. The hell with it! You quit your job, bid farewell to your parents, and get over here as fast as you damned well can. I mean it."

Upon arrival in London, Farley was filled with disgust at its foul smells and thick smog. With the help of his London publisher, he found sanctuary at Coombe Farm, near Litton Cheney, Dorset, on the south coast. His landlord, who had the surname of Percival, was,

Farley rejoiced, also déclassé: a married man, he had impregnated his girlfriend in order to force his wife to divorce him and had married his beloved two weeks before the baby's birth.

On December 21, Farley wrote to Barbara and Angus with instructions for Claire: "I'm here. And wish to hell I wasn't. Imperturbable Mowat. Four thousand miles from the subject of his perturbation. She'd better get a move on, or I'll be ossified, paralysed, petrified. Tell her that."

As Farley's letter of January 2, 1962, to Jack McClelland makes clear, Jack disapproved of Farley's liaison with Claire, probably because he felt it might keep him from writing: "I wish to Christ you'd stop disapproving of my plans for Claire. You disapprove, I disapprove, everybody damned well disapproves, but I've committed myself to it now." Originally, Farley had wanted Jack to keep an eye on Fran, but on February 10, he told him he need not bother: "Don't worry about Fran. Angus has the affair in hand."

The situation with Claire opened up a fissure in Farley's close friendship with Jack because the publisher looked upon sex as a casual matter, divorced from genuine feelings of love and marital commitment. Annoyed by such attitudes, Farley lectured his friend:

> Well, bugger you! You big, blond, bifurcated bastard! Because you have no more goddamn romance in your soul than a rorqual, is no reason for being so bloody snotty. Patiently, gently, calmly, rationally, I have done what little I could do, over the long years, to inculcate in you some faint understanding of a primal fact, that it is possible to love more about a woman than her twot . . . Love, my son! . . . You don't know, of course . . . You're goddamned right I want my golden girl, and if you weren't such a fathead, you'd appreciate her value to both you and me. Properly indoctrinated by a master mind like yours, she might even be able to get some useful writing out of me. And think, you numbskull, with her as a resident blotter to soak up my psychiatric aberrations, what a load will be off your fragile little shoulders.[42]

More than a casual amount of traditional male bonding can be glimpsed in this aside: "Next summer, if you want to sail all male, it's OK with me, and I'll park Claire ashore. If you want to bring a companion, you can have the vessel for the two of you, for as long as you want."

Despite their overwhelming love for each other, Farley and Claire could quarrel. On January 12, almost two weeks before Claire arrived in England, she sent him an angry letter which, paradoxically, cheered him up: "The cheer lay in the exposure of a little raw emotion, and in the recognition (and belief) that we are suffering together, that our need for one another is at least equivalent. I talk too much of how I feel; Claire does not talk enough, but this time she was distrait enough, and mad enough, to open up, which is a damned good thing for both of us."[43] Claire's departure was delayed because her father had just been diagnosed with leukemia; her anger was generated by the fact that Farley ignored her concern for her father and continued to bombard her with "the blackest, most despairing letters" imaginable.[44]

Although certain his alliance with Claire would assist him to put his writing career back on track, Farley could not work, so great was his anticipation of the arrival of his beloved:

> Since I've done no real writing for two years, it is going to be a rough go. But it is *going* to be a go. To hell with situations as they are, and the death wish, and the decay of civilization etc. ad nauseam. I am going to write a story about good people, admirable people who work for, deserve, and find, a modicum of happiness, and who know what love is. God help me, I have a terrible hunch it's going to grow up around the core of Claire and my experiences. We shall see.[45]

Some days, Farley's melancholia got the better of him:

> We are both so damned self-analytical, and so immersed in our problems that it may well be impossible for us to alleviate the problems of the other. I am no longer depressed—depression is

at least an emotion—I'm neither optimistic, nor particularly pessimistic about our chances. Rather neutral. And, if the truth be told, fed up to the teeth with too many weeks in limbo. Hell is more endurable than limbo.[46]

Meanwhile, Angus, acting once again as a go-between on his son's behalf, tried to persuade Fran to accept the situation. On the question of allowing a divorce he found her obdurate, as he reported to his son that February: "1. Fran knows now that you are not coming back; 2. She faces this truth but cannot help hoping. She does not want to give you a divorce because this will end even the hopeless hope. She said she would wait five years, hoping that some kind of arrangement could be made, etc." Specifically, she hoped that if she did not allow a divorce and if Farley tired of Claire, he might return to her. After her meeting with Angus, Fran broke down completely and fell into self-recrimination: "I don't blame Farley. I am defeated. I did try hard. I probably tried too hard. But I just failed and now I am defeated." She burst into tears and had to be comforted by her two small sons.[47]

After what seemed an eternity, Claire arrived at Southampton on January 25, 1962, aboard the *Ryndam* and was whisked away by her lover to Coombe Farm, where they lived until March, making side trips, one to the Channel Islands, to gather historical material for Farley's proposed book on the history of Newfoundland. On March 14 Farley told Angus and Barbara, "To the great surprise of all, most particularly me, we've been working like sin on the Newfoundland book, unearthing some fantastic old bits of stuff in unlikely places. The [war] novel is mothballed, but not quite dead. Only somnolent."

In March and April, the couple rented a car and drove through England and Wales. In Dartmouth, Claire and Farley called on Christopher Robin Milne, to whom Farley had written as a child. "Holed up in Dartmouth where he owned a little bookshop," Milne did not normally receive tourists, but considering the special circumstances in the past, he relented, and Farley confronted a portion of his past. No romance remained: "Shortly a tall, thin, nervous man with thick glasses appeared. It was hard to imagine that this shy, bookish man should be the subject of books that are known the world over."[48] They then drove on to Caithness in Scotland, where the Mowats had come from originally. There, Farley met and got on famously with Sandy and Elizabeth Mowat, crofters who were repositories of all kinds of knowledge about the ancestry of the Mowat clan.

In March, before Farley and Claire headed north, Helen Mowat and her sister, Frances, visited them in London. Helen was again taken with Claire's warmth and charm. On March 28 Farley wrote to Angus and Barbara, "Got Helen away at Euston on Tuesday, she pretty chipper and anxious to get back 'because Angus needs looking after.' Did our best to persuade her to stay over . . . but she wasn't having any. Duty, you know. Hmmmm."

Fran's response to his request for a divorce was negative, he reported to them, but not hostile: "I don't know what the hell goes on in her mind. Have to find out. But if she remains adamant we'll nip down to Mexico in the winter and get a Tortilla Divorce. Either that, or Claire will have to change her name by deed poll."[49]

Their time together in England and Scotland had proven to Farley and Claire that they were inseparable. When they sailed back to Canada on April 24, they knew that there was no longer the shadow of a parting over them. And yet Claire, tough-minded when she had to be, was aware that some crucial barriers still stood in their way. She told Farley,

> I am beginning to wonder if you would love me if I were defiant. You are dismayed that I am beginning to disagree with you so much in public. And yet at the same time I am required to buck the tide of public opinion and tell the world to go to hell and let me live my own life.
>
> I think a lot of our present difficulties were bound to arise. The very nature of our relationship—one of love but without pieces of paper—makes the establishment of some kind of base important. I would never suggest for a moment that a base of

any sort would hold together any relationship which should not be held together. But our love, as it is not based on a legal agreement, needs to have a harbour, a snug harbour if you like, for windy days.[50]

9

Farley Mowat

1962–1965

AFTER Claire and Farley returned to Canada in May 1962 on the *Laurentia*, they spent three weeks at the ramshackle Mowat family cottage, Indian Summer, near Brighton, Ontario. It had been built by Angus, who labelled it a jerry-built affair. "Even the summer breeze whistled through it," he fondly recalled. There, Farley completed work on *The Black Joke*, a novel for young adults set both in Newfoundland and in St-Pierre and Miquelon. Very much in the tradition of *Treasure Island*, the story concerns the adventures of Peter and Kye, who foil a gang of bootleggers. It was completed by mid-June, and Claire and Farley drove to Beachy Cove, Newfoundland, in her ancient Morris Minor to visit Harold Horwood.

A month later, Claire and Farley relaunched the *Happy Adventure* at Milltown and cruised westward along the southwest coast of the island, stopping for a few days in Ramea. They headed vaguely in the direction of Grand Bruit. Then, when their ship drew abeam Boar

Burgeo, by John de Visser, 1967

Island, which marks the entrance "to the intricate maze of runs and tickles between the Burgeo Islands," fate intervened. Their engine failed. Forced into Burgeo for repairs, they were not ready to leave until the weather had turned nasty. They were thus harbour-bound in a place they had originally intended to avoid because they had heard that the recently built fish-packing plant—a series of plain wooden buildings from which, every seventeen days, fish was loaded onto a refrigerated vessel bound for the United States—had corrupted the character of this outport community.

The eastern part of Burgeo was dominated by the factory, the roar of its machinery deafening, the stench suffocating. When Farley and Claire mentioned to the friendly locals that they were looking for a place to winter, they were whisked away to Messers Cove, an enclave of fourteen families of fishermen at the western end of the village. The houses, in an assortment of bright colours, lined the harbour. Perched high on a granite boulder was a small white bungalow, six years old but half completed, whose windows looked south over the islands and beyond to the ocean. The house was for sale. Farley and Claire wanted to rent it, but the owner refused. Having fallen in love with this part of Burgeo, they threw caution to the winds, bought the house, travelled to Ontario for about six weeks and then returned in November to take possession of the house. For both of them, an outport community was the closest they could imagine to living a basic, simple existence away from the crushing demands of the kind of modern life they both loathed.

For Farley, the purchase of the house was a momentous event since after Palgrave, the mere idea of any fixed habitation unnerved him. Cruising dreamily along the Newfoundland coast was one thing— buying a house was another. And yet he knew that he and Claire needed a "snug harbour" to protect them and their love. He told his father, "I seem to have a deep-seated aversion to ever again putting roots into anything, except the good salt sea. Claire deserves a cave as much as any woman, and though she makes no fuss about it, I am aware of the fact. But every time we see a house, or a place to roost, I get panicky at the prospect of another Palgrave in the offing. And yet without a roost, I can't work at all."[1]

The tallest tree in Burgeo was shorter than any man there. Since the only entrance into Burgeo was by sea, most people there had never seen a car. The mail came in once a week on Mondays and one of Claire's tasks in winter was to take a toboggan with her for the one-mile journey to fetch it. There were no telephones, no stores as such. The nearest store, belonging to their next-door neighbour, was in a room tucked away behind an unmarked storm door. The only consistent lifeline to the outside world was provided by CBC Radio.

The kitchen in their new home was by far the largest room; there was a small parlour intended for ceremonial use only. The two bedrooms were tiny, neither with a door in the frame. There was a minuscule room which was awaiting transformation into a bathroom once plumbing and water were installed. Furniture and all kinds of miscellaneous household sundries had to be ordered from Eaton's and from the same Sears catalogue Claire had helped design and assemble. Farley and a local handyman installed doors and floor- and base-boards; Claire painted walls and cupboards. Once the foundation was boarded in, a large, bright office was constructed in the half-basement for Farley. Quite soon, Claire became accustomed to cooking on the spacious iron range in the kitchen and even became expert at local specialties such as cod, halibut, scallops, lobster and crab.

Claire and Farley, outsiders to Messers Cove, were a source of

Farley and Claire in the kitchen, Burgeo,
by John de Visser, 1967

endless curiosity for their new neighbours, to whom they were as strange as zoo specimens or circus freaks. In outport homes, kitchens were considered public property, and quite soon a variety of visitors—usually untalkative—would suddenly appear in the renovated kitchen and then, as quickly, vanish. In time, the day bed—standard in all outport kitchens—received a steady flow of youngsters from neighbouring homes.

Farley, as he told a friend, became fascinated by the sociology of his new community. With tongue in cheek, he wrote, "We are also greatly enjoying the local citizenry. There is a wedding every week, sometimes two or three. The last four brides have been of a tender age, 14, 14, 13 and 15, respectively, and of these, all were pregnant. . . . Nobody, but nobody, marries a woman until she has been tested and found capable. The [federal government's] baby bonus [payment] looms too large to admit of any other procedures. Come to think of it, nobody marries a woman—only little girls; Lolita is old stuff in Burgeo. . . . Claire says she feels bloody well decrepit."

The locals remained inquisitive and, at certain times, were exhibitionistic. During the Christmas season, "mummers" appeared. One evening someone pounded on the back door. Claire padded into the kitchen in her stocking feet, "switched on the light and pushed the door open against the gale. In front of me stood a solitary grotesque figure—I couldn't tell what age or sex—asking me in a hoarse, contorted voice if he, or she, could come in. This ghostly apparition had its face covered with a length of white cloth, secured by a fisherman's rubber sou'wester. An enormous oilskin jacket covered a padded bosom the size of Aunt Jemima's. Overly long sleeves hung down over hands that were covered by pink lace gloves."[2] Mummers, wandering bands of musicians and actors, had vanished from England in the early eighteenth century, but this custom had survived intact in the outports. Once the identity of a visitor was correctly guessed, the mask would be gleefully removed.

Farley and Claire were generally accepted by their new neighbours and attended many weddings and funerals, but they remained outsiders despite the fact that their closest friends included Simeon (Sim) Spencer, the proprietor of the tiny general store, and his

Farley relaxing at home, Burgeo, by John de Visser, 1967

teenaged daughter, Dorothy. The Mowats' own social group was formed by other intruders from "outside," such as Spencer Lake, the wealthy fish plant owner, and his wife; the husband-and-wife doctor team; the nurse; and the RCMP constable and his wife.

Spencer and Margaret Lake spent six months of the year in Burgeo, the other six in Massachusetts. Most of the fish plant owners in Newfoundland lived in St. John's, but the Lakes were excluded from that society because Spencer, a Protestant, had left his first wife to marry a Catholic. When in Burgeo, husband and wife, three small children and two full-time servants lived in baronial majesty. The doctors, recent immigrants from Scotland, considered themselves to be the real top of the social ladder. When they and their children went riding, they dressed impeccably in riding costumes. As Farley recalled, both these families "were united in their determination to impose the social standards of country gentlefolk on the Burgeo background, and they competed mercilessly for top billing, using the tools of conspicuous consumption. Thus when the doctors bought a jet-propelled speedboat which would do thirty knots, the plant owner responded by purchasing a cabin cruiser of regal splendour."

Unlike industrialists and physicians, writers are hard to place on any kind of social scale. Farley and Claire moved between the two worlds of insiders and outsiders, although they were uncomfortably aware of the vast discrepancy in income between the two groups.

Despite the growing intrusion of the modern age, Burgeo had, as Claire recalled, a pristine stillness:

> You could never count on the same weather for more than a few hours, but even during the storms I loved the long walks back to our house at night. We trudged up the main road—past Middle Class Row, the name Farley had given to the three identical split-level bungalows that housed the plant's managerial staff. Then we walked on past the plant buildings . . . until we came to the end of the road. Then we climbed up a hill and reached a stretch of frozen barrens which led us to Long Pond and Short Pond—the winter shortcut to Dog Cove. Since this was marshy ground for most of the year, no houses or other buildings could be built anywhere nearby. If we stood on the ice in the centre of Long Pond on a winter night, out of sight of people and far enough from the fish plant not to hear the constant roar of the engine room, we could fantasize momentarily that we were standing in a virgin world that had barely emerged from the last Ice Age.[3]

Although for the previous two years Farley had remained productive, his writing career had really been on hold. Then, that winter, Farley wrote one of his most celebrated books, the genesis of which can perhaps be traced to a letter Max Wilkinson had written him in January 1960: "You could do a whale of a boy's book about a boy who for reasons to be supplied finds himself living a season with a wolf family. I [have in] mind those excellent observations you once made [in a piece] about the habits of wolves. Eh?"[4][*]

Never Cry Wolf, the third of Farley's books devoted to his experiences

---

[*] Farley has noted, "I originally planned *Never Cry Wolf* at Brochet in 1948/49."

in the Arctic, is completely different in tone from the previous two. More comical and more subjective than *People of the Deer*, this narrative is centred on Farley's early preoccupation with animals. In a sense, the first two Arctic books were a distraction; he wrote them because he was deeply moved by the plight of the inland Inuit. But Farley had originally gone to the Arctic to study birds and mammals; during his second trip to Keewatin, the Dominion Wildlife Service had told him to investigate "wolf—caribou—predator–prey relationships"; he was especially to study the impact of wolves on the decline of the caribou population. To what extent were the wolves accountable for the decline in caribou and thus indirectly responsible for the starvation of the Inuit?

Overjoyed at having found, at last, another topic worthy of his talents, Farley allowed himself to joke, "I am at work, not on a respectable book of course, but on a spoof about scientists and bureaucrats, based on my brief career as a wolf-spy for the Wildlife Department in the Arctic." He also correctly labelled his new book a "potboiler."[5] A spoof and a potboiler *Never Cry Wolf* may be, but it also contains a passionate defence of the wolf, one of whose sources of food is mice; caribou are killed by the wolves, but the victims are usually the weaker members of the band—in Darwinian terms, the wolves cull the weakest of the caribou and thus help to ensure the survival of the fittest of the species. The book also has elements of a love story: the narrator falls in love with his main animal characters, George and his mate, Angeline (the book's dedication reads, "For Angeline—the angel!").

Although based on the field notes Farley made during his trips to the Arctic, the character and behaviour of the wolves is rendered vividly, in language literary rather than scientific. As he grew attuned to the wolves, he could not maintain a scientific distance from them:

> I found myself calling the father of the family George, even though in my notebooks, he was austerely identified only as Wolf "A." George was a massive and eminently regal beast whose coat was silver-white. He was about a third larger than his mate, but he hardly needed this extra bulk to emphasize his

air of masterful certainty. George had presence. . . . His wife was equally memorable. A slim, almost pure-white wolf with a thick ruff around her face, and wide-spaced, slightly slanted eyes, she seemed the picture of a minx. Beautiful, ebullient, passionate to a degree, and devilish when the mood was on her, she hardly looked like the epitome of motherhood; yet there could have been no better mother anywhere.

The lively comedy in the following passage is derived in large part from the use of anthropomorphism, which has been so well established in the text:

It was difficult to believe my eyes. [George and Angeline] were romping like a pair of month-old pups! The smaller wolf took the initiative. Putting her head down on her forepaws and elevating her posterior in a most undignified manner, she suddenly pounced toward the much larger male. . . . He, in his attempt to evade her, tripped and went sprawling. Instantly she was upon him, nipping him smartly in the backside, before leaping away to run around him in frenzied circles.

There is also a deft use of irony when the narrator castigates the "disgusting exhibition" of the female wolf. By making the mating ritual of George and Angeline a part of the battle of the sexes, Farley makes them human—and thus much more sympathetic—to his readers.

The Farley Mowat of *Never Cry Wolf* is a bumbling young man of good heart. At various times, he can be exasperated by Ottawa officialdom, prepare and eat concoctions made of mice—including *souris à la crème*, which, in addition to the rodents, consists of white flour, sowbelly, cloves and ethyl alcohol—and urinate to mark his boundary (in the process making it distinct from the land claimed by George and his family). Because Farley the narrator inhabits two worlds—the human and the animal—he can lay claim to an understanding of the Others, those creatures of the natural world that had fascinated him since childhood.

Peter Davison, thrilled to see Farley back in his finest form, wrote to say how delighted he was with the book, but he did sound some warnings:

> I love the new book. . . . It is terribly funny yet affectionate at the same time. Others have written about the wolf, even with admiration as you do; but no one else in my experience deals with the wolf in the manner of equals; and I am sure that no one else has gone so far as to share their diet of mice . . . but from time to time your tendency to lecture the reader creeps in; and I think that in this book of all books it is out of place. The reader is going to be persuaded to take the wolf's side in an unequal battle because you have aroused his affection, not because of your invective; and I think that wherever possible you should let the reader come to his own conclusions without taking him by the scruff of the neck.[6]

Farley heeded Peter's strictures. Angus, when he read an advance copy of the book, was ecstatic, as he told Barbara: "If you haven't read *Wolf*, please don't. Not till we are together and can read it together. Am sure it is one of his best—[it has] satire—truth—indignation and, I fear, despair. I *laughed* out loud and got a lump in my throat and was angered—all in one sitting."[7] Harold Horwood was "pleased to see— and green with envy—that the Wolves had been selected by the Book of the Month Club. Hope you make a million."[8]

Newspaper and magazine reviews of *Never Cry Wolf* were enthusi- astic, but, as usual, Farley fell foul of the academic reviewers, who disputed the book's accuracy. In *Canadian Audubon*, Douglas Pimlott claimed that Farley misrepresented the attitudes prevalent in the Dominion Wildlife Service in the late forties, the time period in which the book is set; these attitudes, he observed, had been shaped by the research of Adolph Murie and Lois Calder, who had made many of the same claims as the new book. Frank Banfield, who had fired Mowat from the Dominion Wildlife Service, reviewed the book negatively in *The Canadian Field-Naturalist*, ending with this sarcastic remark: "It is certain that not since Little Red Riding Hood

Dust jacket, Never Cry Wolf

has a story been written that will influence the attitude of so many towards those animals. I hope the readers of *Never Cry Wolf* will realize that both stories have about the same factual content."

Jack McClelland, delighted that the book was proving so controversial, penned a defence of it in a letter to the *Edmonton Journal*:

> I have read with great interest the lively controversy in your Dissent Page regarding Farley Mowat's *Never Cry Wolf*. . . . Ever since his first great book *People of the Deer* was published, Mowat has been subjected to attacks from unimaginative individuals who have been unable to understand his commitments and his purpose. Mowat is first and foremost a writer. As such he has felt it his primary concern to write well and write truth. Mowat is perhaps the most sincere and honest human being that it's been my privilege to know. He is concerned with reality, with truth, but with the underlying truths that are the concern of every creative artist. In his view, facts are important only as they relate to truth, and in themselves meaningless.[9]

Later, also in Mowat's defence, Thomas Dunlap pointed out in *Saving America's Wildlife* (1988) that the book is really a fable based on a spiritual experience. In essence, he observes, the story is about a would-be scientist who, having removed himself from the natural world through his education and training, learns about man's deep connections to the animal world; the enemy is "an impersonal administrative program sowing the land with poison. . . . Mowat is overwhelmed by a sense of his own failure to reach the moral level of the wolves and to enter their world. Beneath that is anger and contempt for those who destroy nature."

The humour in the book—based mainly on the narrator's ingenuousness and naivety, and showing Farley's considerable ability to poke fun at himself—sugarcoats the pill, which is a highly moral reflection on our dubious claim to be the lords of nature when we are often really the destroyers of nature and thus of our own places in the chain of being.

Never Cry Wolf sold more than three hundred thousand copies in

Canada and the United States, in the process making Farley a true celebrity in both countries. No longer regarded simply as a popular Canadian writer, he became known—along with Rachel Carson, a great admirer of the book—as one of the truly great crusaders defending the integrity of the planet against all kinds of government and corporate interests. He now became "Farley Mowat," a latter-day prophet who railed against the rapid destruction of humanity's bonds to animals, plants and the earth itself.

In December 1963, Farley and Claire acquired Albert, a five-month-old Newfoundland water dog born at La Poile, not far from Burgeo. Although these dogs look very much like the black Labradors they are ancestral to, they have webbed feet and usually have dabs of white—in Albert's case, a great blaze of it on his chest and at the end of his tail. In his appearance, Albert was, Farley recalled, like a creature in a Rembrandt etching: "He was as angular as a goat, as swaybacked as a

Albert

donkey. He appeared ungainly and somehow out of balance. His hindquarters were so skinny they appeared to have suffered from atrophy, but his forequarters seemed much too massive for a dog of his size, and his broad white-waistcoated chest would not have disgraced a bull. His two ends seemed only loosely connected because of his sag in the middle." He had a "truncheon of a tail, better than half the rest of his length—straight, heavy, formidably muscled." Albert's head was also slightly asymmetrical, one eye slightly lower and smaller than the other. His ears were exceedingly small, stiff and pointed, much different from the drooping earflaps of Labradors.

During his first trip to Newfoundland, Farley had encountered four such water dogs at the harbour at Grand Bruit—alert, bright-eyed, impatiently waiting for the steamer to come in so they could dive for bones flung overboard for them by the cooks—and several at La Poile, where they acted as "wharfingers," taking the lines from incoming boats in their mouths. Of the fourteen families in Messers Cove, three had water dogs: Lady, a gundog who lived in a ramshackle shelter with the local poacher; Jumbo, who lived next door to the Mowats; and Rover, who was a fishing dog (his specialty was catching flounder). Aspiring to ownership of such a dog, Farley wrote to a man in La Poile who bred them. But no reply came, and Farley abandoned his search.

Then a heavy wooden crate mysteriously arrived at Burgeo harbour:

> The only clue to its contents was the long black otter-like tail which stuck up straight through a hole in the top slats. . . . We had to use a crowbar and an axe to get the puppy out of the box which had been built strong enough to ship a lion halfway round the world, but while we worked the inhabitant kept on with his indefinable noises, a sort of resigned muttering, and when we finally pried the heavy lid off his box I could hardly credit the animal within. He was a small lump of blackness, quite unprepossessing except for his white shirtfront and his amber colour eyes, lit by an inner light that stared into mine. His gaze, then and thereafter, was incredibly direct and incredibly aware.

The fellow assisting Farley to open the crate exclaimed, "Farley me son, I t'inks dat's some knowing pup. Don't say there'll be many gets the best of he!"

Claire, as she told Barbara, was very fond of the little fellow, although he could be a bit troublesome: "At first he was called wee Albert, but I have named him wee-wee Albert. However I think he is finally catching on that we don't like him to make puddles on the kitchen floor. . . . When he is full grown, he'll spend most of the time outdoors, but right now I haven't got the heart to keep him out too long."[10] On board ship, Claire was thankful, Albert proved to be "a true sea-dog. He lies quietly on the deck, never interfering with the running of the ship. At night he sleeps below in a little after hold that contains extra ropes. Farley rows him ashore for a pee when we are moored, and only once did he forget his manners. But even then he did it over a hole that runs down into the bilge."[11]

Farley had owned other dogs after Mutt, several at Palgrave, but without doubt, Albert was his favourite. Since Albert had been born in an outport village, he was de facto a Newfoundlander, a strong recommendation for Farley. This dog was also uniquely from the Rock: such canines—now virtually extinct—do not exist anywhere else.* Albert was also an extremely forceful, curious and intelligent canine. Territorial, he would relentlessly attack other male dogs. His skills in orienteering were extraordinary. Peter Davison, a great admirer in general of creatures feline and canine, considered Albert one of the most remarkable animals he had ever met. When Peter was staying at Burgeo in 1965, he and Albert would go on long walks together, with the implicit understanding that Peter followed where Albert led. These hikes were always circular, though they varied. During a typical outing, Albert might pause to attack a passing dog, but he would then return to guide Peter. Albert was also a consummate retriever, fisherman and firewood collector. Although he ambled on land in a jerky way, he

---

* These water dogs are not to be confused with the famous Newfoundland dog, which, according to some, is actually a cross made in England in the nineteenth century between water dogs and Great Pyrenees sheepdogs.

Farley and Albert, by John de Visser, circa 1967

moved like a seal in water, holding his head high as he glided nimbly through the water.

Albert had not been an only puppy, but he acted as if he had been. This may have been one source of his strong bond with Farley, who greatly admired the dog's tenacious yet charming desire for both power and preference. Farley witnessed first-hand in Albert that a dog was an animal whose rank was determined by its position in the pack's pecking order—and Albert was determined to lead his own family pack.

In human society, as Farley had observed, few are leaders; most, as in canine society, are followers. From time to time, Farley day-dreamed about organizing a commune of like-minded individuals into a close-knit pack with himself as the leader.

Farley gained other new insights while writing *Never Cry Wolf* and while being owned by Albert. Among these was that human beings, despite the airs they give themselves, are good animals only when they behave as natural animals. This view of nature holds that all parts of nature are in a delicate interrelationship and that any breaking of this balance threatens the entire fabric of the planet. According to Farley Mowat, we do not understand that our self-interest lies in consistent, careful, long-range stewardship of the planet. Rather than thinking in decades or centuries, modern human society has tended to seize upon short-term exploitation of nature. For example, rain forests are razed and converted into grazing land for cattle because beef has become an important commercial commodity, whereas the true value of such forests is that they enhance the survival of all life in their own regions and, ultimately, of the entire planet. The realization of short-term human goals can result in long-term global disaster.

In *Never Cry Wolf*, Mowat suggests that the tendency to demonize—and then destroy—wolves occurs because we consider ourselves the proper owners of the caribou:

> Antiwolf feelings at Brochet (the northern Manitoba base for my winter studies) . . . were strong and bitter. As the local game warden aggrievedly described the situation to me: the local people had been able to kill 50,000 caribou each winter as recently as two decades past, whereas now they were lucky if they could kill a couple of thousand. Caribou were becoming scarce to the point of rarity, and wolves were unanimously held to be to blame. My rather meek remonstrance to the effect that wolves had been preying on caribou, without decimating the herds, for some tens of thousands of years before the white man came to Brochet, either fell on deaf ears or roused my listeners to fury at my partisanship.

The human species has been a dismal failure as steward of the earth, Mowat claims; moreover, our actions are not only destructive but self-destructive. If we continue on our present course, nothing will be left worth preserving, including ourselves. "I contemplate," he observed in 1967, "the physical and psychic degeneration of the beast called Man. . . . More and more I come to the inescapable conclusion that the beast we are is nearing the end of its tether. As I get older, I revert to my old interest in biology but with man as the prime object under the microscope. In fact, were I a god, and a betting one, I'd lay no odds upon him."[12]

* * *

Since Farley now saw his two sons infrequently, letters became his principal way of keeping in touch. To share with his sons his enthusiasms about the natural world, he wrote at length about his excursions away from Burgeo. One such adventure was seeing Newfoundland from the air: "The Buchans Mine pilot took me inland and I spent several days flying with him in a Beaver airplane. One of the things we did was drop supplies to a pair of prospectors in the mountains. The plane was on floats and there were no lakes to land on, so we 'bombed' their camp."[13] In September 1962, he gave details of a walking and canoeing trip into the interior of Newfoundland:

Most of the time we couldn't use the canoe but had to walk across the country with backpacks. I had a fellow called Dolph Benoit with me. He is half Mic Mac Indian and so tough that he can just about run as fast as a caribou. We were looking for caribou but they are rare now. So many of them have been shot. But after two days we found some. There were five of them on the shore of a little sandy lake and we spent all day crawling through the bushes to get close to them. Two of them were bucks with big spreading antlers. We were within fifteen feet of them before they saw us. The bucks jumped to their feet, snorted, and tossed their big antlers in the air and I thought they were going to charge us. But then they turned and ran. There were two does and a young fawn with them.

We also saw twenty or thirty moose. They are very common in the Barrenlands of Newfoundland and are so unused to people that you can walk up to them as if they were cows in a barnyard. We also met a black bear. He was picking berries on a hill. We were picking berries too and we never saw each other until we were pretty close. I don't know who was the most surprised. . . .

The main thing I was looking for was camp sites of the Beothuk Indians who used to live in Newfoundland. They were all killed by the white people and the last Beothuk died a hundred years ago.[14]

Many of Farley's travels in Newfoundland at that time were in search of the remains of the mysterious Beothuk, major characters in a Newfoundland historical project he had been researching for several years. As he told his sons, the result, *Westviking: The Ancient Norse in Greenland and North America* (1965), was to be his first "real" book about Newfoundland—as opposed to the two books which dealt with the salvage boats peopled by Newfoundlanders—and would centre on the first explorers to reach North America:

> This Newfoundland book is all about the Norsemen from
> Greenland who discovered North America about 500 years
> ahead of Columbus. I have been tracing their story for a long
> time now, and I finally decided that they had come to
> Newfoundland in 1001 A.D., which is 962 years ago. I had an
> idea I knew where they had landed and where they built their
> first settlement, and it looks as if I was right. It is at a place called
> St. Paul's Bay on the west coast of Newfoundland. A Norseman
> named Thorfinn Karlsefni tried to make a settlement there in
> 1002. He stayed there three years and his wife had a child born
> there. His name was Snorri, and he was the first white child ever
> born in North America, nearly a thousand years ago. But
> Karlsefni and his people got into a war with the Beothuk Indians
> and finally they gave up and went back to Iceland.[15]

In another letter to Sandy and David, Farley provided more information on the kind of research—so different from his field work in the Arctic—he was now pursuing:

> One trip was to a place called Rencontre Island which is not
> very far from Burgeo. It is a mountain sticking up out of the sea,
> with no trees on it. Nobody lives there either. But a very long
> time ago it must have had trees and people too. The people
> were the extinct Beothuk Indians. The last known Beothuk died
> in 1814, which is a long time ago. The Beothuks were a kind
> and gentle people who did no harm to anyone, but, as in most
> parts of North America, the white men wanted their land and

didn't want a lot of Indians arguing about it so they just killed them.

I have heard of another cave at Cape la Hune. This is a very big cave. The ice never melts in it, and sometimes fishermen used to go there to cut ice in summer. But one day they found part of a frozen human body in the ice and this scared them so badly that no one ever went back there. I think this too may have been a big Beothuk burial cave and next week, if the weather improves, I am going to sail to Cape la Hune and explore this cave.

One very strange thing—I think I have discovered traces of *Eskimos* on the south coast of Newfoundland. These were probably an Eskimo people that we call Dorsets, and who vanished a long time ago—maybe a thousand years ago. But it looks as if at one time they lived right around the coast of Newfoundland. In early August I am invited to spend two weeks with a trained archaeologist from the USA at a place called Port Aux Choix on the northwest coast of Newfoundland. This man has found the ruins of a big Dorset Eskimo village and he is excavating it. I think that these Dorset Eskimos were the "Skraelings" who are mentioned in the Norse sagas of the exploration of North America in 1004 A.D.[16]

In spite of his field trips, Farley had to rely much more on published scholarship in writing *Westviking* than he had for any of his previous books. On these very grounds, Peter Davison from the outset had grave concerns about the direction this project was taking Farley. In September 1964, the editor told his author that he had been thinking about this predicament: "I don't think there is any point in our pretending that it is not a dilemma." He added, "You have been writing seriously now for almost twenty years. You have had some quite considerable successes and a few books which were not so successful, both in artistic and commercial terms. You have changed your way of life considerably. And you are twenty years older."

Farley was being reminded that he was at a transitional moment.

Almost all his writing had been based more or less on personal experiences in the Arctic and at sea. In the next twenty years or so, it was unlikely he would have such dramatic experiences to write about. "More and more," Peter told Farley, "your writing is going to have to seek out a different kind of source."

Part of the difficulty for Farley in writing *Westviking* was, Peter reminded him, that it raised a crucial question: Was it the right kind of book? "For the first time, you are having to depend primarily on other peoples' scholarship to tell a story."

> If there is a pattern in your work from beginning to end, it is that you have always been profoundly concerned with the confrontation of man and nature—whether tragically, as in *The Desperate People*, or comically, as in *The Dog Who Wouldn't Be*. In the Norse book as you originally conceived it, you have, I think, allowed yourself to be dominated by the notion of history as a chronicle, the story of what happened next and then what happened next after that.

Clearly but politely, Peter was telling Farley that he should not be writing books such as *Westviking*—a book very much in the mould of the earlier *Regiment*—in which his own point of view or involvement was minimized. According to Peter, the strength of Farley Mowat the writer resided in his ability to interpolate fact with fiction; yet, the editor observed, "I have felt you were a bit worried even by the relation between fact and fiction in *Never Cry Wolf*." He added, "I am the last person in the world to recommend a slavish attention to the literal outline of fact, but if fact is to be distorted, the writer should distort it in order to reveal a deeper meaning. This is what you have always done in your successful work."

Perhaps it was time for Farley to acknowledge the fictional basis that underscored his best writing and to move in that direction. Peter reminded Farley, "As long as the events in a work of fiction have a harmonious relationship to one another it matters little what the events *are*."

> In *People of the Deer* you wrote about the community of the
> Ihalmiut. In *The Serpent's Coil* you wrote about the community
> of the salvage men. In *Never Cry Wolf* you wrote about the
> community of wolves. Could you write a book, whether fiction
> or non-fiction, based on the sense of community in a fishing
> village threatened by a civilization which recognizes neither
> villages nor fishing in the old style?[17]

In October 1964, Farley, looking for a new project, seriously
discussed the possibility of purchasing the rights to Angus's third
(unpublished) book, called "Green Hands and Grey Seas,"* and
rewriting it under his own name. This venture was soon discarded.[18]

At the same time that Peter Davison confronted Farley about his
future as a writer, Farley's association with Jack McClelland was
thrown into doubt. Jack's sensitivity to criticism from authors with
whom he had formed a close attachment was excessively high. In
October 1964, he wrote to Farley about discontinuing their publishing relationship: "To put things bluntly, we have reached a point
where it no longer makes sense to continue our business association."

> The problem was initiated by your memorable comment at
> [Jack's cottage at] Foote's Bay. It would be pleasant to think that
> it was a spur of the moment thought. I know that you regretted
> the statement as soon as you had made it and it would have been
> out of character for you not to have regretted it. . . . You had
> come to Foote's Bay intending to say it. Whether you were
> right or wrong, whether you had justification or not, it is my
> view now (as it was then) that you had come to believe in the
> opinion that you expressed.

The "memorable comment" which initiated this correspondence
could not be recalled later by either man, but it likely was something

---

* This was Angus's account of a voyage in *Scotch Bonnet* from Montreal to Halifax,
to New York, through the Erie Canal and back to Ontario. Farley sailed with his
father to Halifax and kept his own journal.

about Farley's enormous debt to Davison and to the fact that M&S—without much work—was gaining advantage from Farley's success.

A significant part of the dispute centred on M&S's internal Brock Hall agency, which now negotiated Farley's American and foreign rights. Earlier, Farley had fired Max Wilkinson, who had undertaken this responsibility with great aplomb; it was, Farley realized, a direct conflict of interest for Jack to have M&S acting as his Canadian publisher and as his worldwide agent.

Jack, as he informed Farley, was deeply hurt by the manner in which his author had revealed his discontent:

> In one sense I don't feel you were entitled to that opinion. Spoken in jest it would be fair enough. Spoken in seriousness, it was a negation of everything we have attempted to do. But you held the view and if you held it, you certainly had the obligation to express it. And if you held it, it had to mean either that I had done my job too well or too poorly. Either way it meant to me that we had outlived our usefulness to you.
>
> . . . It is this, chiefly, that makes it necessary for us to go our separate ways. We started as business associates. We became friends. Perhaps the only way that we can remain friends is to forget the business. There is nothing revolutionary in that. I've told you many times that I consider publishing a service business. The publisher exists only because he offers a service to authors. If a Canadian author feels that he is losing money by publishing with us, then to hell with it. I don't wave the flag quite that much. It has always been my belief that Canadian authors make more money by dealing with us and by listening to our advice.[19]

In the same letter, the editorial side of Jack could not resist commenting—in a manner similar to Davison's—on the typescript of *Westviking*:

> None of the foregoing, Farley, has any relation to the Norse book or to any other book. I think the Norse book is a bad one.

At no time have I been the slightest bit concerned about it from the financial point of view, or from the standpoint of it not being a potential best seller. I'm aware, too, that many worse books are published. However, unless the revision has been extensive, I would be concerned about the effect of the book on your reputation. If published in anything close to its original form, it is my view that it would damage you to a degree that I don't even like to think about.[20]

Despite the fact he could not recall the actual remark that had upset his friend so much, Farley was repentant:

Your letter shook me badly. I had not had any idea that you had been harbouring a dart in your vitals these past six months, and was annoyed with you for what I took to be a lack of concern with the problems I was having with the Norse book. I see that I was wrong. There is probably no point in attempting to disillusion you of your conviction that I have an abiding distaste for M&S. I can, however, assure you that I have not the slightest recollection of whatever heinous remark I evidently made at Foote's Bay. I recall getting very drunk, very gloomy, and busting a glass on the wall . . . Whatever was said, was not meant. I have no real quarrel with you, or the Company, apart from the usual picayune bitchings which all authors indulge in . . . I do not know (since you refrained from telling me) either what I said . . . I like you as a business associate, quite apart from how I feel about you as a friend . . . I would be very sorry indeed to leave M&S and even sorrier to lose you as a friend. And, despite what you may say, the friendship would certainly not survive the rupture.[21]

Claire intervened in the contretemps, writing to Jack on November 3, 1964. She was at pains to point out that Farley sober and Farley drunk were two different people:

I want to tell you about an odd and unpleasant side of Farley's character. He has the capacity, when he's drunk, to be outrageously abusive, untruthful and cruel in what he says to those close to him. I don't mean the sort of lusty, bawdy behaviour of his that we're all familiar with. This is something quite different and it almost amounts to congenital lying. For instance: Whenever we return from a party at which Farley has managed to get drunk, he launches at me a tirade of abuses. He has vigorously accused me, on various occasions, of being childish, grossly selfish, incompetent, stupid, frigid, frivolous and joyless. I am none of these things. Some guys beat their wives. Others get the same kick from verbally beating them. The first few times it happened I was pulverized. I now recognize it for what it is. Now this unsavoury little tidbit of our domestic life is of no importance to you, Jack. I merely mention it to make a point. Farley, when he's sufficiently drunk, is not responsible for what he says.[22]

Jack had to deal discreetly with yet another Mowat-related matter when Angus asked for his assistance in procuring the services of an abortionist. When Barbara became pregnant in 1965, she did not wish to have the baby—she knew by then that she was a carrier of hemophilia. Jack found someone to perform the operation, and Beryl Gaspardy accompanied Barbara to Toronto for the procedure.

Jack accepted Farley's apology for his outburst at Foote's Bay, the threatened rupture was averted, and Farley appointed Ivan von Auw, at Harold Ober Associates in New York City, to be his agent.

Claire's observations to Jack about Farley contained a vivid description of his dark side, that part of his nature which was easily threatened, suspicious and vulnerable, that portion of Farley's character she had learned to both defy and challenge. From childhood, Farley had fled from intimacy with others. This tendency may have been due to—or exacerbated by—the sense that he could never be quite good enough for his father. Farley might be able to accomplish many things, but would they ever be the right things? Consciously and unconsciously, this question haunted him. When drunk and thus uninhibited, his fears were unleashed and then voiced. In such moments, he pushed other people, such as Jack and Claire, away lest he should once again fail at being the person they wanted him to be, furious at them for making demands upon him to be someone he could not be.

In the autumn of 1964, Farley had to confront not only his own inner demons but also Angus's when Barbara called Farley's attention to the difficulties she and his father were having in maintaining their relationship, he in Port Hope with Helen, she in Smiths Falls:

> I have a horrible feeling that, gradually, Angus has worked himself into a chronic state which is going to keep producing glens and deeper glens. Each time he has to find something a little more far-fetched to accuse me of until it gets ludicrous. It has finally dawned on me that he has made a little world for himself in Port Hope in which only he and I live and where he has really no communication with anything or anyone around him. He has made no really good friends in Port Hope even though we need someone who would diplomatically accept my letters [so that they could be hand delivered to him without Helen being aware of what was happening]. Friends he had he is now quite indifferent to. He is really an emotional recluse. He is obsessed and this makes him both supremely happy and so unbearably miserable that it frightens me. . . . The end result is that he is frightened, jealous, suspicious and possessive. . . . He is really jealous of all the time I am not with him, which means really that he is jealous of everything, my job, my social life and the few community responsibilities I have had to accept. While he is in Port Hope thinking about nothing except me I am in Smiths Falls working and trying to make my life without him as bearable as possible. He doesn't really understand how I could possibly love him and still have some kind of passable life away from him. I think somewhere in the back of his mind he has the idea that one must suffer in order to prove one's love. Since I obviously don't suffer as much as he does, it follows that I don't love him as much.

At Port Hope, Angus and Helen often quarrelled bitterly. One day, as Angus informed Barbara, Helen announced she had given up her attendance at prayer meetings. Startled, Angus asked why. She told him: "(a) 'Because of Farley's sin [leaving Frances and living with Claire] I am not worthy.' I shouted out that this was nonsense. She then said, (b) 'Because you have always opposed my meetings and my God.' "[23]

The cosy foursome was also beginning to unravel. Convinced of their own intellectual superiority, Angus and Barbara were conde-scending in their assessment of Claire's many abilities.[24] Angus wrote critically of Claire to Farley, who replied,

> I have heard your brief word of advice and am not sure what to make of it. Having nerved yourself to say anything, you should have said more. No, I'm not dense. But I am aware of the fact that C. shows to very bad advantage in your company, and with others of high intellect, even if they are female. Nervousness, partly, and partly a sense of mental inferiority I suppose. But this much you no doubt have guessed—you must have been perceptive enough to see it, which makes me wonder at the vehemence of your comment. What do you know, or what conclusion have you reached, that has escaped me? Hell, me son, I know C. is no fit mate for a God, but then who in the devil is a God? Not me, I fear, though you and some others do seem to have an exalted idea of my capabilities.[25]

The implication of Angus's evaluation of Claire's abilities was that in the choice of the perfect mate he had bested his son. Yet Angus could even be flirtatious with Claire, as can be seen in a comic turn she offered in a letter to him and Barbara:

> Yes, dear, you and I could get married I suppose. But have you really stopped to consider all the possibilities? I mean would Barb and I still be friends if I were your wife and she were your True Love? And then, would Farley still love me if I were his mother? . . . We had better not rush into this. I would, person-ally, like to think it over for a while.[26]

A continuing source of vexation for Farley and Claire was Fran's steadfast, stubborn refusal to grant her husband a divorce. Since Canadian law refused to sanction marital breakdown as grounds for divorce, Farley's hands were apparently tied.

It was a family built on secrets. Not until 1964 did Farley's stepsister and stepbrother, Rosemary and John, learn of Barbara's existence. This happened when they visited Burgeo, accompanied by Angus. For some years, John had suspected that Angus was a womanizer. One day, when both Angus and Helen were away, the teenager had answered the door at Port Hope to be confronted by an extremely anxious woman who asked if Angus was in. Just then, Angus appeared, looked very chagrined and quickly ushered the woman away. After John learned about Angus's protracted relationship with Barbara, he was, out of a sense of duty to Helen, outraged, but when he secretly met Barbara in August 1964, he "liked her very much." He told Farley, "It made me feel real good to see Dad so relaxed and happy. I was only there the one night and hope to return soon. (Boy what a family!! You living common law and my father doing the same whenever he can. Oh well, who cares except those narrow-minded hypocrites and holy do-gooders)."[27]

In the spring of 1963, Farley and Claire sailed from Burgeo on the *Swivel* to Gloucester, Massachusetts, stayed with Peter Davison and his wife in Boston and then went to Dartmouth College in New Hampshire, where Farley did further research for *Westviking*. That summer, they travelled by car to the west coast of Newfoundland as far north as St. Anthony, then went by boat to Quirpon and L'Anse aux Meadows, also in aid of *Westviking*. That August was spent on *Happy Adventure*. In the autumn, Farley spent four weeks in Toronto, much of this time devoted to publicity for *Never Cry Wolf*. As he had done in 1959, Farley made some films for CBC Television: *Boy on Vacation* (about St-Pierre and Miquelon) and *Portraits from the Sea*. He also got involved in local politics when he opposed plans to connect Burgeo to a proposed highway and to install a television receiver.

Much of 1964 was spent writing *Westviking*, although there were further trips to Boston and Toronto. That August, Farley and Claire cruised along the south coast of Newfoundland, going as far as Grey River. Earlier in the summer he had to break some bad news to Jack McClelland, the co-owner of *Happy Adventure*: "It will come as no surprise to you to hear that *Happy Adventure* sank during my absence. Honest to God. Joe Warren had her ashore to paint her bottom and let a stone puncture her hull. He never noticed, and when the tide rose, she sank. But she is afloat once more, and reasonably seaworthy. It's a damn good thing you don't have to pay your share of maintenance costs on her."[28]

Farley also began to work on his third novel for young people, *The Curse of the Viking Grave*. He cheerfully told Barbara and Angus: "In between [work on *Westviking*] I've written another boy's book. Boy's? It's got a handsome Injun maid. At Chapter Sixteen she was beginning to look pregnant. I fear this may be a best seller on the teenage list. Teen sex books are all the rage. I even hear that pre-teen sex books are icumen in. Thank God I am of the avant garde."[29]

Claire began teaching art at the local school, typed Farley's manuscripts and drew the maps for *Westviking*. As far as she was concerned, Burgeo and the other outport communities were secrets best kept from the rest of Canada and the world. She loved living there. Farley was uncertain. Occasionally, he thought of leaving Burgeo but, in general, he knew he was thriving.

In 1964, in the face of Fran's consistent refusal to sue for divorce, Farley and Claire decided to travel to Mexico, obtain a divorce there and marry in the United States. In November 1964, Claire informed Barbara, "Yes. Mexico. I think we're going to get married—but don't count on it just yet. . . . If we do get married, we will come and see you after that for a big celebration. It should be just about sugaring-off time, and we will settle for a jug of maple syrup for our nuptial present. . . . We may not even get married—I hate to count my chickens before they're hatched."[30]

Early in January 1965, Farley and Claire flew to Boston, where they were soon joined by Harold Horwood in his Ford Comet. For a few days, Farley and Peter worked night and day to complete the final revisions to the typescript of *Westviking*. Then Farley, Claire and

Harold headed south to Mexico. They went by way of Alabama, Louisiana and, as Harold recalls, the coast of the Gulf of Mexico in Texas, where everyone they saw, "blacks and whites, looked equally ragged and poor, many of the children without shoes. Just at dark we drove through an oil field where the air was rank with sulphur dioxide, and the flames of burning gas lit the landscape like a scene from Hieronymus Bosch. As we emerged from the smoke and fire we came to a small shack town named Sabine Pass, where we got beds in the local whore house." The next day they drove many miles along the hard sand beaches on the Texas barrier islands and stopped at the Aransas Wildlife Refuge, where they saw whooping cranes.

At the Mexican border, the trio explained to the border guards that Farley wanted to be in Mexico for two months because he was writing a book about their country, Harold was his research assistant and Claire the typist. Their travels took them to Sierra Madre, Cuidad Victoria, Quinta Chila, Tula and Mexico City, which was so smothered in a haze from gasoline fumes that they could not get a glimpse of the sky. Farley wrote to Angus from Villa Juarez, telling him how much he hated Mexico:

> Illusions die hard. I foolishly re-read *The Plumed Serpent* a month or so before we set out on safari. But both Lawrence and Quetzalcoatl have vanished from the land, if indeed they were ever here. . . . We have been rocketing back and forth from the Pacific to the Atlantic with frenzied and useless rapidity. When we find the sun, it is at an altitude of 9,000 feet, where the air is quite cold enough to freeze the knockers off a brass llama. When we find the sea, it is grey, growling and full of sharks. The best sands are in the centre of the Senora desert but are already in the possession of an inhospitable mob of Gila monsters, diamond backed rattlers and assorted scorpions.

There were two other things of interest—roosters and diesel trucks, neither of which had any sense of restraint in the sound they produced. The Mexicans were a mysterious lot, in some ways rather "like Canadians in that, much as they hate Yanks, they feel compelled to tolerate them because of Ford Fairlanes, television sets and Coca Cola." The Mayans and Aztecs were, according to Farley, "a humble people who ate a lot, drank gallons of pulque [beer made from cactus] and apparently spent the balance of their time manufacturing porno-graphic figurines."[31]

A month later, ensconced in the small port city of Manzanillo, where the three found cloudless days, warm sea water and spacious beach cottages, Farley realized he had been too hasty in his condem-nation of Mexico:

> After weeks of searching we at last stumbled on the sort of tropi-cal paradise for which we were searching. Manzanillo. It is a small seaport on the west coast—first settled by Cortes, and it was here that the Spaniards built the galleons which first sailed west into the Pacific to discover the Philippines. . . . It is a deep, semi-circular bay with a broad sand beach all round it (some seven miles in length) and a minimum of winter visitors. A handful of Yanks and Canucks. . . . We rented a little bungalow on the beach and cook our own meals—mainly shrimp and fruit. Both are abundant and luscious. The days are all the same. Clear, brilliantly sunny, and with a steady, brisk westerly off the open sea to prevent death from sunstroke.

Nobody had to do much except dodge the occasional shark in the sea and avoid sunstroke. Claire had become a "nut brown maid, and Harold has turned Conradian beachcomber, tattered pants, white shirt, panama hat and all."

In Mexico City, Farley engaged the services of Señor Federico Martinez Montes de Oca, who arranged for the divorce, which came through towards the end of March. As soon as the document arrived, the three drove to Corsicana, Texas, where, after the obligatory Wasserman test for syphilis proved negative, Farley and Claire were married by Judge "Tip" Tipton on March 29, 1965. Harold, of course, was Farley's best man. The bride, aged thirty-two, wore a simple blouse and skirt and canvas shoes that had once been white. The groom, aged forty-four, was also casually dressed. Along with a

Farley and Claire on their wedding day,
March 29, 1965

marriage certificate entwined with yellow roses, she received a gift from the state of Texas: a kit containing a book of housekeeping hints, a can of scouring powder, a box of laundry detergent and a bottle of Aspirin. Shortly afterwards, Harold began his long drive back to Newfoundland, while Farley and Claire boarded a train for Chicago and then flew from there to Toronto.

10

Keeper of the Whale

1965–1967

UPON arrival in Toronto, Farley and Claire got in touch with Angus and Barbara to have a celebratory drink at the roof bar at the Park Plaza Hotel. But Barbara had other ideas. She laughed in Claire's face, insisting (incorrectly) that she and Farley were not really married because a Mexican divorce had no legal status in Canada. An upset Claire fished the Texan marriage certificate out of her purse and handed it to Barbara, who remained steadfast in her assertion. The document, she crisply announced, was "not worth the paper it was printed on."

Respectability was a crucial matter to Barbara, who had led her brothers and sisters, whom she saw infrequently, to believe that she and Angus were married all along. All of a sudden, any sense of equilibrium in the relationship between the two couples had vanished. Farley and Claire were no longer "living in sin," whereas Angus and Barbara were still conducting a clandestine relationship. Before, Barbara had tried to be a substitute mother for Farley; when Farley met Claire, lived with her and eventually married her, Barbara's role in his life shrank markedly. Barbara obviously resented this alteration, and her remark to Claire may have been generated by that change.*

For Angus's sake, Farley and Claire attempted to maintain a cordial relationship with Barbara, but their affection for her was considerably diminished. Barbara, they now noticed, used a divide-and-conquer approach to family relationships. She habitually made negative remarks about Farley and Claire but attributed those remarks to other members of the family; sentences would begin, "When John Mowat was here last week, he said that you were. . . ." Often, when she and Angus invited Farley and Claire to a tiny primitive cabin called "Pinchpenny" that Angus had built north of Kingston as a convenient meeting spot between Smiths Falls and Port Hope—somewhere Angus and Barbara could spend time together—Barbara, who had a hypochondriacal side, would be too sick to prepare a meal. So Claire would have to cook in a strange kitchen while Barbara, reclining on the chesterfield, was barely visible behind the smoke from her cigarette.

Angus, of course, became aware that something was disrupting the good feelings once shared by the four. In December 1965 he wrote his son, "I understand that you were both unhappy when you were at Pinchpenny, but I didn't understand it quite, or even guess it, until you said so in your letter. I suppose I just don't know how anybody could be unhappy at Pinchpenny. But I did know you were . . . and was troubled and fully mystified by same."[1] In order to maintain what had become a precarious peace, Farley pretended that nothing disruptive had in fact occurred.

The relationship between Angus and Barbara finally became known to Helen in April 1966, as Angus explained to Farley and Claire:

There have been a great many stupidities in this world and I have committed my share of them; but this time I have sounded the nadir of all stupidities. This time I have done it.

---

* Farley comments, "The simple fact was that Barbara resented that Claire and I now had a legal marriage—and she did not and never would have because Angus wouldn't make it possible."

Claire wrote an understanding kind of letter to Barbara, just one of our letters that pass back and forth. I took it (against Barb's better judgement) to Port Hope. And there was another letter, either from Claire or Farley, that came to Port Hope. I had them both on my desk. When leaving for Pinchpenny, [I thought I had left] the innocuous letter [from Farley and Claire] on P.D.H.'s desk—she having already read it. But in the incredible stupidity of me, I left Claire's letter to Barb there instead.

When he returned to Port Hope and was confronted by an angry Helen, Angus tried to lie his way out: "Oh, it was only a joke-letter from Claire," he dismissively observed. His wife replied, "That was a nice try, but it didn't work."[2]

For some time, Helen had been convinced of the existence of the "other woman" and had been willing to tolerate this demeaning fact of life. She only reached breaking point the following year when Rosemary, now living in Toronto, revealed to her that she was privy to the arrangement between Angus and Barbara. Helen, who had never really gotten along with her adopted daughter, had to face the sad fact that Rosemary had formed a friendship with Barbara. Completely humiliated, Helen, who did not approve of divorce, insisted that she and Angus legally separate. According to the agreement negotiated by their lawyers in 1967, Helen retained the house in Port Hope for her lifetime and Angus, who now lived with Barbara in Pinchpenny, agreed to provide her with two hundred dollars a month.

Farley and Claire returned to Burgeo from May until September 1965, at which point he began touring Canada on behalf of *West-viking*, which was published that autumn. Just before he set off, his stomach gave him problems, the source of which doctors in neither St. John's nor Toronto could agree on, although the patient was labelled "ulcerous." Four months later, as he informed Angus, Farley was diagnosed as having a propensity to "duodenal ulsters, as we say in Burgeo, and I get them from smoking too much, mainly pipe. It is the juice. The nicotine juices combine with the gastric juices, and all hell pops. I get boils on the inside of my stomach."[3] Although the tour disrupted work on *The Curse of the Viking Grave* and his ailment made travel more arduous than normal, the trip was a success.

During this tour—and many others following it—the "public" Farley Mowat was very much on display. At readings and parties, he was often dressed in a kilt and sometimes he would ostentatiously remove his underpants and throw them away. He claims that he performed such actions to shock others and "substantiate my own ego, to reinforce my own evaluation of myself." The "evaluation" was a declaration that he was a cheeky rebel and would-be revolutionary, someone who did not think in predictable ways. His public stance also generated publicity and book sales, but in the process he took the risk of trivializing the claims he was making in some of his books. Particularly in the case of the scholarly *Westviking*, he seemed by his conduct to be suggesting that the book should not be taken too seriously.

However much Farley was willing to perform in Canada, he was decidedly shy about doing so in the United States, where the drive for attention in the publishing industry is both more sober and more relentless. Peter Davison's blood boiled when Farley proved uncooperative in spending even a few days in Manhattan. Although long convinced that Farley was not an author who fit into any easy American pigeonhole, he had counted on Farley's cooperation in promoting the book there.

For one thing, there had been considerable interest in the United States in the new book, especially from the industry's two powerful advance-of-publication reviews. *Publishers Weekly* described the book as a "graphic retelling of the history of the ancient Norse in Greenland and North America"; *Kirkus Reviews* was even more positive: "Imaginative readers will find this a vivid history which constantly reveals primitive visions and attitudes foreign to a modern mind. . . . This is a bold, absorbing story." The publicist for Atlantic–Little, Brown could have placed Farley on the much-watched *Today* show, provided the mercurial author had been a bit flexible. When this was not the case, Peter wrote his recalcitrant author, who had complained about the treatment he was receiving: "I frankly was a little bothered by your last letter expressing annoyance that we had not been able to arrange major television appearances for you in New York on November 15, 16, or 17, particularly because on October 21st you said 'I do not want to spend a week frigging about south of the border unless it is of some value.'"

Specifically, Farley had complained that Jack McClelland had easily arranged a full packet of engagements for him. Davison, who was continually reminding Farley that the large population base in the United States meant that both publishing and publicity dates had to be arranged well in advance, was a trifle exasperated:

> Since you never gave us any dates at all until October 18th, I see no point in comparing a proposed three-day stint in New York on very short notice with what McClelland & Stewart have been able to arrange with six months' notice to fit into a period of three weeks. We had no difficulty whatever in finding engagements in New York, but we agreed with you that you shouldn't have to come down if the appearances weren't important.
>
> As I wrote you, the *Today* show was very eager to have you, but they were all committed on the three days you were available. Aside from the *Today* show few appearances seemed to us to make much difference, unlike in Canada where you are a public figure. Well, I hardly expect you to be consistent. If you were, it would be a new departure.[4]

Davison, who continued to be perturbed by the *Top of the World* trilogy (the Arctic anthologies), had also tried to turn Farley's attention to a new, potentially lucrative project: "Those waterdogs are great beasts, and surely worthy of a book from you. And think how pleased Albert would be. You could even write the book for adults with children only secondarily in mind, like Mutt."[5]

Farley had also been asked to write a general book on Newfoundland, a task he found difficult to formulate. More than a year later, in 1967, Peter remained obdurate: "*The Water Dog*. This can and will, I think, be your next 'real' book. I think we agreed it is very important that your next book be something you can really get your teeth into and not a hack job. My hunch is that *The Water Dog* is the book because it will not have an ounce of reportage in it, and because it will give you an opportunity to embody your feelings and your true emotional resources as a writer. Neither you nor I have the foggiest idea of the form this book will take, and it cannot possibly be outlined or planned very much in advance. It should and can have a real spontaneity to it."[6] The publisher also told Farley that the advance for the Newfoundland book could easily, if he wished, be transferred to the dog book.

By the end of 1965, Farley, at loggerheads with plant owner and mayor Spencer Lake over his treatment of his workers, considered moving back to Ontario: "I have it in mind that one bright day I might even hole up in Port Hope. When Burgeo gets too hot for me. It is hotting up all the time. Lake and his peers no longer speak my way. They may, though, when the CLC [representatives of the Canadian Labour Congress invited by Farley] arrives in here after Christmas to organize the fishermen on the south coast. I should think he *may* speak then. Softly, no doubt, and in parables."[7] On a visit from Burgeo in 1967, the Mowats briefly rented an apartment on College Street in Toronto, just opposite the Toronto Public Library at the corner of St. George Street (the rental was for six months and they occupied it for only one month in the spring and one month in the fall).

In terms of the future of Newfoundland, Farley was a Luddite. He did not want the ancient way of life of the outport villages to be destroyed; he did not want Burgeo to be accessible by automobile; he was hostile to the introduction of television. He felt strongly that the fish-packing factories should be unionized and the owners forced to pay higher salaries to their workers—in his opinion, this might allow fishing, the heart and soul of the outports, to thrive. Farley's vision was in direct conflict not only with Spencer Lake's but also with that of Joey Smallwood, the premier who had by a narrow margin brought Newfoundland into Canadian Confederation. Lake's motto was:

"What's good for me is good for Burgeo." Since the town council was chosen for the most part from among his employees, or his sycophants, he encountered little opposition. . . . The people of the Sou'west Coast, and of Burgeo in particular, were "hauled into the 20th century" so speedily that few of them had any understanding of what was happening to them. The age-old patterns of their lives collapsed in rapid succession. The inner certainties which had sustained them in past generations were evaporating like water spilled on a red-hot stove.

Early in 1965, Farley, who should have known better, made overtures to Smallwood, hoping that the short, ruthless but utterly charming (when he wanted to be) former journalist and union organizer could be made to see reason and return to his early left-wing principles. Farley should have recalled the Badger tragedy of March 1959. In that small town, striking loggers clashed with police officers; one member of the Newfoundland constabulary was clubbed and later died. Smallwood, who had decertified the union a few days before, made the dead man into a martyr. As premier, Smallwood was determined that Newfoundland was not to be "left far behind by the march of time."

As part of an attempt to seduce Smallwood, Farley told him he was seriously considering centring his Newfoundland book—the one which he'd contracted with Atlantic–Little, Brown—on the premier and his struggle to bring his province into Confederation. Smallwood was mightily intrigued but exceedingly coy:

If I may say so without sounding like a gushing schoolgirl or a thoroughly qualified politician, Newfoundland gets distinction from the fact that you are living here and basing some of your writing on us. . . . About the idea of a biography. I don't see how anyone could write as good a book about me as I could do myself, and although that is a pretty quotable statement for a politician to make I do so in the firm belief that the only thing worth writing about me is the effort I made in the campaign to bring Newfoundland into union with Canada. Certainly, I know more about that than anyone else does. However, is there anyone in Canada who wouldn't want a book written about him by Farley Mowat? Of course I would.[8]

Even though Farley had previously made statements against Small-wood, he now attempted to mollify the premier:

[Your flattering comments were] somewhat unexpected. Being a romantic I have been much exercised by the recent, rapid plunge of Newfoundland into the Brave New Yankee World. It can hardly have escaped your notice (or am I flattering *myself*?) that I have frequently, and sometimes rather vehemently, deplored in public the decay of the old Newfoundland and the elder Newfoundlander. I am an apolitical man in the sense that I consider all parties to be tarred with the same ghastly brush of expediency, and I have never been backward in stating my convictions in this matter. But then, if I have at times made intemperate statements about your government, I have done so about every other government which has come within my notice.

Having labelled himself a malcontent capable of "intemperate" statements, Farley told the premier, "I do agree that you are the best man to write your biography and I have always assumed that you would do so when, and if, you should retire. The book which my publishers had in mind would have been more in the nature of a study in change: the sudden thrusting of Newfoundland into the Golden Age. . . . I am happy indeed to leave this field to you and I'm sure you'll do a fascinating job. The fact is that I am a lazy sod, and there are so many books ahead of me that I would like to write that I am always grateful when somebody else writes them first."[9]

The real reason for the brief accord between Smallwood and Farley was *Westviking*. Although prominent archaeologists from the United States and Norway had shown great interest in Viking exploration of Newfoundland, Farley was the first prominent Canadian to turn his hand to the task. Always on the lookout to publicize the Rock—and fully aware of Mowat's status as a celebrity actually living in his province—Smallwood wanted to take advantage of the situation. Farley, who had met the premier in the autumn of 1965 while criss-crossing Canada doing a hundred radio, TV and print interviews—was singled out for special attention, at a state dinner in his honour.

When the invitation came, Farley, as he telegraphed Smallwood, was fearful only of the weather:

I AM FED UP WITH TYPEWRITER AND WOULD WELCOME EXCUSE PLAY TRUANT TO ST. JOHNS EVEN THOUGH YOUR DINNER PLANS SOUND TERRIFYING TO ONE OF MY RETIRING NATURE STOP ONLY PROBLEM IS UNCER-TAINTY WINTER TRANSPORTATION TO AND FROM BUT I MEEKLY LAY THIS DIFFICULTY AT FEET OF QUEENS MINISTERS STOP WOULD YOU WIRE DATE OF THE EVENT SOONEST SINCE THIS HOUR HAS SEVEN DAYS [the public affairs television show] WISHES ME TO MAKE ASS OF MYSELF ON TV FROM ST JOHNS[10]

Farley did not have to worry about transportation: he and Claire were flown to St. John's in a government helicopter to the dinner, which was held in the Memorial University dining hall on March 3, 1966. As it turned out, Smallwood now wanted Farley to write his biography; Farley countered with the suggestion that Smallwood engineer a writer-in-residence post for him at Memorial: "The main advantage to me, apart from the pleasures of St. John's, would be ready access to the available research material. . . . Besides which—Claire yearns for the City Lights. I doubt she was born to be an outporter all her life."[11] But Farley had decided that writing Small-wood's biography was a task he did not want to take on.

From the beginning, Harold Horwood had been deeply skeptical of what he considered to be Farley's attempt to "sleep with the devil":

Watch Joey! Watch the fucker! He has designs on you, and you're not beyond the power of flattery any more than the rest of us. I should say that he wants you for one of two projects:

Either as his Minister of Culture (he has been toying with the idea of a Ministry of Culture, under that or another name).

Or as the author of his biography—perhaps even as the editor of his Life and Works.

Maybe for both.[12]

Farley's assessment of Smallwood was resoundingly negative. He was deeply critical of the man who would

> industrialize at all costs. This meant that all the island's mineral, forest and human resources were to be made available, virtually as gifts, to any foreign industrial entrepreneurs who would agree to exploit them. Smallwood demanded that Newfoundland turn its back on the ocean which had nurtured the islanders through so many centuries.
>
> "Haul up your boats . . . burn your fishing gear!" he shouted during one impassioned speech directed at the outport men. "There'll be three jobs ashore for every one of you. You'll never have to go fishing again!"
>
> Many believed him, for he was a persuasive demagogue, and he had the silver tongue.

A month after the state dinner, Farley flew to Spence Bay in the Northwest Territories, having been commissioned by *Maclean's* magazine to cover the Soosie murder trial. Jack Sissons, who had presided at Kikkik's trial in 1958, was the judge. The charge was that Shooyuk and Aiyaoot had murdered thirty-nine-year-old Soosie on July 15, 1965, at Levesque Harbour. The crown attorney, acting on orders from the Department of Justice, reluctantly brought the charges against the two men, who had shot a deranged, menacing Soosie dead. Once a champion of the rights of her people, Soosie (christened Susannah)—together with members of her band—had been moved as a child, as a young woman and as a middle-aged woman many times on orders from the government in Ottawa in its various schemes to settle her people in "suitable" locations. No spot ever proved to be the right one. Eventually she broke down emotionally and became a threat to members of her immediate family and tribe. Farley described her torment:

> The woman who had struggled so fiercely to preserve her
> people now threatened to become their nemesis. Raging
> through the camp, tearing her hair out in handfuls, screaming
> threats at those she met, she brought a new dimension of terror
> to a people who were at the end of their tether. Picking up her
> baby daughter, she flung the child to the ground. She pursued
> other children, pelting them with rocks. She struck against the
> very stuff of life by destroying the hunting and fishing gear.

Although Aiyaoot was acquitted, the jury found Shooyuk guilty of manslaughter but recommended mercy. In a voice shaking with compassion for the convicted man and contempt for the federal bureaucracy of which he himself was a part, Sissons suspended Shooyuk's sentence and told him, "Try to forget the things that have happened to you and try to live a good and happy life."

In both Newfoundland and the Northwest Territories, Farley was confronted by what he considered the basic inhumanness of all government systems. In large part because Farley had alerted it to the injustices perpetuated against the Aboriginal peoples, the federal government—which had inflicted every Inuit person with an identification number—now took what it considered a more enlightened hand in dealing with indigenous persons. In reality, though, the government either interfered with the lives of these people or overwhelmed them with paternalism. No serious attempt was made to allow the Native peoples of the North—their lives altered for the worse by the white man—to return to their original ways. Similarly, in Newfoundland, Joey Smallwood believed that "progress" was the only way forward; in his view, the island province had to industrialize or be destroyed.

In each instance, Farley's point of view was crystal clear: the indigenous peoples and the outporters required the assistance of their government, but such help had to be on a hands-off basis that allowed each group to retain its character. And in each instance, Farley's words went unheeded.

Upon Farley's return from the Northwest Territories, Jack McClelland, realizing that Farley's interest in the Arctic had been renewed, invited him to write the text for the volume on the Arctic in the lavishly illustrated Canadian Centennial Library series, edited by Pierre Berton. In late July 1966, Farley flew to Churchill in northern Manitoba to board an Otter chartered to take him to thirty-three settlements, a journey of ten thousand miles. Upon his return to Ontario in late August, he spent almost a month at the McClelland cottage at Foote's Bay drafting the book, called *Canada North*.

Unlike his previous books set in the Arctic, *Canada North* (1967), a relatively short text tied to many colour and black-and-white illustrations, is intended as a very general look at various aspects of its large subject (geography, natural history, geology, exploration and Native peoples). Despite the restrictions of space and form, Farley managed to make some controversial remarks in his prologue, called "Myth and Reality":

> This North, this Arctic of the mind, this frigid concept of a flat and formless void of ice and snow congealed beneath the impenetrable blackness of the polar night, is pure illusion. Behind it lies a lost world obscured in drifts of literary drivel, obliterated by blizzards of bravado and buried under an icy weight of obsessive misconceptions. The magnificent reality behind the myth has been consistently rejected by Canadians since the day of our national birth and is rejected still. Through almost a century the Far North has meant to Canadians either a nightmarish limbo or an oppressive polar presence looming darkly over southern Canada and breathing icily down our necks.
>
> . . . The pattern is old and well established. A century after the nation's birth, about three-quarters of the exploration and exploitation of the Canadian North is being carried out by consortiums controlled by American, European and Japanese companies. Military occupation of the North, while nominally a joint undertaking, remains effectively American. Until the middle of the twentieth century almost the *only* Canadians in the Arctic were Indians and Eskimos; but they were people

born to the reality and in any case were, and are, "Canadians" only by courtesy.

Once again, Farley reminds his readers that the Canadian North, both ignored and misunderstood, has never been seen as the repository of anything valuable or priceless—for most Canadians, it is an icy waste-land and a very heavy burden that no one willingly shoulders. Farley's point is that once upon a time the Arctic and its people had functioned well on their own terms, that its delicate ecosystem had been wrecked by the explorers and those who followed them and that the best way to deal with the Arctic was to give it the financial and material resources to renew itself.

At the end of the war, Farley had considered the Union of Soviet Socialist Republics a major threat to world peace; his early awareness of its potential dominance in what became the Cold War had been one of his chief motivating factors in collecting high-tech German military equipment. But after the death of Stalin in 1953 and the rise of the more liberal Khrushchev, many intellectuals in the West— hostile to capitalism—were once again attracted to communism, particularly its defence of workers' rights and its promotion of soli-darity among ordinary peoples worldwide. In 1966, Farley, who was socialist but not communist in his political leanings, was eager to learn how the USSR managed its Arctic territories, painted in the Western press "as a wilderness of trackless forests and snow-covered tundra inhabited mainly by ravening wolves and doomed political prisoners."

Farley also had a number of roubles to spend from the sales of his books in translation there—*Never Cry Wolf* (translated as *Wolves! Please Don't Cry!*) in particular had been an enormous success and had even influenced government policy in the treatment of that species. And since the Soviets did not allow book royalties to be exported, Farley had to use these roubles in the USSR.

The actual invitation came from thirty-five-year-old Yuri Rytkheu on behalf of the Soviet Writers' Union. Yura—the affectionate form of Yuri—is how the Mowats always addressed this writer, with whom, as Farley recalled, he had much in common:

> He was a Chukchee—a member of a native people living in the extreme northeastern corner of Asia almost within sight of Alaska. Born in a *yaranga*—a sod shanty roofed with walrus hide—Yura grew up in a primitive coastal village where he attended the first school to be built in Chukotka. He did so well that he was chosen to go on to higher education which, in his case, meant Leningrad University. Even before graduation he had begun to write, first in his own language and then in Russian. When I met him he was already the author of twelve novels. Erect, a trifle portly, with wide, mobile lips and a pair of horn-rimmed glasses which glittered inscrutably from an impassive face, he had the natural dignity of an Asiatic princeling.

On October 15, 1966, Claire and Farley set sail on the *Aleksandr Pushkin* for Leningrad. During the crossing, Farley completed work on *Canada North*. At the outset, Claire and Farley knew only that they would be sightseeing and meeting with writers in Leningrad and Moscow. Upon his arrival, his Soviet hosts asked Farley what other places he wished to visit. He immediately replied that he had a great longing to see Siberia. He expected that the Soviets would say no, since it was well known even at that time that political prisoners were banished there. He was surprised when his request was quickly granted.

During that visit, the Mowats went to Irkutsk, Yakutsk, the mouth of the Kolyma River, Lake Baikal and Novosibirsk in Siberia, as well as Tbilisi in Georgia. There were impediments, however. Since all airports in the USSR were on Moscow time, they arrived and landed in some places in the middle of the night, where, exhausted, they were received by local officials and expected to eat and drink to the full. Another difficulty was the practice of not heating airplanes until they were in the air. On many occasions, Farley and Claire anxiously awaited the departure of their aircrafts in penetrating coldness.

Almost immediately upon his arrival in Siberia, Farley was

(top) *Farley at Irkutsk, 1966*
(above) *Claire, 1966*

astounded to hear that concerned citizens had banded together to stop the building of a giant cellulose and wood-chemical combine on the south shore of Lake Baikal: "In the Soviet Union, that closed society where, so we are told, the voice of the individual is never heard, there arose a thunder of protests from individuals in every part of the land. . . . To my western mind," Farley observed, "the scope of the victory seemed staggering." The wooden houses of Irkutsk were a moving sight: "long streets of them, even near the centre of the city. They were beautifully constructed of squared logs, and many stood three stories high. Each was a work of loving labour and of art, decorated around doors and windows and under the eaves with scrolls and fretwork."

In Siberia, Farley beheld a society far different from the one he had read about for many years. Individuals could protest meaningfully against bureaucracy: the ecology of Lake Baikal had been preserved. The glorious architecture of the past was allowed to survive even though Siberia was in the process of being transformed into a viable manufacturing and industrial complex.

There were many moments of comic drama, such as the time in Georgia when Sasha, one of Mowats' interpreters, twice leapt precipitously from their car to be sick. Each time, Farley attempted to help him, and each time, as Claire later told Farley, he had left her at risk:

> The first time you got out, the Georgian interpreter grabbed me as if I was his long lost love and kissed me so hard I nearly suffocated. I thought I was going to be strangled. Then you came back and I had a chance to catch my breath and collect my wits. I didn't want to say anything to you, because . . . well, it would have been embarrassing. Then, before I could stop you, you jumped out again. I was just going to jump after you when old pointy-beard turned around, grinning like a goat, and pushed his paw up under my skirt. It took me two seconds to get out of the car but they were the longest two seconds in my life. Georgian men! Don't you dare get out of arm's reach again until we leave this place!

Farley's kilt attracted a great deal of attention when he wore it, but he did not remove his underpants in public during this journey, which included visits to state farms, cooperatives and universities, as well as the obligatory concerts and ballet performances.

The most memorable encounter in Siberia was with thirty-six-year-old Victor Nazarov, "moon-faced, tug-voiced, hairy as a mammoth, strong as a cave man and utterly and absolutely indefatigable." As Farley recalled, "he took Claire and me into his ebullient heart with such rampant enthusiasm that he nearly killed us both." Born of Russian peasant stock in western Siberia, Victor and his family were banished to the Aldan goldfields of Yakutia after his father had a disagreement with the Stalin regime. After his father died in the Second World War, Victor supported his family by working as a driver-mechanic; he also became a champion weightlifter. He subsequently took correspondence courses, which eventually allowed him entry into the university at Sverdlovsk, where he graduated with a degree in industrial transportation. After joining the Communist party in 1955, he ran the truck transport network during the building of the diamond mining centre of Mirny, and in 1962 he was dispatched to the mouth of the Kolyma to take charge of the construction of the new Arctic town of Tchersky, where the Mowats encountered him.

Upon the Mowats' arrival at Tchersky, Victor heaved Farley and Claire into his tiny Bobyk, a jeep-like small car, and while they careened at fifty miles per hour over non-existent roads, he provided them with a nerve-wracking tour of the settlement:

APARTMENT HOUSE FOR FIFTY FAMILIES GOES THERE. . . . THAT IS BEGINNING OF BIGGEST SCHOOL IN SIBERIA. . . . PALACE OF SPORT WE ARE BUILDING HERE. . . . POWER STATION OVER THERE. . . . FARLEE! OVER THERE WE MAKE NEW AIRPORT—BIG ENOUGH FOR JET PLANES—AND CLAIRE! LOOK THERE! WE MAKE NEW NURSERY SCHOOL.

Although Victor was committed to the remaking of Siberia as a viable industrial unit in the modern USSR, he also took Farley and Claire on a helicopter flight to visit a huge reindeer farm, where the nomadic peoples were in charge of the breeding and maintenance of the animals. Farley was given a scroll declaring him to be an "Honorary Breeder of Reindeer."

For Farley, the fact that Victor Nazarov's mission was compatible with a policy of allowing the indigenous peoples to retain their ancient way of life proved that the Soviets—unlike the Canadians—were on the right track. He held this belief even though he realized that the face of Siberia was being irrevocably transformed: "*Sibir*, the Sleeping Land, the Void of Darkness is no more. Where, so recently, the Siberian tiger, the wild reindeer, Baikal seals, Yukagir, Chukchee, Yakut and all forms of life, obeyed the implacable but impartial rule of that omnipresent force we refer to vaguely (and so often superciliously) as Nature; now there is a new ruler, and a new law. One of the last remaining primaeval regions of the earth is being rapidly re-shaped. Nature, who was the mother, has been relegated to the role of step-child." Although he was skeptical of the new creed of technology and the godhead of the machine, Farley nevertheless saw a glimmer of hope in the way the Soviets dealt with their indigenous peoples:

> One of the most exciting and heartening things I found in Siberia was the growing tendency to reject, or at least to question, the mechanistic blueprint for the future of our species. And the genesis for this rebellion (for that is what it is) indubitably lies with the native races; those once forgotten Small Peoples who, under Soviet rule, have not only been enabled to survive as strong and viable segments of society but who have been permitted to retain their deep and subtle awareness of themselves as natural men. *Their* roots have not been severed. They remain a proud and integral part of the continuum of life.

Claire and Farley returned to Canada on a non-stop flight on Aeroflot from Moscow to Montreal. But their experience in Siberia left them far from prepared for the savagery they soon witnessed in Burgeo.

★   ★   ★

Farley and Claire remained in Montreal for two weeks while Farley edited the tapes of a series of radio talks on the Canadian Arctic he had prepared for CBC Northern Services. Their crossing of the Cabot Strait to Port aux Basques from North Sydney took a storm-filled twelve hours rather than the usual six. Their final piece of transport home—aboard the shabby, old *Burgeo*—was uneventful; they saw a few whales feeding in the usual places.

Having been absent from Burgeo for long stretches of time in 1966, Farley was forcibly struck in January 1967 by how much had changed since he had first settled there. Thirty-seven cars and trucks rattled over the few miles of goat tracks which led nowhere; there were a few snowmobiles; non-returnable pop and beer bottles littered the shore. A fish-meal reduction plant spewed out noxious odours. Telephones had become part of the way of life. That January, Farley told his father that he was getting ready to say "farewell for aye to Buggaree. We really must depart this place. The atmosphere gets gloomier and gloomier as TV and cars and probably a road sweep in upon it. I think we might try Nova Scotia or maybe New Brunswick or, possibly, even Prince Edward Island."[13]

Farley's farewell was speeded up considerably when, on January 20, a seventy-foot-long female fin whale became trapped when she followed a school of herring into the sea cove called Aldridges Pond on the outskirts of Burgeo. Five plant workers began shooting at the whale with rifles on the following day. On the third day, a Sunday, when Farley and Claire were out watching bald eagles, more than thirty persons were using the whale for target practice while a large crowd watched from the shore. On the fifth day, two fishermen told the Mowats about the trapped whale. All of a sudden, Farley was aware of a "conspiracy of silence"; before this, their friends and neighbours had been "ready, not to say eager, to keep us informed of everything that happened in Burgeo."

Immediately committed to saving the whale, Farley found little or no support from the management of the fish plant, the federal fisheries office or the local RCMP constable. In desperation, Farley called the Canadian Press office in Toronto, where the CBC picked up the story and sent a crew to cover the event. Joey Smallwood, in response to Farley's plea for assistance, sent two telegrams:

DELIGHTED TO BE ABLE TO TELL YOU MY COLLEAGUES HAVE ACCORDED MY REQUEST THAT WE PAY UP TO ONE THOUSAND DOLLARS TO THE FISHERMEN OF BURGEO TO ENABLE THEM TO SUPPLY HERRING FOR YOUR WHALE STOP WOULD YOU UNDERTAKE TO ORGANIZE CARE AND FEEDING OF YOUR CATCH

I HAVE THE PLEASURE AND HONOUR TO INFORM YOU THAT YOU ARE APPOINTED KEEPER OF THE WHALE STOP THE OFFICIAL DOCUMENT RECITING YOUR APPOINT- MENT WILL BE FORWARDED IN DUE COURSE

Although Smallwood had been trying for some time to revive the whale hunting industry in Newfoundland, he knew that his best interests, as far as public relations were concerned, resided with supporting Farley. The premier had a special genius for manipulating tricky situations.

Singularly lacking in this regard himself, Farley suddenly found himself at odds with his neighbours. Particularly bitter was his recol- lection of how he was shunned when he went to the Pond to tend to the whale: "Some people averted their eyes as they passed our dory. I do not think this was because of any guilt they may have felt—and many of them *did* feel guilty—it was because *I* had shamed *them*. . . . The stranger in their midst had spoken his heart and displayed his rage and scorn. We could no longer pretend we understood each other." Although many of the villagers were sympathetic to the whale and her unhappy plight, they were horrified by the unfavourable notice given to Burgeo by the outside world; they also felt that they were rendered guilty by association, branded as a group of blood-thirsty yahoos. Although the maiming of the whale stopped, she would not feed on the herring with which she was provided to try to persuade her to return to where she came from; she was also badly infected by her wounds and died before antibiotics could be administered.

(top) *The trapped whale, Burgeo, 1967*
(above) *The dead whale, Burgeo, 1967*

To his father, Farley summarized the sorry situation:

Whatever else you may do, and you no doubt will, I beg of you, take heed, to be warned and do NOT ever take up with a Fin Whale. It is a heavy task. It has all sorts of unexpected concomi-tants. Nobody seems to gain much from the experience, although it may be assumed that the bloodthirsty bastards of Burgeo who filled her full of lead will smart for a while. They have had a pretty good national roasting, and when I am finished, they will be charred.

So, we lost her. I should have known we would. But I just didn't realize the damage she had sustained. When I examined the corpse it was riddled. I should think she carried up to 800 rounds of high velocity slugs, mostly army issue .303, and she survived THAT for ten days before septicaemia killed her. She was also, so the experts say, probably pregnant and would have calved in a month or two if she had lived.

The whole affair has pretty well disgusted me with Burgeo. And, likewise, I think Burgeo has had about enough of me. So be it.

The aftermath is dreadful. I would guess I will have a total of ten thousand letters from all over the bleeding world to answer. . . . As a small revenge the worthy butchers have hauled the corpse to Rencontre Island, in front of Messers and into my favourite little harbour of a summer's day. There we shall have to dynamite the monstrous body which already can be smelled within a two mile range.[14]

Although Farley alienated himself—and felt alienated—from the townspeople of Burgeo, he took pains not to blame them for what had happened. In his re-creation of the first shots fired upon the help-less mammal in A Whale for the Killing, he denounces the corrupting influences of the world "away":

Although these men had all been born on the Sou'west Coast, they had all spent some years either in Canada or the United

States. Returning home for one reason or another, they had rejected the vocations of their fisherman forefathers and had instead sought wage employment at the plant as mechanics, tradesmen and supervisors. They were representative of the new Newfoundlanders envisaged by Premier Smallwood—progressive, modern men who were only too anxious to deny their outport heritage in favour of adopting the manners and mores of 20th-century industrial society. . . .

The five men wasted no time. Some dropped to their knees, levering shells into their rifles as they did so. Others stood where they were and hurriedly took aim. The crash of rifle fire began to echo from the cliffs enclosing the Pond and, as an undertone, there came the flat, satisfying thunk of bullets striking home in the living flesh.

For Farley, the tragedy of the trapped whale was a deeply human one: "The whale was not alone in being trapped. We were all trapped with her. If the natural patterns of her life had been disrupted, then so had ours. An awesome mystery had intruded into the closely circumscribed order of our lives; one that we terrestrial bipeds could not fathom, and one, therefore, that we would react against with instinctive fear, violence and hatred. This riddle from the deeps was the measure of humanity's unquenchable ignorance of life. This impenetrable secret, which had become the core of our existence in this place, was a mirror in which we saw our own distempered faces . . . and they were ugly." Once again, humankind had shown itself incapable of protecting the natural resources it claimed was entrusted to it. In Farley's mind, there was a stark contrast between what he had seen in Siberia a few months before and what he had just witnessed in his native country.

In his prescient, opportunistic way, Jack McClelland smelled a best-selling book. He told Peter Davison, "Farley's next book will probably be about the goddamn whale . . . a huge finwhale—it may run to 75 feet and about 80 tons and is possibly pregnant—trapped itself in a small natural aquarium near Burgeo. It went in at high tide over a shelf and it now appears there is no natural way for it to get out. Farley has been appointed Keeper of the Whale by Joey Smallwood and is administering a fund to feed it."[15] Sometimes grossly insensitive, Jack, after the death of the whale, made a joke of the situation: "I think the plan for freeing the whale was fantastic, but not nearly as imaginative as mine. My own scheme involved a huge plastic tank in which we would have floated the whale up to Expo. My theory was that at a dollar a shot we would have cleared thirty million dollars at Expo. The cost of getting the whale up there might have been two and a half million, so we could have netted twenty-seven and a half million which, as a matter of fact, I could use right now."[16]

Even the more empathetic Davison, desperate to get Farley started on a worthwhile new project, could not resist. Having read about the whale in the *New York Times*, he wondered if it could be the subject of a children's book. Then he changed his mind: "I think I may have been wrong in suggesting that a separate book should be written about the whale. I can in fact imagine the whale episode as being beautifully incorporated in *The Water Dog*. What would interest the Water Dog more than a whale? The whale could take its place in the saga of the Water Dog just as the owls were part of Mutt's story."[17] A bit later, Davison offered more frank advice: "Do you really want to write a scientific, as it were, book on the cetaceans? I think you might well find it a bore. . . . That's my advice, for what it's worth. I think now, as I have thought for some time, that your most fruitful next step, both for the short run and the long haul, is to write *The Water Dog*, or at any rate a book about Newfoundland and its people. You may have forgotten that you are very good with people, uncanny in fact. I think the reason you want to write about whales is that they can't write back."[18]

The irrepressible, taunt-filled Max Wilkinson, who still sold the occasional short piece for Farley, informed him he had "turned on my telly for the news and got a very good picture of you looking over the biggest landlocked salmon I've ever seen. Unfortunately the sound department of my boob tube was mute so I could not get any of the details. Is the thing a pet? Was the water your private loch? If you tagged the brute, Farley, and I hook him off Shelter Island next summer I'll send you a piece of his liver."[19]

*　　*　　*

Just when Farley's time in Burgeo was winding down, he finally found the right vehicle for the Newfoundland book that had proven so elusive.

When John de Visser immigrated to Canada from the Netherlands at the age of twenty-two, he worked in banking and retail advertising. Ten years younger than Farley, tall, outspoken, gruff but deeply amiable, he became a colleague of Claire's when they both worked at Simpson-Sears, where he pasted up flyers and other promotional material. His big break as a photographer came in 1957–58 when *Maclean's* printed sixteen pages of his colour photos; he became a full-time photographer in 1959.

In 1965, during a visit to St. John's, de Visser spotted Farley and a woman getting into a taxi. He followed them in his rental car, anxious to introduce himself to the famous writer. De Visser was amazed when it was Claire who stepped out of the taxi. After shaking hands with him, she introduced him to Farley. During that first encounter, Farley and de Visser talked of the possibility of working together on a book. Later, in 1966, he wrote to Farley, "While it has been some time since our chance meeting and consequent few happy hours in St. John's, they are nevertheless just as clearly remembered as if they were last week. . . . How is the Newfoundland project coming? I would still love to be at least part of it, if it should come to pass. How about getting somebody interested in a first class combined text and photo book of the place?"[20]

Subsequently, de Visser visited the Mowats at Burgeo, which he found magically removed from the twentieth century, a place filled with superstitions. He recalled that the local children considered him to be the "bogey man" simply because he was a stranger from away. Both children and adults would walk into snowbanks rather than confront him on a path. Even though Farley was distraught at the "progress" made in Burgeo by 1967, de Visser considered it still to be an exotic place which offered his eye all kinds of opportunity for stunning photographs. In 1967 he was staying with the Mowats at the tail end of the whale episode. Farley, aware that he himself would soon have to depart Burgeo, suggested that he and de Visser think of a collaborative project celebrating the uniqueness of the Rock.

Although de Visser's photographs were taken before Farley's text was written, Farley took notes while they travelled the south coast of Newfoundland in February and March 1967.

The trip for Farley was a sad one, made even more poignant by an encounter in a warm, comfortable kitchen of a fisherman's home in the village of François. Farley and de Visser had spent most of the day photographing the men hand-lining the cod from dories that veered wildly in gales of winter wind. The talk that evening was about the future.

> After a while there was silence; it was the silence of men who, for the first time in their lives and, perhaps, for the first time in the lives of their people, were experiencing the ultimate bewilderment that had come upon them with recognition of the truth that they were completely helpless to save themselves.
>
> The woman brought a pot of fresh tea to the table where we sat and filled our mugs. As she returned to her seat by the stove to begin combing her daughter's hair, her husband broke the silence.
>
> "It's been fine you came to visit us. I hopes your snaps turn out just what you was after, and that you'll make a good voyage out of them—a prosperous voyage, you know. But still and all, I'm wondering could you, maybe, do one thing for we? Could you, do you think, say how it was with us? We wouldn't want it thought, you understand, that we never tried the hardest as was in us to make a go of things. We'd like for everyone to know we never would have left the places we was reared, but . . . we . . . was . . . drove! Aye Jesus, Jesus God, but we was drove!"

The elegiac poignancy of this passage—its lament for a way of life passing away—reflects in large part Farley's own feelings about the prospect of being "drove" away from a way of life that had given him great pleasure and peace.

That July, after house hunting in Ontario, Farley and Claire returned to Burgeo in order to pack up and set sail in *Happy Adventure* for Port Hope via the Bras d'Or lakes, the Northumberland Strait,

Gaspé and Expo 67. True to itself, the ship proved to be completely mercurial. When Farley became convinced it would decide to sink, it proved resolute; as soon as he became certain of its good health, it would precipitously determine to commit suicide.

For Farley, Ontario was very much second best, a place to which he would return, but with a real sense of defeat. At first, house-hunting proved fruitless: "Scoured Cobourg and Bowmanville and found them hopeless. Scoured Port Hope and at the last minute (Monday morning) found a house we really liked. . . . The Hope Chest, on John Street. Very old brick house, once a doctor's home, right on the street, right downtown, no neighbours except a tailor and the Loyal Orange Order."

This spacious but cosy 140-year-old house had many wonderful touches: a grand staircase, a fireplace and multiple guest rooms. In the upstairs bathroom over the toilet, there was a print of Edward VII in the uniform of colonel-in-chief of the 1st Prussian Dragoons of the Guard, while a portrait of Queen Victoria scowled over the tub. The downstairs washroom was crammed with books on polar exploration. Although there was an office on the ground floor, Farley could not work there. For three winters, he wrote on a tailor's table in an unused loft he rented nearby. Like all the houses inhabited by Farley and Claire, 25 John Street was comfortably and pleasantly furnished. However, they always lived simply, without the least hint of pretentiousness.

In an attempt to preserve cordial relations with his father, Farley had assured him whose side he was on: "Anonymity inside the big city. Potential visitors can visit without danger of being surprised. Except, of course, by PDH [Helen]. But I laid down the law on that one. 'Bug me, and we'll move the hell away from Port Hope in a hurry.' She got the message—I trust. I may have to hammer it home a bit, but what will you?"[21] Of course, Farley could have said he would not take sides and left his parents to deal with their conflicts. Consciously, this was his desire; unconsciously, he continued to act as a co-conspirator with his father against his mother.

In moving back to Port Hope, Farley now had to deal delicately with his estranged parents. Although husband and wife had a legal separation spelling out Angus's financial obligations to Helen, there was much bickering between them. Helen required money to pay for other expenses, but feeling much beleaguered, Angus would stick to the letter of the law. Farley now had the thankless task of acting as the referee between the sparring parties, although he found PDH difficult to deal with; he also had to keep his negative feelings about Barbara in check. At one point he attempted to position himself on his father's side after raising the question of divorce with his mother, much as Angus had petitioned Fran on his behalf:

> H. is not disagreeable but pointed out that this might take several years. Meantime, I think you need the new separation agreement to set her mind at rest. It should spell out the assured income she will get after your death. . . . I also explained to her, in some heat, that you haven't got any money, that you are supporting Barbara and yourself. . . . The general consensus seemed to be that you were filthy rich and squandering vast amounts on booze, women and boats. Hmmmm. . . . She's woolly—period.[22]

For Farley, moving back to Ontario also meant having to deal with Fran more frequently. Since divorce papers had never been served on her, Fran considered herself to be still married to Farley. More than a year earlier, in January 1966, Angus had reported after a visit to Palgrave that he was not sure of Fran's reaction to an article in the *Toronto Star* which had referred to Claire as Mrs. Farley Mowat:

> No chance to talk to her alone, and I doubt she'd have mentioned it, nor do I know how to get it mentioned, anyhow. But I wonder if it's of much significance anyhow? After all, Fran knows, must know, that it was she who made it impossible for you to stay with her; and she must know that a man doesn't live wifeless. So, though it may be unfeeling to say it in open words, she has only brought it on her own head. . . . The more I reflect upon it the less I feel troubled about what Fran may *think* or *feel*. What does trouble me though is what Sandy may think or feel—or surmise—or ponder.

Angus advised Farley to make certain that there were no more articles about Claire that Sandy could read until Farley had told both his sons that he had remarried: "So there I am, telling somebody what to do. Please don't feel you need to express your gratitude. I know all about that." Although Angus's advice might seem to be anti-Claire, this was not the case: "Plainly, Claire gave you a good hand holding when you needed it pretty badly. So I love Claire."[23]

As far as Claire was concerned, some of Farley's conflicted feelings about Sandy and David would be alleviated by the move back to Ontario. Back in February 1966 she had told Angus, "My God but I wish Farley would get those kids out of there [Palgrave] once in a while. But he's all wound up in guilt complexes and won't make any kind of a move that might 'upset' Frances."[24] Only at Expo 67 in Montreal did Farley inform his sons he was divorced from Fran and introduce them to Claire. When Farley drove the children back to Palgrave, they immediately told their mother what they had learned. A very upset Fran ordered the children to go after the car and bring Farley back so that she could confront him. A reluctant and dejected Farley returned to the house with the children. Once again, Fran and Farley exchanged recriminations.

At Burgeo, Farley had confronted many difficulties, particularly the sad death of the fin whale; in Ontario, he felt smothered in emotional quicksands.

11

Wayfarer

1968–1970

FOR Farley and Claire, Port Hope was at best a compromise. As Claire told Angus and Barbara, "Living this close to the centre of things has undoubtedly had its benefits in terms of Farley's work. . . . Several good interviews he has had, some personal appearances he's made, would not have been possible had we lived in Burgeo still. But . . . when will he ever get time to write?" She answered her own question—somewhat tentatively: "Winter is the time to write. I still think we should be spending our winters in the Arctic or some other cosy place where there is no temptation to do anything but stay indoors and work."[1] For many years, Farley had written in the colder autumn and winter months and revised in the spring and summer; that pattern continued in Ontario, but he was no longer as completely cut off from civilization as he would have liked. For both Mowats, the loss of Burgeo was an amputation, a severing from a style of life with which they had grown comfortable.

In a letter to her father-in-law, Claire declared, "I know these are

Farley's best years—best that is in terms of earning a living, which is a matter that cannot be overlooked altogether. I wonder if either of us would be happier if we had stayed in Burgeo, or some place like it, hidden from the world except for Farley's books which would appear intermittently. . . . It is not easy to live the way we do. We have to play it by ear all the time. . . . And what of Port Hope, our compromise home? It is still the best bet, I suppose."[2] One advantage to living in Port Hope came in 1976 when Farley's elderly aunt, Fran Thomson, aged seventy-eight and long retired from the salvage company, began working as his secretary (she undertook this responsibility for eight years). Shrewd, precise and energetic, she answered correspondence and prepared Farley's manuscripts for submission to publishers.

Away from Newfoundland, Farley imagined his former home in more romantic terms than he had while living there. Undoubtedly the most lyrical of all Farley's writings, *This Rock Within the Sea: A Heritage Lost* (1968) conveys vividly the sheer physical beauty of the island province.

> Newfoundland is of the sea. Poised like a mighty granite stopper over the bell-mouth of the Gulf of St. Lawrence, it turns its back upon the greater continent, barricading itself behind the three-hundred-mile-long rampart that forms its hostile western coast. . . . Until a few generations ago the coasts of the island were all that really mattered. The high, rolling plateaus of the interior, darkly coniferous-wooded to the north but bone-bare to the south, remained an almost unknown hinterland. Newfoundland was then, and it remains, a true sea-province, perhaps akin to that other lost sea-province called Atlantis; but Newfoundland, instead of sinking into the green depths, was somehow blown adrift to fetch up against our shores, and there to remain in unwilling exile, always straining back toward the east.

In the last hours before Confederation in 1949, "the Coast was a land of vigorous men and women . . . quick, confident, eminently successful survivors." Into this paradisaical setting came a serpent, one Joseph Smallwood, "once a union organizer and once a pig farmer, but always and forever a political animal; combining messianic visions with the essential ruthlessness of an Alexander, or a Huey Long." King Joey "tried to transform his island kingdom into an industrial principality. . . . 'Off with the old and on with the new' was his guiding principle, and he applied it with a vigour and a haste that made no reckoning of the psychic and spiritual havoc it created in the lives of his own people."

De Visser's photographs, a perfect accompaniment to Mowat's text, emphasize a primitive way of life of mythological proportions; together, text and illustrations are reminiscent of Canadian-born Robert Flaherty's documentary film from 1943, *Man of Aran*, which celebrates a pristine, sometimes almost savage way of life, cut off from the modern world.

Although deeply impressed by the book's achievement, Jack McClelland, as he told Peter Davison, was unsure of its potential in the marketplace:

> The real problem with this one is cost versus market. Although it is going to be a beautiful and impressive book, and in that sense is worth publishing, it is something that we clearly shouldn't be doing except as an indulgence as far as Mowat is concerned. He is most anxious to have the book published, partly because of what it represents, but also I think to help his friend John de Visser achieve further recognition. . . . We estimate a very small market here for a number of reasons not the least of them being that Farley has effectively killed any hope of selling copies to Joey Smallwood and there are no other special markets for the book. Newfoundland itself is a hopelessly small market with only about two bookstores of any consequence in the whole province and even they don't really deserve the name bookstores. . . . I feel badly about this book. I think it is a good one. The text is well done. The pictures are superb, but it's a long time since we have faced a book with comparable marketing problems.[3]

To a civil servant in the Newfoundland government, McClelland was even more candid: "Delighted that you liked the Mowat–

de Visser book. I was very pleased with it although I do, to a degree, share your reservation about the Mowat point of view. Migod you should have seen the original draft. I love him dearly but his opinions are sometimes hard to live with."[4] McClelland was wrong about the book's marketability, though—it became a huge best-seller in Canada. And in the United States, where expectations were not large, the book achieved enormous critical success.

De Visser was not to be Farley's only collaborator. At a party in Port Hope, Farley met and later became friends with the painter and printmaker David Blackwood, twenty years his junior, who was teaching at Trinity College School in Port Hope. Born to a seafaring family in the outport of Wesleyville, Blackwood had already developed the stark, masterful style in which he would render his mother's birthplace, Bragg's Island. Like the Mowats, he was fascinated by the mummers, the subjects of some of his best work. Thinking of a possible collaboration along the lines of that with de Visser, Farley met the painter in St. John's and took him by car to Wesleyville.

Davison, meanwhile, very committed to Farley though he was, was continually dismayed by his wayward author's refusal to listen to reason. When *The Polar Passion: The Quest for the North Pole* (1967), the second volume in the *Top of the World* series (the anthologies of writings by Arctic explorers), was severely criticized in *The New Yorker*, he curtly observed, "I won't say I told you so."[5] Peter had been at pains to call Farley's attention to the fact that his vehement criticism of Robert Peary, one of America's great heroes—criticism manifested in giving him comparatively little space in the anthology and in supporting the counter-claims (largely discredited by many scholars) of Frederick Cook to be the first explorer to reach the North Pole—gave some reviewers the chance to claim the anthology was not an accurate, unbiased collection of Arctic documents.

Early in 1968, wanderlust—very reminiscent of Farley's earlier attempts to run away from domestic life—reasserted itself. Briefly, to McClelland's utter dismay, Farley considered writing a book subsidized by a left-wing, anti-Smallwood consortium about the controversial Churchill Falls, Labrador, development scheme whereby hydroelectric power was sold by the government of Newfoundland to Hydro-Québec. McClelland told Davison, "I thought he would reject the idea out of hand but he hasn't. He continues to baffle me. A couple of weeks ago he was complaining that his income was getting too great, but now his essential financial insecurity comes to the surface again and if they are prepared to pay a big enough dollar, he is going to go for this project."[6]

When the Churchill Falls project fell through, Farley, in an attempt to find a suitable new subject, accepted an invitation to monitor the controversial seal hunt in the Gulf of St. Lawrence. In February, he observed seal herds from the air. On March 12, he told Sandy he was flying to the Magdalen Islands to witness the hunt there: "The seal hunt opens on Monday, and I will be flying over the ice in a helicopter with the inspector from the Society for the Prevention of Cruelty to Animals. We will land wherever we see a crew of men killing seals, and photograph them, and see they are not butchering the young seals."[7] Almost three weeks later he told his son, "The seal hunt was interesting. I didn't fall in once but three photographers who were on the ice all went seal-hunting, though not on purpose. The seals must have been amused. It was pretty gory in places but not nearly as bad as we have been told it would be. I felt just as sorry for the sealers as for the seals. Anyway, it looks like I might write a book about the whole story of the sealing—way back a couple of hundred years to the present."[8]

On a sailing ship, accompanied by John de Visser, Farley later witnessed what was supposed to be the "most tightly regulated operation of its kind anywhere in the world." What he observed was frightening: "On one occasion, de Visser watched a hunter club his way through a patch of about thirty pups, killing six and wounding a number of others before leaping to another pan and abandoning his victims. On two occasions, I saw pups returning to consciousness while being skinned alive. When I remonstrated with a ship sealer for clubbing to death a female that had elected to try to save her pup, he grinned at me and replied, 'We got to protect ourselves, now don't we?'" In April, Farley sailed aboard the Norwegian sealer *Brandal* while Canadian government scientists collected samples from a moulting patch of harp seals.

For Farley, the seal hunt raised two issues. First, there was the wanton cruelty inflicted on the animals, although some of the hunters acted professionally in carrying out their tasks. Second, there was the real possibility that the number of animals killed in the annual "harvest" was so great that it could lead to the destruction of some seal species.

Part of the winter of 1968 and much of the summer of 1969 were spent at Indian Summer, the cottage near Brighton on Lake Ontario, which had been purchased from Helen in 1968. Angus told a friend, "Farley says he has to have quiet. No telephone, no mail, no people."[9] On a trip to Newfoundland that summer of 1969, Farley worked on a film for the CBC, *Voyage to the Sea of Ice.*

During his visit to the Gulf of St. Lawrence in the winter of early 1968, Farley had encountered Brian Davies, a thirty-eight-year-old Welsh-born immigrant, who supported himself as a student teacher while working part-time for the New Brunswick Society of the SPCA.

> During the years that followed [Farley later recounted], Davies was to find himself pilloried by government authorities, the sealing industry, and some of the media as a self-seeking, self-serving fanatic of dubious morality and questionable ethics. At the same time he was being elevated to the god head by animal lovers everywhere, who saw him as a latter-day St. Francis of Assisi. Davies waged his war to save the seals mainly by manipulating the media, and he did this with such skill that, almost single-handedly, he transformed the image of the dark-eyed, soulful-seeming whitecoat [a young seal with white fur] into an international symbol of revolt against the old established, merciless and selfish view of non-human life. Eschewing reason, he frankly played on emotions in the belief that this was the only way to defeat the forces arrayed against him. These forces

responded not only by savage vilification of the man and his supporters, but by attempting to bury him, together with the truth about the seal slaughter, under an avalanche of persiflage.

Farley's admiration of Davies was partly based on the fact that he himself, an astute manipulator of the media, had been treated to similar "savage vilification" by establishment forces since the time he published *People of the Deer*. Nonetheless, he soon placed his proposed book on the seal hunt on the back burner.

In 1968, Farley's attention was focused more on another kind of destruction—the Vietnam War. The year before, he had spoken out against the American side in the book *Authors Take Sides on Vietnam*. To show support for the North Vietnamese, Farley now made tentative arrangements to travel to Hanoi. Once this arrangement had been fixed, his friend Ivan Shpedko, the Russian ambassador to Canada, warned him that it was too dangerous to go. Claire put a humorous turn on the situation in a letter to Angus and Barbara: "Still I suppose if Farley was slaughtered by the Yanks he could become a folk hero in Canada, something like General Brock."[10]

In March 1968, the *Ottawa Citizen* reported that Farley had declined an invitation to command the Colonel J. Sutherland Brown Volunteer Brigade, the purpose of which was to defend Canada against an invasion from the United States. This Regina-based group had arisen in response to U.S. Strategic Air Command (SAC) bombers that were making training flights at five hundred feet over the Saskatchewan prairie. When the group asked Farley for advice, he provided it:

> I suggested they acquire a quantity of the large red balloons used by weather recording stations, hide them in convenient gullies and coulees along the flight paths followed by the bombers, and release them at the appropriate moments. I estimated that the sudden appearance of these great crimson globes wafting upward in front of them would make even the most case-hardened

bomber pilots claw for altitude. It followed with iron logic that, if they could not fly low without having the wits scared out of them, they would buzz off home and leave Saskatchewan to the wheat farmers, gophers, and grasshoppers.

Farley refused the command not because—as was later reported—the volunteers refused to use live ammo but because he was engaged in other projects. Although Farley was a great admirer of the one-time chief of the Canadian defence staff Colonel "Buster" Brown (1881–1951) and his hatred of the United States, he later reflected, "I like to talk a good battle." The *Ottawa Citizen* article also revealed that Farley once claimed to having shot his .22 rifle at SAC planes flying five miles above his backyard in Burgeo.

Farley certainly talked a good battle in the essay "Letter to My Son," which he contributed to *The New Romans: Candid Canadian Opinions of the U.S.*, an anthology edited by the poet Al Purdy and published in Edmonton in 1968 by the strongly nationalist bookseller-turned-publisher Mel Hurtig. Responding to the actions of the Americans in Vietnam, the volume, with contributions by Mordecai Richler, Margaret Laurence, Margaret Atwood, Michael Ondaatje, Robert Fulford, James M. Minifie and many others, attempted to provide, as Purdy put it, "strong meat for a public accustomed to hasty disavowals of anti-Americanism on the part of our politicians and daily newspapers."[11]

Still badly stinging from his exchanges with Joey Smallwood, Farley re-creates a conversation with him: " 'What the U.S. wants, it will get,' he told me. 'And if we don't give them what they want, they'll take it anyway. And what they want—is most of what we've got.' " Infuriated both by the American takeover of Canada and by the war in Southeast Asia, Farley pulls no punches in attacking the United States and its supporters within Canada:

My naivety—if such it was—lay in my continuing conviction that the *people* of this country would not forever continue to acquiesce in piecemeal betrayal of themselves and of their country. . . .

I ask you to consider the reality behind the American claims

. . . to being the world's greatest defenders of democracy. Democracy? My God, it is to laugh . . . but bitter laughter it must be since demonstrably the United States is currently engaged in almost every form of domestic and external brutality, aggrandizement, degradation of the individual, and destruction of freedom which, so the U.S.A. maintains with a straight face, are the *singular* hallmarks of the beast called communism.

And what, you say, is this tirade in aid of? Well, it is intended to ensure that you harbour no further illusions about living in a democracy or of being protected by one. . . . You must rid your-self of this delusion because, as I see things, there is no guarantee that the privileged position presently enjoyed by Canadians as "most-favoured serfs" will last. The day is near when the Yankees will see no further need to pamper us—they'll own us outright.

Back home at Port Hope, Farley had to be more involved than he wanted with his parents' ongoing disputes, as Claire told a friend: "We've had a few problems with PDH this week past. She has found out about Angus & Barbara's new house [at Northport near Picton and thus close to Belleville] and is outraged that Angus should choose to move so close to home, as it were. She's also convinced that this is one more of Angus's plots to swindle her out of her money. We've explained repeatedly that it was bought with Barbara's money but she just doesn't want to believe it. We've both listened to long earfuls over the phone. We both feel sorry for her, but what can we do?"[12]

Another problem in the autumn of 1968 was Harold Horwood's intense dislike of *This Rock Within the Sea*. Motivated to some degree by his strong conviction that Farley was treading on his personal turf, Horwood was also appalled by what he considered the book's overly romantic and sentimental view of his native province. He responded by writing a blistering review, which, naturally enough, aggrieved Farley. The friendship cooled considerably and was set back on track only when Farley penned a tit-for-tat negative notice of Horwood's *Newfoundland* (1969), a traveller's guide to the province made up from a recycling of the writer's magazine articles and broadcasts.

Farley came against yet another writing challenge in the autumn of 1968. He had been working hard on the water dog book. Albert had even assisted his master that August by "testing out my theories in the water. Yesterday he dived to a depth of ten feet, and the day before he learned to rescue people (me) by hauling the bodies to shore with his tail."[13] In part to accommodate research on the water dog book and in part to begin a dynasty, Farley and Claire acquired Victoria (Vicky), a purebred black Labrador puppy. She did not get off to a good start with Albert, who bit her on the nose when she walked into his dinner plate. However, once reassured he was still top dog, he grudgingly accepted his new companion.

Peter Davison was not pleased when he read what Farley had written about Albert, and he asked Farley to do the book over again. As Claire told Angus and Barbara, "That hasn't improved F.'s mood at all. He was quite depressed about it for a few days, and I think he will shelve the whole thing."[14] That is exactly what Farley did. In this instance, he decided to write instead the long-postponed book about *Happy Adventure*, in response to Claire's suggestion that he write a humorous narrative in the manner of Jerome K. Jerome's 1889 classic, *Three Men in a Boat*.

That autumn Farley told McClelland, the ship's co-owner, that *Happy Adventure* was leaking once again in her new home, the harbour at Deseronto: "I'm tired of throwing good money after bad. If nobody buys her, I'll strip her this winter and abandon the hulk."[15] A little while later, things were looking up: "We've found the bloody leak. Yes, and plugged it, with an old Kotex pad, and the boat is dry. . . . So I won't yet sell."

As work on *The Boat Who Wouldn't Float* advanced during the winter, Farley sent McClelland an update in February 1969: "You are getting funnier and funnier. The sequence where you and your corset wrestle with all seven of Neddie's daughters is uproarious. You'll love it! But the real kicker, so far, is where you try to jack off the . . . engine. You are going to be famous at last, me son."[16] McClelland responded by rejoicing that Farley had made such wonderful progress but pleaded, "for Christsake I want to see this one before it is beyond recall. I am in fear and trembling."[17] Delighted to have a potential best-seller on his hands, McClelland was—and remained—ecstatic, even though he had been made into a fool by his friend. Years later, when he re-read the book, some of the "scenes from *The Boat* [still struck him] as hilarious even though I had forgotten what a complete ass Farley made me out to be."[18]

As his forty-eighth year approached, Farley began to see himself as some sort of Romantic poet who had lived far too long. "I'm never gonna see 50," he told the *Globe*'s Blair Kirby. "When any animal passes its point of maximum productivity it should crawl off into the bush and die."[19]

Despite the comic front he presented to the public, Farley was in the late sixties a deeply worried man, concerned with the lack of permanence of all things human. In an interview for *Maclean's* conducted by Alexander Ross, he was brutally frank about such feelings:

> Human contact with another individual is only a transient alleviation because we've lost something that other forms of life have. We've lost the ability to maintain the bond between individuals as an immutable fact until death do us part—we use the phrase, but it doesn't mean anything. But a number of other forms of life can do this, you know. Many forms of geese do this.
>
> *Maclean's*: How do geese compare to your present marriage?
>
> *Mowat*: Well, my present marriage, I would say, is better than average. It seems to me that if a male and a female can survive one another for eight years without the love or attraction between them being permuted into active dislike or hatred, they are lucky.

His marriage was soon to be tested when Farley and Claire decided in 1968 to have a baby. Although he welcomed the prospect of a new child, he did not intend to have the arrival of a baby deter him from a second trip to the USSR, which was in the works. In February 1969 Claire told a friend, "I don't know what Farley and I will be doing this summer. Well obviously I'll be busy looking after a little baby, but Farley has a lot of tentative plans. For one thing, he finally got permission to go back to Siberia in July. I can't say I'm happy about him going so far away and me at home with a tiny baby. I don't know a thing about babies and I'm scared to death. Farley, having already raised two children, knows more about them than I do!"[20]

A month later, Farley, as he informed Jack, was devastated: "Claire got labour pains last Thursday. Took her to hospital, where she gave birth on Friday, son, who died shortly thereafter. C. proceeded to try and follow suit, by bleeding to death. Two operations didn't stop it, but finally a specialist managed to halt the flow, just short of a hysterectomy. She is now recovering in Port Hope hospital. This will modify my summer plans."[21] In his relationship with Claire, Farley had achieved the loving intimacy that had previously eluded him. Now, he was faced with the prospect of losing that person, of having everything taken away from him.

On the same day that he wrote to McClelland, a very relieved Farley told Angus that Claire's prognosis was good: "As of tonight she is physically in the clear. Bleeding has stopped. She is, of course, somewhat down in the mouth and could stand some cheering up. I figure Barb can be of aid in this. Claire seems to think she would like to have Barb with her without men, for a little while. Can't think why she doesn't want them."[22]

Although Farley was grateful that his much-loved wife had been spared, an emotional chasm between them had been created. When at the end of the year, Claire, finding it difficult to cope with the loss of the infant, mentioned the possibility of consulting a psychiatrist, her husband was not sympathetic. He confided to Jack,

How would you like to dig up a psychiatrist for Claire? She has claimed to be in need of one of these past, lo, many years. She may be right. . . . What is required (as I, dimly) understand it, is a father confessor figure who will be able to assess her unplumbed wells of guilt, deal kindly with her, listen to her woes, and somehow get me off the hook. Also, it should be done under OHIP [the Ontario Health Insurance Plan], since there is no way I'm going to pay a quack fifty bucks a week for the rest of my life. Cheaper to get a new wife. Am I serious? Very. This has gone on long enough and if you want more books from me, with which to make yourself unbearably rich, you will heed my plea.[23]

This letter represented one of the darkest sides of Farley, his ability to disconnect himself completely when intimate demands were made. Threatened, his instinct was to protect himself by objectifying the situation and by removing himself from potential pain as soon as possible. And yet the fact was that Farley was desperately afraid of losing the one person he loved above all others. When she proved to be vulnerable, he may have withdrawn from her for the simple reason that she was human and all things human can die. If he withdrew first, perhaps he himself would not be so helpless.

In order to justify to himself what he was doing, Farley concocted an elaborate quasi-psychological, somewhat absurd explanation of his relationship with women: "My women—you know, the people that I really love—I love them, but most of the time I'm eating them. I just can't live with them in terms of absolute harmony, giving of myself, or just loving. I've got to *eat* them all the time, I've got to chew them, I've got to prove to them that they're wrong, they're inadequate, that they just aren't what they ought to be. I'm an eater!"[24]

Although Farley may have seen himself as an eater, he was really a runner. Like his father when Helen gave birth to a stillborn baby daughter, Farley put emotional distance between himself and Claire by embarking on a series of liaisons, mostly of short duration. Such exploits—removed from the domestic sphere he found so difficult to operate in—gave him the momentary illusion of freedom, of being unbound from ties that connected him to the possibility of what he most feared: losing Claire, whom he genuinely loved. In 1960, he had thought he had found a sense of permanence in his relationship with Claire; years later, he was no longer convinced this was the case. Once again, Farley felt cast adrift; once again, he was the wanderer, a man desperately searching for some sort of meaning to his increasingly fragile sense of existence.

Looking back on their marriage, Claire was able to put this difficult situation into perspective. She told Farley,

> The trouble with making great cataclysmic changes in your life, like leaving your spouse and moving far away and starting life over with someone else, is that you always think back and wonder if you weren't better off in whatever the situation was before you did it. I think that's what plagued the first years of our marriage. For me, it was a beginning; for you, it was an upheaval. I couldn't figure out why you weren't happier with me because I loved you so much. I understand now, but I didn't then.[25]

That May, Farley and Claire travelled to Nova Scotia and the Magdalen Islands looking for a summer property. Much of June and July 1969 was spent in the Magdalens making a film for the CBC; the couple spent the remainder of the summer at a rented place at Breton Cove, Cape Breton, with Sandy and David Mowat and Dorothy Spencer, their young friend from Burgeo.

Farley's second trip to the USSR began that September. In preparation for that visit, Farley and Claire—as well as Angus—had dinner at the Russian embassy in Ottawa in the winter of 1967, over a year earlier. This was a night of great merriment, which reached its climax on the roof with Angus inducting Ivan Shpedko, the ambassador, and Vladimir Semenov, the first secretary, into the Mowat clan, the Sutherland.

This "induction" was actually concocted, Farley observed, "to subvert the loyalties of these unsuspecting Russians. My father and I had both come to dinner kilted, and we now persuaded our hosts that they should allow themselves to be inducted. We then inveigled them into exchanging their formal black trousers for our kilts. Since both Russians were tall and heavyset, and Angus and I were small and lean, the fit left something to be desired. We capped it—literally—by putting our Scots bonnets on their heads."

Then, as Farley also recalled, "we went out onto the balcony. It faces Charlotte Street and across the street is an old Victorian house that's been shuttered up and vacant for years. It's generally assumed to be an RCMP observation post." Angus, in top form in the role of sergeant major, introduced his new recruits to the "stirring music of a pibroch, which he played, without benefit of pipes, by holding his nose with one hand while beating on his Adam's apple with the other and at the same time emitting a high-pitched squeak." Upon Angus's order of "About Face. Eyes Right. Thumbs Up," the assemblage gave thumbs up in the direction of the darkened, empty building. A few months later, when Farley spoke publicly about the ceremony, Angus, as he told Shpedko, was perturbed by his son's indiscretion: "Of course we all understand Farley and the way he has of letting his imagination carry him away; but I am worrying lest his absurd (and to me funny) account of the kilt episode might prove embarrassing to you. . . . When I wrapped my kilt on you and 'solemnly' made you a clansman in Clan Sutherland, it was in a moment of amusement for both of us, and in good fellowship and, above all, it was *in private*."[26]

The impetus for Farley's second visit to the USSR came from Alexandra Yakovlevna Ovchinnikova, the chairperson of the Yakut Autonomous Soviet Socialist Republic, nicknamed the "Snow Queen" by some Russian journalists. Farley met her at a reception at Expo 67: "Simply dressed, her jet hair combed close to her head; dark eyes very alert, and her face devoid of cosmetics but glowing brown, she was a natural woman, and a handsome one, in a swarm of vastly unnatural diplomats." During this trip, Farley and de Visser flew northeast from Moscow to Shelekov, the Sea of Okhotsk, Yakutsk and many other places, visiting sites as diverse as an aluminium smelter, a leather plant, a diamond mine, a hydroelectric plant, a burial mound, an agricultural college and a spa. Once again, Farley visited the camp of the reindeer herders at Tchersky, where a 107-year-old woman shaman blessed him. At a celebration to which Alexandra Ovchinnikova invited him, Farley drank fermented mare's milk.

Impressed once again by how well the technological advances in the Russian Arctic were being integrated with the area's Native peoples and ecology, he praised the Siberians' lively sense of skepticism about politics, in the process singling out their remarkable connection to the earth: "*Their* roots have not been severed. They remain a proud and integral part of the continuum of life. It is not inconceivable that these enduring peoples may some day be the seeing eyes to lead the rest of us into a better day."

At a meeting with Farley and de Visser, the chairperson, blushing like a schoolgirl, was reluctant to have her picture taken; she had absolutely no hesitancy, however, in expressing her opinion of how Canadians were treating their portion of the Arctic: "When are you Canadians going to start acting like real men and women and stop behaving like simple little children? Don't you realize you are giving away your country to anyone who wants to steal a piece of it? Haven't you the will to fight for what is yours? Oh, you make me furious!"

Such encounters made de Visser extremely angry. Deeply anti-Soviet, he felt that Farley was being manipulated by the Russians to suit their own devious Cold War purposes. If they could get a prominent Canadian author on side, de Visser imagined, perhaps he would write in such a way as to support the Soviet position against the American one. Of course, Farley's fierce anti-American feelings would have prevented him from taking the American side in any case. But in 1968, he attempted to define his attitude towards the Russians in purely personal terms: "Well, I like them. Almost everything I know about them as individuals I like. And I'm not concerned with politics at all. I operate at about 50 percent higher intellectual and emotional activity when I'm with Russians than when I'm with Canadians."

Although Farley never considered himself either a communist or a communist-supporter, before, during and after the trip, de Visser was vehement in his disgust with Farley's left-wing sentiments, and Farley responded with equal fervour in attacking de Visser's right-wing attitudes. Upon their return from the USSR, an RCMP officer contacted the photographer, who was perfectly willing to undergo a debriefing. Farley was furious at de Visser when he learned what his friend had gladly subjected himself to.

De Visser, whose understanding was that he and Farley were collaborating on a book similar in format to *This Rock Within the Sea*, became even more upset when, at a meeting at Port Hope, Farley, McClelland and Davison viewed his photographs, retired from the sitting room and returned ten minutes later to inform him that none of them would be used inside the book, which would be devoted solely to Farley's text. McClelland and Davison felt that the use of a significant portion of the de Visser photos would make the book too expensive; as a compromise, McClelland suggested an independent book of photos with captions by Farley, but he cautioned he could do such a book only if he found an American publisher for it; he had no luck in this regard and so no such volume was published. Despite de Visser's disappointment, this friendship remained intact for a time because of de Visser's respect for Farley as a man and as a writer and because he felt Farley had given him a big break by collaborating with him on the Newfoundland book.

That autumn, Farley, often accompanied by Claire, crossed Canada promoting *The Boat Who Wouldn't Float*. Back from that chore, he worked on a book, *Sibir*, encapsulating both his trips to the USSR. In the spring of 1970, he received an honorary degree, his first, from Laurentian University (he has since received eight more). He was awarded the Stephen Leacock Medal for Humour for *The Boat*; at the award ceremony, Farley, in response to a dare from Pierre Berton, distinguished himself by hitching up his kilt to reveal the bare facts. He was also given the Canadian Authors Association's Vicky Metcalf Award for his contribution to Canadian writing.

In the summer of 1970, Farley and Claire finally found the summer home they had been seeking, on the northeast tip of the Magdalen Islands (les Îles de la Madeleine) at Grande Entrée, Quebec (they purchased it a year later). Apparently named after Madeleine Fontaine, the wife of the islands' first seigneur, the islands were the site of the first battle in North America between the English and the French, in 1597. The first significant colonization of the islands began in 1755, when Acadian settlers and several English-speaking families settled there. Eight years later the Treaty of Paris gave all North American French possessions to England, and in 1787 George III bequeathed the islands to Captain Isaac Coffin, whose seigneurial reign was so severe that many islanders were forced into exile on Quebec's North Shore. Only in 1895 did the government of Quebec enable the islanders to buy back their land and resettle there. Red

The Mowat house in the Magdalens

sandstone and grey cliffs dominate the islands, many of which are linked by long sand beaches.

On August 9, Farley, in a triumphant mood, told Angus and Barbara, "So far, it has worked like a charm. We bought the house and find it increasingly delightful. Fantastic weather—sun every day, but cool breezes too, and we brown like buns. The locals are excellent, friendly and charming albeit they DO take a droppie now and again. [The dogs] Bert and Vicky are worn to shadows from fetching half a million wooden ducks a day. . . . Claire is in good fettle, madly making bread, picking wild strawberries, and redesigning the interior of the old house. It is in surprisingly good condition and is light, airy and comfortable. Big, too. Four bedrooms. Big workshop, and a barn in which I can pretend to keep a cow."[27] In a more raucous but poetical mood, he characterized his summer home as "Old, big, rotten house full of rum. Hot sun, cool breezes, wide seas, fresh cod. Long grassy hills, red cliffs, curlews crying."[28] A year or so after settling on Grand Entrée, Farley remained deeply pleased, even in the midst of a fight against Irving Oil when one of the company's barges sank near the islands, fouling the water and beaches with oil.

The Isles are really great. Our house is big, modern (inside) and comfortable and lots of room for guests. Great beaches, nice people (French–Acadian), lots of seafood, good weather, swimming, sailing, and almost no tourists, and NO Yanks at all! I'd like to spend eight months of the year there, but C. isn't so keen on that. Frankly, the sooner I get out of Ontario for good, the happier I'll be. If we HAVE to live in a totalitarian state, and we will be doing that in a few years, I'd prefer it to be as remote as possible from the centre of the Bastille.[29]

At Grand Entrée during the summer of 1970, Farley worked on an NFB (National Film Board) film about Newfoundland with the humorist, novelist and short story writer Max Braithwaite, a friend of many years for whom he had protective feelings.

Braithwaite is perhaps best remembered for *Why Shoot the Teacher?* (published by Jack McClelland in 1965), an autobiographical novel which tells of his experiences teaching in a one-room Saskatchewan school during the Depression. In 1972, Braithwaite was very upset about the sales of *The Night We Stole the Mountie's Car*, published the year before. He did not tell Jack about his discontent; instead, he left this unpleasant task in the hands of Farley, who felt uncharacteristically awkward about broaching the matter with McClelland: "Max is very depressed [over low sales]. . . . Now don't get prickly and don't go all defensive. . . . He [Max] cannot afford losses due to inefficiency on production and distribution. As a result of very poor sales of Mountie he is close to being strapped."[30]

Farley was expecting a hostile letter by way of reply from McClelland; he was very surprised by what his publisher told him:

Max's book was not the only one that suffered from an incredible backlog in Canadian binderies last fall. . . . I can tell you that more money was spent on the promotion of the Braithwaite book than all but a handful of Canadian titles published in 1971. . . . I know it to be a fact that retailers across the country lie like troopers to defend their own position when they haven't ordered enough copies of a goddamn book. . . . I am sorry that you and Max feel badly about it. Frankly I don't. I think we did our best by it, and I think it was a damn good best and at most I think he lost the sale of a couple of hundred copies. . . . I have great affection for Max and great respect for him as a writer. His books are best-sellers by Canadian standards, but I think he must recognize that his books are not as popular as yours and as those of a handful of other authors. . . . It was a self-indulgent book where he paid more attention to what he wanted to say, than he did to the interests of the reader. . . . I am, by the way, sending a copy of this letter to Max. . . . I don't by the way blame him for bitching. Every writer does. It is part of the game. . . . I have been listening to author frustrations for 25 years. . . . I've never claimed to be the perfect publisher.[31]

A somewhat stunned Farley responded, "At least nobody can say you don't take authors' 'bitchings' seriously. Which is one of the reasons you still have a lot of good authors despite the obvious inadequacies of M&S's publishing organization."[32]

In 1970, Farley and Max had a third collaborator, Farley's young cousin from Montreal, Andy Thomson, the son of Helen's younger brother, Arthur. On August 20 Farley told Andy, "All goes exceedingly well. Max is here now and we are working like stink on the film. Will have a full story outline for you on arrival, and Max will be able to produce a detailed shooting script by the end of September."[33]

Three years before, in 1967, Andy Thomson had written his master's dissertation at Acadia University about his famous relative, who had cooperated with him fully. Thomson had even gotten in touch with A.E. Porsild, who had severely criticized *People of the Deer*, requesting an interview. In his letter of refusal Porsild showed that his animosity towards Farley had not diminished a whit: "Tear up your thesis. . . . I have shown that most of Mowat's sensational claims were deliberate falsehoods, as Mowat well knows."[34] Later, when Andy worked for the NFB, he and Farley talked of doing a film together. This led to the Newfoundland project, whereby Farley was assisting Braithwaite to obtain work and at the same time doing a favour for Andy.

Quite soon, there was acrimony between the cousins, based mainly on the fact that Farley and Max felt Andy was too unseasoned to be single-handedly directing and producing a feature film. In fact, Farley telephoned Andy's boss at the NFB to complain, unaware his cousin was in the room when the call came through. Andy upbraided Farley for going over his head and, in turn, received a sharp letter:

> I'm not sure [the film] will be made in an adequate manner now. That's up to you. But my general feelings on this matter are that I have no further interest in a collaboration which has turned out to be, in essence, a one man operation intended to enable you to leap from obscurity as an embryonic film maker, into sudden prominence as a successful producer of feature films, at the expense, and on the shoulders of, your peers. Hard words, but they do not require modification. You now have what you set out to get, and I don't really feel that you care very much about the consequences of how you achieved your objective.
>
> Drop in any time, but as Cousin Andy, not as a film maker.

In retrospect, Farley says, "Max and I complained to Andy's superior in an attempt to save the film. But the damage had been done and the film was cancelled." This dispute was papered over—but it would cast a long shadow into the future.

That autumn, *Sibir* was published and there was another gruelling cross-Canada tour. Claire informed Angus and Barbara that the book was selling well, "despite the lousy review in *Globe & Mail*. The guy who reviewed it is a pompous academic who has just written a book himself about the Canadian north which is pompous and academic. That kind of guy, in Canada anyway, is always out to clobber Farley. Anyway I'm glad the book is selling. I hope we make a huge pile of money and then Farley can quit for a while. The pressure of producing two major books in two years, and all the attendant publicity that goes with it, is just too much."

Pompous reviewer or not, *Sibir* is one of Farley's weakest books. It is so because it is largely a detailed travelogue directly lifted from travel diaries. A habitual keeper of diaries throughout his career, Farley often employed them as the basis for books, but in most cases, he lifted the essence of an incident and fictionalized it, in the process breathing life into it. In writing this book, however, he pursued another approach, composing it, he joked, "almost entirely from Claire's journals." He added, "I have no compunction about it. I steal from her. But I pay her a good salary for it—which she spends on gigolos." *Sibir*, which shows little evidence of the transforming hand of Farley Mowat, is exactly the kind of book that critics such as Porsild had maintained that he should be writing.

Farley's new book also left open the door for Angus to make this rather snide complaint: "I have read the first review of your new book [a favourable one]. . . . So I had one of my thoughts. Since you can neither spell nor punctuate and, further, since Jack McClelland cannot afford an editor, why do you not permit me, without 'expense to the public' [to] edit your mss with respect to those two items and also, of course, to remove the 'hopefullys' and the 'meaningfuls' over which you occasionally slip. I'll make a writer of you yet."[35]

As he had confided to Andy prior to their falling out over the film project, Farley was having a lot of problems with his father: "Angus is drifting out of the world, and that means he is losing touch with all of us—not just with you. I have not had a meaningful conversation with him for lo, these many months. I don't know what he has in mind for himself, but sharing something of the Mowat ability for moody self-dramatics, I suspect he is now living the role of Old Angus, the doddering old decrepit, Who Is Out of It All. It probably gives him pleasure. He probably won't maintain it forever."[36]

Increasingly, Farley did not like to be around Barbara, whom he now found loathsome. Even the exceedingly tolerant and gentle Claire pronounced her company jarring: "Last time we were [at Northport]," she told Andy, "I was on the verge of telling her to go to hell and mind her own G.D. business. I think I would have if Farley hadn't got drunk and fallen asleep, which meant we had to stay the night. She is determined to manipulate people and tell them how to run their lives, and then admonish them if they don't do what she advises." The Mowats also felt that Barbara's "mysterious poor health" was exerting a harmful influence on Angus: "I just hope that Angus survives it all, but as Farley says, he has the ability to withdraw into himself and ignore the surroundings."[37] Farley also felt guilty about the way he had treated his mother; after all, he had for a number of years cooperated fully with Angus in concealing his father's relationship with Barbara. And he was aware that Angus did not completely approve of his writing career.

Barbara provided Andy with her own view of the complex interactions between father and son: "You can't really talk of Farley as an individual because Angus and Farley are so mixed up together that you can't really separate them. The relationship is so close that I've never seen anything like it in my life. It's uncanny. The two are just like two peas in a pod. Somehow or other, there's a peculiar understanding that exists without ever anything having to be said. A complete rapport, almost a complete identification."

Is it really rapport, though, when two individuals are so bound together? Where does the father end and the son begin? This was the very uncomfortable position in which Farley was placed. In a 1968 interview, he put a good face on his relationship with his father: "One of his great influences has been he has stepped ahead of me. He is roughly thirty years older than I am and he enables me to see in myself a kind of freedom. I can live thirty years in advance without being frightened. I don't see in him somebody who has given up, someone who has become crystallized, and this is great. This is why he is the guru." If one's father remains the guru, what kind of breathing room does this give the son? This was the disturbing question Farley now asked himself.

His Father's Son

1971–1977

AT the beginning of 1970 Farley was, as he observed, "in a terrible state of confusion—worse than usual—trying to write two books at one time. The long seal book, and a short book about Moby Josephine. It is apparently time for the whale story to surface. I dream about it, so I guess I'll just have to write about it."[1] Yet a year later Farley still could not get down to work and was, as Claire told Angus and Barbara, "in a gruff mood" early in 1971.[2]

The seal book would be a long time in coming. Not so *A Whale for the Killing*. Angus may have withheld praise for *Sibir*, but he was deeply touched when he read a typescript of the whale book that January: "This, my son, is a great book. I state that flatly. You must give me some of the time [to suggest changes and corrections] you couldn't give yourself because you wrote hot. And so you should."[3]

Upon completing *A Whale for the Killing*, Farley still remained deeply unsettled, unsure of what to do next. His uncertainty was both professional and personal. At this crossroads in his son's life, Angus offered his usual counsel:

> I have never been one to offer unsolicited advice and that's what I'm writing about but I don't know how to do it. I am much worried about the state you are in. Oh yes I know; you aren't. But you are. And nipping out to Vancouver Island or nipping out to the Magdalens isn't going to help at all. The nipping itself is a symptom. Running from place to place like a chicken without a head. You'll have to give up writing for a while. . . . If you think it is too hard a bullet to chew then you'll just have to think again. "Fame" has never been anything but the one thing, a hard climb up and a fast slide down and you are too damned good to slide down. But you are the only one who can stop it, and it has begun.[4]

Angus's frankness released a corresponding, intimate one in Farley, who much appreciated his father's concern:

> Of course you are right, but you are also wrong, in that you seem to think that I am not aware of what is happening. I am. Very much so. But there are a good many complicating problems, including female ones. Do you know about them? Female complications, I mean. It strikes me that you should.
>
> What I am doing now is marking time and staving off (as well as withdrawing from) the whole frenetic business. It will take time. There is no nice, pat solution to what I need.
>
> One of the basic problems is that the kind of people I have always enjoyed most, are now all but extinct, and if they aren't, they are in desperate straits, and falling apart, within and without. I went to Frobisher [on a short trip] mainly to see if the arctic held any new Windy River for me. It doesn't. It was an appalling experience, and infinitely depressing. Now then. *You* can, and do, live in insulation from most of the reality of what is happening in the world. I can't and don't. It weighs heavily upon me.

But I'll work things out. I suspect the direction is right away from Man, and back to my initial loves, the birds and the bees and the bustards etc. I think *Whale* points the way. It's a matter of respect. To be frank, I do not much respect my own species (individuals? oh hell, of course) nor do I find much affection for homo sapiens, per se. Well, you can beat a dead horse, with or without effect, but you sure as hell can't love one.

Take it easy. I'll survive. Will you? Will any of us?

A Whale for the Killing, published in 1972, had taken Farley back to his earliest interests: animals. Perhaps he had been diverted—in his books on the Inuit, the salvage operations, Siberia, the early settling of North America and Newfoundland—from his most fundamental preoccupations. Moreover, there was the whole problem of running away from involvement with others when it became complicated. "Nipping away" from Claire had now become a preoccupation.

In March 1972, Farley asked Jack McClelland to assist him in the invention of some excuse, upon returning to Toronto from Paris, not to return directly to Port Hope with his wife: "What I need is a good solid reason for being in Toronto on May 22/23. Assuming that I arrive back the evening of May 21, which is my plan. The fucking problem is that May 22 is a Sunday, and the 23rd is also a holiday. What possible reason could I have for being there then? And only just back from Paris? What I hope to be able to do is send Claire and luggage home to Port Hope by cab from Malton. Well, if you can't dream up something, nobody can. The letter of invitation should reach me [in London], not later than April 20."[5]

Seventeen months later, on July 16, 1973, Farley requested his publisher to call an "emergency" board meeting of McClelland & Stewart, of which Farley was now a director: "Quickie note. I think I need to get the hell out of here [Magdalen Islands] for a few days, say about July 27th. Can you think up the spring board sequence? Call me, or send a wire, but not sooner than the 20th, to allow me time to see if it is a good time to go to old TO."[6] The requested letter was immediately forthcoming: "You will have had my telegram. It would be really helpful if you could break into your summer holiday and come to

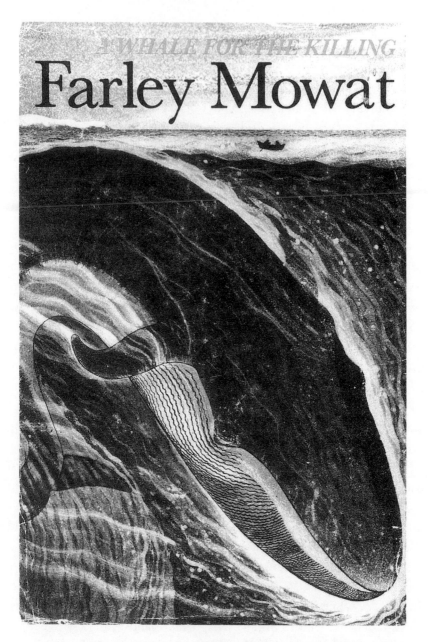

Dust jacket for A Whale for the Killing, *illustration by David Blackwood*

Toronto for the Directors' meeting on the 27th of July. . . . We have a great many serious matters to review. . . . The other members of the Board feel that it would be really helpful if you could be here."[7]

In 1971 and 1972, Farley's drinking increased markedly, to the extent that he sometimes allowed cruel remarks to escape his lips. He told a person who had just had an artificial eye installed that he looked terrible with it. At one wedding reception, where he was an otherwise splendid master of ceremonies, Farley called upon Claire to make a speech. She upbraided him afterwards: "How it is that you can have known me for eleven years and not know how terrified and incapable I am of speaking in front of a large group of people is beyond me."[8]

Farley found it almost impossible to reconstitute what he saw as an increasingly fragile sense of self. In despair, he sought escape in drink and women. There was one serious relationship with another woman in the early seventies; she often accompanied Farley to public events, such as book signings. But this manic activity inhibited his ability to work, and so he became quickly ensnared in a vicious circle.

In an astute comment made in 1977, Jack McClelland observed that it had been "almost five years since Farley has done anything seriously." He wondered if Farley had become "too bloody wealthy" for his own good, but he pinpointed the problem more precisely when he made another interpretation: "I really think though that the serious part of his current writing block is that he can't write with Claire around and that he doesn't want to face the prospect of life without Claire beyond the short term."[9] Farley—who always preferred to have his workspace as separate as possible from his living quarters—imagined he would be able to write if he was separated from Claire; but once actually separated from Claire, he became extremely melancholic. Time and again in her letters from Port Hope to her husband when he was in the Maritimes, Claire expressed her hope they could find a way to live comfortably in each other's presence:

> I miss you my love. It is lonely here without you. The one thing I long for most is that we can be together somewhere and be happy. Where? Where can we be content?[10]

And I sit and wonder if we will ever find a more peaceable way to live. We must. It is a major priority. Everything else comes second. Your health and survival, my mental health and *our* marriage are all contingent on our finding some peace.[11]

Peace evaded Farley because he knew that he was extremely dependent on Claire; to overtly recognize such a need would open him up to enormous grief if she were to be removed from him. And so he evaded the entire question by not dealing with it. Claire, a person with a good understanding of herself and others, knew exactly what her husband was doing, but she was unable to assist him to see the truth.

In an attempt to return to animals, his "initial loves," Farley became active in conservationist causes in the early seventies. He investigated reports of a raid on the breeding grounds of double-crested cormorants on the Magdalens; some locals claimed that these birds were consuming a disproportionately large amount of fish. Farley also met with Jack Davis, the federal fisheries and environment minister; the two negotiated a ban on the hunting of large whales off Canada's Atlantic coast. And he became an active member of and founded a Canadian branch of Project Jonah, an international group committed to the welfare of whales, in particular to their preservation from hunters.

Although Farley recalls first meeting Ed Schreyer, the then thirty-five-year-old premier of Manitoba, in 1973, the politician is convinced that they first met in 1972 at a Project Jonah conference in Winnipeg. In any event, the relationship between the two began in 1973 when Farley heard of the proposal by a tourist lodge operator in Churchill, Manitoba, to set up expeditions to hunt the beluga whales that populate the harbour there. Thirty-seven years earlier, when he had accompanied Frank Farley there, he had seen these small whales being picked off for fun. On the way to Lethbridge, Alberta, to receive an honorary degree at the university there, Farley stopped in Winnipeg to discuss the situation. Schreyer immediately put a stop to the entrepreneur's scheme.

Although the sometimes outgoing Farley Mowat and the sometimes bashful Ed Schreyer seem an unlikely couple, the handsome young NDP premier had a lifelong interest in climates similar to those in Manitoba and Farley's political sentiments have always been left-wing. The two men immediately found they could speak frankly to each other about issues such as protection of the environment and alternative methods of energy. Farley soon realized that Ed's quiet, pensive habit of mind complemented a side of himself he often kept hidden from public view; at the same time, Ed became aware that Farley's extroverted personality was an aspect of his own character he did not often display in public. From these realizations—and the rapport which soon developed between two other seeming opposites, the sometimes shy Claire Mowat and the often effervescent Lily Schreyer—a close friendship was formed between the couples.

Farley travelled to Manitoba several times in 1973 to speak at rallies on behalf of Schreyer and the NDP, who were fighting (successfully) for re-election. Not unexpectedly, Farley's mischievous side asserted itself: "There was a brief but bizarre visit to Churchill, culminating in the disappearance of the Premier whom I had inveigled into joining an all-night party out on the tundra and resulting in a RCMP search being mounted for him after a rumour got around that he had been carried off by a polar bear."[12] Farley hated the airplane used, dubbed *The People's Plane*: "It was *sans* toilet, an oversight that led to the famous incident of the Premier's Piss in which I was a major partissipant."[13] Farley even became a dollar-a-year man who offered his advice to his friend's "Red" Cabinet, as they jokingly referred to themselves.

Having grown dissatisfied with the Magdalens, the Mowats even considered settling in rural Manitoba. Claire and Farley spent two months towing a caravan and living a nomadic existence searching for a new "mooring" in the central and southern parts of the province, catching their breaths between outings while parked in the Schreyers' backyard just outside Winnipeg. The caravan remained at the Schreyers' for a year. In the autumn of 1975, Farley, accompanied by his son Sandy and by Max Braithwaite, drove the caravan east to Port Hope. "This was," Farley remembers, "a madcap voyage made memorable by Max doing moons out the car window at U.S.

hunters, and by an encounter with the moody spirits of prehistoric Indians in the Nipigon country."

In February 1974, Farley, persistently drawn to the idea of establishing or being part of a rural brotherhood, told Sandy, "I have been seconded to the Manitoba Indian Brotherhood and will be working to help establish a Free Indian State in northeast Manitoba. An Israel in Canada, by god. It sounds like a hell of a lot of fun and just the sort of nutty thing I enjoy. So I'm bound back there tomorrow for about three weeks."[14]

There were many other projects to distract Farley from writing. He was one of the founders of the Writers' Union in 1973. He spent a great deal of time sorting his papers for donation to McMaster University in Hamilton, Ontario. In July 1974, the Mowats and the Schreyers took a flight to Greenland from Frobisher Bay; the highlight of this trip was an exploration of the Godthaab Fjord, the western settlement of the Greenland Norse. Politically, the trip was fascinating because the Home Rule movement against the Danish government was at its peak. A year later, in 1975, Farley and Sandy travelled to Scotland so that Farley could introduce his son to his Mowat ancestry. As he had done before, Farley stayed at the Mowat croft at John O'Groats. Father and son went lobster fishing and several times talked late into the night at the local pubs. So smitten was Farley by what he saw that he nearly purchased a croft of his own, having already failed to buy the ruins of the ancient pirate stronghold of Bucholie, which had been the Mowat seat between 1200 and 1630.

When Kildare Dobbs interviewed him in December 1973 for the *Toronto Star*, Farley spoke frankly of the difficulties he was having in settling into a new writing project. Observing a meticulously crafted scale model of the *Foundation Franklin*, the subject of *The Grey Seas Under*, Dobbs asked who had made it. "I did," Farley replied. "I spent weeks on it, to avoid getting down to work on the book. I hate writing."

That December, the recently published *Wake of the Great Sealers*, illustrated by David Blackwood, had been so popular that it was no longer available; M&S could not get paper of sufficient quality to reprint the lavish book. More importantly, sales of the paperbacks of

Angus, circa 1975

Farley's previous books were so successful that each easily outsold its original hardback printing. Dobbs joked with him: perhaps he was on the verge of outselling Pierre Berton, with whom he had a sort of sibling rivalry? "Beat Pierre?" Farley rejoined. "Now there's an interesting thought. Well, it wouldn't be by a frontal assault. You might say I'm sort of encircling him!"[15]

Farley undertook more projects for CBC Radio and Television, and he was active in the production of and wrote the script for *Angus* (1971), a short NFB film directed and produced by Andy Thomson in which Angus is seen repairing his boat at Pinchpenny, north of Kingston, and singing folksongs. Farley's voice-over, tender, elegiac and lyrical, celebrates his father as the prototype of the rugged, romantic individual who lives life to the full, even in old age.

Angus displays a very real side of Farley's deep love for his father. Absent from the film, though, is the bickering that had overtaken their relationship. Since Farley and Claire found Barbara insufferably bossy and interfering, they did not like to be around her; as a result, Farley saw his father far less often than he would have liked.

A letter sent to Helen on Angus's behalf caused additional acrimony when Barbara put her name down as "Mrs. Angus Mowat." Deeply affronted, Helen complained at length to Farley and Claire, who were convinced Barbara had perpetrated the stunt in order to insult and humiliate Helen (from whom Angus was never divorced). As he told Farley, Angus completely brushed such an interpretation aside:

> There is one thing that I neglected, actually forgot, to bring up during your visit the other day. You have been labouring under a misapprehension about an envelope that Barb addressed to Helen on which she put, for the return address, "Mrs. Angus Mowat." I'm sorry and so is Barbara that you automatically assumed that this was, as you say, "a quite unnecessary knife thrust" and "petty harassment." The truth is that it happened innocently and by accident at a time of stress.[16]

Angus interpreted Farley's hostility towards Barbara as perhaps having another component—disguised hostility towards himself. On this score, he confronted his son:

> I am writing in sorrow and with a heavy heart. I shall not answer your letters in detail since there is no use talking against a wall; better hold my peace. You have gone very far away from me—and that not suddenly—but the love I have had for you all your life is still strong; so, if you want to come back to me, later, I'll be here. One thing though, if you do, you must let me know ahead of time. This is for Barbara's sake. Barbara, although she has been generous and is blameless, has the conviction that her very presence with me has been to blame. I think she is wrong but her conviction must be respected. So if you come back she must be given time to make herself scarce and

leave the two of us alone. That in itself speaks clearly enough of a generous nature.[17]

Even more complex was Angus's continuing involvement with Farley's writing career. When *Canada North Now: The Great Betrayal* was published in 1976, Angus offered enthusiastic support, even though he felt that the book was a significant departure from Farley's earlier books dealing with the Arctic: "You have done an important book, you have done it timely, and you've done it well, you have backed up on a broader scope what you had to say before on a more familiar and personal scale. If I miss some of the warmth or closeness I can remind myself that *Canada North Now* isn't the place for it; and for that I can always go back to *People of the Deer* and *The Desperate People*. Which I quite often do, you know."[18] And yet Farley felt his father in the end disapproved of him, did not bestow unconditional support, because Farley had never become a literary novelist, the highest calling to which, in Angus's opinion, a writer could aspire.

There was also the way in which Angus joked. When Farley walked off after introducing Angus to Ed Schreyer, Angus turned to the premier of Manitoba and asked him, "How could anyone such as yourself get on with someone so erratic and unpredictable as Farley?" At the time, Schreyer thought the tone in Angus's voice was one of bemused approbation, but he later wondered if there had been a cutting edge to the question. In June 1974, Angus and Barbara wrote to the Schreyers telling them how much they had enjoyed meeting them: "It gives us something to be grateful to old Farley for."[19] Angus also, Farley and Claire noticed, started to develop the habit of walking away from them if he felt he was not getting sufficient attention—for instance, at a CBC film shoot—without giving them the least indication that he was going to do so.

Then there was a fight over a maple chest of drawers owned by Angus but kept at Farley's home in Port Hope. When Angus told Rosemary the chest was hers, she asked Farley to send it to her. He did not reply at once, which led her, in a downcast frame of mind, to broach the matter with her father a second time. He replied, "I'm not quite sure what you mean when you say you have no rights in family matters. I'm still head of the family, you know; and you'd know, even if I hadn't told you in plain words, where you stand with me. Farley isn't the family you know."[20] Rosemary repeated her request to her brother, whereupon he sent the chest to her.

In the midst of Farley's troubled dealings with his father were his difficulties with his mother, who sometimes complained to him about how Angus mistreated her. As Farley became increasingly alienated from his father, he drew closer to Helen and began to see her point of view more clearly, even though he found the PDH side of her character irritating. Farley also continued to feel guilty about the way he had, years before, assisted Angus in concealing Barbara's existence from his mother.

Farley's much-beloved Albert was easier to deal with, although he proved less than enthusiastic when asked to sire a litter of puppies. "Finally, in despair," Farley told Angus, "we took the baster which normally bastes roasts, filled it with Albert's sperm and gently introduced it into Vicky! What a way to get laid!"[21] The result, in August 1971, was "eight new Alberts." Farley was not certain what to do with them—perhaps a "dog team? Maybe I'll train them all as fishing dogs and live off the profits."[22]

Just before the birth of the Victoria and Albert pups at Grande Entrée, there was a visit from recently married fifty-one-year-old prime minister Pierre Trudeau and his young wife, Margaret, who "dropped into the backyard in a helicopter last Saturday and spent the day." Farley was a bit intimidated before the Trudeaus arrived. He lamented, "It appears that hizzoner is going to drop in upon us on Saturday for lunch. He must be mad. Or maybe it is we who are mad. However, I have high hopes for a hurricane on Friday night."

Although the confrontation was a bit tense at first between the sometimes haughty politician and the sometimes prickly writer, the two men, both quite capable of extending enormous charm when so inclined, got along well. Albert immediately took to the prime minister and shamelessly showed off for him. But the ice was completely broken when Margaret, observing that if she and Pierre were having a baby they might as well have a dog, asked if she could have one of Albert's offspring as a companion for the baby she was expecting.

Immediately after the visit, without any intent on their part, Farley and Claire found themselves in hot water with their neighbours. Claire told Angus, "We discovered that we had incurred as much hostility as we had goodwill. The English community was mad that Trudeau had spent his day in the French community. The fishermen were mad that Trudeau didn't spend his day listening to them and trying to settle their problems."[23]

Among the puppies were Red Star (presented to Premier Kosygin of the USSR) and Farley Trudeau, who later distinguished himself by peeing on the prime minister's Tibetan prayer rug and chasing deer at Harrington Lake. Claire and Farley kept Edward and, for a while, Alice; the other pups found homes locally.★

In the spring of 1972, Farley and Claire went to Europe. The chief purpose of their trip—which included stops in London, Caithness and Paris—was to visit Peter Davison, his wife Jane and their two children in Rome. Peter's father had recently died, and the editor-publisher had decided to take a sabbatical from his duties at the Atlantic Monthly Press in order to write poetry. During that visit, work on the editing of *A Whale for the Killing* progressed smoothly, but Peter noticed that Farley was mortally distressed by Rome. The noises, smells and theatricality of one of Europe's great cities were a continual affront. In a diary he kept during his nineteen-day stay, Farley recorded that repugnance in no uncertain terms: "The City, citta, civitas, civilization—all one and *all* wrong for Man! What frantic, frenzied efforts we make to believe in what is in fact our damnation—civilized man and all his works. . . . Rome is an asylum filled

★ In 1972, Victoria (Vicky) was given away; Albert died in January 1975; Lily arrived in the fall of 1976 and died in 1991; from a litter between Edward and Lily came Tom, who died in 1991 at the age of thirteen; Edward died in 1982; Millicent (Millie) was adopted in 1990, Chester in 2000. The only purebred black Labrador ever owned by the Mowats was Victoria; all the other Mowat dogs have resembled black Labradors, as did Albert, a black Newfoundland water dog.

with aimless and lost (in the living animal sense) men and women, infested with those who eat their shit."[24]

Farley's sense of any large city as a barometer of the corruption of so-called civilized man was absent from *A Whale for the Killing*, published in 1972. Instead, the new book was about evil in an apparently paradisaical setting. Farley lambastes the young men who return corrupted to their outport communities; he regrets the shame inflicted, in part by himself, on the residents of Burgeo; and yet he also casts a very cynical eye on himself when he describes the last days of the wounded, dying mammal:

> She was on the surface and moving very slowly. Almost all of her great length was exposed. She could easily have been mistaken for one of those colossal sea monsters which decorate ancient charts. The illusion was intensified by the vagueness given to her outlines by the drifting snow.
>
> I hardly know how to describe or explain my reaction. Instead of feeling sick with disappointment as I realized she was still a prisoner, my spirits rose. I felt something akin to elation. The only explanation I can offer, and it is no easy one for me to accept, is that if she *had* managed to escape without my help, it would have made a travesty of my attempts to save her. Or was it, perhaps, that I needed her continuing presence in the Pond to justify my own actions and attitudes towards those who had tormented her? Had I come to rely on her presence in order to maintain my rôle? Had *my* need of her become greater than *her* need of me?
>
> I have no answer to these questions, and I think I want none.

Afraid that he has his own self-aggrandizing agenda, Farley calls his behavior into question and, in the process, subtly attacks himself. Always interested in analyzing his motivation, for instance, for wishing to help the Inuit, he does the same here. But the feeling in this passage is different from what occurred earlier. The reader can now feel the self-loathing that invaded Farley in the seventies. Uncertain of who he was and what he wanted of life, he was filled with rage at those close to him and, more importantly, at himself.

Farley had to contend with the fact that McClelland & Stewart was increasingly on the brink of bankruptcy, and he also did frequent battle with Pierre Berton, the popular historian who, apart from the biographer and political commentator Peter C. Newman, was his only real best-selling rival at M&S. Not unlike Farley, Berton usually had a long list of complaints about the inefficient way business was conducted at McClelland & Stewart; unlike Farley, he voiced his reservations with great frequency.

Chief among Berton's annoyances was his increasing sense that publicity at M&S was poorly handled, and he was certain that Catherine Wilson, the firm's director of publicity, was inept. In order to counter her, Berton had his agent, Elsa Franklin, oversee the publicity campaigns for all his books. The problem was that Wilson and Franklin were often working at cross-purposes to promote the same Berton book because Wilson was still responsible for posters, print publicity and party invitations. Knowing how much of a perfectionist Berton could be, Jack McClelland attempted in August 1971 to warn Wilson before things had a chance to get out of hand: "Needless to say the guest list for this [Berton launch] party submitted by Elsa bugs me in the same way and to the same degree that your average guest list for parties bugs me. I say that to make you feel good. Elsa will get the same snarly reaction from me that you usually get. I get more and more crotchety I guess, but when the names of guests are improperly spelled, it absolutely drives me up the wall and I wonder if any part of it is right and will be handled properly."[25] However, Berton was certain that Wilson had messed up yet again when she scheduled a country bacchanal—Food, Poetry and Wine in the Woods—for the poet John Newlove on the very same night Franklin was holding an event to celebrate the revised edition of *Klondike*, originally published in 1958. Berton was on the verge of asking Jack to fire Wilson, who claimed to know nothing about the other event.

Farley, on the other hand, felt Wilson had done an excellent job in promoting his books, and he contacted friends in the industry to tell them Berton had demanded Jack let Wilson go. In turn, Berton was furious about Farley's interference and about his passing on incorrect information as to what Berton had (or had not) asked of McClelland. Berton demanded an apology from Farley.[26]

The dispute about Catherine Wilson ignited some pent-up antagonisms between the two men, both of whom were directors of McClelland & Stewart. Jack, caught in a three-way conflict not of his own devising, fired Wilson before Berton asked him to do so. In this instance, as he told Berton, Jack was more on his side than Farley's:

> I have no hesitation in saying that I agree with your letter and particularly with its moderate tone. I hope Farley will respond in an appropriate way. I have some reservations about your request that copies of his apology be sent to everyone to whom he has made statements . . . I don't know how many people are involved, but I am concerned that a sort of round-robin apology might in fact have the reverse of the intended effect and exacerbate the situation . . . Leaving aside all considerations that relate to McClelland & Stewart and publishing, I now find myself in the cross-fire between two old and valued friends. Unless all three of us are extremely careful there will be three losers. . . .
>
> I am sending a copy of this letter to Farley. I think and hope you both know that regardless of the outcome, I won't take sides in the matter. Maybe I'll be the big loser. To me the term friend is absolute and degrees don't exist. I ask you both, as I have asked myself, what is the end-product here and what can any of us achieve? I am certain that not one of the three of us wants to do any hurt or harm to Catherine Wilson. I am equally sure that not one of the three of us wishes to destroy our mutual friendship because I handled her essential departure from McClelland & Stewart in a manner that left much to be desired. I suggest we cool the whole thing.[27]

The actual firing was done by Peter Taylor, Catherine's boss, and not by the tender-hearted Jack. The night before she was summoned to the breakfast meeting at which she was dismissed, Catherine had been—together with McClelland—at a party at bookseller Louis Melzack's home in Montreal to celebrate the publication of Mordecai Richler's *Shovelling Trouble*. McClelland, who obviously knew she was going to be fired, said not a word to her about this matter. When she subsequently consulted lawyer Sam Grange about the manner of her dismissal, he got in touch with M&S and with Bob Martin, the firm's lawyer. Although Wilson never returned to work, she was kept on the payroll for six months and received back the company car which had been taken away from her. During the negotiations between lawyers, she was startled to receive a phone call from an inebriated Jack, who told her he was upset about what had happened. He claimed he had had to do what he had done because Berton had him by "the short and curlies."[28]

Farley felt he—along with Wilson—was the innocent victim of Berton's animosity. He wrote to Jack,

> I have read Pierre's letter and it just plain makes me mad. Somebody has done a hell of a lot of lying about the whole mess, and I'm damned if I'll take the buck. I phoned Pierre, but he was in New York. . . . He is an arrogant son of a bitch, and I am half inclined to xerox the whole of the correspondence and distribute it to the authors concerned. . . . Well, chum, I won't initiate anything more (unilaterally) but neither will I grovel to Pierre. You might call it The Last Straw. As far as I'm concerned any friendship I had with him is at an end. It now remains for him to decide whether we part on a basis of neutrality, or wage war.[29]

This dispute blew over, but it left a permanent mark on the friendship between Berton and Mowat. And Farley insisted Wilson act as the publicist on a freelance basis for his next McClelland & Stewart book.

Then a new dispute arose. Berton was publicly critical of Farley's unsympathetic response to the arrest by the Soviets of author Aleksandr Solzhenitsyn. On December 20, 1973, Farley told his publisher, "Hope to talk to you today about Pierre. I am really outraged by his actions and I will have nothing to do with him, nor will I sit on any board with him until he has publicly apologized to me. Either he or I will have to leave the Board [of Directors of M&S], and since I am aware that he isn't going to be the one to leave, then I shall have to do so. He is a megalomaniac son of a bitch."[30] The situation was remedied when Berton offered a full, eloquent apology: he was sorry he had given the impression that he felt Farley's stance was conditioned by the fact he had been a guest of the Soviet Union. Of course, Farley was defending the USSR he had seen on two visits and knew that Solzhenitsyn had his own agenda—the restoration of what would be essentially Czarist Russia.[31] Realizing that he had exposed himself to a drubbing from anti-communists, Farley confided to Sandy, "Sure got my ass in a wringer over Solzhenitsyn, didn't I? However Pierre Berton apologized to me on CKEY [radio] yesterday, so all is not lost. He had to. I was about to sue the SOB. Anyway, if it is possible to get one's tits caught in the wringer, I will somehow manage to do it."[32]

Farley often exercised restraint in his public dealings with Berton because he and Claire as well as Pierre and Janet Berton were sometimes a part of the "*Maclean's* gang," the nucleus of which was a group of freelance writers and their spouses or partners who had once worked together at the national magazine: June Callwood and Trent Frayne, Scott Young, and Max and Aileen Braithwaite. Other members of the "gang" included the broadcaster Fred Davis, the novelist Arthur Hailey and his wife Sheila, the architect John Parkin, the artist Harold Town and, later, the publisher Anna Porter and her husband, lawyer Julian Porter. Well into the seventies, this large group would gather on summer weekends at the McClelland cottage, the Hailey cottage or the Davis cottage. Pierre and Farley—having quarrelled the previous night—would make up and then begin imbibing at breakfast time.

Farley's fierce anti-Americanism reached fever pitch at the prospect of McClelland & Stewart failing and at the possibility of the Canadian publishing industry being taken over by American interests. He spoke for many other Canadians when he lamented the desperate situation M&S had reached: "McClelland & Stewart is one of the last bulwarks of Canadianism in this country. And it is being forced to the wall by a total lack of interest by people who pretend to govern this country and who are no more than spokesmen for U.S. interests in Canada. If we allow McClelland & Stewart to be destroyed [by being sold to the United States] we deserve to become second-class citizens of the U.S."

On one score, Farley and Berton were firmly united: their opposition to the dumping of remaindered American editions of their work at the chain stores, such as Coles, to be sold to the public at prices ridiculously lower than the corresponding Canadian editions still in print. Such sales earned no royalties for their authors.

So angry were Jack, Pierre and Farley at Coles that in January 1975 they were on the verge of entering one of the chain's stores, destroying the American editions of Berton and Mowat titles from which they received low or no royalties and getting themselves arrested. In many ways this alliance would have been a monumental undertaking, considering that the two authors often felt like hitting each other. In the past, booksellers in Canada—notwithstanding the glaring loopholes in the Copyright Act—had usually respected publishers' contractual territorial arrangements and obtained their stock of a book from the legitimate Canadian rights holder. Coles had successfully challenged this arrangement in court and won. As far as proprietor Jack Cole was concerned, the issue was cut and dried: "Being retailers we feel an obligation to represent the interests of the public by offering books at the lowest cost. The publishers are trying to create an artificial price situation. How long will they be allowed to continue operating at the public expense? The taxpayer has to pay to subsidize the publishers and pay again through artificially high book prices. I say that's desperately wrong."[33]

Also "desperately wrong" for Jack and Farley in 1975 was the importation into Canada of American Penguin paperbacks of *A Whale for the Killing* and *Sibir* (the American title was *The Siberians*). Farley received a royalty of 4 per cent of the retail price on the Penguins, as opposed to the 15 per cent he would have received from M&S. Farley's loss of earnings on these two books, Jack estimated, was as much as fifty thousand dollars.

There was a slight adjustment in the seventies in how Farley's new books were to be handled. Farley, who had been happily edited in

Boston by Peter Davison, was now to have the same function performed in Canada also, by Lily Miller, who had worked as an editor in New York City at Macmillan, McGraw-Hill, and Lothrop, Lee and Shepard before joining M&S in 1972. The largest audience for Farley's books was in Canada, and it seemed appropriate to Peter, who initiated this scheme, to make this change in order to give Farley's books additional attention. There were a number of teething problems that had to be worked out in this new arrangement, but ultimately it functioned very well. In *The Snow Walker* (1975), Farley thanked Miller for her "unremitting, gentle but implacable persistence" in improving the book.

Unbeknownst to Davison, Jack McClelland decided, in light of the new arrangement, to shift Farley from his American publisher Atlantic–Little, Brown in Boston to Alfred A. Knopf in New York City; he told Angus Cameron, a senior editor at Knopf, that Farley "is very fond of Peter Davison who is his editor at Atlantic but apart from that he's very upset about the Little, Brown performances. . . . In my function as Farley's unofficial agent but mainly as his friend (he is one of the very few people I really care about) I would say he is up for grabs, if you people were really prepared to publish him."[34] This plot never took off—Knopf was not especially interested in adding Farley to their list—but the story has a strange coda.

Davison, unaware of Jack's scheme, flew to Toronto to meet with Farley and Jack. Since he could be away for only the day, Peter arranged for the two to meet him at his hotel, the Inn on the Park, for a working lunch. At the appointed time, no one showed up. Two hours later, Jack called to say he and Farley would be along shortly. A few more hours went by without an appearance by either man. Then the phone rang again. Jack was in the foyer of the hotel; he asked Peter to join him. Davison took the elevator downstairs and was greeted by McClelland, who took him to his car, where a completely drunk Farley was sprawled on the back seat. Realizing he could not conduct any sort of business because of Farley's condition, and aware that his flight was leaving in less than an hour, a very hurt Davison mumbled a hello and then excused himself. Not surprisingly, Farley cannot remember this incident.

There was another publishing imbroglio in 1975, this time between Jack and Claire. The publisher felt Claire had a duty to act as a hand-maiden to her celebrity husband and should forget her own ambitions to pursue a career as a writer:

> I've been brooding about the fact that I seemed to have caused a stoppage of progress on your manuscript. That wasn't my intention. I wish we had taken the opportunity to discuss the whole thing at greater length the other night. . . . My comment was that of all the careers that you could have selected, it seemed to me that writing would perhaps be the least suitable. . . . But, for God's sake, this does not mean that you should, having started a book, be discouraged from finishing it.
>
> I came to understand that evening that the writing of this particular book was not really the start of a separate career for you—as I had first understood it—but rather something that you wanted to do to occupy your time and to tell a story you wanted to tell. That's fair enough. . . . My concern related to the long-term prospect of a wife developing a career that parallels her husband's.

His apology—although a genuine one—betrayed his real feelings about the book, *The Outport People*, which he would nonetheless publish in 1983 to rave reviews.

Precarious though his own writing career and McClelland & Stewart already seemed in the mid-seventies, Farley further complicated matters when he announced that he wanted to publish a volume of verse and told McClelland he had Davison's complete support in this undertaking. Jack fired off a letter on August 15, 1977: "Surely you're joking! Have you and Peter both gone out of your minds at the same time? . . . I've only glanced at a couple of the poems. . . . It may be possible to destroy your whole literary reputation with one slim volume. The whole thing sounds suicidal and masochistic to me. I don't mean the—poems—I mean the whole activity." Two days later, after he had read more of the poems, he was a bit more temperate in his response: "I'm honestly baffled. This type of thing isn't my cup of tea exactly—and never has been—but I don't think a book of these poems would be the crown in your literary career." Three weeks later, Jack took a slightly different—but nevertheless sarcastic—tack: "How could I have been so wrong? The material is fabulous. . . . Complete the manuscript as soon as possible. I am negotiating with Picasso at the moment re illustration. So, it is my fault and I am sorry. I think you should [also] do a book about rabbits fornicating."[35]

The poems sent to Davison and McClelland were, in part, excerpts of "beastie verses" from "Mowat's Bestiary for Unnatural Children." One of them reads,

There once was a rooster named Ern
Who made love to a chick in a churn.
    The result of their flutter
    Was ten pounds of butter
And slivers all over his stern.

Although Farley was hurt by Jack's peremptory dismissal of the proposed book, he was consoled by Peter's more wait-and-see attitude: "I think you are really on to something, and by God you've learned to scan since I last saw your stuff. But this could be a very charming change of pace, and I applaud it. Let's see more."[36]

By the end of the year, a very relieved McClelland teased Davison, whom he suspected—incorrectly—of not having been completely serious in backing Farley's verse: "I think we'll never know whether he [Mowat] has abandoned the verse because you encouraged him or because I told him it was outright crap. It could become a problem that literary historians wrangle over for centuries. Who cares?—the important thing is he has abandoned the verse."[37] However, Farley now threatened to undertake a biography of McClelland: "The truth is you are yellow. Scared to death that the truth will out. . . . It has to be done. At any rate, please do start getting some of it down on tape. . . . Otherwise I'll have to make the whole thing up, and you know what that will mean."[38]

Peter Davison's poet-to-poet letter led to a renewed and even greater intimacy in his relationship with Farley. That August, Farley described to his publisher-editor the rough emotional tangles in which he was involved, tangles which had led to a serious disruption in his ability to write:

> The truth of the matter is, as you undoubtedly well know, my domestic and personal life has hung me up. It is virtually impossible (virtually? Hell, it is impossible) for me to achieve the kind of ambience that will enable me to concentrate my so-called energies on any one subject long enough to make a job of work. . . .
>
> I know this will sound like a thinly disguised plea for what? Advice? Help? Soothing syrup? Well, fuck it, maybe that's what it is. But you are a singularly sapient son-of-a-bitch and so you will read me without the need for any elaboration. But I am N O T asking for assistance. Jasoosie Cristoosie! If I can't figure out how to save myself from drowning, how in hell can you?[39]

After *A Whale for the Killing* (1972), Farley published four more books in the next six years: *Tundra: Selections from the Great Accounts of Arctic Land Voyages* (1973), the last in the *Top of the World* trilogy; *Wake of the Great Sealers* (1973); *The Snow Walker* (1975); and *Canada North Now: The Great Betrayal* (1976). This is not an impressive number given the fact that the first title is largely a collection of the writings of others and the third is largely a collection of previously published magazine pieces. Even *Canada North Now*—which Farley correctly termed a "violent tirade, tract, etc. [that] will blow some lids off"[40]—is an updated version of *Canada North* (1967) and reaches many of the same conclusions as the earlier book, although it announces that conditions in the North have gotten far worse in the intervening decade. Farley also correctly called this book a "violent, old-fashioned Mowat attack on government, big business, and you name it. Ought to start a riot."[41] More importantly, none of these were signature Mowat books in which his distinct sensibility—in either a comic or a tragic mode—is effectively shown. The truth was that Farley was afraid that he had somehow lost his way, was perhaps debarred forever from writing a book of the quality of, say, *People of the Deer* or *Never Cry Wolf.*

In July 1974, Peter Davison—well aware of the difficulties Farley was having in finding a new project worthy of him—suggested he write "No Man's Land," which would tell of Farley's 1947 canoe trip with Charles Schweder. "I think," he told the writer, "that part of your restlessness these past two years . . . comes from a sense, no matter how unconscious, that your talent has outgrown the sort of thing that in the past has presented itself to you to write." All of Farley's books, with the exception of *Westviking*, the salvage books and the various anthologies, were based on investigations he had carried out himself. "I hope you can move on to more thoughtful, less instinctive writing. You couldn't lose your narrative gift if you tried, and I wouldn't think of suggesting that you try. But I think you could reflect more deeply and patiently on your experience and that your writing will be the better for it."[42]

The fragility in Farley's dealings with his father and with Claire and the anxiety he felt about his writing career spilled over into uncertainties about where he wanted to live. Not really happy in Port Hope, he looked forward to the summers away from Ontario, but after two years of spending his summers in Grande Entrée, Farley was thinking of leaving. He was dissuaded from doing so because his Palgrave friends Arnold and Vi Warren bought a property nearby. By 1976, however, Farley was determined to find a summer home elsewhere. For one thing, the growth of French-speaking tourism on the Magdalen Islands dramatically increased the tension level between residents; the English-speaking minority often felt overwhelmed and threatened. The Mowat and Warren properties were on the water, and their land was frequently invaded by tourists and, most significantly, by all-terrain vehicles. Although there was plenty of room for walkers to access the beach on both properties, the Mowats and the Warrens constructed a fence and gateposts as a barrier to prevent vehicles from entering both properties. Farley's summer home was no longer the simple retreat he had wanted it to be.

There was another complication. Farley antagonized some locals when he opposed the Quebec government's plan to establish salt mines on the islands; this proposal required the dredging of the lagoons and had the potential to ruin fishing as a local industry.

Although the fishermen appreciated his support, many other locals—in need of employment—resented his opposition to the government scheme.

In April and May 1974, Claire and Farley, after sixteen days looking for a farm to buy on Prince Edward Island, purchased one a few miles inland from the Wood Islands ferry terminus: "ninety acres, 60 cleared, good barn, fair house, backed into a thousand acres of forest."[43] The Mowats were sure they had found a place that would be impregnable by tourists and local politics.

Two years later, however, Farley bought yet another house and piece of land in Nova Scotia. He was ecstatic in describing the muskeg spruce that covered Brick Point: "Well, we found it. 150 acres at St. Peter's Bay on the east coast of Cape Breton. Facing the sea, but only a mile or so from the canal leading into the Bras d'Or Lakes. Over a mile of shoreline, an island, and 120 acres of forest. Terrific place."[44] The property in Prince Edward Island was eventually sold.

In 1976, the Mowats moved house within Port Hope when Helen decided, after seventeen years, to move into the senior citizens' apartments owned by her church, St. Mark's, and Farley and Claire took over 18 King Street. Since their new home—an 1840s wooden Ontario cottage built for farm workers—was a bit on the small side, the Mowats, a year after moving in, converted the old veranda at the back of the house into an enclosed sun room which could be used as a den. When the house that abutted their backyard went up for sale, they purchased it to store their ever-increasing mountain of books and to have a place where Farley could write. Later, they added a full-width shed dormer to 18 King Street to convert the four tiny bedrooms into a large master bedroom, a bathroom and an office for Claire.

No matter where he lived, Farley remained uncomfortable. In a letter to Arnold and Vi Warren in March 1977, Claire commented on the uncertainties that plagued her husband: "Farley changes his mind daily about what he intends to do during the rest of 1977. One day he is going to Cape Breton to build a house. Another day he is going to tour Canada interviewing people about the current state of the nation. Another day it's something else. I feel as if I'm living in a cage with a very restless tiger."[45] In an aside in a letter to Sandy, Farley

(top) *Brick Point, Nova Scotia*
(above) *18 King Street, Port Hope*

observed, "I am trying to get back into a working posture and it ain't easy."[46] Unfortunately, writing was to remain difficult for a long stretch of time.

Farley's melancholia was augmented by Albert's bad health throughout 1974 and his death on Monday, January 27, 1975, at Indian Summer, at the age of twelve. The dog had three massive seizures over the preceding weekend, each one leaving him progressively wobblier. Farley took him to a vet in Cobourg on the day he died; he received a lot of drugs, but either despite them or because of them, he passed away that night. Andy Thomson was visiting the Mowats, and he and a tear-filled Farley dug the grave in the midst of a grove of small cedar trees. Claire told Angus and Barb, "He was an old dog, we have to remind ourselves; arthritic, going blind, and a heart murmur for the past year and a half. We were so lucky to have had him for so long. I do feel we had the best years of our lives together."[47]

Seven years before, Farley had tried to write his book about Albert, but he had become nervous when he looked down and saw his subject staring back at him with limpid eyes and had abandoned the venture. Seven months after Albert's death, in September 1975, Peter Davison, who was staying with the Mowats at Grande Entrée, urged him to begin the book again. On September 30, Farley told Sandy, "I'm starting work on Albert. Or, rather, he is starting work on me. He has decided to write his autobiography, using my typewriter and my paws. Thank God he can spell better than me (better than me can?). So we'll see what happens. If he fails me I can always revert to the war museum story but, truthfully, I can't find a book to hang on that one. Lots of fun, but what's it all mean? Sound and fury, maybe. Well, I'll give it a chance later, but meantime, old Al seems to have a grip on my testicles."[48]

Within two months, Farley had written two hundred pages of a quick first draft and summoned a very excited Peter Davison to take a look at it. Some of the material—all done in Albert's voice—was brilliant, some dreadful. Nevertheless, as he informed his colleagues, Peter was excited:

For years now we've been hoping and waiting, hoping that
Farley would write a book about his marvellous water dog, and
waiting for him to start. Farley kept putting the book off during
Albert's lifetime. I've been accused of sometimes overselling
projects. Well, trot out all your suspicions on this one: do your
worst. No matter how sceptical you are that a short bearded best-
selling Canadian in a kilt can write the autobiography of a dog in
his own voice, I know he can, like the little train that could. [49]

But despite his initial enthusiasm, the Albert book defeated Farley,
who even tried switching the voice in the book from first person into
third. Once again, he abandoned the project.

June 1977 provided Farley and Claire with a liberating escape from
the "picayune hassles of home," a trip to Bulgaria to attend a conference of 150 writers, including the English novelist C.P. Snow, the
American novelist John Cheever and the Russian poet Yevgeny
Yevtushenko. The VIP treatment—the best rooms in the best hotels,
good food and wine, a trip to the Black Sea, visits to ancient monas-
teries—allowed both Mowats to relax completely. Flowers, especially
roses, were everywhere. "Bulgarians," Claire told Arnold and Vi,
"aren't like Russians. They are certainly far less evangelical about
their communism than the Russians. Political posters and slogans are
scant compared to the USSR and not once did anyone try to tell us
about the virtues of communism."

That summer, Farley and Claire were in Cape Breton getting Brick
Point ready for habitation, living in a trailer while the old farmhouse
was being renovated. As Claire said, she and Farley had not yet formed
any real impression of their new summer home: "I have nothing to say
about the place after five days. It just feels very odd not to be in the
Magdalen Islands. We were there, after all, for eight summers."

One consolation provided by Cape Breton was Farley's friendship
with his neighbours, Ervin and Janice Touesnard. He was also
delighted to make the acquaintance of the journalist and writer
Silver Donald Cameron, who had settled at nearby D'Escousse on

Isle Madame. An irate, tired Cameron, clad in overalls, was digging out a disintegrated septic tank when all of a sudden a "curiously tentative" Farley, who had been given Cameron's name by Harold Horwood, popped his head around the corner and asked if he wanted to have a drink. Ever since that encounter, the two men have seen each other frequently.

Cameron, fifteen years younger than Farley, admires his friend's human touch, his willingness to concede that some writers have tackled a topic better than he had or could have done. "As a young man," he points out, "Farley nailed down a lot of big issues." He adds, "He has a quality of manliness not seen very often nowadays. He has a distinctively brave way of doing things, a courtly manner that was once associated exclusively with masculinity."

During their first encounter, Farley mentioned that he and Claire were living in the trailer. "We don't answer the phone. But you know what happened the other day? I just happened to be at the house washing some dishes and the phone rang. Like a fool I answered it. It was the bloody *Globe and Mail*! How the hell they got hold of the phone number I'll never know. By the way, I'll write it down for you."

Flummoxed, Cameron asked, "Isn't that a sort of contradiction. You come down here to get away from all that, and one of the first things you do is seek out the only other full-time writer for miles and give him your unlisted phone number." Without skipping a beat, Farley replied, "I'm not hiding from you! I'm hiding from the bloody tour buses who used to stop at my gate in the Magdalens and announce, 'This is the home of Farley Mowat, the famous writer.'" Despite his best intentions at times, Farley's habitual friendliness usually comes to the fore.

Claire and Farley stayed overnight with Angus and Barbara at Northport en route to Cape Breton in 1977. Since 1975, when Albert died, Angus had been slowly dying of cancer in the brain and chest. A very sad Claire now told the Warrens, "He has lost ground since our previous visit one month earlier. Very frail and very weak and his eyesight is failing, as well as his co-ordination. I have the feeling we're on 'stand-by' to go back there before the summer is over. Very very sad to see him this way."[50] At that meeting, Angus called his son aside and plaintively confessed that he wished that they lived near each other.

As Angus's physical condition slowly deteriorated in 1976 and 1977, father and son attempted to come to terms with the fallout from Helen's decision to move into the St. Mark's apartments, where she had to pay rent. When Helen offered to give 18 King Street to Farley, he refused. Instead, he purchased it from her at full market value and made arrangements to increase the bequest in her will to John and Rosemary; this resulted in a substantial lowering of the amount of money to be left to Farley. In turn, Farley asked his father to maintain his original payment of two hundred dollars a month for Helen's support; if he did this, Farley offered to ensure that there would be no shortage of further financial support should Helen require it. In concluding his letter outlining their mutual financial obligations to Helen, Farley attempted to make peace with his father:

> This is not a "curt" letter, but it is too formal a letter. I have sounded formal only because I want to be sure that the facts are clearly presented. The best thing, I'm sure, is to talk it over once again and so I'll bring a copy of this letter with me when next I come down, and we can go over it point by point, together, and in amity and harmony. There is no reason at all why there should be grounds for irritation between you and me and I don't intend, this time, to allow irritation to enter my soul. I know you won't either. It would be so damned silly.[51]

And yet "irritation" had entered the souls of both men.

Part of the problem was that Barbara became deeply anxious as Angus's death approached. One day she telephoned John Mowat at the bank where he was employed and asked if he realized that his father was at death's door. John immediately left work and drove to Hotel Dieu, the hospital in Kingston where Angus was a patient. Since his condition had not changed at all in the past few days, a perplexed Angus told John he had wasted his time by arriving out of the blue to see him. Even Beryl Gaspardy, a close friend of Barbara's, sometimes found an increasingly distraught Barbara difficult to deal with. For example, despite the fact that Farley and Claire had visited Angus on their way to Cape Breton, Barbara told Beryl that they had not done so.

When Angus died on September 21, 1977, Farley and Claire were at Grande Entrée, clearing out their house. Without consulting them, Barbara arranged for the funeral to be held at Sophiasburg cemetery, near Picton, at noon on the twenty-third, even though she knew that travelling from the remote Magdalen Islands in the Gulf of St. Lawrence routinely took fifteen to twenty hours, even by air.

However, Farley and Claire barely managed to get back to Ontario in time for the funeral. When John Mowat and Claire and Farley arrived at the Picton Bay Motel on the evening of the twenty-second, it was almost eleven o'clock at night. Farley was shocked to learn that Barbara had notified very few of Angus's friends and former associates of his passing; he was even more distraught when he learned that no arrangement had been made for a colour guard from the Hasty Pees or for a piper to play.

Although Farley was told by Barbara that Angus had asked for the simplest possible funeral, he was not sure of her veracity. He later said, "I do know that I could not stand by, nor could John, to see him disappear anonymously—put down like a dog."[52] There followed some frantic efforts on Farley's part to contact the Hasty Pees by telephone:

> Since there was no phone book in the room I went to the proprietor, Mr. Rudy Scheidthauer, and asked if he could provide me with one. His reply was that he would not, since customers stole the phone books. Only after considerable discussion did he agree to allow me to take a phone book to my room for a "few minutes." It was then close to 11:00 P.M. I completed two local calls but, on the third, the proprietor did not answer the switchboard. I went to his office and explained that I still had important calls to make. He informed me that the switchboard

was closed as of 11:00 P.M. and that he would not operate it for me until the next morning.

Understandably, I believe, I was annoyed. I told him that I would report his attitude to the Department of Tourism and returned to my room. He followed me there and was abusive to me, my wife, and John Mowat. When I asked him to leave the room, he responded by ordering us to leave the motel. It is to be clearly understood that he had been informed of the nature of our predicament regarding my father's funeral.[53]

Scheidthauer later told the press that he had thrown Farley out because "he did not act like a gentleman. He had been drinking." From the Picton Bay Motel, the trio made their way to the Sportsman's Motel near Picton, where Farley was allowed to make his phone calls. Given the lateness of the night, he could not arrange a colour guard; he did, however, hire a piper to play.

Things did not get much better after the simple, sparsely attended funeral the next day, where the poet Al Purdy, a local resident, spoke at Farley's request. For once, the poet was at a loss for words. He simply said, "Angus Mowat was a wonderful man. I was very fond of him, and I'll miss him very much." No minister was present, only an undertaker. At the reception held at the Mowat home in Northport, two groups formed on opposite sides of the living room: friends of Barbara's and friends of Farley's. There was almost no communication between the two camps, but the tension was palpable. Finally, Farley removed a chair and a tam-o'-shanter from the house. Barbara told Beryl Gaspardy and others that Farley had begun removing things from her home and had persisted in doing so even after she told him to desist. Subsequently, Farley informed Rosemary of what had really happened:

I did not wish to remove anything belonging to him. Barbara insisted that I take some family papers, and then the chair. The chair was not under her control. Helen had willingly allowed John and I to take it down there [a few years earlier], at Angus's request. But under the terms of the separation agreement, and

the will, it belongs to Helen until her death and so was only
being returned to her. It was *not* a "gift" to me.

Ah yes. The Bonnet. This was mine. I had worn it back from
Scotland at which time I brought another bonnet as a gift for
Angus. He didn't much like its colour, so I took mine off and
put it on his head. He never wore it—preferring his old one.
The day of the funeral I put it on as a sentimental gesture when
John and I went to pay our private respects at the grave in the
afternoon. To be accused, at 11:00 P.M. by telephone, of effectively stealing something of Barbara's was N O T the most pleasant
experience of an unpleasant day.[54]

In the aftermath of Angus's death and the acrimonies surrounding
the funeral, Farley and Claire became ill with flu-like symptoms.
Their health remained so bad that they had to abandon their project
of clearing out the house at Grande Entrée (they finished the packing
up only the following summer). But despite the weariness and sickness that engulfed him, Farley was able, three months later, to tell
Peter Davison of a strange psychic change:

Am in much better fettle and can't quite see why. Ah, but I
suspect it is the departure of Angus. I hadn't realized how he had
been riding my psychic back. You know the old thing: got to
please the old man, and work like hell to extract some measure
of approbation. He has made it easy for me by taking off and
leaving a mess behind him which I have to handle. Left everything to Barbara, and nothing at all to Helen (me either) which
means all sorts of shit to be shovelled.

In any event, I truly do feel much more myself, able and even
willing to go to work.[55]

PART THREE

Visionary

13

Prophet of Doom

1977–1984

"ON the whole, I think this book will be a great departure for you, because of the personal involvement of a man who was once Farley Mowat."[1] This was Peter Davison's response in November 1978—thirteen months after Angus's death—when he read a draft of what was then called "One Man's War," Farley's graphic account of his own ordeal of war in Sicily and Italy.

The Regiment, Farley's earlier account of battle, had been a historical chronicle centred largely on the experiences of the Hasty Pees in Sicily and Italy; Farley himself is absent from what is largely an objective piece of writing. After completing that book, he had thought of writing a novel about the war (perhaps in the manner of Earle Birney's scatological, semi-autobiographical *Turvey*) but abandoned that project. He had also considered writing a satirically minded account of the war museum venture.

After Angus's death, Farley's imagination turned once again in the direction of a comic, autobiographical history of his early days in the Army. But the book quickly swerved away from his conscious control to become a gut-wrenching account, in three parts, of the author's own experience of the horror of war. While his father was alive, he had been unable to write of his sense of being a coward, a man consumed by fear of death. Although war and its aftermath had drawn father and son closer together, Farley had been ashamed, both during and after the war, to tell his father of such feelings, obviously afraid (probably incorrectly) that his father would reject him if he was candid about them. Angus's passing liberated Farley's imagination, finally making it safe for him to speak about emotions previously kept hidden. Now uninhibited, Farley was suddenly able to reveal a side of his character hitherto concealed from the reading public.

Farley had many obstacles to overcome in moving in this new direction in his writing career. Soon after Angus died, Farley, on Helen's behalf, became embroiled in a bitter legal battle with Barbara over Angus's pension. Barbara finally won this battle when her status as common-law wife was given precedence over Helen's as widow. Then Barbara began to spread untrue stories about Farley's treatment of his father. And when these efforts were not listened to, she took up a new line of harassment: she paid a surprise visit to Frances Mowat at Palgrave, told her that the Mexican divorce meant she was still married to Farley and recommended she sue Farley. Since Frances and Farley had remained on good terms after their initial traumatic parting and Farley had continued to support his ex-wife and children since the time of their legal separation, Frances brushed aside Barbara's suggestion.

At the same time that Farley was discovering another level in his imagination, he was withdrawing further from Claire. Since he felt he needed to be alone even more than before, he would go down east by himself to work, often during the winter. He sometimes became annoyed when a very lonely Claire, in search of solace, called him. On July 9, 1978, she told him, "I'm sorry I phoned you the other night in my sad state. It is so stark and terrible sometimes that I break down and call you, even though I vow I won't." In Port Hope, Claire had an additional burden—taking care of Helen, whom she found excessively self-centred: "She thinks she listens to me. She does, for about five minutes, maybe six. After that we go back to flowers, or to you, or to Angus. All very ritualized."[2]

Also very ritualized was Farley's need for solitariness. As he wrote about his experience of war in a new, raw way, he came uncomfortably back into touch with thirty-year-old traumas. And as those sufferings were reactivated, he acted in what was in many ways his habitual way of dealing with difficult or demanding situations: he tried to run away. When he was in such a state, no amount of love or affection ever seemed enough. Claire wanted to comfort him, but he often spurned her. He did not wish to push her away—he simply did not know how to use the consolation offered to him. Realizing that the problems between herself and her husband could only be rectified through confrontation, Claire warned him in July 1978 that they must be "prepared for a fight within the first few days of my arrival [in Nova Scotia]. Now I know you're going to say, no, no, no, it's unnecessary and preventable and all that, but it will happen anyway. Let's face reality."[3]

But psychic realities were something Farley wanted to evade. If one difficult part of the burnout of war consists of a conviction that everything is meaningless, fear that any kind of human contact is worthless can result. On a daily basis, Farley relived the war in setting it down on paper; he could not run away from that reality if he wanted to write the book that was demanding to be written.

For instance, he remembered a stretcher-bearer, an "older" man of thirty-five, who had been with the Regiment since the autumn of 1939:

> I was descending the north slope, numbed and passionless, drugged with fatigue, dead on my feet, when I heard someone singing! It was a rough voice, husky yet powerful. A cluster of mortar bombs came crashing down and I threw myself into the mud. When I could hear again, the first sound that came to me was the singing voice. Cautiously I raised myself just as a star shell burst overhead, and saw him coming toward me through that blasted wasteland.

Stark naked, he was striding through the cordite stench with his head held high and his arms swinging. His body shone white in the brilliant light of the flare, except for what appeared to be a glistening crimson sash that ran from one shoulder down one thigh and dripped from his lifted foot.

He was singing "Home on the Range" at the top of his voice.

In this portrait, the absurdity and madness of war is chillingly rendered; and as he wrote this passage, Farley was aware that he too had long been a victim of such events.

Peter Davison, realizing how difficult a project the new book was for Farley, nevertheless saw the challenge as a breakthrough opportunity for a writer who had been unable to return to top form. He sent his writer detailed instructions on how to proceed; Peter had often stayed with Farley while editing his work, and he was staying with him at Port Hope in November 1978 when he offered more hands-on advice than usual, writing a long memorandum to Farley:

> In a few flashbacks scattered through the book you should give us glimpses of the untrained, sensitive but uncalloused boy who enlisted in the Army, his father's son, at the early part of the war; the boy whose outdoor training actually fitted him to be a fairly skilled soldier; the boy who would be crushed into man's shape by the events of the war. Part I, in Sicily, will be his blooding; Part II, in southern Italy, will be his bloody plunge into the crusher of war; and Part III will be his disillusionment.

Having expressed his confidence in the material he had read, Davison was aware of just how arduous the task was for Farley, who usually wrote quickly and well:

> You still, as you know better than I, have an enormous amount of work to do in spite of the large number of pages you have accumulated. There is a lot of material here, but a structure and an inner, ultimate meaning have still to be found. I have great confidence that you will find it, that this book like the best war books

will ultimately be a story of "What the Self Saw." And of what the Self became, what was lost in the boy, and what in the man was scarred. I'm keeping a copy of this memorandum. I trust it sums up most of our several long conversations about the manuscript. After you've read this, we'll decide whether you want me to edit a couple of the draft chapters before I leave here.[4]

Ten months earlier, Farley, who had taken himself off to Brick Point in Nova Scotia to work on his war book, did something uncharacteristic. Although he had always been a dutiful keeper of journals—especially when travelling—those documents were largely observations of and reflections upon what he saw. But in January 1978, Farley finally turned his eye upon himself, explored his own struggle to create, and in the process forced himself to confront the slump that had overtaken him.

Monday, January 23
Still fine, bright weather. A new start on the [war] memoirs this AM, and I hope to God this one takes. . . . Mail today including further word of the machinations of Barbara the Bitch. Got me riled up again even though I am fairly sure she is a mental case.

Thursday, January 26
Somewhat depressed. So far there is no fire in what I am doing. Hasn't been much since *A Whale for the Killing*, really. Little spurts here and there. For some reason I am changing, or have changed, from an activist to a passivist. The interest level is low, and not easily sustained. To what does one attribute this? Ageing process? Too much success? Or too much personal stress these past several years? Past not important. What is important is how to reverse the process, if it is reversible. Well, we shall see.

Friday, January 27
Back at it this morning, and this time with some results. Have quit trying to begin at the beginning. By now, I should know better.

Saturday, January 28

Turning point! Wrote most of a full chapter, and it is not bad at all. Crossed fingers—the block seems to be broke. There will, of course, be innumerable setbacks ahead, but I am underway at last!

Tuesday, February 7

Finished Chapter 3. And am even able to start cutting back on my smoking as a result of having some accomplishment to show myself. [Receives news of Barbara.] The woman really has to be sick. I am thinking back to earlier events, too, and conclude that she had Angus completely under her thumb several years ago. He was not allowed to visit us, or to see us without her being present, and, of course, she made us as unwelcome as possible. . . . Perhaps she was jealous of my position, fame, etc., and was simply seeking to cut me down through any means at her disposal. Hence her attempts to alienate me from the members of the family; her espousal of people whom I did not like or who had done me a disservice; her belittling of my work, and that of the people I admired; her attempts to strike at Helen and so, at me. . . . But I am still puzzled about Angus. Did she actually persuade him I am a louse and an ingrate, etc.? Else why did he not leave me some message, or send me something to clarify the issue, at least after he was gone? . . . Instead of which all he left was a coil of ugliness for me to sort out. . . . what good memory can I hold of him? Must I look back on his last incarnation as a foolish weakling, so self-indulgent that he would sacrifice me to ensure that he went out in comfort?

Tuesday, February 14

I took a nose dive. Unable to work at all. Sure the book is no good. Gloomy about my age, health, marriage, etc. . . . My essential problem is that nothing *excites* me any more. . . . At 57 a man is hardly the big-eyed enthusiast he might have been in his twenties or thirties.

Wednesday, February 15
Short lived depression. . . . Really missing *my* Claire these days. Not cut out to be a hermit *all* the time, though I have to admit this is the way to force myself to write. No alternatives.

Wednesday, February 22
Last two days working out the details, and outline, of my war year in England. Quite fascinating how the reconstruction grows: little forgotten driblets of memory flow into place and the picture takes form.

Monday, February 27
Finished Chapter 9. Must have about 35,000 words to date, at the end of the first month of work. Which ain't bad.

Sunday, March 5
. . . Claire descended from the train, and I whisked her home. Big fire, good meal, wine and lamplight, and so both of us to bed in cuddlesome mood. Been a long time sleeping alone.

Saturday, March 11–Wednesday, March 15
The old conundrum remains unaltered. I am not happy or able to function in the urban milieu, and Claire is not able to do likewise in the rural one. There seems to be no middle ground where both can operate. In the meantime writing work is at an end and we are doing very little of anything except eating, sleeping, and putting in time.

Saturday, March 18
Another good evening by the fire. C. to leave on Tuesday and I shall miss her.

Tuesday, March 21
Both of us full of angst, as always one is on a departure day.

Tuesday, March 28

A week since Claire's departure and I miss her. The writing goes in spurts but is improving as I settle back into habits but, alas, my no smoking campaign is in ruins. The smoke rises in direct proportions as the tension rises, and I am back to being a volcano.

Thursday, March 30

This day I got a letter from [the novelist and essayist] Hugh MacLennan—an excellent, fine note extolling the virtues of *A Whale for the Killing* and of my role as a non-fiction writer. This is the second time Hugh has given me a great boost when I needed it. The first was with *People of the Deer.*

Friday, March 31

Spent most of the working day reading my war letters from 1944, which only intensified a depression that has been coming over me for the past several days. Unidentifiable. I lack energy, incentive, and am gloomy about the point and purpose of things. Nothing new about this, but the mood hasn't bothered me for some weeks. . . . I begin to understand Claire's problem. It is so damned difficult to keep at the business of starting to build anew every few years. I've been doing it all my life, and it is unnatural and in every way exhausting.

Sunday, April 2

In evening called Claire who sounded most despondent. . . . Decided I had better pack it in and head for Port Hope. Have drafted some 14 chapters of the book, maybe 55,000 words, which is a good start. Will now put it in abeyance for a time.[5]

During the winter and early spring of 1978, while he struggled valiantly to write his war book, Farley confronted many of his inner demons: his distress at growing old, his suspicion that his powers as a writer were waning, his struggle to stay connected to Claire, his deep unhappiness at the disintegration of his relationship with his father, his hatred of Barbara. Farley wanted to mourn his father and to put that loss into perspective but the rage he felt towards his father's common-law wife impeded him. Even her closest friends admitted that Barbara could be exceptionally difficult, harsh and controlling. Yet by focusing his rage on Barbara, Farley let his father off the hook and, in the process, was unable to grieve properly. As a result, he paid a high price in depression and anxiety.

He confronted his inner demons, however, and won. Although the battle had been a difficult one, the long drought since *A Whale for the Killing* was over, and a rough first draft of one of his finest books had finally been wrested from the psychic garbage. And although Peter Davison's hand was needed as never before to bring *And No Birds Sang* to completion, Farley was the real architect of this triumph.

Still, many problems remained in the manuscript. When Davison read the penultimate draft in the early months of 1979, he found the book a "strong, deceptively simple narrative of what happens to men in war. Beginning in light-hearted, almost old-fashioned Imperial style, it descends gradually into the grinding horror of modern warfare." Yet the book "steeps itself too wholly in the war ambiance without relief, without memory, without nostalgia." He suggested that Farley insert "an interlude or two, in the spirit of harmonica music rising from the trenches in a movie, or the strains of Lili Marlene."

Another of Davison's reservations was about the ending: "You ask if it's too abrupt. Yes, I think so. An epilogue is needed. . . . If you can write [such a piece], tell us what indelible impressions—beyond those you have obviously recounted—your war left you with." Finally, there was the title. Davison hated the working title, "One Man's War," and he found Farley's original title, "No Birds Sang," too poetical; he suggested "The Worm That Never Dies" or "The Old Lie."

By the middle of May, McClelland & Stewart decided to call the book *And No Birds Sang*. On May 29 Farley told Davison, "Herewith one contract. Signed. Unsealed. And NO epilogue. But that is for you to make—the termination. Peter the Terminator. I simply can't work on the damn book any more—not a word, not a line." By June 14,

Davison had written a draft of "An Anti-Epilogue" for Farley's scrutiny:

> There should perhaps be an Epilogue to this book, telling why I wrote it, and what happened to me next. My publisher seems to think so. But to me it would be a violation of the dead, and a violation of time. For decades my war has been so wrapped in the cotton-wool of protective forgetfulness, that unwrapping it has been enough to recall the boy that I was, and the man I began to become. Does it matter that after the events I have just recounted I went away from the Regiment at last, to take that previously despised job at Brigade headquarters? Does it matter that my war, after that, was both an anti-climax and a gargantuan joke? Does it matter why I have set down this record of events that took place thirty-five years ago? It does not matter that I have changed so much that I can barely remember the young lieutenant I was in Sicily, nor that it was the war that set those changes into motion. What matters, I suppose, is only my firm conviction that there are, and can be, no good wars. My war was one of the best and a bloody damn thing it was. Perhaps it only matters that we can remember our bad dreams and hope they will never come back.

Moved by Davison's intuitive understanding of *And No Birds Sang*, Farley extensively revised his editor's words to construct the anti-epilogue that concludes the finished book. In this version, the personal elements in the book are downplayed considerably. It concludes:

> Let it be said that I wrote this book in the absolute conviction that there never has been, nor ever can be a "good" or worthwhile war. Mine was one of the better ones (as such calamities are measured), but still, a bloody awful thing it was. So awful that through three decades I kept the deeper agonies of it wrapped in the cotton-wool of protective forgetfulness, and would have been well content to leave them buried so forever

. . . but could not, because the Old Lie—temporarily discredited by the Vietnam debacle—is once more gaining confidence; a whisper which soon may become another strident shout urging us on to mayhem.

Dulce et decorum est pro patria mori!

Spawned in Hell long before Homer sanctified it, and goading men to madness and destruction ever since, that Old Lie *has to be put down!*

If there must be a specific purpose to such a book as mine . . . let this be it.

On April 3, 1980, Farley wrote to Peter, "Thanks for the continuing flow of reviews of *Birds*. I note, with a slight taste of crow in the gullet, that almost all refer favourably to the epilogue. Good man, you." Jack McClelland paid Farley one of his back-handed compliments: "Well, I have read *Time* and I have read *Newsweek* and I am overwhelmed. They both seem convinced that it is your best book. I can't argue with them. I didn't really think it was your best book, but I feel I must send you belated congratulations."[6] But no notice gave Farley as much pleasure or satisfaction as the letter he received from Helen, who showed she had a good understanding of the psychic forces that had conspired against him, both during the war and afterwards:

> My very dear Son—
> I've been listening to you reading [on the radio] and it breaks my heart. You were so young, so sheltered—what can I say? Those experiences don't fade out with time. They are always there, too painful to allow being brought to the surface of consciousness or touched by other hands.
> I love you very much,
> Mother—[7]

One friend, Silver Don Cameron, recalled hearing Farley read from the book: "Glasses low on his nose, he reads too quickly, shy about his work and its reception. But the images of the pounded, churned Italian countryside, the slithering tanks and ruined men, the worm of fear: These are so strong, so vivid, that they overmaster even the author's anxiety. As the last words hang in the air, Farley is crying. He's not alone."[8]

When *And No Birds Sang* reached its final stages of readiness early in 1979, Farley wanted to get to work on another book, but he was not exactly sure either of the subject matter or of the form that a new book should take. In fact, he wondered if he should move in a completely different direction, as he told a business associate: "The book situation and the publishing situation everywhere in the west seems to be rapidly deteriorating. I am seriously thinking of shifting most of my effort to film-making in future."[9]

During the remainder of 1979 and throughout 1980, Farley realized he wanted to write a novel set in the Magdalen Islands that would be about the destruction of the natural world at the hands of European explorers. The book, to be tentatively called "Killing Ground," would be fresh territory for him. In August 1980, Davison responded to the proposal for such a turning point in Farley's writing career:

> This book more than any other Mowat will have to depend for its pace and its appeal on the flesh rather than the bone, on the texture of the prose and the detailed satisfaction of the reader's curiosity rather than on the unfolding of some plot. Your plot is simple enough: the boy and the woman are made captive and violated (it doesn't matter whether the violation is literal or sexual) by European conquistadors; they escape and make their way through the earthly paradise of the Magdalen Islands; they form a new society based on their own instincts, a society of two which may—or could—be destroyed by the death of one of them. The boy (or the boy and the woman) survives happily enough, surrounded by the Eden-like fertility of the place, and companioned by animals of land and sea alike. The conquistadors return, and the inhabitants return, and the inhabitants

struggle and die, along with the teeming population of the islands.[10]

Five months later, Farley had decided to abandon any attempt at a fictional format in favour of a non-fictional one: "A series of separate accounts (chapters, whatever) dealing with some score or so of bird, fish, mammal species that, at c. 1500, were abundant (to super abundant) in the Gulf of St. Lawrence basin, including Newfoundland, south Labrador and the southern shore." As he explained to Davison, his research into the situation in the Magdalens

> led me to uncover more than the mere tip of a horrendous story
> of death and destruction of living beings on a scale that even I
> had not suspected. And it can't be told properly in the frame-
> work of the original book idea. I'm not sure how it will finally
> be told, but I am close enough to a solution to begin, in my own
> inimitable way, groping my way toward it on the typewriter. I
> suspect the "chapters" will be linked closely, from one species or
> group of beasties to the next, on an "ascending" scale beginning
> with the fishes and finishing in a burst of bloody horror with the
> Beothuks. As far as I know the concept is unique . . . to carry
> the modern reader back some 400 years and show him what
> Eden was like, then to let him see in detail the rape of Eden.[11]

Davison did not like Farley's new ideas and told him so. Bloodied but very much unbowed, Farley continued on with the book, which he now called "Age of Slaughter." By September 1982, however, he was sufficiently depressed by the book he was struggling to write that he decided to abandon it:

> What I think is that I have finally, and irrevocably (until I
> revoke it) had it up to here with weighty tomes designed to
> influence homo sapiens to behave a little less like a totally
> deranged species. Fuck it. I am sixty one, and I have enough
> money, reputation, etc. So. No more crusades. No more foolish
> attempts to be a literary gent. I am going to take some of the

advice I gave you—get out of the bloody rut and learn to live, larf, and make Mary when, if and where I can find the bitch.

Actions which follow upon this: 1. Age of Slaughter is effectively dead. I will try and find some way that the data, and the written sections, can be used. But I am not going to wade in blood and blubber, death and destruction any longer. 2. I am going to continue writing but only for my own pleasure and delight, and if there be no pleasure and no delight, I will cheerfully stuff it.[12]

Instead of wasting his time on preaching, he was "going to have fun!" His new book would be an autobiography, to be called "Born Naked."

While wrestling with his next book project, Farley had plenty of activities to keep him busy. Briefly, there was the possibility of collaborating on a book with Sandy, who, using a tape recorder and a camera, wanted to do a book on the survivors of the hippie generation. Farley received the Curran Award in 1977 for his contribution to animal preservation; was presented with the Queen Elizabeth II Silver Jubilee Medal in 1977; was obviously involved in 1980 with Andy Thomson's NFB documentary *In Search of Farley Mowat*; and was made an Officer of the Order of Canada in 1981.

Early in 1978, Farley and Claire visited England, Scotland and Iceland. In some ways, this was a sad trip because the Mowat who had been somewhat like Farley's adopted father or older brother, his croft Farley's adopted home, had recently died.

After Ed Schreyer was appointed governor general in 1979, the Mowats attended his installation and visited with him and Lily at their official residence, Rideau Hall, in Ottawa. In the summer of 1979, the Schreyers and their four children—plus round-the-clock Mounties—spent twenty-six hours at Brick Point. During that year, Farley continued to lobby on behalf of seals and whales. A year later, the Mowats accompanied the Schreyers to Lahr in West Germany in an Armed Forces 707, then to Milan in a Dash 7, and from there toured

Farley clowning with Ed and Lily Schreyer
at a vice-regal ball, circa 1980

northern Italy and Austria in a minivan chauffeured by an RCMP
inspector. The party was then flown to Holland and England before
being flown home in the private saloon of the 707.

Peter Davison, hearing that Jack McClelland planned to publish a
one-volume selection of Farley's work, wrote the Canadian publisher
that year with his list, "off the top of my head, of passages I can
remember from twenty-two years . . . which I would like to see in
the book."[13] For his trouble, Peter became the editor of *The World of
Farley Mowat*, which was published in 1980.

The most surprising event of 1979 was the dramatic reappearance
of the *Happy Adventure*. In the intervening years, it had been
purchased and sailed to Owen Sound by Jerry LeClair, a sailor who
had worked on the Great Lakes. Now he phoned Farley and told him
he was planning to sail it to Cape Breton and then back to its birthplace, Newfoundland. When Farley told Jack what had happened,
the publisher was determined to purchase the boat as some sort of

"interesting tourist attraction."[14] Farley did not want the boat back but was persuaded by Jack to buy it. On July 30 he told McClelland, "*Happy Adventure* is getting closer, and I shudder at the prospect."[15] A little more than three weeks later, Farley provided his co-owner with a graphic account of what happened next: "I have spent every hour of every day and night for three weeks on that fucking boat you made me buy! . . . And last Sunday we launched her under the cameras of the CBC National News no less. And she floated. While the cameras were on her. And the next day she began to sink. . . . She will never, never float!"[16] A year later, on June 7, 1980, he asked McClelland, "Should I sell HA again? Why don't you ask Ontario Place [a provincially owned waterfront park in Toronto] if they would like to splurge. We can ship her up to them via flatbed express. I'm too old to fart around with her any longer, and too lazy."[17] A bemused Claire told the Warrens, "I've never heard of anyone buying back a boat 9 years after they had sold it. I guess we can now call it The Boat Who Wouldn't Go Away."[18] The boat was eventually dragged to shore and donated to a local museum, which placed it on its front lawn. Later, when the museum decided it could no longer afford to keep the *Happy Adventure*, it was to be hauled on a trailer to Margaree Harbour on the west side of Cape Breton. It hit a bump on the way and fell to pieces but was resuscitated and is still, in a sad state, on display there.

Another discomforting event was the thunderbolt that struck Brick Point on the night of July 12, 1980. A visitor, "David Blackwood, was tossed right out of bed onto his ass," Farley reported. "Very undignified. My Volvo was sprayed with brick shrapnel until it looks like it had barely survived World War III. . . . A huge hole was blasted in the roof, and a 6 inch rainfall at the same time didn't do the ceiling any good."[19]

At Port Hope around this time, Helen's deteriorating physical condition became a major worry, and she began to suffer from senile dementia in about 1981. During this time, Farley drew close to his mother as never before.

★ ★ ★

There were some refreshing interludes. In March 1981, Farley visited the set near Whitehorse in the Yukon where *Never Cry Wolf* was being filmed. The movie, produced by Lewis Allen and Joseph Strick, was the first time in the history of the Walt Disney studio that it used independent producers. The director was Carroll Ballard, whose *Black Stallion* Farley admired in part: "Liked the photography and effects, but the story died when boy and horse left the island and Disney took over. But the island mood was very good." When he arrived in Whitehorse, Farley was offered a cameo role as a bartender who had to say a simple line and gulp some beer. After more than twenty-five takes, he was too inebriated to say the line "Sure, I know who you want. Rosie" correctly, confusing the woman's name with the stripper-turned-author Gypsy Rose Lee. After a while Farley could only mouth expletives and cusswords, and the scene was cut from the film. His hopes were dashed: "I had visions of Hollywood beating at my door and thousands of beautiful women falling at my feet," he wistfully recalls.

The author did, however, make a close and lasting friendship with the young Los Angeles–based actor Charlie Martin Smith, previously one of the stars of George Lucas's *American Graffiti*, who played Farley in the movie. When the film was released in 1983, Farley, Claire, Jack McClelland and the Schreyers were among those attending the gala.

This time Farley was pleased—as he had not been by the 1980 ABC television movie of *A Whale for the Killing*, which turned the book into a mawkish romance about an architect and his wife who encounter a Soviet whaling ship while sailing off Newfoundland: "I wouldn't give a damn what they did as long as it was pro-whale. But it isn't even that. I hope it bombs."[20]

Farley's most interesting trip of this period was planned in January 1981 while he and Claire were visiting the Schreyers at Rideau Hall. The vice-regal couple, it was announced, would be visiting five Scandinavian countries that spring. Ed asked the Mowats to accompany them. Intrigued but wary, Claire turned to Lily: "You're not going to be travelling by yourselves. You'll have all those External Affairs people as well as your household. I doubt if there would even be room for us."

"Of course there's room," Lily assured her. "And besides, I have to

Farley and Lily Schreyer, circa 1980

choose a lady-in-waiting. That's it! Claire, I want you for my lady-in-waiting."

When Claire demurred, Lily was insistent: "You don't need experience. All you have to do is be charming. And get all dressed up."[21] As Claire later recalled, dressing up was not her husband's normal way of being: "Farley would be obliged to buy something he had never owned, a three-piece, pin-striped suit. In fact, he didn't even own a two-piece suit. His wardrobe was a modest array of comfortable sweaters and slacks, with jackets made of tweed or corduroy. His only quasi-formal outfit was his Scots regalia: kilt, velvet jacket, sporran and shoes with silver buckles. But that ethnic costume would not satisfy protocol."[22]

At the start of this almost three-week venture (May 18–June 5), Farley had some misgivings—misgivings which he quickly overcame: "C. has got herself euchred into being the Lady in Bloody Waiting to her Ex[cellency] for the journey. Me, I am merely the Husband of the Lady in Waiting, and travel separately in an ox cart somewhere behind the Vice Regal party. But, for once, Claire has top billing. . . . Sounds to me like a bloody drag, but what the hell, I shall have a chance to get drunk in all five Scandahoosian countries at one fell swoop." In fact, Farley was given by Schreyer the official, and unique, position of "gentleman-in-waiting" to the governor general and as such took part in the festivities.

Despite his trepidations, Farley very much enjoyed making his way, in settings of jet-set glamour, through Sweden, Finland, Norway, Denmark and Iceland. Ed Schreyer's fondest memory is of Farley's encounter with the King of Norway:

"Your majesty, do you have a job for me at your court?"

"Doing what?"

"Court jester?"

"Too late. I just appointed a new government so I have plenty of those around me."

An encounter between Farley and Queen Margrethe of Denmark was more sober. Knowing of Farley's book *Westviking*, she asked him, "How is it that the Greenland settlers could have built seaworthy ships when there is no ship timber in Greenland?"

"Your Majesty, historians don't agree about the answer to that," Farley began cautiously.

Farley, circa 1980

"Ah, but historians seldom agree about anything!" laughed the queen.

Farley took courage. "Personally, I've concluded that the Greenland Norse were sailing to Canada for wood, and a lot of other useful things, for hundreds of years. Of course, that's a minority opinion."

"I like minority opinions," said the queen frankly.[23]

In Norway, when Claire was totally exhausted and an event was sprung on Lily, Farley volunteered to act in his wife's place. "Farley, my ever-ready lady-in-waiting," proclaimed Lily. "Just call me an equal-opportunity employer."[24] In Copenhagen, Claire slept through an event at the Tivoli Gardens. She was flustered: "But I was supposed to be there! What did Lily say?"

"Don't worry," her husband assured her. "Lily was fine. I took over as lady-in-waiting. I even carried her bouquet."

"Thanks," Claire responded, "but damn it, that's a famous place and I've always wanted to see it. Tell me what it was like."

"A lot of phoney baloney," he snorted. "Part circus, part Disneyland. Hot and noisy besides. Not my kind of place."[25]

A few times Canadian tourists recognized Farley and shouted greetings to him. In Finland,

> two attractive young ladies [from his Finnish publisher's office]
> had met him at the palace gates where they greeted him with a
> kiss—right in front of the palace sentry. Then they summoned a
> taxi and drove him down to a pier on the waterfront where,
> among yachts and seagulls, a crew from Finnish television was
> waiting with a water taxi. Equipped with a cooler of white
> wine, the party sailed off to a nearby island where a young man
> conducted an interview with Farley for a local television show.[26]

Two years later, another trip provided a dramatic confrontation with the past, when Farley and Claire returned to Burgeo as part of a vice-regal visit from July 30 to August 3 to the south coast of Newfoundland and Prince Edward Island. Claire's *The Outport People* had been published that spring, and she was disturbed by the discrepancy between what she had known and written about and what she now witnessed:

> The place has changed out of all recognition. I've never been back to any place that's changed so much. Triple the population. Roads and cars and trucks everywhere. Houses built cheek by jowl, tighter than in a city. A new fish plant (which went into bankruptcy ten days after we were there). Our former house painted turquoise green. Nobody threw a fish at Farley or tried to throw him off the wharf.[27]

In 1982, the year before, the Mowats had gone to Greenland, returning on time for Sandy's wedding on October 8. Sandy, after completing his degree at Erindale College at the University of Toronto and before obtaining work at the CBC, had stood for Parliament in the Toronto Rosedale riding as a candidate for the Apathetic Party. Sandy's theory, a proud father explained, was "that there are more apathetic voters than there are Liberals, Conservatives and New Democrats together."[28] Although father and son saw each other only intermittently while Sandy was growing up, a close relationship developed between the two. Sandy, who resides in Palgrave near his parents' former home, explains it this way: "As a child, I didn't see my father very often, but I really treasured the times we were together. After Dad and Claire got together—and I lost my initial reserve around her—my father and I saw each other more often. And it was then that we discovered that we could be good friends."

Farley's relationship with David has not been as serene. As a teenager, David had a penchant for getting into trouble and became alienated from both Farley and Fran. But although Farley and David, who lives in Alberta, have not seen each other in a while, their relationship is cordial.

With his brother, John, Farley has maintained a good friendship over the years. John, a former banker turned financial advisor, handles many business matters for Farley. And while Rosemary and

Farley have had their differences, based chiefly on her affection for Barbara Hutchinson, they have recently drawn closer together.

Although Farley was later to claim that no book gave him greater anguish to write than *Sea of Slaughter* (1984), that distinction probably actually belongs to *And No Birds Sang*. Nonetheless, writing *Sea of Slaughter* was a daunting experience. In 1982 Claire told the Warrens, "Farley slaves away every day on his tome about extinct sea mammals. It's a big undertaking, and will probably take another year."[29] A year later, she told them that the end was still not in sight: "Farley is still working like a Trojan to finish his epic by the Fall. He is sick to death of it after three years."[30] Claire further lamented: "Farley is still working on that same &%#!!% book which he's been immersed in for years. Right now, he is hiding out at Indian Summer [the old Mowat summer cottage] in order to finish some significant chunks of it. It has to go to press this summer if it's to be published this year, so we can't leave for Cape Breton until he's done."[31] One day, when Harold Horwood phoned to tell him that he had been severely depressed for six days, Farley rejoined, "Hell, I've been depressed for six years!"

Earlier, in April 1983, a somewhat despondent Farley wrote to Peter Davison, "Yup. I'm working like an SOB. *Sea of Slaughter* is moving well, which will not delight you I know. But there it is. I expect to finish the manuscript by autumn, and have it in print next autumn, though I might opt for spring pub. We shall see. We should also talk about that, because I suspect you and Little, Brown might be as happy if you weren't saddled with it, and I might find it easier too to place it elsewhere. . . . The main thing is that I would not want it published reluctantly, just to keep me sweet. That can be the kiss of death for a book."[32] When he received the letter, Peter immediately phoned to tell Farley that his fears about Atlantic and Little, Brown were "nonsense." But that did not mean that Peter approved of *Sea of Slaughter*.

The ever-loyal Davison had always maintained that Farley's

strongest books were those he wrote from his own experiences with the Inuit, animals and war, and thus from within himself. He was especially averse to any attempt by Farley to write a "thesis" book like *Westviking*, where the tone of scholarly methodology replaced the multi-layered idiosyncrasies of Farley's personality. He had similar strong feelings about *Sea of Slaughter*, a series of powerful, loosely linked essays that take up in turn the destruction of, for instance, the great auk, shore birds, polar bears, brown and black bears, cod, salmon, walruses and various kinds of whales. Having read one report of the destruction of a species, the reader goes on to the next, and so on.

In his introductory remarks, Farley faces the book's problems squarely: "Some who read this book in manuscript found the stories it tells so appalling that they wondered why I had committed myself to five years in such a pit of horrors. What did I hope to accomplish? It is true that this book describes a bloody piece of our past— it records what we have accomplished in one special region during 500 years of tenure as the most lethal animal ever to have appeared upon this wasting planet." But then there was the real reason he had bothered to write the book: "But, perhaps, with luck, this record of our outrageous behaviour in and around the Sea of Slaughter will help us to comprehend the consequences of unbridled greed unleashed against animal creation. Perhaps it will help to change our attitudes and modify our future activities so that we do not become the ultimate destroyers of the living world . . . of which we are a part."

Sea of Slaughter is a jeremiad, a book-length list of woes and lamentations. In the manner of an Old Testament prophet or a fire-and-brimstone preacher, Farley catalogues man's raping of one part of the natural world. He began working on the book in a spirit of optimism, hoping that it might have the sort of effect that Rachel Carson had achieved in 1962 with *Silent Spring*, her attack on the indiscriminate use of pesticides and weed killers. However, while writing *Sea of Slaughter*, he became—and remains—convinced that we, the most successful of all animals, are also the most stupid, something that is plainly evident in our wanton destruction of the natural world. His relentless cataloguing of human degradation gave Farley little pleasure, although he did take some satisfaction in the fact that he had never joined the enemy.

Throughout the long years of writing *Sea of Slaughter*—and even before—Farley dreamed of abandoning writing and substituting film-making in its place. In 1981, he and Jack McClelland formed Norwolf, a company which, in cooperation with the NFB, had a mandate to make films about the Arctic. He had hoped to spend the next twelve to eighteen months making a series of hour-long television films documenting the past, present and future of the whale; he would write the scripts and do on-camera narration. In September 1982 he told Jack McClelland, "I want the film projects to move, and I will participate in them to the degree that they pleasure me thereby." He hoped that the filming of *Never Cry Wolf* might interest other parties in making his other books into films: "I am no longer lackadaisical about the film things. I am hot to trot. I do NOT intend to let another couple or three years of iffy/maybe be the pattern for the future. I want *action* and I want it in 1982, even if I have to go out myself and huckster the deal."[33]

Not surprisingly, work on *Sea of Slaughter* exacted a heavy price in domestic harmony. So consuming was the research for the book that Farley was more oblivious than ever to his surroundings; he was also more acerbic than usual. Claire had found Brick Point lonely during the first four or five years that she and Farley summered there: "Farley seems happy enough with [life at Brick Point]. It doesn't seem to bother him that our only close friends are the young couple down the road with whom we have a kind of partnership pertaining to lobster fishing and dairy farming."[34]

Even more than before, Farley claimed that he needed to be by himself in order to write. In March 1982, Claire told her husband some of her worst fears:

> What worries me about us as I sit here . . . is that we may grow into something like Helen and Angus. I'll live in a cosy little

world within the framework of civilization as I understand it, and you'll disappear with increasing frequency to the wilds. It sounds so much like the days of PDH and Pinchpenny. Just an updated version. And then of course some much younger woman will decide to join you in your hideaway and you'll be sure you're in love and that she couldn't possibly be after your money, and then you know the rest.

I hope not. I hope we can figure out a way to grow old together. You are my best friend and I'm your best friend. It's just kind of sad that we've never found a home that suited us both.[35]

Sometimes, Claire could even make her points in a comical manner: "I'm feeling crestfallen at the moment, utterly, and not because I fear literary criticism, not because I'm growing old, not because our marriage is on shaky ground. Nothing as simple as that. It is because I missed the date to renew my Canada Savings Bonds this year."[36] But Claire, whose love for Farley had always included an intimate knowledge of—and acceptance of—his shortcomings, felt in 1983 that she was reaching the breaking point. Courageously, she confronted him:

I don't know what to say to you. We've been together for twenty-one years. I do feel that the end of our long relationship is near. Perhaps that doesn't bother you. Perhaps this is what you have had in mind for some time. What am I to think? . . . Maybe you don't want me to join you this summer. I try to imagine my life without you and that adds a lot of grief to the load I'm already carrying. But the truth is that you don't miss me. . . . I desperately need your help. I'm begging for water and you're giving me vinegar.[37]

Farley would have preferred to have offered wine, but the sad truth was that he was thoroughly depleted as work on *Sea of Slaughter* began to come to a conclusion.

Both *And No Birds Sang* and *Sea of Slaughter*—books filled with

Farley and Claire

man's inhumanity to man and man's inhumanity to animals—had simply worn him down. On the occasion of his sixtieth birthday in 1981, he put on a brave face for a writer for the *Toronto Star*: "I feel very good about myself as a writer. I've lost the doubts and the bitterness." He made this claim even though he was well aware that the literary establishment "dominates everything and it only goes for novels and poems. I've tried to write novels but I just lose interest in them." At about the same time, he told another journalist that he no longer enjoyed writing: "The only pleasure is in the cessation."

After his father's death, Farley claimed over and over again that he no longer needed to "perform" in public, to present a cardboard personality to the world. The truth was that he clung to his persona because it gave him breathing room, space in which to hide some raw and unpleasant feelings. It also allowed him to outwit interviewers. He composed rules for such occasions: "Don't talk about your book. The book is *death*. Be outrageous, tell stories, insult the interviewer. Hold your audience. If you deliver a good show, the interviewer's going to be eager to have you back. Talking about the book makes you sound like a cheap promoter."[38] This persona of the devil-may-care hell-raiser may have been wearing thin, but it was second nature. He tried again and again to shake it away, but he found it deeply ingrained, impossible to cast aside.

His persistent sense of gloom was heightened when his mother died on February 24, 1984. On the day of the funeral, after a major snow-fall, there was concern that those travelling from out of town would not arrive on time for the ceremony at three o'clock. But the weather cleared and, in fact, a strong beam of light descended on the coffin during the service at St. Mark's.

Farley's public success was now vast. By the early eighties, 103 translations of Farley's books had been published in twenty-two languages.* These foreign-language sales amounted to four million books. *The Dog Who Wouldn't Be*, for instance, had sold 780,000 copies in the Japanese version. Farley's English-language editions had sold 1,300,000 copies in hardcover and 1,600,000 in paperback. The sales of his books in mass paperback editions had begun to make him wealthy.

Farley was one of the most celebrated Canadians of his time. And yet he was struggling to keep his creativity alive, to maintain his marriage and to keep himself sane. He felt more desperately alone than ever.

* In 2001, there were 460 translations in twenty-four languages.

Keeper of the Faith

1984 to the Present

"I BECAME a writer primarily because it seemed to be the only way of making a living open to me where I would not be constantly trampled upon by other people. It only seemed that way. I have probably been trampled on even more as a writer than if I had become managing director of the Bank of Canada."[1] Farley made what he thought was a lighthearted comment in a 1981 letter to a fan. In the eighties and nineties the truth behind this wry remark came home to roost in unexpected ways.

Early in 1984, the Mowats visited the Schreyers in Australia, where Ed had been appointed high commissioner. Farley attended a writers' conference and gave some talks sponsored by Canada's Department of External Affairs and International Trade. After returning from what had been a pleasant sojourn, Farley readied himself to do something he hated: a book tour to promote *Sea of Slaughter* in the United States, beginning in California and ending in Seattle. A year before, Michael Bauman, a professor of English at

California State University at Chico, a bit north of Sacramento, had invited Farley to discuss his work with his students. Funding for this trip was to be supplied by External Affairs, but their support was suddenly and mysteriously cancelled in March 1984. But Atlantic–Little, Brown offered to pay Farley's expenses, and the tour went ahead.

On the morning of April 23, Farley arrived at the U.S. Customs and Immigration section of Toronto's Pearson Airport, where he was subjected to a variety of interrogations. First, there was the encounter with the customs officer, who asked if he had anything to declare. "Nothing but good intentions," he replied optimistically.

"Open the bag!"

The man was aghast when he saw the kilt of the Sutherland clan. "This is a *skirt*?"

"No. It's a kilt."

"You wear that thing?"

"I do, indeed. And proudly."

Then there was the encounter with the immigration official:

"Your name is Mao-it?"

"*Mo*wat—as in poet."

"So. Your first name Fairley?"

"*Far*ley. As in barley."

Then there was an additional series of questions by another official:

"Have you ever been turned back at the U.S. border?"

"Never!"

"Have you entered, or attempted to enter, the U.S.A. illegally?"

"Of course not!"

"Do you have a criminal record?"

"Certainly not!"

Finally, just as Farley's plane was about to leave, this official, a trace of a grin on his face, informed him, "You are excluded from entering the United States."

"I *what*?"

"You are not permitted to enter the United States of America."

"Why in blazes can't I?"

"I can't tell you that."

"You *know*, but you bloody well won't tell me?"

"You could say that."

A very exasperated Farley telephoned Jack McClelland, who collected him at the airport and drove him to his own home in Kleinburg; they contacted Peter Davison, who confirmed that the Justice Department declined to say why they were refusing entry.

Farley became convinced that he was being kept out of the United States because of his visits to Siberia in 1966 and 1969; Jack thought the anti–gun control, pro-hunting lobby was angry at the author of *Sea of Slaughter*. Finally, Peter was told that Farley was being barred under the provisions of the McCarran-Walter Act, whereby enemies—especially communists—were not allowed entry into the United States.

On the following day, Farley and Jack gave print, radio and television interviews. Joe Clark, the secretary of state for external affairs, got in touch to say he would contact the appropriate U.S. immigration officials. He never called back. Prime Minister Brian Mulroney personally telephoned and offered his condolences but did not seem to understand what the problem was.* Farley only found out the real reason for his exclusion from a reporter from the *New York Times*, who told him that Mowat's FBI file mentioned that he had threatened to shoot down—and had actually taken a shot at—a United States Air Force bomber that had flown over his house in Burgeo (the FBI had acquired a copy of the *Ottawa Citizen* story of March 22, 1968, which related this "incident").

Under pressure from public opinion, the Justice Department decided Farley could "enter" the United States, although he would not be "admitted." In turn, Farley—long a sworn enemy of bureaucratic double-talk—demanded complete vindication or nothing. During May and June of that year, Farley worked on a small (125-page) book-length investigation of this fiasco—called *My Discovery of*

* Earlier that year, on January 29 and 30, Farley, Pierre Berton and the environmental activist David Suzuki had taken part in a brainstorming session in Ottawa on Canadian symbols. "A Mulroney bullshit exercise," Farley labelled it.

America (the title nods in the direction of Stephen Leacock's *My Discovery of England*)—which was published in the autumn of 1985.

In 1985, Farley travelled to a place disdained by the United States: Cuba. The Mowats joined Margaret Atwood, Graeme Gibson, Ron Graham, M.T. Kelly and some other writers on a birdwatching expedition there. Farley resisted the tempting offer by Ramon Castro, the ruler's brother, to write an account—to be called "The Great White Udder"—about the country's prize cow, which had been a gift to Cuba from Canada. Farley returned from that trip to discover that the Canadian Wildlife Federation (CWF) was launching a suit against him.

Much-needed good news came early in 1986 when Farley and Claire were entertaining a neighbour from across the street, Wade Rowland. Jack McClelland called in the middle of dinner with an offer he claimed Farley could not refuse: an extremely lucrative invitation from Time Warner to write a biography of the American-born gorilla conservationist Dian Fossey, who had been brutally and mysteriously murdered in 1985, perhaps by one of the poachers who constantly attempted to kill her charges, perhaps by another scientist, perhaps on orders from the Rwandan government. Farley—who had always been reluctant to take large advances, preferring that his books earn their royalties—told Jack he would think the matter over and then proceeded to discuss the matter at dinner. Rowland, who worked as senior producer at CBC TV's consumer-oriented *Marketplace* but had been anxious to make a career change and become a writer, expressed his interest in such a project. When Jack called back, Farley told him, "Sure I'll do the book—if Wade can work on it with me." Jack agreed, and the two men worked out a sixty-forty split of the advance (the larger portion going to Farley), whereby Rowland would do much of the research and Farley would do most of the writing and pay all travel and research expenses.

Rowland conducted a large number of interviews in the United States, England, Rwanda and Germany; in Africa he found two of Fossey's diaries, which he photocopied. That discovery convinced him there were many more such documents and he eventually found them in a storage depot in Ithaca, New York, where Fossey had placed them for safekeeping when she had been lecturing at Cornell University on sabbatical from her primate research. Although he had the permission of Fossey's mother and stepfather to examine these documents, a legal injunction prevented him from taking this material out of the United States. Rowland would go to Ithaca for three or four days at a time; sometimes he stuffed material under his shirt, took it home for photocopying, and then returned it surreptitiously.

Rowland drafted much of the first third of the book, but Farley cut most of this material, choosing to foreground Fossey's experiences in Africa rather than dealing at length with her childhood, education and early career. Sometimes Farley would rewrite conversations recorded by Rowland. When Rowland called his attention to this, Farley labelled him "Mr. Holier-Than-Thou" but—sometimes after heated discussions—restored the research material supplied to him to its original state even though that material was not usually as dramatic as he would have liked. Through the entire collaborative process, Rowland found Farley amenable to compromise. He also discovered in Farley a "consummate professional" who worked very hard to meet the deadline imposed by the American publisher (the book was published in the autumn of 1987).

Although Farley had been initially doubtful about attempting a book so completely removed from his own experience, his identification with Fossey is evident throughout. Like him, Dian had been an eco-warrior who battled the establishment to protect her charges. At one point in *Virunga: The Passion of Dian Fossey*, Farley observes, "She was not afraid of legal action if she exposed the sleaziness of the internecine wars engaged in by players in the 'conservationist' game." Biographer and biographee shared a tendency to prefer animals to people. In relating Dian's love of the monkey Kima, he observes that this animal was no mere child-substitute for Fossey "as some have said. She was a being whose needs kept Dian's capacity to love alive through years of disappointments with her own species."

So perfect was the fit between himself and Dian that Farley allowed his subject to co-write the book with him by interweaving her intimate diary, in bold type, with his own text. This experimental technique allowed a remarkable and often moving convergence of author and subject. In a very early passage, Farley's lingering memories of his own childhood are palpable:

> Like many lonely children Dian loved animals and took comfort from their undemanding acceptance of her; yet she was not permitted any pets of her own except for a goldfish, upon which she lavished the affection that had few other outlets. The death of the fish left her desolate.
>
> **I cried for a week when I found him floating belly up in the bowl in my room. My parents thought it was good riddance, so I never got another. A friend at school offered me a hamster, but they considered it dirty, so that was out.**

In the following passage, one of her assistants reminds Dian that she should not be upset by a failure to meet up with the gorilla Effie and her baby, Maggie:

> **I had gone out with Rwelekana; and when we were coming back (I was totally exhausted), he very seriously said, "Yesterday the gorillas had to come a long way to say hello and greet you near camp. Today they have to go on with their own business." I absolutely choked up at this idea, but he was serious.**
>
> The effect of the [eventual] reunion with Effie's clan was transcendental—and enduring. Whatever doubts Dian may have had about her future place in the scheme of things had been resolved.
>
> **I now know that I've truly come home. No one will ever force me out of here again.**

Fossey's obsessive love of the gorillas, her hatred of the poachers, her heavy drinking, her refusal to take proper care of herself—all these themes are orchestrated to present a portrait of a dedicated woman who was sometimes her own worst enemy.

After completing the internationally acclaimed Fossey biography,

Farley was more inclined than ever to attempt an autobiography, the book he had long before labelled "Born Naked." Work on that book proved incredibly difficult, although Farley was game to try his hand at it, as he informed Davison in June 1988:

> I have been running around like a rabbit with its pecker cut off ever since you were here trying to organise my unorganisable life. I haven't made any real effort to concentrate on the biographical book since I was fully aware that if I started on it, I would get confused and might develop a distaste for it. . . . The more I deal with the world as it is here and now, the more disturbed and distressed I become. It will be a pleasure to retreat into the past.[2]

That withdrawal was postponed when another venture attracted his attention.

For some years, Farley had thought of changing the direction of his career by moving away from books into film production. Because the writing of *And No Birds Sang* and *Sea of Slaughter* had come at heavy personal cost, *My Discovery of America* and *Virunga* proved in their different ways to be excellent projects. But when he finished work on *Virunga*, Farley felt disconnected from the writing process and did not wish to venture into a new project that might be as personal and as bitter as either *No Birds* or *Sea of Slaughter*.

Farley and Jack had put their film company, Norwolf—a venture that had been specifically formed to make films about the Arctic—on the back burner. But Farley was aware that Andy Thomson was itching to leave the NFB. Thomson had demonstrated his competence with his film *In Search of Farley Mowat* (1981), and now—although he had a good salary at the NFB and was the head of a production unit—he was ready to become an independent filmmaker.

This was the background to Farley's decision in 1984 to do something about relaunching Norwolf and, in the process, making it a viable enterprise. It took two years to get this new venture off the ground. By that time, McClelland had withdrawn from Norwolf and a new partnership had been formed: ⅓ Farley Mowat Ltd., ⅓ Andy Thomson and ⅓ Atlantis Films (Michael MacMillan). Farley would provide properties, ideas and scripts; Andy, who would be managing director, would draw a salary; and Atlantis would contribute working capital and market and distribute the films. Farley once told Thomson that he would be prepared to invest one hundred thousand dollars in Norwolf; instead, he pledged the use of his literary properties.

From the outset, there was an unexpected series of setbacks. Farley soon discovered that the grind of day-to-day filmmaking was both onerous and tiring for him; for example, he did not enjoy making filming arrangements in Moscow, where he journeyed with Michael MacMillan, and he later found the filming of the company's first project, *The New North*, excessively demanding of his time and involvement.

Although he was awarded a Gemini Award for Best Documentary Script for *The New North*, he was a bit disdainful of the award because little of his actual writing was left in the film. Then there was the problem of Farley's friendship with Andy. Years earlier, there had been a patch of trouble regarding the Newfoundland project at the NFB, when Max Braithwaite and Farley found Andy too inexperienced to be in charge of it. Thomson says he found Farley increasingly difficult to deal with; Andy got on Farley's nerves.

Farley's previous uneasiness with Andy surfaced within a year of the re-establishment of the Norwolf initiative. In succeeding months, the issues concerning the partnership became extremely muddy. Farley was displeased when Andy independently formed Great North Communications to produce a film about dinosaurs. Andy told his cousin that he had decided to become involved with the dinosaur venture because it would provide him with a larger salary and with the possibility of finding future lucrative projects which could be useful to Norwolf.

At this point, Farley decided to dissolve Norwolf. Andy was furious. He wrote to Farley,

> I think *you* should be reminded that *The New North* was not
> financed because of your name alone. Otherwise you and Jack
> would have been able to get it off the ground years ago when
> you first began to market the idea. It was a combination of your
> name and prestige, my experience and my relationship with the
> NFB . . . and Atlantis's track record and reputation at Telefilm
> that enabled it all to come together. We were all equally respon-
> sible for that particular source of income. . . . This was not and
> could never have been a one man show, no matter who that one
> man might have been.[3]

Although Andy felt put upon by his cousin, Farley felt *he* was the
one who had been betrayed. He was convinced that his name and
reputation had been misused; he now realized that he was essentially a
writer who worked in solitude, and he now knew that filmmaking
was, for him, a mistake. He deeply resented the character assassination implicit in Andy's letter:

> When you did decide to leave the NFB, you made your reasons
> for doing so very clear. You left, so you said, because you
> believed you could rise no higher in the film production side of
> the Board and you did not want promotion into the purely
> administrative area. You wished to get into the action in
> commercial film making. I supported your plans and ambitions
> in every way I could. True, I did not invest $100,000 in the
> project (for which I am devoutly thankful), but I did everything
> else I could to help you and, of course, to further my own hopes
> for filming my properties.
>
>   The cold, inescapable fact is that the decision was yours alone.
> No amount of double talk can get you off that hook. Accusing
> me of seducing you away from your comfy job is a gutless
> evasion of the truth.
>
>   Your venomous personal attacks upon me, including your

characterization of me [in a letter to Claire] as a "bitter, angry, resentful and paranoid old man" and your accusations that I have betrayed and robbed you reveal much more about you than they do about me.

Your final remark, in which you blame me for everything that has gone awry with your professional life in the last year, should echo loudly in your own ears. *The responsibility for and the solution to your problems rests solely with you.* I hope that, for your sake, you can muster the courage to shoulder your own burdens instead of attempting to unload them on others. I hope that you will also learn, before it is too late, that friends and associates will not remain with you as long as you attempt to manipulate them for your own ends.[4]*

A year after the debacle with Andy came another painful imbroglio, the dissolution of Farley's close friendships with John de Visser and David Blackwood. Years earlier, in an interview with Kildare Dobbs, Farley had been asked why he "always quarrel[ed] with his rural neighbours." Farley—referring to incidents in Burgeo and the Magdalen Islands—replied, "Well, I have this habit of telling them how to improve their lives. Sometimes, without consulting them, I go and get their lives improved for them. Funny thing—people don't seem to like that! They resent it!"

In the closed, confined world of a small town such as Port Hope, it is quite common for townspeople to know each other's secrets. Sometimes idle talk becomes a pastime. In such settings and situations, alcohol can be a dangerous ingredient because it loosens inhibitions about speaking the truth. Without drink, Farley has never had a problem speaking his mind; with drink, he can speak his mind in a belligerent way. Although Farley had been generous in fostering the careers of both de Visser and Blackwood and had strong feelings of affection for them, he had very decided opinions and often did not hesitate to speak his mind, sometimes on intimate matters. Over the

* In 1990 and 1992, respectively, Michael MacMillan's Atlantis Films produced television adaptations of *Lost in the Barrens* and *The Curse of the Viking Grave*.

years, Farley's outspokenness may gradually have worn at the two men, no doubt leading to the strange episode that concluded these friendships.

Farley had collaborated with de Visser on *This Rock Within the Sea* and with Blackwood on *Wake of the Great Sealers*. When Peter Davison prepared *The World of Farley Mowat* in 1980, he published excerpts from both books without consulting the photographer or the artist since none of their work was being reproduced in the new book; no complaints were registered by de Visser or Blackwood. Seven years later, in 1987, when Farley assembled *The New Founde Land* (published in 1989), a selection from his works dealing with that province; he too did not feel it necessary to ask permission of either de Visser or Blackwood since the work of neither man was to be used and since both had authorized the reproduction of their pictures in the two original books. However, someone from McClelland & Stewart telephoned Farley at Brick Point in the summer of 1988 and suggested such permissions should be obtained. Farley told that person that he thought that both men would offer no problem "signing off." When the same person from the publishing house called Anita Blackwood, who acted as her husband's agent, and told her that she and her husband would, at Farley's insistence, be sent some documents whereby they could "sign off," she was offended and told the caller she would consult her lawyer. After de Visser spoke to the Blackwoods, he decided to follow the same course of action. In both cases, de Visser and Blackwood felt Farley was treating them badly, the implication being that he might be obtaining royalty income at their expenses. The truth was that the cause of concern about (unnecessary) permissions had been raised by a functionary at McClelland & Stewart.

When the Mowats returned to Port Hope in the autumn of 1988 from a long, arduous book tour of England, Scotland and Ireland to promote *Woman in the Mists* (the American and British title of *Virunga*), they were startled to find that the Blackwoods and de Visser were threatening legal action. Although the friendships with both men had gone through bumpy periods, those difficulties had eventually been resolved. Suddenly, these friendships ended. Although the phone call from McClelland & Stewart precipitated the crisis, it would be erroneous to consider that incident as the entire cause of the breach: the truth is that a lot of hitherto-suppressed bad feelings were released by the incident. For de Visser and Blackwood, Farley's failure to consult them was symptomatic of an arrogance they felt he had long maintained in his dealings with them.

A domino effect was also at work. The Blackwoods were close friends of Andy Thomson and had witnessed the disintegration of the cousins' business association. They chose to be on Thomson's side. And David Blackwood was de Visser's closest friend.

In order to understand the collapse of these three close associations in 1987 and 1988, some other factors have to be weighed. As a child, Farley had been enabled by his father; as he got older, the son realized that he paid a heavy price for such empowerment. And yet Farley had a tendency to be like Angus in his generosity. He wanted to foster Thomson's, de Visser's and Blackwood's careers in much the same way that his own talents had been furthered by his father. But there was a catch. Without being fully aware of what he was doing, Farley may have leaned on these three "adopted children" in a way that mirrored his father's treatment of himself. And like Farley before them, these men were resentful and jealous of the father-figure at the same time that they claimed to be deeply grateful to him. In 1988, de Visser and Blackwood split with Farley over what was superficially an exceedingly minor affair. From Farley's point of view, he had attempted to assist three younger men and wound up being badly treated.

Earlier, Farley and Harold Horwood had quarrelled openly, but their friendship remained steadfast; Peter Davison sometimes found Farley difficult to deal with, but they always found a way to relate creatively and positively with each other; Farley's friendships with Ed Schreyer, Arnold Warren and Max Braithwaite always maintained a steady course; Farley and Jack McClelland often had to agree to disagree. These six relationships, each durable over a long period of time, amply demonstrate Farley's ability to maintain friendships. What differentiates these relationships from those with de Visser and Blackwood is that they have always been conducted as dealings between equals, a vital element in any friendship.

Starting in 1984, bright, energetic but sometimes self-effacing Mary Elliott, twenty-two years younger than Farley, assumed Frances Thomson's responsibilities as his assistant. Although Mary had approached him looking for work by letter in 1982, he did not respond until he phoned out of the blue two years later to ask her to assist in readying *Sea of Slaughter* for publication. He told her, "Don't worry [about getting everything exactly so]. It doesn't have to look like a bride going to her wedding." At the launch party for the book at Stop 33 at Toronto's Sutton Place Hotel, he escorted his jittery helper around the room, finally stopping before two men: "Mary, these good-looking fellows are Jimmy Smith and Peter White." Mary, recognizing the two men as Jack McClelland and Pierre Berton, chatted with them as Farley wandered off.

Over the years, Mary has become expert at using computers and e-mail; she sometimes does research for Farley using the resources of the World Wide Web. Farley, mechanically inclined in the maintenance and repairing of VCRs and telephone answering machines, is a proud Luddite when it comes to anything to do with Macintoshes or Toshiba laptops, both of which have at various times been given to him. Instead of allowing the machines house room, he donates them to Mary.

Mary soon learned that Farley was a shy man who often pretended to be otherwise. Like her boss, she is hard-working, disciplined, methodical and organized. Over the years, she has been touched many times by her employer's acts of generosity: "Years ago," she recalls, "when he and Claire were visiting me, we were watching for birds. When he discovered I did not own binoculars, he quietly slipped off the old ones he had brought along and put them in my hands, saying he was finding them a bit too heavy nowadays."[5]

★   ★   ★

Since Farley and Wade Rowland had worked well together on *Virunga*, they agreed to collaborate on a project Farley had envisaged about eco-warriors, those individuals who actively and sometimes angrily call governments and corporations to task for destroying rain forests, the ozone layer and other crucial aspects of the environment. The two men—who had separate contracts—were each to write one half of the book. Farley was to conduct a series of interviews which were to be printed as such; Rowland was to write five essays, investigative in scope. Ultimately only Farley's portion of the project, *Rescue the Earth! Conversations with the Green Crusaders*, was published, in 1990. The poor sales of that book—and the author's feeling that the book was inadequately publicized—gave Farley pause about his publisher, and were one factor in his eventual decision to leave McClelland & Stewart, which had been his Canadian publisher for thirty-eight years. In 1985 that firm, close to bankruptcy, was purchased by Avie Bennett, a real-estate developer. Although Jack McClelland remained with the firm for two more years, Farley was from the beginning distrustful of Bennett and his connections within corporate Canada.

When he abandoned publishing, Jack became a literary agent, and Farley, who had functioned without one for some time, insisted on being added to his list. Although Jack McClelland the literary agent was not averse to selling to his former firm, he was obliged to garner the highest possible price for his authors. Quite soon after taking over Farley's dossier, Jack decided that Farley had to write a multi-volume autobiography, for which he, as his agent, could demand a great deal of money. Farley, uncertain whether he wanted to write any sort of autobiography, was reluctant to assent to this venture, although he wrote the detailed, forty-three-page outline ("Travels with Farley: Being a Brief Outline for a Long Memoir in Three Volumes") requested by his agent. On September 12, 1989, Jack told Farley that he hated to take him "away from McClelland & Stewart, [but] I am hoping we can announce that Farley Mowat's memoirs have been sold to English-language publishers for over one million dollars and that will rank you up there, as a literary figure, with Danielle Steele and Marlon Brando."[6]

Houghton Mifflin, the firm to which Peter Davison had recently moved (still in Boston), had made a bid lower than—but competitive with—one made by Bantam and Key Porter. However, McClelland & Stewart had presented an extremely low offer on the memoir, an offer which Jack had told Avie Bennett on August 18, 1989, wasn't "even remotely in the ball park. Is it a deliberate low-ball or should I read this as something approaching your final offer? . . . You may be somewhat misled by the fact that Farley has always been prepared to accept fairly modest Canadian advances in the past. Those figures are not a realistic guide. They represented the fact that Farley was on the Board of McClelland & Stewart and a close personal friend."[7]

On September 17, Farley, after much soul searching, refused an offer from Bantam and Key Porter of $925,000—because he wanted Houghton Mifflin to be his American publisher (so that Peter Davison could remain his editor) and because he was extremely uncomfortable taking a large sum of money for books he had not even begun to write. He also had other concerns, as he told Jack:

> I am very worried about the fate of my backlist. Those books are flesh of my flesh, and they epitomize the best of whatever I may have contributed during my lifetime. I do not want them placed in jeopardy and, regardless of what financial logic has to say about the likelihood that McClelland & Stewart would continue to nurture them in my absence, I am frightened for them. . . .
> McClelland & Stewart remains a *Canadian* company when almost all the others have fallen into foreign hands. . . . Money matters much less to me than do other considerations, such as whether or not I feel comfortable with my publishers and easy in my mind that they will serve *my* purposes.[8]

Although Jack was disconcerted, as he told Farley on September 22, he was not completely surprised by this turn of events:

> Someday I may learn that my instincts are usually right. You will remember our lengthy discussions regarding the issue of whether

or not I should represent you. My instincts were against it. I should have listened to them. . . . As I know you suspect but don't want to believe, your letter of September 18th [refusing the Bantam and Key Porter offer] placed me in a completely impossible position. It is precisely that simple. I have no alternative but to say that of this date we [JM and Associates Inc.] no longer represent you. Having taken that step I can then inform Bantam and Anna Porter [publisher of Key Porter] that we bargained in bad faith and without full authority and we cannot honour our commitment and as a result no longer represent you. At that point you can deal directly with Houghton Mifflin and McClelland and Stewart in any way you see fit. . . . I would also add that I feel unhappy, on your behalf, if Farley Mowat really can't write at his best without Peter holding his hand editorially. . . . I have great respect and admiration for Peter. He has been a friend for many years and I think will always be one, but I do not share your views on this issue.[9]

Despite the disagreement between the two men, their friendship remained as strong as ever. Seven months later, Farley told Jack, "My general feelings about McClelland & Stewart are cooling steadily. I think that I will now gradually phase myself out of their clutches."[10]

In contemplating a switch from McClelland & Stewart, Farley was responding to the fact that he had already been less than pleased with Avie Bennett; moreover, Farley had also been put out when Bennett and publisher Douglas Gibson had visited him and Claire at Port Hope early in 1989 to apprise them that the Mowats' much-loved Canadian-based editor, Lily Miller, was about to be fired. This event may have been the real turning point, although Farley also felt that McClelland & Stewart had put little effort into promoting Claire's book *Pomp and Circumstances* (1989), her account of her experience as a lady-in-waiting during the 1981 vice-regal tour of Scandinavia.

During 1990 and 1991, Anna Porter, who had almost landed Farley as an author in 1989, courted him again. The balance tipped in her favour when she organized a seventieth birthday party for him in July

1991 (his birthday is in May) at the Canadian Booksellers' Association convention. Porter held the birthday celebration in her capacity as the publisher of a paperback line, Seal Books, under which many of Farley's titles were readily available. Not one person from McClelland & Stewart attended this event.

On February 4, 1992, Farley broke the news to Doug Gibson: "Why [am I going to] Key Porter and not [staying with] McClelland and Stewart? Primarily because I feel I owe it to Anna since she made the highest bid for the autobiographical series that Jack was handling. . . . A second point is that I no longer feel that McClelland and Stewart is greatly concerned as to whether or not I continue to publish under that imprint. Who knows, the firm may even breathe a collective sigh of relief."[11] In subsequent years, Gibson has approached Farley and Claire several times to ask them to come back to McClelland & Stewart.

My Father's Son began accidentally. In the summer of 1991, Farley had been scheduled to take a Society Expeditions cruise from Churchill, Manitoba, to Greenland. When that trip was cancelled, he found himself with nothing much to do, so he began to read both sides of his wartime correspondence with his father. In so doing, he rediscovered one side of the man whose death had caused him so much pain and conflict. Once more he saw Angus as a "loving friend whose steadfastness and infinite understanding helped me to endure and to survive the roughest years of my life." Nonetheless, the healing was not yet complete: "Despite his extracurricular activities, he and Helen remained together until, at the age of seventy-two, he abandoned my mother for a lady librarian thirty-three years his junior. Although he never returned to Helen, she bore him no grudge. Whether he ever forgave himself is another matter." Helen may have remained angry with her husband well after they parted, though she seldom voiced such a sentiment; there is no evidence to suggest that Angus ever regretted his decision to leave Helen and take up with Barbara Hutchinson.

Evidence for the eventual healing of the rift between father and son suffuses almost every page of the book to which Farley finally turned after the publication in 1992 of *My Father's Son: Memories of War and Peace*. In *Born Naked* (1993), Farley's affection for both parents finds full expression in a narrative that tells of the comradeship the child and young adult experienced in their company—even while it speaks openly of Angus's amorous inclinations. The writing of his autobiography gave Farley great pleasure. He was appalled by how limited his actual memories were, but he was "also delighted by how they could be stimulated into new life by small things such as newspaper clippings, letters and photographs. Anyway, it's a hell of a lot of fun exploring the distant past which is becoming ever more distant day by day."[12] In both books, Farley recaptures his childhood and early manhood before the marriage of his parents fell apart.

In writing *My Father's Son*, Farley experienced many sad days when he had to retrace the terrain he had recreated earlier in *And No Birds Sang*, although this new war book amply displayed the support Farley's parents had given him during the war. While working on *Born Naked*, he would be filled with moments of great joy, as he recalled many of the happiest moments of his childhood.

Born Naked, in its emphasis on the joyful side of Farley's childhood, does not do justice to the dysfunctional aspects of his early family life. And yet working on the latter book forced Farley to confront—and deal with—some of the lingering demons of his past. By writing about Angus and Helen, he came to terms with both of them, although it can be argued that he evaded some of the more difficult parts of his youth. He certainly realized in a new way that Angus's failure to become a successful writer had caused his father to transfer his thwarted ambition to his son. Farley also now perceived that his own profound restlessness had been inherited from his father.

Farley's revisiting of the landscapes of childhood and young adulthood led to a revitalization in his marriage, almost as if he could return to Claire in a new way only once he had overcome some impediments that had stood in his way for a long time. In a letter of March 3, 1993, she told him, "I wish you were here to discuss the plot [of the] story [which Claire was working on]. I wish you were here for lots of reasons! Soon, I hope you will be."[13] Sentiments he had expressed in 1979 became truer in 1989: "Claire is the one thing I fear to lose. Cancer, radioactivity, all the things that destroy the flesh are nothing compared to aloneness." Ultimately, when Farley forgave Angus, he was able to forgive himself for some of his own, similar frailties and therefore to renew his claim on Claire's heart. Claire's gentleness and steadiness were now seen in a fresh light by her husband, who responded by becoming more courtly towards her. He became less restless, less inclined to need long stretches of time by himself.

Nonetheless, Farley and Claire's search for the perfect place to live—intensified after Helen's death—had led them to commission in 1988 the building of "High Dudgeon," a one-storey, window-filled modernist house overlooking Rice Lake, forty minutes from Port Hope. Once the building had been completed and the Mowats had moved a few pieces in during April 1989, they realized the house's austere modernity did not really allow the cosy living conditions in which they had previously lived; moreover, they were certain the neighbourhood would always be resistant to their becoming part of it. The few visits they made to their new home in 1990 convinced them they should get rid of it. They rented it out and sold it in 1995.

The Mowats continued to travel, flying to Fiji and then Australia to spend Christmas with the Schreyers in December 1987. Farley was actively involved with the filming of (and provided the voice-over for) Sea of Slaughter, produced and directed by John Brett in 1988 and 1989 for the CBC TV series The Nature of Things; this involved visits to the Magdalens, Newfoundland and Labrador. Sea won the Conservation Film of the Year at an ecological film festival in Bristol, England, and Farley was given an award of excellence at the 1990 Atlantic Film Festival in "outstanding achievement in narration" and the 1990 Canadian Achievers Award by Toshiba Canada. Around this period Farley also received the first Take Back the Nation Award from the Council of Canadians for his contributions to Canadian nationalism and environmentalism.

In March 1992, Farley had an alarming experience when the train he was taking to Brick Point derailed in New Brunswick. There were no serious injuries, but there was a great deal of anxiety on the part of all the passengers until they were rescued by trucks and snow-ploughs from the wintry depths of the forest where they were stranded. In July 1993, Farley and Claire returned to visit St-Pierre and Miquelon, and two years later, they were aboard the *Alla Tarasova* for almost the entire month of July on a northern cruise that began at Frobisher Bay and took them south along the Labrador coast, along the west and south coasts of Newfoundland, and then to St-Pierre, from which they flew back to Cape Breton. Early in 1995, Farley finished his book dealing with his trip to Europe in 1953, *Aftermath*, and throughout 1996 he worked on his Alban book, *The Farfarers* (published in 1997).

That April, Farley suffered a slight stroke (Wallenberg's syndrome) and had some problems walking; there were no lasting effects except for the loss of the sense of hot and cold in his right leg. Before that, the only relatively major health problem he had encountered had been almost a decade earlier: a dislocated elbow from a fall from a ladder in August 1987.

In the autumn of 1995, a publicist at Key Porter asked Farley if he would consent to an interview from a writer from *Saturday Night* magazine about *Aftermath*. During the ensuing day-long interview at Port Hope with John Goddard (author of a single book, the well-researched but neglected *Last Stand of the Lubicon Cree*, published in Vancouver by Douglas & McIntyre in 1991), that journalist led Farley to believe that the commissioned article would deal with his entire career. Later, Goddard requested a second meeting, this one held in Toronto in the presence of the Key Porter publicist. "What ensued," Farley later recalled, "was not an interview, but a taped interrogation during which I was accused . . . of misrepresenting aspects of *People of the Deer*, and was forcefully urged to admit as much." On the evening of April 4, 1996 Goddard telephoned Farley in Port Hope, "requiring me to account for my actions in central Keewatin during June of 1947. He also informed me at that time that he had retained the services of a private investigator."[14] Anticipating that a defamatory article on him was about to be published, both Farley and Anna Porter intervened with Kenneth Whyte, the editor of the magazine—to no avail.

In the spring of 1996, however, although Farley was feeling vulnerable, he was not really prepared for the onslaught he was about to face. When "A Real Whopper" was published in the May 1996 issue of *Saturday Night*, it created a sensation, much of which can be attributed to the digitally enhanced photograph on the cover of the magazine, the now infamous Pinocchio-nosed portrait. The magazine had asked Farley to sit for a portrait, but he had not been informed that the resulting photograph would be embellished.

The article itself repeated many of the allegations made against Farley by A.E. Porsild years before. Goddard also made use of documents in the National Archives of Canada in Ottawa and the Mowat archive at the McMaster University Library. The papers in Ottawa were supposed to substantiate the charge that the federal government had acted much more compassionately to the inland Inuit than Farley had depicted, and the papers in Farley's own archive were used to show (accurately) that he had sometimes been impatient with the Inuit and that he had been so emotionally distraught in the summer of 1948 about the state of his marriage that he had ventured, without permission, to Toronto in order to retrieve Fran and bring her back up north with him.

Like Porsild before him, Goddard accused Mowat of stretching the facts in *People of the Deer* and *Never Cry Wolf*; in particular, Farley had not spent the amount of time in the Arctic he had led his readers to believe. Completely neglected in this article was *The Desperate People*, which corrects many of the factual errors in *People of the Deer* and which provides a great deal of evidence about Farley's cooperation with the federal government. Also overlooked—although Goddard could have done nothing to remedy this deficiency—were the embargoed portions of Farley's archive, which reveal, among other things, that Francis Harper had specifically asked Farley not to write about him and that Farley, in the aftermath of the controversy surrounding his first book, had exchanged many letters and had established cooperative relationships with various officials in Ottawa. And the original policy statements by various federal government officials which are cited by Goddard contradict but never destroy the original allegations made by Farley.

Upon publication of the article, a grinning Whyte was unrepentant: "It was a great story and good for the magazine," he told the *Globe's* publishing reporter, Val Ross. He was also condescending: "[Mowat's] the Clown Prince of Canadian literature." At first, Farley told Ross, "I felt I'd been knifed badly. But it doesn't matter that John Goddard has attacked me personally. What I'm upset about is that he has left the impression that people didn't starve, that there wasn't a program to cut the wolf population, that a holocaust didn't happen."

When Ross herself looked up past copies of the *Globe*, she found an article dated October 8, 1946, which quoted federal health officials warning of malnutrition among the Inuit. A piece on August 11, 1947, reported that "a tiny colony of Eskimo [were] threatened by starvation," with Ottawa mounting a "flying relief expedition." Although this evidence supports *some* of Goddard's claims, she later found evidence that at least four Inuit died of starvation in the winter of 1946–47. Marie Bouchard, the organizer of the Baker Lake Fine Arts in the Keewatin district, told the *Globe* reporter, "My personal feeling is that Mowat may have exaggerated the facts, but the important thing he did was to draw attention to the privation. If not for Farley, perhaps the government would have continued to ignore the situation in the North."

Perhaps the most succinct and level-headed account in the press was provided by Robert Everett-Green in a brief notice in the *Globe and Mail*:

> Time and again, Mowat the note-taker contradicts Mowat the author, while in the background, Mowat the grand old man of letters blusters about how he never claimed to be writing anything but "subjective non-fiction." Reading Goddard's uncharitable piece, it's hard to escape the conclusion that Mowat's sense of drama did routinely win out over his respect for the literal truth. But has this self-confessed "teller of tales" really

"muddled public debate on Inuit and wildlife issues for decades,"
as Goddard claims? The charge is thrown out in the final para-
graphs, with no further argument. The fact remains that Mowat
did more to raise awareness about the North than anyone, and
more to convince people that a debate was necessary.

In his letter to the *Globe* (published on May 7, 1996), Gary T. Gallon,
president of the Canadian Institute for Business and the Environment, eloquently describes how the Goddard piece was part and
parcel of the eager willingness of Canadians to tear down—and
destroy—their own cultural icons:

> *Saturday Night* is practising Canada's favourite pastime, bashing
> great Canadians. Heaven forbid that we lionize them. We dare
> not make Canadian heroes out of them. Ignore the fact that
> they've contributed to the human good. I am pleased to see that
> *Saturday Night* has not let Canada down by keeping up the tradi-
> tion of pulverizing anyone who would become great. Farley
> Mowat has become famous around the world for his dedication
> to protecting the environment. His writings call attention to the
> destruction of the ocean fish stocks, the disruption of Arctic
> communities, and to the plight of the wolf and have helped
> Canada and other nations deal with their imperiled environments.

Many times before Goddard's article appeared, Farley had spoken
candidly about his conviction that he had never allowed the facts to
get in the way of telling the truth, that he eschewed trivial details in
favour of genuine authenticity. Twenty-two years before, he had
written,

> My approach to writing, once established, remained and remains
> more or less unchanged. Having early eschewed the purely
> factual approach, I was not willing to go to the other extreme
> and take the easy way out by writing fiction. My metier lay
> somewhere in between in what was then a grey void between

fact and fiction. For many years my work presented an almost insoluble problem to cataloguers who could never quite decide where it belonged. . . . On the other hand reviewers and critics, who were enraged that I should dare to sail the middle ground between fact and fiction, knew where my work belonged, or thought they did, and were not hesitant about saying so. The truth was, of course, that I was simply ahead of my time. When Truman Capote finally "discovered" the middle ground [in the non-fiction novel *In Cold Blood*] it became respectable and acquired a name so that, at last, it could be charted. The void I had been swimming in for lo, those many years, became known as subjective non-fiction. At last I had been pinned down like the somewhat tattered butterfly I was.[15]

Tattered was exactly how Farley felt after the appearance of the piece in *Saturday Night*. Although the charges in the article were glaringly unoriginal, the magazine's cover photograph branded him in the public eye as a liar by associating him with the fairy-tale figure Pinocchio. Reduced in status as he was, though, Farley soon discovered in the many letters sent to him that he had many more supporters than detractors. His greatest fear in the midst of the brouhaha was that the raison d'être of a book such as *People of the Deer* would be lost. He had spent much of his life warning that some of the earth's most precious resources were in danger of being destroyed. In 1996, he witnessed on a daily basis evidence that the environment, sea animals and the Inuit were being further blighted. He had been—and remained—a staunch defender of causes he held dear. He did not want those causes to be further eroded because his advocacy of them was now called into question and in the process ridiculed.

Farley made his strongest personal response to the "Pinocchio" article in 2000, after *Walking on the Land* (2000), his account of his 1958 trip to the Arctic, was reviewed negatively by Goddard in the *Toronto Star*, where Goddard works as a copy editor. When asked by a reporter about both of Goddard's attacks, Farley suggested they were, in part, motivated by envy: "The difference [between himself and

Goddard], according to Mowat, is that his books were 'successful' in drawing attention to a native people in trouble and Goddard's wasn't." In a particularly feisty mood, Farley was quite willing to expand on what he saw as the nub of the issue: " 'It wasn't a very good book,' Mowat says of Goddard's effort. 'His role as a saviour of native people came to nothing and I think that has something to do with it. I think he resents deeply the fact that I've had success with the Inuit.' "[16]

After publishing *Born Naked*—the first volume in the originally proposed three-volume memoir—Farley wrote *Aftermath: Travels in a Post-War World* (1995), *The Farfarers* (1997) and *Walking on the Land* (2000). The first book tells of the visit he and Fran made to Europe in 1953; the second—a continuation of the themes first examined in *Westviking*—proposes the controversial thesis that the Norse were not the first Europeans to reach North America but were preceded by walrus-hunting Northern Scots; the third records his 1958 visit to the Arctic and the tragedy at Garry Lake.

Walking on the Land was suggested by Elisapee, a daughter of Kikkik—whose trial for murder is the central episode in *The Desperate People*—when some new information about her people became available. Farley was agreeable because, once again, he wanted "to help ensure that man's inhumane acts are not expunged from memory, thereby easing the way for repetitions of such horrors." Farley had never written about the starvation episode at Garry Lake, which he had investigated in 1958. He had excluded that incident from *The Desperate People* "for fear a surfeit of horrors would cause readers to shut the book and turn their hearts and minds away." In 2000, he was glad to "make amends for that omission" and to write a book that returned him to the landscapes of *People of the Deer*.

A plurality of projects now claims his attention: the long-postponed book about Albert the water dog, a collection of animal poems, the also long-delayed "canoe" book about the 1947 trek taken by himself and Charles Schweder and *High Latitudes*, the about-to-be-published book (his thirty-eighth) about the ten-thousand-mile exploration of the Canadian Arctic that he made in 1966. In that narrative, he is once again the saga-man. This time, he allows the various "voices" of the New North (priests, ministers, police officers, trappers, Native peoples, mixed breeds) to tell their stories.

Very much the professional writer in his eighty-second year, Farley rises early in the morning, walks the two dogs, Millie and Chester, and then writes for the remainder of the morning. After lunch he takes a nap, revises for an hour or two before supper and then retires early in the evening. He and Claire winter in Port Hope and depart for Brick Point in the spring. Farley hears occasionally from his son David, who lives in Alberta with his two daughters; he sees Sandy, Sandy's wife Kim and his grandson Justin on a regular basis. Farley was often in touch with Fran—they remained good friends until her death in early February 2001. With Mary Elliott's assistance, he answers the fan mail with which he is still deluged.

Although Farley may have slowed down physically, his creative drive and agility of mind are still those of a much younger man. Ron Wright, the novelist and travel writer, and his wife, Janice Boddy, the anthropologist and writer, had been residents of Port Hope for a year when Ron retrieved a message on his answering machine from Farley: "Are you the person who did the book on the Fiji Islands? If so, come over for a drink." The Mowats had read Wright's book on Fiji while staying there in December 1987 and subsequently discovered Ron and Janice were neighbours.

From that encounter a strong friendship soon developed. When Ron showed Farley the manuscript of his first novel, *A Scientific Romance*, and expressed some anxiety about switching from non-fiction to fiction, he soon discovered he was seeking advice from exactly the right person. True to form, Farley was outspoken but also extremely encouraging: "Fuck non-fiction. Give us another like this one!" In his new friend, Ron discovered a person with "great instincts," someone who likes to flout conventions in preferring conversation over chit chat, irreverence over politeness.

Tethered in both Ontario and Nova Scotia to his ancient Underwood typewriters, Farley prepares himself to "write with great

Farley at Port Hope

distress. The process is purely subconscious. Can't program what I want to write. There's a wall between my conscious and subconscious, and I have to wait until a little trapdoor opens. What comes out is something over which I have no control. Can use it, manipulate it and shape it, but can't consciously control it."

Farley may no longer be restless, but he is still as capable as ever of being, as the *Ottawa Citizen*'s Paul Gessell put it, "a pint-sized dynamo ... a real motor-mouth, even with strangers, dispensing hilarious one-liners, gossip and vulgarities on any subject that happens to cross his mind." At times, he is quite capable of despairing about what he has achieved: "In the end, my crusades have accomplished nothing. I haven't saved the wolf, the whales, the seals, primitive man or the outport people. All I've done is to document the suicidal tendencies of modern man. I'm sure I haven't altered the course of human events one iota. Things will change inevitably, but it's strictly a matter of the lottery of fate. It has nothing to do with man's intentions."

Farley's own estimate of himself sometimes borders on the self-effacing, but it is based on a realistic assessment of his own talents and how he chose to use them:

> I was content from the first to be a simple saga man, a teller of tales. . . . My basic problem, or disability if you wish, is that I felt from the first that a writer was most useful when he addressed himself to the people as a whole; when he wrote things that were relevant to or which threw some light upon, the lives of ordinary people and the human condition in general. Because I felt that way I shied away from becoming a writer for Art's Sake, or in the hopes of impressing my literary peers. I would have been of no use at that sort of game anyway, so it was probably a good thing I didn't try.
>
> My own claims for myself are modest. I consider myself an adequate craftsman. I think I have written about people and other animals with some insight and skill. I have never, *never* been the recipient of a grant-in-aid-of. I have contributed largely to the survival of McClelland & Stewart. I have made the name of Canada, and the fame of some of her writers (me, that is) a household word in at least one household in Chukotka, on the shores of the Bering Sea. Finally, I have, almost single-handedly, changed the ghastly drinking habits of a Nation from rye whiskey to Demerara Rum . . . this is the *real* me.[17]

He could have added that writing for him is an almost sacred enterprise in which the most important issues in life are highlighted, discussed, debated and, in various ways, illuminated.

Also forgotten in Farley's own self-assessment are his many acts of private generosity and kindness, the interest-free loans and sometimes outright gifts he has bestowed on friends and acquaintances; one instance is the investment of seventy-five thousand dollars to purchase 1½ shares in the failing McClelland & Stewart in Jack's last years at the firm. When Farley heard in 1987 that the poet Gwendolyn MacEwen, whom he knew slightly, was destitute, he sent her a cheque for a thousand dollars. In Port Hope, he has supported the

fight to keep the tiny Port Hope Hospital open, the restoration of the nineteenth-century Capitol Theatre, the establishment of the Port Hope Friends of Music, the push to prevent the storing of low-level radioactive waste in underground caves near Lake Ontario, the expansion of the local library and the establishment of a local watch-dog-style newspaper.

Some days, Farley is filled with despair at the plight of the world. Silver Don Cameron recalled in an article the day when Farley, seated at his kitchen table, the sunlight gleaming in his copper beard, stared out over the green land and glittering sea at Brick Point and reflected, "Nobody who watches the way human beings behave can possibly doubt it: we're going to destroy ourselves and our environment. And the world will be better for our going."[18] On other days, Farley is a ruthless optimist, one who feels that good sense might manage to prevail. When he lashes out against the stupidity of his fellow human beings, it is frequently possible to hear a tinge of disappointment in his voice, as if he still hopes against hope that his fellow humans will prove his negative assessment of them wrong.

He remains a person of fearless, very decided opinions, although he is always more than willing to change his mind in the give and take of debate. Farley can be bossy, obstinate and grumpy, but more often he is compassionate, sprightly and jovial. In conversation, he talks about himself as acting, "as all animals do," from the vantage point of self-interest and survival, but, then again, he often finds it hard to conceal the generosity and compassion that underlie many of his actions. Farley claims not to suffer fools gladly, but he is an unusually polite and sensitive person in dealing with others.

From the time of childhood and adolescence, Farley was aware of a rapport between himself and the natural world, the world of the Others. As a soldier, he became aware of those forces in the world that are destructive of humankind, the animal world and nature itself. At first he wanted to withdraw from those conflicts. He resisted those impulses and dedicated himself to becoming a writer concerned with our precarious relationship with the world and its other inhabitants. In so doing, Farley not only found redemption for himself, but he also bestowed upon his readers a series of vivid blueprints of how global salvation can be achieved. His books are filled with anonymous heroes—Native people, deep sea tugboat men, Vikings, Atlantic fishermen, outporters, trappers, infantrymen—who have tried either to live in peace with nature or to restore it or to fight for its survival—like himself.

Books by Farley Mowat

1952   *People of the Deer*

1955   *The Regiment*

1956   *Lost in the Barrens*

1957   *The Dog Who Wouldn't Be*

1958   *The Grey Seas Under*

1958   *Coppermine Journey*, editor

1959   *The Desperate People*

1960   *Ordeal by Ice*, Volume One of *The Top of the World* trilogy, editor

1961   *Owls in the Family*

1961   *The Serpent's Coil*

1962   *The Black Joke*

1963   *Never Cry Wolf*

1965   *Westviking: The Ancient Norse in Greenland and North America*

1966   *The Curse of the Viking Grave*

1967   *Canada North*

1967   *The Polar Passion: The Quest for the North Pole*, Volume Two of *The Top of the World* trilogy, editor

1968   *This Rock Within the Sea: A Heritage Lost*

1969   *The Boat Who Wouldn't Float*

1970   *Sibir*

1972   *A Whale for the Killing*

1973   *Tundra: Selections from the Great Accounts of Arctic Land Voyages*, Volume Three of *The Top of the World* trilogy, editor

1973   *Wake of the Great Sealers*

1975   *The Snow Walker*

1976   *Canada North Now: The Great Betrayal*

1979   *And No Birds Sang*

1980   *The World of Farley Mowat*, edited by Peter Davison

1984   *Sea of Slaughter*

1985   *My Discovery of America*

1987   *Virunga: The Passion of Dian Fossey*

1989   *The New Founde Land*

1990   *Rescue the Earth! Conversations with the Green Crusaders*

1992   *My Father's Son: Memories of War and Peace*

1993   *Born Naked*

1995   *Aftermath: Travels in a Post-War World*

1997   *The Farfarers*

1997   *A Farley Mowat Reader*, edited by Wendy Thomas

2000   *Walking on the Land*

2002   *High Latitudes: An Arctic Journey*

Sources

FM = Farley Mowat

IN researching this biography, I have found the following to be of considerable help. There are three excellent books about FM, all of which contain a great deal of useful information: Alec Lucas, *Farley Mowat*, Canadian Writers Series 14 (Toronto: McClelland & Stewart, 1976); John Orange, *Writing the Squib: A Biography of Farley Mowat* (Toronto: ECW, 1993); and Lorraine M. York, *Introducing Farley Mowat's* The Dog Who Wouldn't Be, Canadian Fiction Series 7 (Toronto: ECW, 1990).

The following interviews with FM contain useful information: "Assessing an Outcast," with Suzanne Sandor, *Maclean's* (October 26, 1987); *Canada's Role in Vietnam* (Willowdale, Ont.: Conference for the Arts, 1965); "Farley Mowat," with Alan Twigg, *Strong Voices: Conversations with Fifty Canadian Authors* (Madeira Park, B.C.: Harbour, 1988); "Farley Mowat—Last of the Saga-Men," with Jan Myers, *Canadian Author and Bookman* 52:4 (1977); "Maclean's Interviews: Farley Mowat," with Alexander Ross, *Maclean's* (March 1968); "Mowat's Metamorphosis," with Joan Lister, *Impetus* (February 1973); "On Being Mowat," *Maclean's* (August 1971); "The Way of One Writer: Farley Mowat," *Canadian Library Journal* (February 1975); and "Why Story-Teller Mowat Abhors Facts: They Get in the Way of the Truth," with Wayne Grady, *Books in Canada* (October 1979).

There are many magazine and newspaper articles about FM. The following are especially good: Jack Batten, "The Quintessence of Farley Mowatism," *Saturday Night* (July 1971); Silver Donald Cameron, "Farley Mowat, Prophet," *Atlantic Insight* (October 1979); Joseph E. Carver, "Farley Mowat: An Author for All Ages," *British Columbia Literary Quarterly* 32:4 (1969); Martin Knelman, "Farley on Parade," *Toronto Life* (December 1983); T.D. MacLulich, "The Alien Role: Farley Mowat's Northern Pastorals," *Studies in Canadian Literature* 2 (1977); Betty Martin, "The World of Farley Mowat," *Canadian Author and Bookman* 45:2 (1969); and Scott Young, "Storm out of the Arctic," *Saturday Night* (October 18, 1952).

There are also some excellent television and radio interviews: *Meet the Author*, sound filmstrip, Mead Sound Filmstrips (1986); "Me and Albert," *Telescope*, CBC Television (December 15, 1970); and *In Search of Farley Mowat*, directed by Andy Thomson, National Film Board of Canada (1981). John Orange lent me the tape of his unpublished interview with FM (May 26, 1962), and Ole Gjerstad lent me the complete set of tapes he made in preparing his CBC *Life and Times* video devoted to FM.

Endnotes

INFORMATION for this book comes primarily from three kinds of sources: interviews with FM, Claire Mowat and their friends and associates; the writings of FM; and archival information, most of it in the Farley and Claire Mowat archive at the McMaster University Library and in the Angus Mowat archive at the University of Western Ontario Library. At the beginning of the listing of each chapter's sources, I list the people I have interviewed and the books by FM which are cited. The numbered endnotes are, in the main, reserved for archival sources used in the writing of that chapter.

CHAPTER I   BUNJE (1921–1928)

Sources: Interviews with FM; family records in FM's possession; *Born Naked*.

1 Angus Mowat to Andy Thomson, February 18, 1968; ms: Andy Thomson.
2 Ibid.
3 Angus Mowat to FM and Claire Mowat, July 27, [1971]; ms: McMaster.
4 Angus Mowat to Gill Mowat, undated; ms: Western.
5 Angus Mowat to FM, October 9, 1946; ms: Western.
6 Angus Mowat to Andy Thomson, February 18, 1968; ms: Andy Thomson.
7 Ibid.
8 Ibid.
9 *Born Naked*, 7.
10 Angus Mowat to Andy Thomson, February 18, 1968; ms: Andy Thomson.
11 Angus Mowat to [?] Robinson, December 27, 1951; ms: Western.

12 *Born Naked*, 35.
13 Ibid., 41.
14 Ibid., 13.
15 Angus Mowat to FM, December 12, 1971; ms: McMaster.

CHAPTER 2   PLAUSIBLE IKE (1928–1932)

Sources: Interviews with FM; *Born Naked*.

1 [Angus Mowat], "Better Reading and How to Attain It . . . ," 3; ms: Western.
2 All further citations in this chapter are from *Born Naked*, 46–85.

CHAPTER 3   BILLY (1933–1939)

Sources: Interviews with FM and Marie Heydon Johnston; *Born Naked*; *The Dog Who Wouldn't Be*.

1 Angus Mowat, "Roll and Go," 1; ms: Western.
2 Ibid., 23.
3 Angus Mowat to Andy Thomson, February 18, 1968; ms: Andy Thomson.
4 FM, "Travels with Farley: Being a Brief Outline for a Long Memoir in Three Volumes," 5; ms: McMaster.
5 FM, chronology for 1938; ms: FM.
6 FM, "Travels with Farley," 5.
7 FM, "Annals of Saskatchewan Trip 1939," 9; ms: McMaster.

CHAPTER 4   SQUIB II (1939–1946)

Sources: Interviews with FM, Bette Campbell Cox and Frances Mowat; *And No Birds Sang*; *My Father's Son*; *The Regiment*.

1 Angus Mowat to Andy Thomson, February 18, 1968; ms: Andy Thomson.
2 FM to Helen Mowat, July 11, 1942; ms: McMaster.
3 FM to Frances Mowat, July 17, [1948]; ms: McMaster.

CHAPTER 5   RAGING BOY (1946–1948)

Sources: Interviews with FM and Frances Mowat; *People of the Deer*.

1 FM to Andy Thomson, December 7, [c. 1967]; ms: Andy Thomson.

2 FM to Frances Mowat, July 17, [1948]; ms: McMaster.

3 Ibid.

4 Frances Thornhill to FM, July 18, 1947; ms: McMaster.

5 Francis Harper to FM, April 7, 1947; ms: McMaster.

6 FM to Angus and Helen Mowat, June 30, [1947]; ms: McMaster.

7 Francis Harper to FM, February 23, 1948; ms: McMaster.

8 FM to Francis Harper, February 27, 1948; ms: McMaster.

9 FM to Frances Thornhill, July 17, [1947]; ms: McMaster.

10 Frances Thornhill to FM, July 18, 1947; ms: McMaster.

11 FM to Frances Mowat, July 17, [1948]; ms: McMaster.

12 Frances Mowat to FM, June 13, 1948; ms: McMaster.

13 FM's diary entries also record the fact that he distributed government-supplied milk and supplies to the household leaders of the Inuit living near Nueltin Lake.

14 FM to Frances Mowat, July 17, [1948]; ms: McMaster.

15 Frances Mowat to FM, June 13, 1948; ms: McMaster.

16 Frances Mowat to FM, June 18, 1948; ms: McMaster.

17 FM to Angus and Helen Mowat, July 12, 1948; ms: Western.

18 Angus Mowat to FM, August 12, 1948; ms: Western.

19 FM to T.F. McIlwraith, December 1, 1948; ms: McMaster.

20 FM to Angus and Helen Mowat, November 21, [1948]; ms: McMaster.

21 R.A. Gibson to the head of the Dominion Wildlife Service, October 28, 1948; *Saturday Night*, 64.

22 FM to the Editor, *Atlantic Monthly*, December 1, 1948; ms: McMaster.

23 FM to Frances Mowat, July 17, [1948]; ms: McMaster.

CHAPTER 6   SAGA-MAN (1949–1953)

Sources: Interviews with FM, Bette Campbell Cox, Peter Davison, Frances Mowat and John Mowat; *Aftermath*.

1 Angus Mowat to [?] Robinson, January 4, 1949; ms: McMaster.

2 FM to Angus and Helen Mowat, June 16, [1953]; ms: Western.

3 FM to "Boss," September 20, 1950; ms: McMaster.

4 Max Wilkinson to FM, October 9, 1953; ms: McMaster.

5 Max Wilkinson to FM, June 2, 1953; ms: McMaster.

6 Max Wilkinson to FM, February 15, 1952; ms: McMaster.

7 "How to Be a Canadian Writer—and Survive," typescript, 5. Published in *Saturday Night*, June 1953.

8 Max Wilkinson to FM, April 16, 1953; ms: McMaster.

9 Angus Mowat to [?] Robinson, April 22, 1950; ms: McMaster.

10 FM to Helen Mowat, March 26, [1951]; ms: Western.

11 FM to Angus and Helen Mowat, August 20, [1951]; ms: Western.

12 Angus Mowat to [?] Robinson, November 19, 1951; ms: Western.

13 Angus Mowat to [?] Robinson, December 17, 1951; ms: Western.

14 Angus Mowat to FM, December 18, 1951; ms: Western.

15 Angus Mowat to [?] Robinson, December 7, 1951; ms: Western.

16 FM to Angus and Helen Mowat, November 3, [1951]; ms: Western.

17 FM to Angus Mowat, April 8, [1952]; ms: Western.

18 Angus Mowat to FM, April 18, 1952; ms: Western.

19 Jack McClelland, "My Rose Garden, A Publishing Memoir," 46; ms: McMaster.

20 Jack McClelland to FM, January 28, 1958; ms: McMaster.

21 FM to Jack McClelland, November 25, 1956; ms: McMaster.

22 Jack McClelland to FM, May 27, 1958; ms: McMaster.

23 Jack McClelland to FM, November 30, 1959; ms: McMaster.

24 FM to Jack McClelland, May 8, [1959]; ms: McMaster.

25 FM to T.F. McIlwraith, February 24, 1950; ms: McMaster.

26 *The Beaver*, June 1952, 47-9.

27 "Storm Out of the Arctic," *Saturday Night*, October 18, 1952.

28 FM's only rebuttal was published in the *Montreal Star* on July 15, 1952.

29 FM to Angus and Helen Mowat, September 10, [1952]; ms: McMaster.

30 FM to Angus and Helen Mowat, July 27, [1952 or 1953]; ms: Western.

31 Max Wilkinson to FM, February 15, 1952; ms: McMaster.

32 Max Wilkinson to FM, December 17, 1952; ms: McMaster.

33 Max Wilkinson to FM, March 11, 1953; ms: McMaster.

34 FM to "Boss," September 20, 1952; ms: McMaster.

CHAPTER 7   NOMAD (1953–1959)

Sources: Interviews with FM, Peter Davison, Harold Horwood, Jack McClelland, Frances Mowat, John Mowat, Rosemary Mowat, Sandy Mowat and Vi Warren; *Lost in the Barrens*; *The Dog Who Wouldn't Be*; *My Discovery of America*; *Walking on the Land*; *The Desperate People*; *Coppermine Journey*; *The Grey Seas Under*; *The Serpent's Coil*.

1 *Globe and Mail*, 1957.

2 Jack McClelland to FM, April 13, 1955; ms: McMaster.

3 FM to Jack McClelland, [April 1955]; ms: McMaster.

4 Jack McClelland to FM, August 16, 1955; ms: McMaster.

5 Jeannette T. Cloud to FM, January 19, 1955; ms: McMaster.

6 Dudley Cloud to FM, November 28, 1955; ms: McMaster.

7 FM to Angus and Helen Mowat, April 15, [1955]; ms: Western.

8 "Dog of Genius," *Saturday Night*, 27; ms: McMaster.

9 Harold Horwood to FM, undated but c. 1965; ms: McMaster.

10 Harold Horwood to FM, undated but c. 1964; ms: McMaster.

11 Harold Horwood to FM, undated but c. 1964; ms: McMaster.

12 Harold Horwood to FM, March 11, [c. 1965]; ms: McMaster.

13 Douglas S. Harkness, the minister of National Defence, wrote to Farley on April 5, 1961, about the "scurrility" and "irresponsibility" with which he had accused the Canadian government of storing nuclear weapons on Canadian territory: "You accuse me of adopting the tactics of the late Senator McCarthy. May I suggest that your writings give every indication that you yourself are a strong and ardent supporter of such tactics" (ms: Vi Warren).

14 Jean Lesage to FM, April 23, 1957; ms: McMaster.

15 Max Wilkinson to FM, February 19, 1959; ms: McMaster.

16 FM, "Travels with Farley," 7.

17 Peter Davison to FM, December 2, 1959; ms: McMaster.

18 Peter Davison to FM, November 23, 1959; ms: McMaster.

19 Peter Davison to FM, January 7, 1960; ms: McMaster.

20 Peter Davison to FM, March 27, 1959; ms: McMaster.

21 Peter Davison to FM, July 8, 1958; ms: McMaster.

22 Jack McClelland to Steve Rankin, undated but 1958; ms: McMaster.

23 Hugh Kane to Jack McClelland, undated but probably October or November 1959; ms: McMaster.

24 *Library Journal*, November 1, 1959; ms: McMaster.

25 FM to Angus Mowat, December 5, [1959]; ms: Western.

26 Harold Horwood to FM, June 15, [1960]; ms: McMaster.

27 FM to Jack McClelland, July 4, [1960]; ms: McMaster.

28 Frances Mowat to FM, undated but c. 1959; ms: McMaster.

CHAPTER 8   HAPPY ADVENTURER (1960–1962)

Sources: Interviews with FM, Peter Davison, Beryl Gaspardy, Harold Horwood, Jack McClelland, Claire Mowat and Frances Mowat; *The Boat Who Wouldn't Float*; *A Whale for the Killing*.

1 Anna Porter et al., *Jack McClelland: The Publisher of Canadian Literature* (Guadalajara, Mexico: University of Guadalajara, 1996), 54.

2 Jack McClelland to Elizabeth McClelland, July 28, 1960; ms: McMaster.

3 FM to Jack McClelland, undated but 1961; ms: McMaster.

4 FM to Jack McClelland, January 20, 1960; ms: McMaster.

5 FM to Jack McClelland, April 5, 1960; ms: McMaster.

6 Evan Thomas to FM, April 28, 1960; ms: McMaster.

7 Max Wilkinson to FM, March 23, 1960; ms: McMaster.

8 Peter Davison to FM, March 2, 1960; ms: McMaster.

9 Jack McClelland to FM, March 15, 1960; ms: McMaster.

10 Max Wilkinson to Jack McClelland, April 27, 1960; ms: McMaster.

11 Peter Davison to FM, June 8, 1960; ms: McMaster.

12 Max Wilkinson to FM, November 11, 1960; ms: McMaster.

13 FM, note in response to a query from James King, August 2000; ms: James King.

14 FM to Jack McClelland, November 18, 1960; ms: McMaster.

15 Handwritten comment by Kenneth Littauer, undated but c. November 1961, on Carolyn Blakemore to FM, October 13, 1961; ms: McMaster.

16 Peter Davison to FM, August 31, 1960; ms: McMaster.

17 Peter Davison to FM, October 17, 1960; ms: McMaster.

18 Undated but attached to Peter Davison's letter to FM, October 17, 1960; ms: McMaster.

19 FM to Angus Mowat, September 12, [1960]; ms: Western.

20 Claire Mowat, *Pomp and Circumstances* (Toronto: McClelland & Stewart, 1989) 53.

21 FM to Claire Wheeler, July 10, 1961; ms (carbon copy): McMaster.

22 FM to Jack McClelland, September 12, 1960; ms: Western.

23 FM to Barbara Hutchinson, September 3, 1960; ms: Western.

24 FM to Barbara Hutchinson, January 16, 1961 [postmark]; ms: Western.

25 FM to Barbara Hutchinson, June 7, 1961 [postmark]; ms: Western.

26 FM to Barbara Hutchinson, January 25, 1961 [postmark]; ms: Western.

27 FM to Barbara Hutchinson, January 31, 1961 [postmark]; ms: Western.

28 FM to Barbara Hutchinson, February 7, 1961; ms: Western.

29 Arnold Warren to Claire Wheeler, May 1, 1961; ms: Vi Warren.

30 Claire Wheeler to Arnold Warren, undated but c. May 5, 1961; ms: Vi Warren.

31 FM to Jack McClelland, July 6, 1961; ms: McMaster.

32 Journal Notes, Newfoundland Waters, June 8, 11, 1961; ms: McMaster.

33 FM to Claire Wheeler, July 10, 1961; ms: McMaster.

34 Journal Notes, Newfoundland Waters, August 4, 1961; ms: McMaster.

35 *A Whale for the Killing*, 66–67.

36 Journal Notes, Newfoundland Waters, August 5, 1961; ms: McMaster.

37 Ibid., August 13, 1961.

38 Ibid., August 14, 1961.

39 Ibid.

40 FM to Jack McClelland, August 20, 1961; ms: McMaster.

41 FM to Barbara Hutchinson, November 24, 1961 [postmark]; ms: Western.

42 FM to Jack McClelland, January 12, 1962; ms: McMaster.

43 FM to Claire Wheeler, January 12, 1962; ms: McMaster.

44 Claire Wheeler to Barbara Hutchinson, February 12, 1962; ms: McMaster.

45 Journal entry for December 30, 1961; ms: McMaster.

46 Journal entry for January 11, 1962; ms: McMaster.

47 Angus Mowat to FM, February 4, 1962; ms: Western.

48 Journal entry for March 9, 1962; ms: McMaster.

49 FM to Angus Mowat and Barbara Hutchinson, March 28, 1962; ms: McMaster.

50 Claire Wheeler to FM, September 29, 1962; ms: McMaster.

CHAPTER 9   FARLEY MOWAT (1962–1965)

Sources: Interviews with FM, Peter Davison, Harold Horwood, Jack McClelland, Claire Mowat, Frances Mowat and Sandy Mowat; *A Whale for the Killing; Never Cry Wolf.*

1 FM to Angus Mowat, July 9, [1962]; ms: Western.
2 Claire Mowat, *The Outport People* (Toronto: McClelland & Stewart, 1983), 45.
3 Ibid., 86.
4 Max Wilkinson to FM, January 5, 1960; ms: McMaster.
5 FM to Angus Mowat and Barbara Hutchinson, December 3, 1962; ms: Western.
6 Peter Davison to FM, March 1, 1963; ms: McMaster.
7 Angus Mowat to Barbara Hutchinson, June 29, 1963 [postmark]; ms: Western.
8 Harold Horwood to FM, February 14, 1964; ms: McMaster.
9 Jack McClelland to D.L. MacDougall, *Edmonton Journal*, February 21, 1964; ms: McMaster.
10 Claire Wheeler to Barbara Hutchinson, December 19, 1963; ms: Western.
11 Claire Wheeler to Angus Mowat and Barbara Hutchinson, November 10, 1964; ms: Western.
12 FM to Angus Mowat, January 10, [1967]; ms: Western.
13 FM to Sandy Mowat, August 18, 1965; ms: McMaster.
14 FM to Sandy and David Mowat, September 2, 1962; ms: McMaster.
15 FM to Sandy and David Mowat, March 25, [1963]; ms: McMaster.
16 FM to Sandy and David Mowat, July 6, [1963]; ms: McMaster.
17 Peter Davison to FM, September 9, 1964; ms: McMaster.
18 FM to Angus Mowat, October 10, 1964; ms: McMaster.
19 Jack McClelland to FM, October 6, 1964; ms: McMaster.
20 Ibid.
21 FM to Jack McClelland, October 30, 1964; ms: McMaster.
22 Claire Wheeler to Jack McClelland, November 3, 1964; ms: McMaster.
23 Angus Mowat to Barbara Hutchinson, October 18, 1962 [postmark]; ms: Western.
24 See Angus Mowat to Barbara Hutchinson, May 4, 1963 [postmark]; ms: Western.
25 FM to Angus Mowat, undated but c. 1963–64; ms: Western.
26 Claire Wheeler to Angus Mowat and Barbara Hutchinson, March 12, 1964; ms: Western.
27 John Mowat to FM, August 25, 1964; ms: McMaster.
28 FM to Jack McClelland, June 9, [1964]; ms: McMaster.
29 FM to Angus Mowat and Barbara Hutchinson, October 7, 1964; ms: Western.
30 Claire Wheeler to Barbara Hutchinson, November 24, 1965; ms: Western.
31 FM to Angus Mowat, February 23, 1965; ms: Western.

CHAPTER 10   KEEPER OF THE WHALE (1965–1967)

Sources: Interviews with FM, Peter Davison, John de Visser, Jack McClelland, Claire Mowat and Fran Mowat; *Canada North; Sibir; A Whale for the Killing; The Snow Walker; This Rock Within the Sea.*

1   Angus Mowat to FM, December 11, 1965; ms: McMaster.
2   Angus Mowat to FM and Claire Mowat, April 4, 1966; ms: McMaster.
3   FM to Angus Mowat, January 18, 1966; ms: Western.
4   Peter Davison to FM, November 2, 1965; ms: McMaster.
5   Peter Davison to FM, September 8, 1965; ms: McMaster.
6   Peter Davison to FM, January 13, 1967; ms: McMaster.
7   FM to Angus Mowat and Barbara Hutchinson, November 23, [1965]; ms: McMaster.
8   Joseph Smallwood to FM, May 13, 1965; ms: FM.
9   FM to Joseph Smallwood, May 26, 1965; ms: FM.
10   FM to Joseph Smallwood, February 7, 1966; ms: FM.
11   FM to Joseph Smallwood, July 5, 1966; ms: FM.
12   Harold Horwood to FM, November 30, 1965; ms: McMaster.
13   FM to Angus Mowat and Barbara Hutchinson, January 20, [1967]; ms: Western.
14   FM to Angus Mowat and Barbara Hutchinson, February 10, 1967; ms: Western.
15   Jack McClelland to Peter Davison, February 6, 1967; ms: McMaster.
16   Jack McClelland to Peter Davison, February 24, 1967; ms: McMaster.
17   Peter Davison to FM, February 14, 1967; ms: McMaster.
18   Peter Davison to FM, March 27, 1967; ms: McMaster.
19   Max Wilkinson to FM, February 10, 1967; ms: McMaster.
20   John de Visser to FM and Claire Mowat, June 2, 1966; ms: McMaster.
21   FM to Angus Mowat and Barbara Hutchinson, June 13, [1967]; ms: Western.
22   FM to Angus Mowat, c. 1968; ms: Western.
23   Angus Mowat to FM, January 10, 1966; ms: Western.
24   Claire Mowat to Angus Mowat, February 1966; ms: Western.

CHAPTER 11   WAYFARER (1968–1970)

Sources: Interviews with FM, Harold Horwood, Jack McClelland, Claire Mowat, Andy Thomson and Vi Warren; *This Rock Within the Sea; Sea of Slaughter; My Discovery of America; Sibir.*

1   Claire Mowat to Angus Mowat and Barbara Hutchinson, November 28 or 29, 1968; ms: Western.
2   Claire Mowat to Angus Mowat, November 17, 1970; ms: Western.
3   Jack McClelland to Peter Davison, June 17, 1968; ms: McMaster.

4 Jack McClelland to Edward Roberts, November 11, 1968; ms: McMaster.
5 Peter Davison to FM, May 10, 1968; ms: McMaster.
6 Jack McClelland to Peter Davison, February 27, 1968; ms: McMaster.
7 FM to Sandy Mowat, March 12, 1968; ms: McMaster.
8 FM to Sandy Mowat, April 1, 1968; ms: McMaster.
9 Angus Mowat to Betty [?], January 25, 1973; ms: Western.
10 Claire Mowat to Angus Mowat and Barbara Hutchinson, February 28, 1968; ms: Western.
11 Al Purdy, ed., *The New Romans: Candid Canadian Opinions of the U.S.* (New York: St. Martin's, 1968), iv.
12 Claire Mowat to Andy Thomson, December 21, 1968; ms: Andy Thomson.
13 FM to Sandy and David Mowat, August 20, 1968; ms: McMaster.
14 Claire Mowat to Angus Mowat and Barbara Hutchinson, December 19, 1968; ms: Western.
15 FM to Jack McClelland, autumn 1968; ms: McMaster.
16 FM to Jack McClelland, February 19, [1969]; ms: McMaster.
17 Jack McClelland to FM, March 6, 1969; ms: McMaster.
18 Jack McClelland to Lily Miller, January 21, 1980; ms: McMaster.
19 *Globe and Mail*, November 22, 1969.
20 Claire Mowat to Isabel [?], February 17, 1969; ms: McMaster.
21 FM to Jack McClelland, March 12, [1969]; ms: McMaster.
22 FM to Angus Mowat, March 12, 1969; ms: McMaster.
23 FM to Jack McClelland, November 1, 1969; ms: McMaster.
24 *Maclean's*, March 1968.
25 Claire Mowat to FM, February 22, [c. 1985]; ms: McMaster.
26 Angus Mowat to Ivan Shpedko, February 28, 1968; ms: Western.
27 FM to Angus Mowat and Barbara Hutchinson, August 9, 1970; ms: Western.
28 FM to Andy Thomson, July 31, 1970; ms: Andy Thomson.
29 FM to Arnold and Vi Warren, December 1, [c. 1972]; ms: Vi Warren.
30 FM to Jack McClelland, February 24, 1972; ms: McMaster.
31 Jack McClelland to FM, February 28, 1972; ms: McMaster.
32 FM to Jack McClelland, March 1, 1972; ms: McMaster.
33 FM to Andy Thomson, August 20, [1970]; ms: McMaster.
34 A.E. Porsild to Andy Thomson, January 19, 1967; ms: McMaster.
35 Angus Mowat to FM, October 22, 1970; ms: McMaster.
36 FM to Andy Thomson, January 5, 1970; ms: Andy Thomson.
37 Claire Mowat to Andy Thomson, October 20, 1972; ms: McMaster.

CHAPTER 12   HIS FATHER'S SON (1971–1977)

Sources: Interviews with FM, Pierre Berton, Silver Donald Cameron, Peter Davison, Beryl Gaspardy, Claire Mowat, John Mowat, Rosemary Mowat, Sandy Mowat, Ed and Lily Schreyer, Vi Warren and Catherine Wilson; *A Whale for the Killing*.

1   FM to Angus Mowat, February 15, 1970; ms: Western.

2   Claire Mowat to Angus Mowat and Barbara Hutchinson, March 9, [1971];
    ms: Western.

3   Angus Mowat to FM, January 5, 1971; ms: McMaster.

4   Angus Mowat to FM, February 25, 1973; ms: Western.

5   FM to Jack McClelland, March 1972; ms: McMaster.

6   FM to Jack McClelland, July 16, [1973]; ms: McMaster.

7   Jack McClelland to FM, July 19, 1973; ms: McMaster.

8   Claire Mowat to FM, undated; ms: McMaster.

9   Jack McClelland to Peter Davison, December 7, 1977; ms: James King.

10 Claire Mowat to FM, October 3, 1975; ms: McMaster.

11 Claire Mowat to FM, June 18, 1972; ms: McMaster.

12 FM, "Travels with Farley," 19.

13 Ibid., 8.

14 FM to Sandy Mowat, February 22, 1974; ms: McMaster.

15 Kildare Dobbs, "The Man Who Hates Writing Rests from the Success of It,"
    Toronto Star, December 22, 1973, F3.

16 Angus Mowat to FM, December 25, 1975; ms: McMaster.

17 Angus Mowat to FM, August 8, 1975; ms: McMaster.

18 Angus Mowat to FM, October 17, 1976; ms: Western.

19 Angus Mowat and Barbara Hutchinson to Ed and Lily Schreyer, June 23,
    1974; ms: Western.

20 Angus Mowat to Rosemary Mowat, April 11, 1976; ms: Western.

21 FM to Angus Mowat and Barbara Hutchinson, June 24, 1971; ms: Western.

22 FM to Angus Mowat, August 10, 1971; ms: Western.

23 Claire Mowat to Angus Mowat, September 4, 1971; ms: Western.

24 Ms: FM.

25 Jack McClelland to Catherine Wilson, August 17, 1971; ms: McMaster.

26 Pierre Berton to FM, October 10, 1972; ms: McMaster.

27 Jack McClelland to Pierre Berton, October 13, 1972; ms: McMaster.

28 Information from Catherine Wilson.

29 FM to Jack McClelland, November 10, 1972; ms: McMaster.

30 FM to Jack McClelland, December 20, [1973]; ms: McMaster.

31 Pierre Berton to FM, February 25, 1974; copy in McClelland & Stewart
    archives, McMaster.

32 FM to Sandy Mowat, February 22, 1974; ms: McMaster.

33 Jack Cole, as quoted by Roy MacSkimming, "Authors Tempted to Get
    Arrested Inside Bookstore," *Toronto Daily Star*, January 23, 1975, D11.

34 Jack McClelland to Angus Cameron, March 28, 1973; ms: McMaster.

35 Jack McClelland to FM, September 9, 1977; ms: McMaster.

36 Peter Davison to FM, August 1, 1977; ms: James King.

37 Jack McClelland to Peter Davison, December 7, 1977; ms: McMaster.

38 FM to Jack McClelland, August 1, [1978]; ms: McMaster.

39 FM to Peter Davison, August [1977]; ms: James King.

40 FM to Sandy Mowat, April 7, 1976; ms: McMaster.

41 FM to Sandy Mowat, March 28, 1976; ms: McMaster.

42 Peter Davison to FM, July 8, 1974; ms: McMaster.

43 FM to Sandy Mowat, May 13, 1974; ms: McMaster.

44 FM to Sandy Mowat, June 22, [1976]; ms: McMaster.

45 Claire Mowat to Arnold and Vi Warren, March 29, 1977; ms: Vi Warren.

46 FM to Sandy Mowat, January 20, 1975; ms: McMaster.

47 Claire Mowat to Angus Mowat and Barbara Hutchinson, January 28, 1975; ms: Western.

48 FM to Sandy Mowat, September 30, 1975; ms: McMaster.

49 Peter Davison, Trade editorial report, November 19, 1975; ms: James King.

50 Claire Mowat to Arnold and Vi Warren, July 2, 1977; ms: Vi Warren.

51 FM to Angus Mowat, April 26, [1976]; ms: McMaster.

52 FM to Rosemary Mowat, dated "Sunday"; ms: McMaster.

53 Draft of an undated letter from FM to Claude Bennett, the Ontario minister of Industry and Tourism; ms: McMaster.

54 FM to Rosemary Mowat, dated "Sunday"; ms: McMaster.

55 FM to Peter Davison, December 20, 1977; ms: James King.

CHAPTER 13   PROPHET OF DOOM (1977–1984)

Sources: Interviews with FM, Peter Davison, Claire Mowat, Ed and Lily Schreyer, Andy Thomson, Ervin and Janice Touesnard and Vi Warren; *And No Birds Sang; Sea of Slaughter.*

1 Peter Davison to FM, November 10, 1978; ms: James King.

2 Claire Mowat to FM, July 9, 1978; ms: McMaster.

3 Ibid.

4 Peter Davison to FM, November 10, 1978; ms: James King.

5 This diary is in FM's embargoed papers at McMaster.

6 Jack McClelland to FM, February 21, 1980; ms: McMaster.

7 Helen Mowat to FM, October 4, 1979; ms: McMaster.

8 Donald Cameron, "Farley Mowat, Prophet," *Atlantic Insight*, October 1979, 34.

9 FM to Herta Ryder, November 11, 1980; ms: McMaster.

10 Peter Davison to FM, August 18, 1980; ms: McMaster.

11 FM to Peter Davison, January 5 and 9, 1981; ms: James King.

12 FM to Jack McClelland, September 10, 1982; ms: McMaster.

13 Peter Davison to Jack McClelland, July 20, 1979; ms: James King.

14 Jack McClelland to Peter Taylor, May 2, 1979; ms: McMaster.

15 FM to Jack McClelland, July 30, 1979; ms: McMaster.

16 FM to Jack McClelland, August 25, [1979]; ms: McMaster.

17 FM to Jack McClelland, June 7, 1980; ms: McMaster.

18 Claire Mowat to Arnold and Vi Warren, August 5, 1979; ms: Vi Warren.

19 FM to Robin [?], July 14, 1980; ms: McMaster.

20 FM to Peter Davison, July 1, 1980; ms: James King.

21 Claire Mowat, *Pomp and Circumstances*, 17.

22 Ibid., 19.

23 Ibid., 249.

24 Ibid., 192–93.

25 Ibid., 267.

26 Ibid., 109.

27 Claire Mowat to Arnold and Vi Warren, c. September 1983; ms: Vi Warren.

28 Donald Cameron, "Farley Mowat, Prophet," 30.

29 Claire Mowat to Arnold and Vi Warren, July 3, 1982; ms: Vi Warren.

30 Claire Mowat to Arnold and Vi Warren, July 25, 1983; ms: McMaster.

31 Claire Mowat to Andy and Lynn Thomson, May 24, 1983; ms: Andy Thomson.

32 FM to Peter Davison, April 9, 1983; ms: James King.

33 FM to Jack McClelland, September 10, 1982; ms: McMaster.

34 Claire Mowat to Arnold and Vi Warren, July 3, 1982; ms: Vi Warren.

35 Claire Mowat to FM, March 14, 1982; ms: McMaster.

36 Claire Mowat to FM, November 10, 1982; ms: McMaster.

37 Claire Mowat to FM, May 29, 1983; ms: McMaster.

38 Donald Cameron, "Farley Mowat, Prophet," 29.

CHAPTER 14   KEEPER OF THE FAITH (1984 TO THE PRESENT)

Sources: Interviews with FM, Anita and David Blackwood, Janice Boddy, Peter Davison, John de Visser, Mary Elliott, Jack McClelland, Lily Miller, Claire Mowat, Wade Rowland, Andy Thomson and Ron Wright; *Virunga*; *My Discovery of America*; *Sea of Slaughter*.

1 FM to Leslie Peterson, *Vancouver Sun*, April 6, 1981; ms: McMaster.

2 FM to Peter Davison, June 2, 1998; ms: McMaster.

3 Andy Thomson to FM, July 28, 1987; ms: FM.

4 FM to Andy Thomson, October 2, 1987; ms: FM.

5 Mary Elliott to James King, June 13, 2001; ms: James King.

6 Jack McClelland to FM, September 12, 1989; ms: McMaster.

7 Jack McClelland to Avie Bennett, August 18, 1989; ms: McMaster.

8 FM to Jack McClelland, September 17, 1989; ms: McMaster.

9 Jack McClelland to FM, September 22, 1989; ms: McMaster.

10 FM to Jack McClelland, April 25, 1990; ms: McMaster.

11 FM to Douglas Gibson, February 4, 1992; ms: McMaster.

12 FM to Jack McClelland, December 7, 1992; ms: McMaster.

13 Claire Mowat to FM, March 3, 1993; ms: McMaster.

14 FM to Kenneth Whyte, April 9, 1996; ms: FM.
15 Preface to "The Farley Mowat Papers in McMaster University Library," compiled by Susan Bellingham, *McMaster University Library Research News*, 2:6 (September 1974), 7–8.
16 Paul Gessell, "Farley and the Facts," *Ottawa Citizen*, December 7, 2000.
17 Preface to "The Farley Mowat Papers in McMaster University Library," 11.
18 Donald Cameron, "Farley Mowat, Prophet," 34.

Index